5

...Lake Rd.
Bay Village, Ohio

The Great Books of Russia

THE GREAT BOOKS OF RUSSIA

By Ruth Davies

University of Oklahoma Press : Norman

Library of Congress Catalog Card Number: 67–24613

 Composed and printed at Norman, Oklahoma, U.S.A., by the University of Oklahoma Press. First edition.

For Helen

Prologue: Mountain Through the Mist

After Alexander Herzen, a Russian journalist, escaped from the autocracy of czardom to the haven of London, he made the following statement about his native country:

> . . . Men's eyes involuntarily turn toward the East. There a hostile, menacing empire is seen standing out behind the mists, like a dark mountain; at times it seems as though it is falling upon Europe like an avalanche. . . .
>
> This empire, absolutely unknown two hundred years ago, has suddenly made its appearance, and with no right to do so, with no invitation, has loudly and bluntly raised its voice in the council of European Powers. . . .
>
> Is it credible that on the very eve of conflict nothing is known of this combatant? Yet he stands already menacing, fully armed, prepared to cross the frontier at the first summons of reaction. And meanwhile men scarcely know his weapons, or the color of his flag.[1]

To many modern readers these words seem as appropriate today as at the time they were written in 1851. Russia and the Russians now appear to multitudes in the Western world as the same dreadful, unknown "combatant" of Herzen's description.

But the Russians can be understood. More completely than almost any other people, the Russians have revealed themselves in their literature. "Next to the communism of the peasants," Herzen went on to say, "nothing is so deeply characteristic of Russia . . . as her literary movements." Literature supplies the powerful lens by which it becomes possible to penetrate the mist, if not to see clearly the entire mountain. During the nineteenth century many authors explored and explained their society and their age. This book will introduce the reader to some of the best

[1] *My Past and Thoughts*, VI.

known of these authors and to some of the most significant of their writings.

This introduction to Russian literature is not intended as literary criticism or as a thorough study of any of the authors or works herein presented. So brief a commentary can do no more than suggest the complexity, variety, and richness of Russian literature. The present volume should be a bridge leading to the books it discusses. Apart from their other values, they offer the best background for an understanding of modern Russia.

One of the most striking characteristics of what has been called "The Golden Age of Russian Literature" is the fact that it served the twofold function of reflection and prediction. All the long-repressed forces which began to move toward revolution are mirrored and analyzed by the authors, who played no small part in the ferment of their times. Their prophetic utterances are of particular interest to modern readers, who have already witnessed the fulfillment of many and may be apprehensive about the possible fulfillment of others of their prophecies.

This survey ends with the coming of the Revolution, toward which most of the literature of the previous eighty or ninety years had pointed. The short bibliography which concludes the volume will, however, assist the reader to begin making an acquaintance with the history and literature of Soviet Russia.

All the books discussed here are readily available in English translation. Except when otherwise indicated, the quotations are from the translations by Constance Garnett, because they are the most accessible. New and more exactly translated editions are, however, increasing in number.

Readers unfamiliar with the language often find Russian names a handicap to their enjoyment of the great books of Russia. For such readers, the brief statement which follows may be of some assistance.

RUTH DAVIES

Delaware, Ohio
August 15, 1967

Russian Names

THE RUSSIAN SYSTEM of nomenclature is different from that of western Europe and America. Ordinarily an individual does not have what we know as the "middle name." Instead, he has in that position a name (patronymic) which he receives automatically. A father's first name becomes the middle name of all his children, male and female, the difference in sex being indicated by masculine and feminine endings—[*o*]*vi*[*t*]*ch* (m.) and *ovna* or *evna* (f.). Thus, in the Karamazov family the father's first name, *Fyodor*, is the source of the patronymic of all his sons: Dmitri Fyodorovich Karamazov, Ivan Fyodorovich Karamazov, and Alexei Fyodorovich Karamazov. If these brothers had had a sister, her name would have been, say, Tatiana Fyodorovna.

Further, the surname is not generally used in ordinary conversation or explanation. An individual would not normally be addressed as the Russian equivalent of Mr. Karamazov, but as Dmitri Fyodorovich. Reference to him would take the same form. Among intimates, diminutive or pet names are extremely common and so varied as to cause possible confusion. In the matter of the last name, it is to be expected that a feminine ending will be appended; for example, the wife of Alexei Alexandrovich Karenin was Anna Arkedyevna Karenin*a*.

The reader should not be surprised by variations in spellings of names in the process of transliteration from Russian to English. The two most common variants are *i* and *y* (Son*i*a and Son*y*a) and *v* and *ff* (or *f*; Oblomo*v*, Oblomo*ff*). The fact that the Russian alphabet is quite different from the Roman causes unavoidable irregularities in the attempts to render Russian words—proper nouns included—in English.

The relatively small number of Christian or "first" names which appear in Russian fiction is often a surprise to readers. This limitation may be explained by the fact that in most Russian families, before the Revolution, children were named for the saints, particularly if a child was born on a saint's day (and there were many such in the Russian calendar). It was customary to celebrate the "name day" (not necessarily the day of an individual's birth) rather than the birthday.

Following is a list of "first" names which appear most commonly in Russian literature. The English equivalents and the common diminutives are indicated.

Agrafina	Grusha, Grushenka
Anastasya	Nastya
Anna	Anya, Annushka
Darya	Dasha, Dashenka
Elizaveta (Elizabeth)	Lise, Liza, or Lizanka
Evdoxia (or Avdotia)	Dunya, Dunyasha
Irina (Irene)	
Katerina (Katherine)	Katya, Katusha
Lyubov	Lyuba
Marfa (Martha)	
Marya (Mary)	Masha
Maya (May)	
Nadejda	Nadya
Natalya (Natalie)	Natasha
Olga	
Sophya (Sophia)	Sonia
Tatyana	Tanya, Tanitchka
Varvara (Barbara)	Vanya
Vera	
Alexander	Sasha, Sashenka
Alexei	Alyosha
Andrey (Andrew)	Andriusha
Arkady	Arkasha
Boris	Borya, Borenka
D[i]mitri	Mitya, Mishka
Evgeny (Eugene)	
Fyodor (Theodore)	Fedya, Fedushka

Grigory (Gregory)	Grisha
Ilya	Ilyusha
Ivan (John)	Vanya, Vanka
Mikhail (Michael)	
Nikolai (Nicholas)	Kolya
Pavel (Paul)	Vanka, Pasha
Pyotr (Peter)	Petya, Petrusha
Sergey	Seryozha
Stepan (Stephen)	Stiva
Vassily	
Vladimir	Volodya

Readers should not permit themselves to be distracted by the problem of the pronunciation of Russian names. The following, however, will assist in the pronunciation of the names of the authors with whom this book is primarily concerned:

Pushkin	– *Poosh* keen
Gogol	– *Go* gawl
Goncharov	– Gone tchar *off*
Turgenev	– Tour *gay* nyef (or v)
Dostoevsky	– Daws taw *yevf* (or f) skee
Tolstoy	– Tall *stoy*
Chekhov	– *Ch[y]eh* kawf [v]
Andreyev	– Ahn *dray* yev [f]
Gorky	– *Gor* kee

Contents

The Great Books of Russia

1/ The Loser Won the Duel

When the poet Alexander Pushkin was born in Moscow in 1799, the Czar of Russia was Paul I, son of Catherine called the Great. It is symbolic that the nineteenth century, which witnessed the shaping of revolutionary forces in Russia, had its beginning under the rule of a man who was, if not quite mad, at least the victim of insane impulses and temper. Catherine's death in 1796 concluded an impressive reign, sometimes compared with that of the first Elizabeth in England. This comparison, while misleading, has some claim to validity. Although Russia under Catherine could hardly be measured favorably with the England of Elizabeth, Raleigh, Drake, Francis Bacon, and Shakespeare, nevertheless the Empress made a number of intelligent attempts to reduce the ignorance and despotism that disfigured her country.

Paul I brought with him to the throne not only a long-smouldering hatred of his mother and all her policies, but a habit of brutality and a conviction that the monarch should be absolute. He cancelled or made negative practically all his mother's efforts to give the Russian people more freedom and opportunities for enlightenment. He refused to allow his subjects to travel abroad; recalled Russian students from foreign universities; permitted no importation of foreign scholars, books, or art; closed down virtually all forms of publication; imposed rigid censorship; made himself the head of the church; and demanded universal recognition of his absolute authority.

During the slightly less than five years of Paul's reign, the great giant, Russia, reeled from one stultifying blow after another. Paul's own favorites were not safe from his explosive temper and terrifying changes of mood. Many were sent to Siberia for the smallest failure to submit to his will. Like a savage oriental potentate he required paralyzing subjection. He compelled his subjects to fall on their knees in his presence, even if it meant groveling in the mud or snow. His malice had the terrifying incalculability of madness.

The harshest of despots, however, is occasionally responsible for a constructive regulation. One mitigating feature of Paul's reign was his *ukase* limiting the service that serfs were required to render their masters to three days a week. This law could not be said to have played any significant part in the correction of the peasants' grievances, but it did bring into the open the whole issue of serfdom, the dominating issue of the next six decades. This action was part of Paul's general plan to limit the power of the gentry, a first step in the process which culminated during the revolution, more than a century later, in the triumph of the proletariat and the destruction of the traditional pattern of privilege.

Paul's reign was brought to an end by his assassination in one of the "palace revolutions" which have frequently occurred in Russia. Among the conspirators were several of Paul's advisers who had taken into their confidence his oldest son, Alexander. The latter had apparently agreed that his father must be removed from the throne but had exacted from the conspirators a promise to spare his life. When Paul was killed, Alexander was oppressed by a sense of guilt, but few in Russia felt anything except rejoicing. In his early twenties, Alexander was known as a young man of liberal tendencies. Looking backward across the rude interruption of Paul's fanatic tyranny, the people remembered the reign of Catherine as more liberal than it had actually been. They looked to Alexander with strong hope that he would rule according to the pattern set by his illustrious grandmother.

The Russia of Alexander I, in which Pushkin grew up to become "the father of Russian literature," was full of contrasts. In view of the "enlightenment" of Catherine's reign, it is a shock to discover that at the close of the eighteenth century more than thirty-four million of the country's thirty-six million population were serfs, that is to say, 94.5 per cent. For virtually all the serfs the conditions of existence offered nothing better than desperate poverty, ignorance, and subjection to the authority of the owner —whether private individual or the state. The degree of servility was appalling. The owner could regulate every detail of the serf's life (even marriage), could seize his possessions, judge or sell him, send him to military service, or banish him to Siberia. In short, when Alexander succeeded his murdered father in 1801, he became the ruler of a country more than 90 per cent of whose inhabitants were oppressed by slavery not essentially different from that which stirred the conscience of Harriet Beecher Stowe to the white heat of *Uncle Tom's Cabin*. It is interesting to speculate on what Mrs. Stowe might have written if she had lived in Russia. In the pre-Civil War South there were four million Negro slaves in comparison to a white population of nine and one-half million free men. The number of Southern slaves would have had to be more than doubled for the proportions to come close to those existing in Russia.

During the eighteenth century the intellectuals began to emerge, and by the second quarter of the nineteenth century they had started to play a dominant part in shaping the temper of the country. This development is noteworthy in view of the political repressions which had always made intellectual pursuits difficult in Russia. When Catherine became empress, only one institution of higher learning existed, the University of Moscow, and it was a great change for Russia when from the beginning of her reign Catherine looked with favor upon the spread of education. The increase of contacts with western Europe and the leavening effect of Western ideas provided a strong incentive for the development of a Russian intelligentsia. An astute and educated woman fascinated by Western philosophy and political ideology, Catherine encouraged the importation of foreign scholars, opened a number of schools for the gentry, sponsored the publication of several periodicals, and even permitted the establishment of private printing houses.

Nevertheless, the salient fact about education in Russia at the beginning of the nineteenth century was its strict limitation. All the essentials existed for the production of a small number of scholars, but the gap between the well trained and the masses was almost unbridgeable. Opportunities for education were accessible only to a small fraction of the population. The overwhelming majority remained submerged in the quagmire of ignorance.

The extremes of learning and ignorance were no more marked than the extremes of wealth and poverty. The nightmare incubus of slavery was, of course, responsible for the contrasts of wealth and poverty which existed in the Russia of Catherine and Alexander. The gentry had begun to amass vast wealth and power even before Catherine played into their hands by granting them almost unlimited scope in the gaining of both. Some of the nobles, their holdings in land and serfs having provided them with scarcely credible affluence, were able to live on a scale rivaling that of the monarch. The splendor of their way of life was similar to that of the French nobility before the revolution.

The majority of the peasants, on the other hand, plodded through their miserable existence in circumstances scarcely better than those in which farm animals lived. They were hardly ever regarded as individuals. Often they lived in villages or "communes" where individual liberty counted for little or nothing. D. S. Mirsky wrote about the results of the commune form of organization:

> There can be no doubt that both the commune and the *artel* (i.e., gang of workmen) did breed in the Russian people a different and less individualistic spirit than the European farmer's, and a more clearly felt class consciousness. . . . It was the commune that educated in them that capacity for mass action which made Russian peasant movements so formidably singleminded. A Russian peasant crowd is a real collective organism. . . . But what contributed most to make the peasants' class consciousness so intense

> and clear was the profound legal and cultural rift between them and their masters, whether squires or administrators.[1]

To understand the receptivity of the masses in modern Russia to the forms of communistic organization, it is important to keep in mind the historical prevalence of the commune as the social and economic unit of life.

Alexander I was a favorite of his grandmother's and she had supervised his education, selecting for him tutors who were, for the most part, intelligent and liberal men. Their influence, and that of several liberals among his close friends, was beneficial in shaping his early policies. But in sober truth, Alexander, like Catherine, was essentially a despot, though by comparison with his father's despotism, his had a relatively mild flavor.

At the outset of his reign the handsome, urbane Alexander justified the hopes of his subjects by lifting some of the oppressions imposed by Paul. He removed the restrictions on foreign scholars, books, and travel and lightened the censorship restrictions. He made some generous gestures toward the improvement of education (six universities were founded, along with a number of other schools) and granted more independence to the Orthodox church and more tolerance to dissenting groups. It does not seem unreasonable to assume that the young sovereign had some genuinely humanitarian impulses. He apparently wanted a constitution and a reform program, particularly a program to work toward the abolition of serfdom, but it would have required a more resolute and dedicated man than Alexander to effect any sweeping changes. The weight of opposition and confusion was too much for him to combat. The gentry were solidly against any reforms which might conflict with their interests. Except for some reorganization of government departments and the impetus given to education, little of note was accomplished even during the early and idealistic part of his reign. It was not

[1] *Russia, A Social History*, 219–20.

strange, therefore, that the auspicious beginnings were nullified by Alexander's later swing to reactionary and, to a degree, tyrannical policies.

Alexander's inclinations toward reform were already weakening when external events necessitated a complete change of emphasis. After the first four peaceful years of his reign, the next ten were almost wholly devoted to war or an uneasy balance on the edge of war. In 1804, Russia joined several other powers in a coalition against France. During the next several years the Russian forces met a series of reverses, humiliating to Alexander because he feared unfavorable comparison with his father and grandmother. Finally, exasperated and mistrustful, he performed an about-face. Deserting his allies, he signed an agreement with Napoleon—under melodramatic circumstances on a raft on the Nieman River at Tilsit—which gave both of them the illusion that the world was theirs for the taking. Temporarily the former enemies became allies, but the "peace" was only an anxious interval of parrying between two masters of diplomatic dueling. During this period the two monarchs became increasingly suspicious of each other; and as each pursued his devious aims, they drifted irrevocably toward the war of which the previous conflict had been but the prelude. When the Grand Army under Napoleon entered Russia in June, 1812, the event could not have failed to afford Alexander a certain relief. His appeasement policy had been unpopular in Russia. This was his opportunity to realize his ambitions as a military leader and statesman.

No other account of the Napoleonic invasion of Russia can compare in effectiveness with that of Tolstoy in *War and Peace*. In that novel the war—the battles, monarchs, generals, common soldiers, and common people—becomes a modern epic. The story of the French invasion, the battles at Smolensk and Borodino, and the occupation of Moscow need not be told here. It is enough to recall that in Moscow Napoleon had to choose between remaining for the winter in a despoiled enemy city, with inadequate provisions and small possibility of getting more, or retreating as quickly as possible before his men starved or froze to death. The consequences of his choice of the latter course are well known. What had started as an invading army turned into an ignominious rabble bent on survival. As they fled, they were nearly destroyed by the harrying tactics of the "conquered," by their own disorganization, and by the pressures of distance and climate. When the once "grand" army straggled back across the frontier, it was probably less than one-twelfth the size it had originally been. Thus ended a strange campaign lacking both victor and vanquished. The Russians had not conquered, but they had seen the invader routed. Two things were certain: the prestige of Napoleon had suffered a collapse from which it would never recover, and Russia was given credit for a strength she did not possess. An almost mystic sense of invincibility resulting from this illusory triumph was a partial cause of Alexander's determination not to conclude the conflict until Napoleon had been wholly vanquished.

When Alexander followed Napoleon across the border of his own country with the intention of "liberating" Europe, he had a grandiose sense of his own importance; and he had begun to assume heroic proportions in the opinion of multitudes of his subjects. The result was that he, encouraged by the support of Prussia, refused to conclude the war until the spring of 1814, although England and Austria—the other allies—would have been content on several occasions to make a settlement with France. When the allied forces entered Paris and Napoleon abdicated, Alexander saw himself as the great white hope of Europe.

At the final settlement, Russia received only a portion of the spoils for which Alexander had hoped. Nonetheless, this first Russian Czar of the nineteenth century had achieved, and continued for a time to bask in, an eminence never again approached by his successors. If something was subtracted from his stature by the settlement, it was temporarily restored by his proposal of a Holy Alliance of European powers. For some time Alexander had been swayed by religious influences which gave him the conviction that the affairs of Europe could be conducted according to Christian principles if the sovereigns would agree to rule in a spirit of harmony and justice. Such an attitude, he felt, would insure a new feeling of mutual responsibility and might lead to the preservation of peace in the future. The plan of the Holy Alliance, as drafted by Alexander, was intended to facilitate the realization of these aims. It provided that the individual monarchs should rule according to the finest ethical precepts and that all the monarchs should assist each other in time of need like members of a family. Even though the Alliance was signed by the leaders of almost all the European powers, it may be doubted whether any ruler except the Czar took it seriously. In spite of Alexander's sincerity, at least at the outset, the inevitable development occurred: as a league of rulers, the Holy Alliance became after a few years little more than an instrument for the maintenance of despotism. It is interesting to note that, though American sympathy had been for a time with the Alliance, the United States declined the invitation to membership when the evidence pointed to the autocratic nature of its policy.

After the end of the war and the creation of the Holy Alliance, nothing was left of the youthful idealism of Alexander. Still clinging to an illusion of liberality, he had in fact become pompous and reactionary. The forward-looking program of his ablest adviser, Michael Speransky, now seemed to him too advanced. The problems of serfdom no longer troubled his conscience. In fairness it should be said that he had made some new regulations which perceptibly improved the lot of the serfs. Early in his reign legislation had made it illegal for owners to exile their peasants to hard labor or sell them in the market. Restrictions (later removed) limited the rights of owners to punish the serfs severely. An appropriation of money made it possible for the state to buy large tracts of land from private landlords, whose peasants passed to government ownership. But all this was only a superficial treatment for a deep-seated disease. Many of the abuses

Please type

Russian Names:

pg. IX – X – xi

in the beginning of the book

DiBiasio

continued unabated; in some respects the conditions of serfdom became more unendurable than before.

During the war young Alexander Pushkin was spending his time in a boarding school for the children of aristocrats. This school, located in a wing of one of the palaces, was under the Czar's sponsorship. Though an indifferent student during his six years in the Lyceum, Pushkin distinguished himself from the first by his verses, marked by a stylistic finish and wit far beyond his years. Whether because he had frequent contacts with army officers, because he was periodically close enough to the court to develop a contempt for the monarchy, or simply because the spirit of freedom was in the air, by the end of his school days he had become something of a liberal. He undoubtedly shared the disappointment of other young liberals who had hoped at the end of the war to see their heroic Czar committed to a program for the abolition of serfdom and the reduction of autocracy, but who saw him instead committed to nothing but an alliance, "Holy" in name only. In place of the liberal advisers of his youth, including the enlightened Speransky, Alexander had as his closest mentor during the last years of his reign a reactionary who had held the same position under Paul. This man's brutish spirit and ethics had been appropriate for the regime of the earlier monarch, but his reinstatement in a position of prestige by Alexander offered a sad commentary on the degeneration in outlook of a Czar who had started out to compensate for the despotism of his father's system. In an unpublished section deleted from his famous verse-novel, *Eugene Onegin*, Pushkin fittingly called Alexander

> *A man weak and also cunning,*
> *A fop gone bald, toil's arrant foe,*
> *Whom fame had, by strange chance, been sunning . . .*

In harmony with a policy now strictly conservative, the press was again subjected to outrageous censorship. The universities were placed under surveillance, and all evidences of progressive teaching were severely frowned upon. Throughout the entire country a program was launched to root out "subversive" ideas. Literature was held in overt suspicion. Pushkin himself had hardly got into print before he ran afoul of the authorities. Following his graduation from the Lyceum at the age of eighteen, he received an appointment in the Foreign Office. Since his position, like many other posts in the Russian bureaucracy, was only a nominal one, he had plenty of time for amours and literature. At that period he did not hesitate to set down his opinions freely, even if doing so meant criticizing serfdom, autocracy, and, on occasion, the Czar. His early work is full of his "love affair with freedom." In a poem addressed to a fellow liberal ("To Chaadayev"[2]), he spoke of "oppression's fateful hand," and declared:

In hope, in torment, we are turning
Toward freedom, waiting her command.

And he urged his readers:

While freedom kindles us, my friend
While honor calls us and we hear it,
Come: to our country let us tend
The noble promptings of the spirit . . .

A year later in the poem "In the Country," Pushkin gave even stronger expression to his sentiments. He spoke of fleeing "from all the vice of Czardom's courts" to the quietude of the country, where he could live simply and let his thoughts wander freely. But even in this retreat he could not escape the pain of awareness. Everywhere he encountered the serfs, masked by ignorance and bound by slavery. He described the owners of the slaves:

Blind to all tears, and deaf to every groan,

[2] The poems by Pushkin quoted in this chapter have been translated by the following: "To Chaadayev," "With Freedom's Seed the Desert Sowing," and "Unto Myself I Reared a Monument" by Babette Deutsch; "Message to Siberia" by Max Eastman; and "In the Country" by Walter Morrison.

Chosen by destiny to ruin other lives,
Heartless and lawless, here a race of masters thrives;
Wielding a ruthless rod, it makes its own
The peasant's toil, his chattels and his days . . .

The slaves, he said, were as helpless as if they had been animals yoked to the plows they pushed across the earth for the benefit of masters deaf to all entreaties: "Here all bear heavy yokes till their last hours." He wondered whether he would ever see his nation free, a "lovely dawn," and whether a Czar would someday abolish serfdom. But the tone of the poem is heavy; the poet had small reason for hope.

For these and other "dangerous thoughts" Pushkin was soon transferred (more exactly, banished) from St. Petersburg. He was sent to southern Russia, where, his professional duties existing on paper only, he was free to wander about at will in the Caucasus and the Crimea. The beautiful scenery and the picturesque people (including gypsies) with whom he became acquainted stimulated his romantic imagination; yet Pushkin found this involuntary exile from the social gaiety and the culture of Moscow and Petersburg extremely trying. Although untroubled by duties and always supplied with the means to carry on the dissipated habits to which he was accustomed, he smarted under the veiled supervision which left him no real freedom. Bitterness and disappointment succeeded his earlier optimistic faith in the future. He wondered whether freedom was only a dream, not in Russia alone, but in western Europe as well. Now that he had begun to know "the people," he found them like mute "flocks." During this period he wrote his well-known poem, "With Freedom's Seed," in which he referred bitterly to his efforts to sow the seeds of the love of liberty in the minds and wills of his countrymen. As a result of this endeavor he had learned, he said, "what lost labors are." The poem ends on a tone of indictment mixed with hopelessness:

Should flocks heed freedom's invocations?

Their part is to be slain or shorn,
Their dower the yoke their sires have worn
Through snug and sheeplike generations.

At Odessa, where he was stationed briefly, Pushkin found some relief from the stifling provincialism of the earlier scenes of his exile, but he clashed with his superior, who had the awkward idea that the poet should perform certain official duties. He was soon in disfavor on so many counts that he was dropped from his post. Thereafter he was forced to live under undisguised surveillance on one of the Pushkin family estates deep in the country. Despite the fact that almost all the young man's energies were devoted to literature on the one hand and to amatory adventures and libertinism on the other, he was looked upon with as much suspicion as if he had really taken action against the government.

The inevitable outcome of such repressions as those to which Pushkin was subjected—and his experience was comparatively mild because of the cushioning effect of his widely heralded genius—was an upsurge of the spirit of rebellion. The backward swing of the pendulum was unendurable after the bright hopes which attended the start of Alexander's reign—hopes raised even higher by the auspicious termination of the war. Moreover, members of the gentry and common people who had gone abroad after the war had observed more liberal forms of government, which they began to dream of seeing in Russia. Many were strongly influenced by the revolutionary mood of western Europe. At first the consequent agitation in Russia was confined to secret societies whose aims put primary emphasis upon the development of a constitutional monarchy and the abolition of serfdom. Alexander was kept informed of the workings of these secret societies but was apparently satisfied that the inconclusiveness of their plans made them relatively harmless. Actually, the majority of the members of the societies favored revolution. There seemed no immediate likelihood that they would attempt the realization of their purpose, however, until the death of Alexander provided an unexpected opportunity.

When the Czar died in December, 1825, there was a strange confusion with regard to the succession. While Alexander was still living, his highly respected brother, the Grand Duke Constantine, had made known his refusal to accept the responsibility of rulership, and Alexander had handled the matter of naming his successor with odd indecisiveness. Therefore, after his death some time elapsed before the issue was resolved by the determination of the younger brother, Nicholas, to claim the throne. Known for his open adherence to reactionary views, Nicholas was not admired. Consequently, the period of uncertainty ending with Nicholas' seizure of power was accompanied by considerable disturbance.

At this point in the history of Russia the ranks of the liberals were still thin, and the revolutionary minded were comparatively few. But though few, they were spirited. They saw in the ascent to power of Nicholas a threat to the welfare of Russia and a moment to make a beginning at revolt. On the day designated for taking the oath of loyalty to the new sovereign, at the instigation of some of the revolutionaries a group of approximately 2,000 soldiers refused to swear allegiance. Lacking experienced leadership and with no definite organization, the so-called "Decembrist" uprising was easily put down although the rebels were not suppressed until they had been fired upon by other troops. Nicholas did not hesitate to make his position clear. Using this revolt as a dire warning, he had 120 of the instigators brought to trial. Five were put to death and more than 100 were sent to Siberia, 31 of these to hard labor. When the novelist Dostoevsky was banished to Siberia nearly twenty-five years later for what had been interpreted as an attitude disloyal to the regime of Nicholas, he was the recipient of benefactions from the wives of some of these exiles, long since become symbolic figures.

The Decembrists accomplished nothing tangible. Yet their rebellion and their martyrdom amounted to the turning of a page in Russian history. They openly held up to question the power of the monarchy. Their uprising, though of small magnitude and ignominious conclusion, may accurately be called the prologue to the revolution which matured ninety-two years later.

When the Decembrist revolt occurred, Pushkin was in unwilling rustication. Whether he would have joined the rebellion if doing so had been within his power is uncertain. Pushkin had many of the characteristics of the Byronic hero, and his ardor for freedom was probably secondary to other interests, especially after he had become disillusioned by personal experience. Still, he had a number of friends among the Decembrists, and he was moved by their martyrdom. To the wife of one of them he gave the manuscript of his poem "Message to Siberia," not published until after his death:

Deep in the Siberian mine,
Keep your patience proud;
The bitter toil shall not be lost,
The rebel thought unbowed. . . .

The heavy-hanging chains will fall,
The walls will crumble at a word;
And freedom greet you in the light,
And brothers give you back the sword.

Nicholas I, nineteen years Alexander's junior, made no pretense to liberal views. Born the year his grandmother, Catherine the Great, died, he was brought up without her influence. Because it was considered unlikely that he would be Czar, no effort had been made to give him an education which might have added breadth to his outlook. Like his father he was attracted to militarism and despotism. Unimaginative and lacking in insight and idealism, he was stubbornly honest, stodgy, suspicious, and inflexible. Notwithstanding his having few of the qualifications of a good ruler, he had a strong concept of his duty, which he proceeded inexorably to fulfill. Having set his course, he followed it—to the point of suffocation for his country.

Obviously, Nicholas began his rule under adverse circumstances. The Decembrist uprising fomented widespread agitation which could not be put down as firmly as he had put down the revolt. In his favor it must be admitted that he did not stop with checking the rebellion and punishing the conspirators. Having given sober consideration to the causes of the uprising and the protests of the Decembrists, he immediately set about providing a remedy for the grievances he considered legitimate. One of the criticisms was directed against the outworn, inadequate legal code and the lack of a consistent or just court system. Another pointed out the confusion in finances caused by overissuance of currency. For the correction of these defects the new Czar summoned able assistants who made noteworthy improvements.

The most vehement protests of the rebels had to do with the abuses of serfdom, which, they rightly pointed out, could not be controlled by ignoring them. Honestly concerned with this matter, Nicholas endeavored to relieve some of the most painful pressures. Despite his good intentions, however, the predicament of the serfs was not measurably improved. Like Alexander before him, Nicholas failed to get beneath the surface. The conditions of poverty, ignorance, and injustice in which the peasants were forced to live and die remained essentially unchanged. Enactments which might have been beneficial elicited resistance from the gentry, who often refused to abide by them. Also standing in the way of these and other improvements was the unwieldy machinery of bureaucracy. The government had become a huge complex of officials and bureaus in which inefficiency was rampant and tyranny the order from high to low.

The Decembrists' last major criticism was directed against the sparse educational opportunities and the government's disinterest in raising the intellectual level of the populace. At this point the Czar's response collided with the view of the insurrectionists. He was unwilling to do more than make a few minor concessions, for his whole program was calculated to throttle the spread of enlightenment and the spirit of inquiry. Knowing that the Decembrists had received most of the stimulus for the development of liberal views from the study of Western philosophy and social theory, Nicholas reasoned that to prevent the spread of such views required the suppression of all "free" thought. A few months after he began to rule, he inaugurated a systematic campaign for the control of ideas. Regulations regarding censorship became so severe that it was practically impossible to publish anything which could, by the widest stretch of the innumerable censors' imaginations, be considered other than innocuous. Books on philosophy were altogether forbidden. The interchange of thought between Russia and western Europe was again sharply curtailed. Freedom of discussion in the press was nonexistent. Writers who attempted to convey anything beyond the banal or obvious were forced to have recourse to "double talk." Phraseology in the slightest degree inimical to the monarchy, either past or present, was absolutely banned. The famous historian of Russia, Sir Bernard Pares, has pointed out that even musical notation and rows of dots in print were suspect: "The censor Akhmatov stopped a book on arithmetic because between the figures of a problem he saw a row of dots."[3]

The universities suffered perhaps most seriously from these repressions. Considering them, as Nicholas did, storm centers of radicalism existing for the purpose of threatening his power and raising his blood pressure, he took every possible measure to limit their freedom. The curricula were reorganized to put more emphasis upon everything Russian. The study of foreign literatures and history was almost eliminated and of philosophy either eliminated or emasculated. Professors were spied upon, their oral and written utterances checked as if they were archtraitors. Associations of students were discouraged, because they might provide an environment for the enunciation of radical ideas. A network of spies permeated every phase of university activity, including the debating and discussion societies. Novelist Fyodor

[3] *A History of Russia*, 336.

Dostoevsky's attendance at the meetings of such a group led to his arrest, his imprisonment in solitary confinement, the sentence of death later changed to exile in Siberia, and the loss of ten productive years from his life at the height of his creative power.[4] Opportunities for foreign study were difficult to obtain. To hold down the number of potential malcontents, the czarist agents limited university size to not more than three hundred students, all of whom were expected to be robots with no inclination for freedom of inquiry.

With regard to the general population, Nicholas was convinced that there was safety for him in their ignorance. His arguments have a familiar tone. They were the same as those used in America by white masters who held that even a little learning would be "dangerous" for their black slaves. Whereas early in his reign Nicholas made a few gestures in behalf of the extension of technical education, he was soon so alarmed by the receptivity to any and all types of learning that he backtracked farther than his original position. With repression and curtailment the watchwords for such education as existed, to say nothing of the dense ignorance of the huge mass of peasantry (which in 1835, the tenth year of Nicholas' reign, still composed more than 70 per cent of the population), the populace was in a state of intellectual stupor.

To maintain this condition Nicholas employed a vast police and spy system whose members counted every beat of the national pulse. The eye of Big Brother in George Orwell's *1984* was scarcely more ubiquitous than Nicholas' network of informants. People were arrested for the most trifling and even for imaginary infringements of the regulations. Americans aghast at the repressive practices of present-day dictatorships will discover from even a superficial investigation of the reign of Nicholas that there is nothing really new about modern repressive procedures. Practically every device the Soviet regime has used to control and standardize the population was used for the same purpose and with more deadening effect a century earlier.

[4] See Chapter VI.

Remarkably enough, in spite of general oppression, the era of Nicholas saw an unprecedented intellectual awakening among the few to whom advanced education was available. It was as if the very fact of tyranny forced the growth of what had been rare but now became rich and vigorous. Notwithstanding the stultification within the universities, many students developed a passion for learning and became absorbed by their largely *sub rosa* contacts with western European philosophy, literature, and social thought. Among the professors a number of excellent scholars were dedicated to keeping alive freedom of investigation and a dispassionate pursuit of the truth. The Russian literary genius had already begun to manifest itself in the writings of Pushkin even during Alexander's reign, but in his twelve remaining years under Nicholas, Pushkin laid a magnificent foundation for a national literature. It is not too much to say that he was the Russian Shakespeare, both in the quality of his talent and in his generative influence.

Nicholas himself took an unexpected personal interest in the poet—which at first glance seems out of character but was indicative of his cunning. One day in 1826, a special messenger from the Czar appeared at Pushkin's country retreat to summon him to Moscow. There, in the midst of the coronation celebrations, Nicholas received the long-suspect littérateur. After a lengthy interview, the substance of which was never disclosed, the Czar "pardoned" the poet and offered to become his sponsor (in plain words, his censor). Pushkin refused this "opportunity," but was apparently forced to promise good behavior. Thereafter he was never able to escape the clutches of Nicholas. Russia's foremost literary figure was not permitted to go abroad, to travel freely in Russia, or to join the army. The Czar delegated to the head of the gendarmery the responsibility of being Pushkin's special watchdog and counselor—the hope being not only to control the poet's pen but to harness it to the service of the state. The censorship of all his writings was inordinately strict.

The years of his banishment had added richness and variety

to Pushkin's experiences and given him leisure to write, even if he never freed himself from emotional entanglements. When the poet came back to Moscow, with distractions and dissipations increased, his output was still brilliant though less prolific. He had begun to compose prose pieces which compared favorably with his poetry in charm and excellence of style. Unfortunately, as a result of his uncurbed habits of extravagance, he was soon pressed by debts as well as by harassing censorship. But most perturbing of all was a lengthy courtship of the famous beauty, Natalie Goncharova, an irresponsible, empty-headed flirt thirteen years his junior, whom he was determined to marry. The poet himself scarcely knew with how many women he had been infatuated, but when he married Natalie, he mortgaged all the remnants of his freedom and signed his death warrant.

Pushkin and his wife settled at Tsarskoe Selo (the Russian equivalent of Versailles), where the poet had gone to school. This was the summer residence of the Czar. Coming thus to the attention of Nicholas, Pushkin was again given a nominal post in the Foreign Office with a salary intended to help him maintain his gay and frivolous young wife in a manner befitting her beauty. That Nicholas also noticed and favored Natalie soon became apparent. When Pushkin was made a Gentleman of the Bedchamber, he understood that the inappropriate appointment had been intended to make possible his wife's attendance at court balls. He now found himself in a position doubly insupportable. As a courtier, in debt to and under the inescapable eye of the Czar, he had become subservient to the royal favor. As the husband of a dazzling beauty and court favorite, he was forced into the role of social escort, a glorified gigolo. Any satisfaction he may have felt at having been freed from banishment soon turned to gall.

His debts, his wife's coquettish abandonment to the social whirl, and his shame at being the pawn of a tyrant became a mesh tightening around him. He made several attempts to extricate himself, but all were ineffectual. In a last desperate effort to achieve at least financial independence, he established a magazine, *The Contemporary*; but the high costs, the small number of readers of serious journalism, and, most of all, the censorship doomed the undertaking from the beginning. The despot had won his duel with genius. Meanwhile, the irrepressible Natalie was attracting a swarm of admirers. Rumors of dishonor came more frequently to the harrassed husband. It did not matter to his wife that the greatest of Russian poets was being destroyed by suspicion and despair. Natalie loved intrigue. She had no thought but her own shallow pleasure—as many admirers and as much attention as possible.

Gradually, the slanderous rumors coupling Natalie's name with that of a young officer of the guards became serious. Then they were supplemented by anonymous letters accusing her of infidelity. It became necessary for Pushkin to defend his wife's honor. In the duel between the poet and the young officer, Pushkin was mortally wounded. He died two days later, in January, 1837, at the age of thirty-eight.

Pushkin was the slave of his own passions, the martyr to political tyranny and domestic entanglements. He was the victim of outmoded political and social systems, but he inspired new systems and new ideas. He was an ardent patriot without strong political theories or allegiance. His hopes for liberalism had been dashed even before the collapse of the Decembrist movement. Still, he offered a challenge to the best of the national spirit and became a rallying point in the cause of freedom. The splendor of his genius lit up the darkness of his age like a beacon. He spoke truly of himself when in one of his last poems ("Unto Myself I Reared a Monument," 1836) he wrote:

Not wholly shall I die—but in the lyre my spirit
Shall, incorruptible and bodiless, survive—
And I shall know renown as long as under heaven
One poet yet remains alive. . . .

I shall be loved, and long the people will remember

The kindly thoughts I stirred—my music's brightest crown,
How in this cruel age I celebrated freedom,
And begged for ruth toward those cast down.

Pushkin was followed by another poet, Mikhail Lermontov, also memorable for his challenging insight into his age. Some of Lermontov's poems are significantly prophetic. His novel, *A Hero of Our Time*, accurately analyzes the mood of paralyzing disillusionment which enervated many of the intellectuals who succumbed to the stagnation of the period. Other poets, dramatists, and novelists in large number proved worthy successors. The young Turgenev had begun to write, Dostoevsky had published his first effort, and Tolstoy had taken the initial steps in his career while Nicholas still occupied the throne. No one can guess what talents, or how many, failed to rise above the frustrations of the era. But it is no exaggeration to assert that those which survived had a special brilliance. Their achievements were assisted by the master of Russian literary critics, Vissarion Belinsky, who promulgated a new independence of judgment and added incentive to creative achievement. Around him rallied the best minds of the time—writers, philosophers, historians, journalists, and artists, most of whom drank from the fountain of Western culture. Despite almost insurmountable barriers to free expression, they succeeded in challenging the intellectual isolationism of Russia. Many of the most stirring documents of the times were never published, or if published were quickly repressed, but that did not prevent their serving as fuses to set off the imagination and indignation of the intellectuals among whom they were circulated in manuscript.

During the reign of Nicholas, the intelligentsia, formerly limited almost wholly to the gentry, was extended to include representatives from the middle class and even the proletariat. Since many of the latter knew from personal experience the meaning of oppression as few among the gentry could know, they possessed an intense receptivity to radical political and social theories. This responsiveness made a great difference in the evolution of Russian thought. The power of the thinking minority has scarcely ever been more clearly illustrated than in the Russia of Nicholas I.

In 1842 two peculiarly important events occurred in Russia. The first, the construction of a railroad between Petersburg and Moscow, signalized the material development of the nation. This was a landmark in the industrial progress of the country. The second was the publication of Gogol's searing indictment of the land-owning classes, *Dead Souls*. This novel was by implication one of the first tangible demands for social progress.

Nicholas died in the midst of a struggle which brought him no glory and gave Russia no rewards. The Czar had long occupied a position as the most staunch advocate of absolutism. Before the year 1848 brought the outbreak of revolution to several parts of Europe, Nicholas had become a symbol of reaction, committed to the suppression of democratic movements. In 1848 only one European monarch stood firm—and that was Nicholas. In the autumn of 1854, however, when the siege of Sevastopol began, the inflexibility of Nicholas was no longer enough to hold his power intact. For many people the Crimean War means little except the occasion Tennyson somewhat sentimentally commemorated in "The Charge of the Light Brigade," but it was in fact the last test of the system by which Nicholas had lived and ruled.

He did not survive to witness the collapse of that system. When he died in 1855, he was already an anachronism. To the last he remained a conscientious tyrant, the champion of absolute monarchy. In an age when the people had begun to insist upon the rights of humanity, he never wavered in his position, from which he scornfully looked down upon the masses as the property of the monarch, to be kept abject and inarticulate, to obey but never to inquire. But in the end he lost the duel of monarch *versus* people; he lost to the spirit of freedom of which Pushkin sang.

Visitors to Russia today are not likely to see either statues or pictures of Nicholas (though a statue of him on horseback occupies a prominent position in a small square near the famous St. Isaac Cathedral in Leningrad). But Pushkin is the idol of the Russian people. The palace at Tsarskoe Selo, now called Pushkin, is of interest primarily because one wing has been converted into a museum housing a memorable collection of the poet's writings and personal effects. And one may come upon the likeness of Pushkin almost anywhere. He has even been immortalized in alabaster in one of the stations of the Leningrad subway!

II/ Gogol and the Dead Souls

The effort to seek in literature explanations of the Russian personality and the causes behind Russian history during the past century may well begin with the writings of Nicholai Vassilievich Gogol (1809–52), to whom credit has been given for fixing Russian literature firmly upon the path of realism. Indeed, Dostoevsky once stated that all later Russian literature emanated from one of Gogol's stories, "The Cloak" ("The Overcoat"). To fill the role that Gogol played would seem to have required a man of impressive and magnetic personality, but Gogol was neither impressive nor magnetic. He was a man of nondescript, at times almost ridiculous, appearance. He came from an undistinguished background and was satisfied with a mediocre education. He spent his entire life under the illusion that he had been born to a greatness he never achieved. After a period of popularity as a writer he ran into gales of disfavor and rejection, justified by the early decline of his creative powers and by the reactionary sentiments he expressed in his last years. He lived at intervals on the loans and gifts of friends and died leaving nothing—except a handful of manuscripts which helped change the course of Russian history.

Born into a family of moderate means among the Ukrainian gentry, Gogol never developed the inclinations or pursuits of a country gentleman. He was apparently not influenced at all by his father, who died when Gogol was still a schoolboy. From his mother he derived an excessive religiosity, which took the form of a lifelong attempt to cultivate partnership with the Almighty. This characteristic can best be studied in his correspondence—with relatives, friends, admirers, enemies, and even strangers—all of which is infused with expressions of self-castigation, pietistic sentimentality, and moral exhortation. At school he was often intellectually arrogant but never a genuine scholar. There and later he turned restlessly from one interest to another, always coming back to literature. No matter what direction his moods took him, he always found excuses for himself—for what he wanted to do and what he failed to do—in the convenient mystery of the divine will. His ability to invent excuses was remarkable, and although few of his excuses were credible, his relatives and friends usually took them seriously.

He went to St. Petersburg at the age of nineteen, a young man with no preparation for or visible means of achieving security, but sustained by the assurance that he had been born to a great destiny. He had dreamed of St. Petersburg as a mysterious and splendid city, an earthly paradise for the artistic and sensitive spirit, but the reality proved cold and unresponsive to his hopes. He found that the world not only was not waiting to receive him, but had no concern for him at all. The adolescent poems he had apparently expected to use as heralds of his genius fell with a dull thud. Their only effect was to provide the first of the shocks to his sensibilities, from which Gogol always recoiled as if he had been smitten by an avenging Fury.

His abortive attempts at job hunting led him to the theater, and he made one or two vain efforts to become an actor without realizing that he had not a particle of talent. After several dodges and false starts he spent a short interval in the civil service. In this position his duties (although vague) and observations led him to the conclusion that government work was insufferable, not so much because of the inefficiency and petty tyrannies of the bureaucracy as because having to perform routine tasks hampered his impulse to soar. Later he had one or two teaching posts, including a lectureship in history at St. Petersburg University. This foolish venture quickly became a fiasco since his pretensions to scholarship were not supported either by knowledge or by a capacity for sustained effort. It was typical of Gogol that although his first lecture was eloquent, he never afterward had anything to say; his superficial learning provided no reserves upon which to draw. Before he gave up his post, he had become a caricature of a professor, but he never admitted to himself that he alone was responsible for his failure.

Uncertainty and a sense of unfulfillment, combined with his inclination to flee when he felt injured or unappreciated, drove him to sporadic bouts of traveling whenever he could acquire the necessary funds. He was a lifelong hypochondriac, and although during most of his life the doctors could find nothing wrong with his health, he believed that what he called "the open road" was the only sure means to restoration of physical vitality for him.

He saw something of Russia but was much more inclined toward lengthy excursions into western Europe, where he was particularly attracted to Rome. This refined vagabondage—which he always explained on the grounds of physical, artistic, or ethical necessity—was, of course, a symptom of spiritual malaise. Gogol believed he was searching for something, for a sign or the key to unlock revelation. The probability is that he was always running away from an unacknowledged sense of his own inadequacy. His varied journeys apparently had small effect on the vivid grotesqueries of his imagination, but they certainly deepened his sense of being homeless even in his own country.

Through mutual friends Gogol made the acquaintance of Pushkin, who, although ten years older than he, apparently became somewhat interested in his potentialities. From the beginning of their acquaintance Pushkin perhaps involuntarily exerted a directive influence upon him. In spite of the infrequency of their contacts, Gogol felt that Pushkin understood him as no one else could, and he depended on the poet for stimulation and to some extent for critical guidance. At Pushkin's death Gogol believed he had lost his strongest inspiration and feared that his own literary achievements would suffer. Actually, some of his best writing was done, or at least completed, in the years immediately following the death of Pushkin; thereafter his creative powers rapidly deteriorated.

Even as a schoolboy Gogol had imagined lofty designs for the great works he would produce, but he showed little promise of literary achievement. When he started to write in earnest, he proceeded as if without any design at all. He was like a juggler who tossed into the air the balls of epic poetry, heroic narrative, history, and folklore but was able to manipulate only the latter. His first stories and the historical romance *Taras Bulba*, written in his twenties, reflect the influence of his Ukrainian background. Composed largely of elements drawn from folklore and legend mixed with fragments of history, they have the sprightliness that soon came to be one of the most appealing qualities of his style. They are a strange blend of the fantastic and the real, the former presented in such a straightforward way—sometimes laconic, sometimes droll, and usually with deadpan seriousness—as to seem almost realistic. Their romantic or supernatural material and eccentric characters attracted immediate attention and proved popular. Soon dwarfed by what have long been considered his more significant works, they have received less attention than they deserve. However, when they first rose above the dull horizon of Russian literature, Gogol's tales, *Evenings on a Farm Near Dikanka*, were the cause of excited adulation on the part of most critics. Gogol was, of course, gratified by his quick rise to fame, but it was no surprise to him as it must have been to almost everyone else. After all, he had always assumed he was born to be great. He made it clear, furthermore, that what he had accomplished was only a pale intimation of what was to come.

The three works which brought Gogol immortality are completely different in spirit and material from his earlier productions. One of these, "The Cloak," is the short story mentioned at the beginning of this chapter about which Dostoevsky made such extravagant claims. A drama, *The Government Inspector* (*The Revizor*, 1836), became the best-known and remained the most popular play in Russia until the time of Chekhov at the end of the century. It engendered widespread and intense protest among those whom it held up to mocking scrutiny, but it gave the author temporary financial security. After it was produced, he spent most of his time abroad, particularly in Italy, where he completed the novel *Dead Souls* (1842), the third of his epoch-making trio. Each of these works is a landmark in Russian literature. Together they set a new style which dominated the writing of the entire century.

I.

"The Cloak" is a story, simple not only in language and plot, but, more important, in the personality and circumstances of its main character. It does not deal with a member of the nobility, an aristocrat, or even a landowner without a title. It is the story of a humble and hence an obscure and forgotten man.

Akakii Akakiievich was a copy clerk in one of the government bureaus. No one was sure how long he had been there, but there he always was, bent over his task, wordlessly accepting each bit of copying set before him. Often the other clerks ridiculed him, but only when the ridicule became unbearable would he humbly beg to be let alone. And except for the jibes of his co-workers, Akakii was left alone in solitude and poverty.

The time came, however, when the vacant tranquillity of his existence was interrupted by an emergency—the necessity to do something about his overcoat, a garment so threadbare that it was "no better than the coarsest of sacking."[1] Intending to have the coat patched, Akakii took it to a tailor, who asserted that there was not enough left to sew the patches to. Finally, he pronounced the verdict: Akakii must have a new overcoat.

> At the word *new* a mist swam before Akakii Akakiievich's eyes and everything in the room became a hotchpotch. . . .
>
> "A new one? But how?" he asked, still as if he were in a dream. "Why, I have no money for that."

But eventually he saw that the old overcoat was beyond repair, "and his spirits sank utterly. Really now, with what means, with what money would he make this overcoat?" Fortunately, for

[1] From the translation by Bernard Guilbert Guerney.

years Akakii had made a habit of saving an occasional copper, and his small hoard proved to be half of what the new coat would cost. To get the other half, he had to impose upon himself the most stringent curtailment of his already frugal expenditures.

Although Akakii began his program of added economy with a will trained by life-long necessity, he found it hard at first to live on the bare edge of survival. But soon the new habits were formed, "and everything went well; he even became perfectly trained to going hungry of evenings; on the other hand, however, he had spiritual sustenance . . . the eternal idea of the new overcoat." He became, thus, a man with a purpose, and in anticipation the new coat shone like a light before his eyes. In not much more than a year the dream which had added fullness to his life and brought an occasional sparkle to his eyes was realized: the new overcoat was his.

The other clerks in the department were so much impressed with the coat that they insisted they must help Akakii celebrate, and one decided to give a party. Akakii was startled by such an innovation, but blushingly agreed to attend. The need for absolute economy no longer pressing upon him, he ate his evening meal almost gaily and started out with unprecedented lightness of heart, enjoying the prospect of a walk in his new coat. The party, the merrymaking, and the crowd filled Akakii with wonder. Long after his usual bedtime, when the festivities were at their liveliest, he stole quietly away, happy as he had never been before, for he was no longer solitary.

Even though the night was dark, the enfolding warmth of his new coat made him feel secure as he started out alone. This sense of security, however, was an illusion; the little man in Russia had no security. As he plodded homeward through the silent streets, two ruffians set upon him, knocked him down, and left him lying unconscious in the snow. When he came to himself, he was first aware of the cold and then realized to his horror that his coat was gone. He tried to call for help, but there was no one to hear.

Akakii's predicament provided the opportunity for Gogol to

make an unconcealed attack on bureaucratic officialdom. He shows Akakii, not knowing where else to turn for assistance, going to the justice of the peace, whom he was permitted to see only at the fourth attempt. The justice, of course, had no interest in the matter and would do nothing for him. For a whole day and for the first time in his life Akakii stayed away from his work—this was the measure of his despair. The next day some of the more kindly clerks urged him to appeal to another official who would surely consult with the proper authorities and even, if need be, undertake to help Akakii by corresponding with the proper government bureau.

Numbed by his overwhelming sense of loss and impotence, the poor clerk went to the official, only to be met with such a show of arrogance and brutality that he was "bereft of his senses, swayed, shook all over, and simply could not stand on his feet." This official, like the police officer to whom he had previously appealed, behaved as though Akakii were the offender, not the victim. After this rebuff Akakii realized that there was no one anywhere from whom he might expect help.

> How he went down the stairs, how he came out into the street—that was something Akakii Akakiievich was no longer conscious of . . . he breasted the blizzard that was whistling and howling through the streets. . . . In a second it had blown a quinsy down his throat, and he crawled home without the strength to utter a word.

The despair, the exposure, and the fever were too much for him, and he died, as he had lived, alone:

> And Petersburg was left without Akakii Akakiievich, as if he had never been therein. There vanished and disappeared a being protected by none, endeared to no one, of no interest to anyone, a being that actually had failed to attract to itself the attention of even a naturalist who wouldn't let a chance slip of sticking an ordinary housefly on a pin and of examining it through a microscope; a being that had submissively endured the jests of the whole chancellery and that had gone to its grave without any

> extraordinary fuss, but before which . . . there had flitted a radiant guest in the guise of an overcoat, which had animated for an instant a poor life.

Here for the first time in Russian literature the small man, the man of no importance, commands not only pity but also respect. Cruelly and unjustly wronged, in life he finds no one who will succor or even sympathize with him. But after his death something happens. It is as if the dead had refused to be buried. His spirit demands redress. In ghostly form he takes on a stature and power he could never have hoped for in life and becomes the bane of the unscrupulous, corrupt officials, symbolic of the tyranny that pushes down the little man to abjectness, if not slavery. Only when he has had his revenge will he accept the obscurity of the grave.

Actually, the ghost of Akakii Akakiievich was never laid. His soul went marching on, straight through the nineteenth century until a day in 1917 when it stormed into the winter palace of the Czar and destroyed what it supposed was the ultimate symbol of tyranny. It is not difficult for the readers of Gogol's story to hear the trumpet call addressed to the Russian people. It would be a mistake, however, to imply that Gogol wrote to issue a call to action. It is rather as if he were an instrument, an expression of the will of a people not yet aware of their will.

II.

Gogol's lack of ability as an actor did not prevent him from having a sound sense of what makes good theater. His satiric comedy, *The Government Inspector*, was recognized at once as excellent drama, and the passing of time has not diminished its impact. Modern readers, especially American readers, will find familiar material in the play. Theatergoers have become accustomed to seeing representatives of the existing political regime pilloried on the stage. Such plays as *I'd Rather Be Right* by George Kaufman and Moss Hart, *Both Your Houses* by Maxwell Anderson, and *State of the Union* by Howard Lindsay and Russell

Crouse contain similar material. But those plays were not written in Russia in 1836. Moreover, the wisecracking impudence, the raillery, or even the calculated accusations of these playwrights do not produce the effect of exposing political skulduggery in all its ugly nakedness, an effect which Gogol's satire achieves. True, there is a quality of buffoonery about his play, but it is buffoonery motivated by fear and distaste, whereas political satires on the American stage are usually undergirded by buoyant optimism derived from faith in the future. In political satires the officials are always scoundrels and usually fools. The fact that in the Russian play they are scoundrels by conviction contrasts with the implication of most American dramatists that beneath the scoundrelly exterior, in the breast of every politician lurks that peculiarly American institution, a heart of gold. Most striking about Gogol's characters is their consciousness of their baseness and the complacency with which they plan for, abet each other in, and blame themselves for failing to carry off their villainies.

The play was by no means as much an innovation as "The Cloak." Exposure of corrupt politicians had occurred before, even in Russian literature, but the outspoken sweep of the treatment was something new. The simple plot turns on a case of mistaken identity, which was suggested to the author by an anecdote Pushkin had related about his having been mistaken for a government personage sent to inspect the work of the dignitaries in a certain town. The setting, a provincial town, and the characters, the officials of that town, might have been anywhere and any officials. They are the prototypes of the despicable, petty politicians not only of the period of Nicholas I in Russia, but of all times and places. This universality, bolstered by the rollicking humor, accounts for the power of the drama.

The most original character in the play is the young rogue, Khlestakov, who, mistaken for the government inspector by the town officials, rides the flood tide of their efforts at dissimulation. At first the inadvertent accessory to their villainy, he soon understands and outsmarts them. Khlestakov is not really evil, but he is satisfied to live by his wits and turn events to his own advantage. Obviously, it would have been a violation of Gogolian drollery to condemn the young rake for benefiting from the stupid error of those who practiced chicanery, considering that he was smart enough to outwit them.

Gogol develops the actions of the drama as if in wide-eyed innocence. Without moralizing, the play has an air of gaiety in its disclosure of the meanness, vulgarity, and scheming of its sordid-souled bureaucrats. Indeed, it is difficult for the modern reader to evaluate just how serious Gogol may have been or whether he was serious at all. That he had any expectation of bringing about reform through the medium of his play is unlikely, as is also any intention to hit at particular targets in the government. The fact is that Gogol was not opposed to the czarist regime, and he seemed genuinely amazed that his mockery of representatives of the government was automatically regarded as an attack on the government itself. He tried to make it clear that the individuals he depicted were only incidental by-products and not integral parts of the system. He had simply allowed his mad-hatter imagination to work freely, and he maintained truly that he was neither critic nor ranting reformer. But the more he tried to defend his intention, the louder the clamor grew.

In fact, the play aroused such protest that the censor passed it only at the insistence of the Czar. Nicholas' determination to have the play passed and produced is incredible. Given the personality of Nicholas, it is impossible to propose seriously that perhaps the drama amused him. Perhaps (but not likely) he wanted to show that the shoe did not fit. Whatever his reasoning, his indulgence was not shared by the administrators who had been ridiculed and who rose in their wrath to decry Gogol as unpatriotic, even traitorous. The author commented wryly that those who felt they had been attacked would not have objected so stridently if he had "portrayed monsters," and the inescapable resemblance of the portrait to the subject caused them to make as much commotion as Cerberus.

Whatever Gogol's intention, he did unmask the ineptness and corruption of an officialdom determined to preserve itself at any cost. Here again Gogol served as a mouthpiece for a people coming to consciousness. They could not free themselves from autocracy; they could not evade the finality of censorship; but they could at least recognize the incubus of paltry tyranny for what it was, contemptible and stupid. The bureaucrats had the upper hand, but they could not prevent the people from ridiculing them. These were the officials to whom Akakii Akakiievich had appealed for help but whose ears were deaf to the cry of a human being socially and economically unimportant. In the drama the cry became a guffaw weighted with mockery. In the future, indifference to or stony disregard of such a cry would not be borne with meekness or endured as inevitable.

The response to his play convinced Gogol that Russia could offer him nothing to compensate for the strain of being pilloried by those who believed he had deliberately derided them. His disappointment was the more keen, of course, because of the fact, again incredible, that he had expected the response to be quite otherwise. The absence of the lampooner, however, did not put an end to the lampoon. The play became a permanent fixture in Russian life. It continued to incite angry recrimination, though none could see it without laughing. Never again was the bureaucracy sacrosanct as it had been before Gogol spoke on behalf of "the people." The anguished ghost of Akakii had now been joined by another: that of the government official wearing, like Bottom the Weaver, the head of an ass!

III.

Gogol's productive years were marked by a series of contradictions. His success turned sour because the enthusiastic reception of his major works was countered by hostile criticism and prevailing misinterpretation. Accused of writing what he had not intended, he was driven by the compulsion to explain and placate, but his explanations only added fuel to the protests and detracted from his real achievements. He was haunted by self-mistrust and at the same time intoxicated by the champagne of illusion. It was not unusual for him to work for months on a manuscript and then abruptly throw it into the fire when his friends criticized it or he saw how far it fell short of his hopes. His expectations with regard to his creative abilities were presumptuous and overambitious, yet he was able at times to transcend all his limitations and bring his kaleidoscopic images into a focus that outdistanced even his illusions. After the success of *The Government Inspector* he was terrified by the ebbing of his power over words, but just when it appeared certain that he could not duplicate that achievement, the book which ensured his immortality appeared.

Gogol's *Dead Souls* has been described as everything from a comic masterpiece to a plea for moral and social regeneration. Brilliantly witty, it contains some of the sharpest and cleverest observations regarding human nature to be found in print. A magnificent sense of dramatic irony, of the ridiculous, the unexpected, and of anticlimax; an understanding of the foibles and follies of human beings; and a capacity for observation seldom equalled are mixed in a tangy brew that evokes laughter at the same time that it produces queasiness.

The plot of the novel (for the germ of which Gogol was again indebted to Pushkin) is only a framework. Pavel Ivanovitch Tchitchikov, formerly a government clerk who had lost his post because of misappropriation of funds, had conceived a scheme by which he expected to recoup his losses and also to provide security for his future. He wished to become a "man of property." His plan was to buy a number of slaves, or "souls," at the cheapest possible price and to use this property as a means to gain more. The possession of slaves would ensure his acceptance as a landowner—for what man would own slaves and not own land for them to till? As soon as he became an owner, he would be, like the creatures of Noah's ark, in a situation in which he might expect to increase and multiply.

This intention sounds unremarkable enough, but the plan did not end there. The slaves Tchitchikov proposed to buy with his limited capital were not to be *living*, but *dead* men. (Women didn't count in Russia at this time. They were not worthy of being listed even as chattels.) He was, to be specific, expecting to establish his fortune upon a foundation of *dead souls*.

He had little doubt that the owners of these souls would be glad to sell. The census was taken only once every ten years, and during the intervening time every landowner had to pay a government poll tax on all souls, living or dead, listed as his property. Obviously, with Tchitchikov glad to assume the burden of the poll tax, the owners could be expected to dispense gladly with property that had become nonexistent. Some would even be willing to give away the dead souls to cut down the tax.

The plot follows Tchitchikov's maneuvers to transform his plan into reality. Gogol relates this gargantuan hoax as if it were the most natural thing in the world. Having established a mood of easygoing familiarity, he invites the reader to join him in a chummy consideration of amusing circumstances. Tchitchikov is presented, not as a rogue or a villain, as, for example, Ben Jonson presented Volpone and Molière presented Tartuffe and the Miser, but as a pleasant fellow who could hardly be expected not to take advantage of any opportunity to get ahead, even if he has to create the opportunity in a vacuum. Tchitchikov's major characteristic is complacency. Although he does not advertise it, he is almost candid about his dishonesty. Further, he is often as indulgent of others' vices as of his own. His matter-of-fact opportunism reminds one of Sancho Panza; the difference is that whereas Sancho waits for the future to come, Tchitchikov leaps toward it. Some of these leaps, of course, result in mistakes and miscalculations despite his native shrewdness. The plan of *Dead Souls* also brings to mind *Don Quixote*; both books are constructed on the picaresque model, following the loosely connected experiences of the central figure. But there are only contrasts between the noble Don himself and Tchitchikov. Everything Don Quixote was, Tchitchikov was not.

It is easy to take the story as casually as Gogol seems to have written it—as the ridiculous tale of a "biter bit," of a man who reaches too far and gets slapped. Or it may be regarded as the medium Gogol found most congenial for the exhibition of his extraordinary magic in the creation of characters—personalities infused with the bizarre distortions of his imagination and yet, at the same time, so much like living people that the reader recognizes and knows them well. A long-time controversy has been waged between those who see in *Dead Souls* an earnest social document and those equally or more positive that it came into being for no other reason than that the volcano of Gogol's creative energy simply erupted in this form. Probable as it is that the second of these positions is the more accurate, it is hardly safe to assert, as Vladimir Nabokov does, that the first assumption is completely unthinkable and absurd. Gogol's enigmatic nature encourages guesses but almost defies certainties.

Irrespective, however, of motivation or what the author intended, there can be little doubt that the book does accomplish two things with such impact that Gogol seemed to have said all that needed to be said about either. In the first place, he established the predicament of the serfs. This book elucidates what slavery in Russia really meant as scarcely any other single document does. Secondly, Gogol defines the class against whom those in bondage had to struggle—a landowners' class, holding frantically to privilege but doing nothing to deserve it; a class out of date, corrupt, effete, niggardly, shortsighted, irresponsible, and parasitic; a class whose members became more despotic as they rose higher in the social and economic scale until the absolute symbol of despotism was reached in the figure of the Czar.

Dead Souls is a black record of an anachronistic feudal system based on the assumption that human life has no meaning and no value, that the human being has neither dignity nor rights. It is full of monstrous disregard for human bodies and spirits. The argument (intentional or not) against slavery is built on the convincing evidence of symbols, representatives who stand for the whole. Here are masters so disinterested in their slaves that they really do not know whether the slaves are alive or dead. Here are owners with no other feeling for their dead serfs than resentment because the tax must be paid even though the bodies are underground. Here are traffickers in human beings who haggle over the dead, unwilling to sell lest higher prices for decomposed matter are being paid elsewhere. Against these figures, Simon Legree and the system he represented appear relatively humane.

Gogol establishes what the property- and slave-owning class was like (and hence what slavery was) by a parade of typical landowners. Interesting as they are as individuals—and an uninteresting Gogol character does not exist—it is appropriate here to consider them as types and point out the salient characteristics of each. But for the obscurity in which Russian literature has remained in most of the Western world, several of these types would certainly have occupied a place as familiar and representative as Shakespeare's Shylock, Molière's Tartuffe, or Dickens' Uriah Heep.

The first country gentleman Tchitchikov approached was a sentimentalist named Manilov whose pretense to culture was indicated by his having in his study "a book with a marker at the fourteenth page, which he had been reading for the last two years." Asked about the number of his peasants who had died, he replied that he hadn't the slightest idea—no one would have bothered to count them—but he was willing to secure an estimate from his bailiff. When Tchitchikov made his proposal, the bewildered Manilov inquired whether this arrangement would be a violation of the civil code or a threat to the welfare of Russia. Upon being reassured that the government would be the gainer because it would receive the legal fees, Manilov had no further hesitation and certainly no scruples. Instead he felt respect for

Tchitchikov's business acumen, which operated on a plane he did not understand. When Tchitchikov broached the matter of payment, Manilov, delighted by the opportunity to render a service, expressed his magnanimity and a desire for friendship. "Surely you don't imagine," he said, "I am going to take money for souls which in a certain sense have ended their existence?" Later, his purchases satisfactorily completed, Tchitchikov went to the government offices to make them legal. Manilov accompanied him and behaved as if Tchitchikov were a creature rare and precious.

Tchitchikov's next encounter was with the Widow Korobotchka, a wily, calculating old woman who would stop at nothing for gain. Tchitchikov proposed to take her dead souls off her hands, thus saving her the necessity to pay taxes on them, and offered to give her money besides.

> The old lady pondered. She saw that the transaction certainly seemed a profitable one, only it was too novel and unusual, and so she began to be extremely uneasy that the purchaser might be trying to cheat her. . . .
>
> "Really, at first sight, I am afraid that it may be a loss to me. Perhaps you are deceiving me, sir, and they, er—are worth more, perhaps."
>
> "Listen, my good woman—ech, what nonsense you talk! What can they be worth? Just consider: why, they are dust, you know. Do you understand, they are nothing but dust. . . . Come, tell me yourself, what is it of use for?" . . .
>
> "Really," answered the old lady, "I am an inexperienced widow; I had better wait a little, maybe the dealers will be coming and I shall find out about prices."

Finally the old woman decided to make the deal, but she would have preferred to sell this strange young man her hemp, her rye or buckwheat flour, her grain or carcasses, her salt pork or feathers. She agreed to sell her dead souls only on Tchitchikov's promise that he would return for further transactions.

With Nozdryov, Tchitchikov's good luck as a buyer met a

reversal. A liar, drunkard, and gambler, Nozdryov was not only Tchitchikov's match but his superior at knavery and fraudulence. He had no objection to parting with his dead souls, but any kind of deal set off his passion for gambling as a flame sets off a firecracker. Nozdryov would have been glad to gamble the coat off his back, and his skin, too, if that had been possible. He insisted that he would throw the dead souls in extra only if Tchitchikov would buy his stallion, a chestnut mare, a gray horse, or dogs, or even a barrel organ. The wary Tchitchikov sidestepped one trap after another but finally gave in to the gambler's urging that they play a game of draughts. Nozdryov cheated so flagrantly, however, that Tchitchikov withdrew from the game, whereupon Nozdryov became angry, refused to part with the dead souls, and ordered his servants to give Tchitchikov a good beating.

The fourth landlord, one who proved at least temporarily useful to Tchitchikov, was Sobakevitch, who resembled a bear. He was like a bear in behavior, too—lumbering and churlish. Never a word passed his lips that was not ill humored and spiteful. Something about Tchitchikov, however, struck a responsive chord within him. Consequently, Sobakevitch accepted Tchitchikov's proposal about buying dead souls as calmly as if they had been talking about turnips. He readily agreed to sell but asked a high price for his nonexistent merchandise. To Tchitchikov's protestation that he could not and would not pay so much, he retorted: "But why are you so stingy—it really is not dear! Another man would cheat you and sell you some rubbish instead of souls; but mine are as sound as a nut, all first-class."

This statement, which Sobakevitch made in all seriousness, is enough to illustrate Gogol's raffish humor, his sardonic double talk, and—more important—the total blindness of the landowning class.

But there is still another symbolic figure, the miser Plyushkin, Gogol's most alarming commentary on the "dead" souls of the Russian gentry. Here was no sentimental hypocrite, no wily and grasping old woman, no licentious rake, no coldhearted vilifier of humanity. Plyushkin had once been a man of respectable habits and position; a good husband, father, and master, his thrift showing only a slight tendency toward miserliness. His potential goodness, however, had been slowly consumed by the cancer of avarice. Now he lived alone in a house falling into decay, its windows boarded up, everything covered by thick layers of mold and dust, and every inch—house, barns, and yard—filled with an accumulation of junk the old man had laboriously collected during the years without ever subtracting anything. When Tchitchikov saw the old man and the way he lived, he could hardly believe his eyes, and Tchitchikov was no amateur in the matter of avarice himself!

In some obscure way the younger man pleased the miser, who agreed to transfer his 120 dead souls. (He had a larger number than the others, for he allowed his serfs scarcely enough food to survive.) Charmed by the prospect of being relieved of the tax, he volunteered to throw in a few runaway souls, too, for a little additional charge. He was so pleased with the transaction that he had the almost forgotten impulse to offer his guest refreshment. It made no difference to him that the piece of mold-covered cake in the storeroom was left from what his daughter had brought him on her last visit several years before or that the liqueur made by his long-dead wife, "in a little decanter which was enveloped in dust as though in a vest," had all sorts of rubbish in it. When Tchitchikov said he had already eaten and drunk, Plyushkin, thinking the better of his guest for not making a drain on his hospitality, sent the cake back to the storeroom and returned the decanter to the shelf. He was, however, agitated by the necessity of using a whole sheet of paper to authorize the transfer of his dead and runaway slaves.

Plyushkin was a wreck of humanity, in whom evil had become the active agent. Like the avaricious in the *Inferno*, he had become "squint-eyed in mind" and soul. And the same was true of the Widow Korobotchka, Nozdryov the gambler, and Sobakevitch the bear. The latter three would have been candidates for a variety of assignments in Dante's Hell. Even Manilov, bad because he was not good, would have been among the multitude of the damned. Dante would probably have put him among the neutrals, those without principles or convictions, in the suburbs of Hell.

And what of Tchitchikov, who was determined to join this parade of the privileged? He had learned his trade well. He understood people for the most part—their weaknesses and their foibles—knew how to appear plausible and modest, and was careful to avoid extremes. Well tutored in trickery, he was more adroit, more patient, more ingratiating, and more subtle than Khlestakov in *The Government Inspector*. The failure of his opportunistic strategy was not caused by any lack of will or zeal. His downfall was caused by his not being cunning enough, not being able to see the full degree of the deviousness, ruthlessness, colossal selfishness, and unmitigated evil-doing and evil-being of those whom he was forced to use as the means to his end.

Thus Gogol implies, and the validity of his argument is unassailable, that Tchitchikov is not the villain of the piece. What he did was only a response to the success formula of his society. Inasmuch as the right to be classified as successful in Russia in the 1840's was limited to those who owned land and slaves, any blame for the existence of so hideous a standard could hardly be laid at the feet of those who yearned for a place and a position of their own. Gogol would have us understand that Tchitchikov was in many respects better than the majority of those who had been born to the position he ardently desired.

Never throughout the entire book does Gogol speak other than disparagingly about the privileged classes in Russia. They are unable, he says, to "admit that they are to blame." The men spend most of their time deciding what to eat until they are so stuffed and dyspeptic that they must go to Karlsbad for a cure. The women are cheap scandalmongers with roving eyes, loose tongues, and no principles whatever. And no wonder, for the only education available to them is a smattering of French and pianoforte and learning how to knit "purses and other surprises." In Russia, "where everyone prefers to expand rather than contract," there is such class consciousness that different tones of voice are used for addressing landowners, depending upon the number of their serfs. The facility of members of the upper class for making such distinctions far exceeds what is possible for any German or Frenchman. Those who already own far too much live for nothing but to get more. There is no culture, but ignorance, filth, and malignity abound. Even the landscape is depressing, but the landscape is the least depressing part of Gogol's Russia in *Dead Souls*.

Even if the emphasis of the novel is nonpolitical, it adds a strong postscript to the commentary of *The Government Inspector* on officialdom. Knowing that he could do nothing without being in their favor, Tchitchikov cultivated the acquaintance of the most important people, beginning with the governor, who was "a very simple and good-natured fellow, and sometimes actually embroidered on net." The bunglesome mechanism of official procedure is graphically illustrated when Tchitchikov set about having his newly purchased souls legally transferred to him. The best thrust is Gogol's account of the panic of the local officials when, after Tchitchikov's scheme had been exposed by the vindictiveness of the Widow Korobotchka and the drunken raucousness of Nozdryov, it occurred to them that the new governor-general might hear about the unsavory business which had been going on in their community:

> "Why," thought the local officials, "if he finds out that these stupid rumours are going about the town, his fury may be a matter of life and death." The inspector of the medical board suddenly turned pale; he imagined, God knows why, that the words "dead souls" might be a reference to the patients, who had died in considerable numbers in the hospitals and infirmaries of an epidemic fever, against which no proper precautions had been taken, and that Tchitchikov might have been sent by the governor general to gather secret information. He mentioned this to the president of

the court. The president answered that this was absurd, and then grew pale himself.

This debunking of officialdom reaches its climax in the last scene of the novel. Fallen from hero and idol (because of his rumored millions) to outcast, Tchitchitkov was hoping to make an unobtrusive departure from the scene of his triumph-turned-sour when his carriage was stopped by a funeral procession. It was, he learned, that of the prosecutor. He feared his carriage might be recognized, but no one paid any attention to it. All were concerned about the new governor-general. They were wondering what he would do, what he would think of them, or whether he would find them out. Tchitchikov ruminated that "they will write all sorts of nonsense" about the dead prosecutor; ". . . and yet if one goes into the facts of the case, it turns out on investigation that there was nothing special about you but your thick eyebrows."

IV.

What has been said about *Dead Souls* refers only to Part I. The confused second part was never finished. Gogol worked laboriously for years, but was so dissatisfied with it that he consigned all or parts of it to the flames several times. Apparently he had in mind a three-part development to constitute a kind of prose sister to Dante's *Divine Comedy*. That the first part is a convincing delineation of an inferno is beyond question. But the fragments of the second part, most of them rescued and assembled by his friends, prove that when Gogol attempted to explore the possibilities of regeneration, he needed talents he did not possess. Like Dante and Milton, Gogol could depict evil more convincingly than good.

Perhaps Gogol was hopelessly confused by the paradox of his position. In *Dead Souls* he had delivered an incisive and irreparable blow to a system to which he was not opposed. He was trapped by the predicament of hating the symptom but accepting the disease. It seems never to have occurred to him that the system itself was responsible for the evil of the individual masters and the catastrophe of slavery. He had thought he was exposing the part, but he had really laid bare the whole. Having succeeded beyond his intent, he could not reclothe the hideous skeleton in seemly attire. Moreover, there was no place in the second part of the book for the humor which lifts many passages of the first to the plane of the superlative. Gogol's humor grows out of a perfect blend of innuendo, understatement, and anticlimax, and none of these was appropriate to an effort to present Tchitchikov sympathetically.

Gogol lived for ten years after the publication of the first section of his great novel, years marked by the tragic falling away of his powers and by the pitiable, deluded effort to find rest for his spirit in religious mysticism. In an effort to attain the inner peace for which he longed he journeyed to the Holy Land, but even Biblical scenes could not bring quietude to his soul. He was haunted by images of hell. His nose had always been his dominant feature, and in his last years it looked still longer as his face became thin and his eyes gazed more and more inward upon a private inferno more dreadful than the one he had created for readers.

Gogol's last writings, a betrayal of his earlier, better self, should be left to the oblivion which mercifully enshrouds them. Unfortunately, he published in 1847 a volume called *Selected Passages from Correspondence with Friends*, which was his final public effort to vindicate himself. The same irony which attended the publication of his great works still prevailed: the book produced an effect quite different from what he hoped. It convinced even his friends that he was looking backward instead of having the courage to look toward the future that he invoked in "The Cloak," *The Government Inspector*, and *Dead Souls*.

Never having fulfilled his dream of a unique destiny, he died as he had lived, a lonely, disappointed man. In the last months of his life, indeed, he seems to have willed his own death, convinced that the clouding of his soul made impossible the spiritual fulfillment which he had always expected of himself. Perhaps his personal disappointment accounts for the demoniac cry with which his laughter is edged.

Modern scholars have for the most part stripped from Gogol the aura thrown about him in his successful years by some of his contemporaries who saw him as a humanitarian. At one point the critic Belinsky hailed Gogol as an apostle of indignation, a great-hearted denouncer of existing abuses, one who laughed "through tears." Modern critics maintain that Belinsky and other admirers of Gogol read into his work what they wanted to find there and that Gogol wrote, not from humanitarian motives, but out of spite against a society in which he was not appreciated as he thought he ought to be. Be that as it may, whether he wrote from conviction or only provided the score which genuine humanitarians interpreted as a protest and a challenge, the results were the same. Intentionally or not, he became the conscience of his time.

To understand the circumstances which made revolution in Russia inevitable, it is not necessary to look beyond Part I of *Dead Souls*. In this "comedy" may be seen the institutions and the individuals who made Russia a chamber of horrors: the autocratic governing class, the decadent patriarchal system with its parasitic and degenerate gentry, and the slaves imprisoned by the system as well as by ignorance and poverty. The book brings to mind the last part of *Gulliver's Travels*, except that there are no noble Houyhnhnms. Gogol saw his country as a land defiled by Yahoos. Small wonder that when Pushkin listened to Gogol's reading of the first part of the tale, in spite of his natural buoyancy the poet was filled with foreboding and is said to have exclaimed, "God, what a sad country our Russia is!"

Gogol's mournful insight and the timeliness and appropriateness of his mockery cannot be questioned. His influence was as dominant as Dostoevsky asserted. There was something of the prophet about him, too. He was only one of many Russian authors who, although critical of their country, were at the same time convinced that Russia was destined to be supreme. This faith in the messianic destiny of Russia was so strong in Gogol and later in Dostoevsky that it caused them to believe Russia would become the master, and thus the savior, of all other countries. Consider the sense of exaltation of the following passage which appears among the fragments of the incomplete second part of *Dead Souls*:

> And, Russia, art not thou too flying onwards like a spirited troika that nothing can overtake? The road is smoking under thee, the bridges rumble, everything falls back and is left behind! The spectator stands still struck dumb by the divine miracle: is it not a flash of lightning from heaven? What is the meaning of this terrifying onrush? What mysterious force is hidden in this troika, never seen before? Ah, horses, horses—what horses! Is the whirlwind hidden under your manes? . . . They hear the familiar song over their heads—at once in unison they strain their iron chests and scarcely touching the earth with their hoofs are transformed almost into straight lines flying through the air—and the troika rushes on, full of divine inspiration. . . . Russia, whither flyest thou? Answer! She gives no answer. The ringing of the bells melts into music; the air, torn to shreds, whirs and rushes like the wind, everything there is on earth is flying by, and the other states and nations, with looks askance, make way for her and draw aside.

III/ Goncharov and Oblomovism

In *Dead Souls,* Nikolai Gogol demonstrated that the end of the long-continued patriarchal system of land and slave ownership could not be far off. It was challenged by external forces which proved it an anachronism and was doomed from within by the Manilovs, the Korobotchkas, the Nozdryovs, and the Plyushkins—and by their slaves. Both the owners and the owned were symptoms of deterioration. But Gogol did not speak the last word about this decline. That was left to the author of the book *Oblomov,* published seventeen years later (1859). In this novel Goncharov set forth another representative of the landholding class destined to extinction. When he finished with his character Oblomov, the case against the gentry was almost complete.

Whereas Gogol's characterization produces the effect of ruthless debunking, Ivan Goncharov bestowed upon Oblomov a grave and at times affectionate pity. Knowing that Oblomov must die, Goncharov still wished he could be saved. The book is a strange mixture of criticism and nostalgia. Most of the time Goncharov sympathized with Oblomov, who was on the losing side in the clash between the old and the new. The reader, too, will sometimes be sympathetic, but at other times exasperated and unbelieving. One thing is certain: having made the acquaintance of Oblomov, he will not again need to wonder why (to paraphrase the title of Sinclair Lewis' novel) it did happen in Russia.

Ivan Alexandrovitch Goncharov (1812–91) was born into the family of a wealthy merchant, but he was educated as if he were a member of the gentry, and he always considered himself as of that class. Except for one lengthy trip which took him to the opposite side of the world, his life was uneventful, providing the perfect environment for the conception and bringing to life of an Oblomov. After the completion of his studies at the University of Moscow, Goncharov became connected with the civil service, in which he held a succession of posts that did not demand from him more than minimal exertion. The one interruption to this bland existence occurred when, apparently against his inclination, he was sent with a group of other officials on a government mission to Japan. This journey—everything he saw and did—bored him, although he made full use of the details in an account of the experience, *Frigate Pallas*, which was popular among Russian readers starved for information about other lands. Goncharov published three novels, the first and last of which are dull, verbose, and cloudy (*A Common Story*, 1847, and *The Precipice*, 1869). But *Oblomov*, the second, is one of the rarest treasures of Russian literature. The book is like an etching in its painstaking detail, a near perfect engraving of the minutiae of impotence and decay. Goncharov himself must have been a partial Oblomov. There can be no other explanation of his absolute understanding of the character and of the lucidity and comprehensiveness of his treatment.

Paradoxically, after being regarded during his writing career as one of the foremost of Russian novelists, his popularity exceeding that of Dostoevsky with many readers, Goncharov and his books passed into such obscurity that *Oblomov* was not even available in English translation until 1928. It is regrettable that this intensely significant novel has been little known to English and American readers. Apart from the delight to be found in the book—the delight of recognizing a perfect blend of form and substance—it has the added significance of offering a new perspective on what happened to the social structure of Russia during the past century.

I.

At the death of his parents Ilya Ilyitch Oblomov had become the owner of an estate of moderate size (350 souls) from which he could expect a comfortable income as long as he lived. He had grown up in the country under the indulgent eyes of his parents, relatives, and servants, who considered the satisfaction of his slightest wish the chief of their pleasures. In this sheltered life Ilya, "protected like an exotic flower in a hot house,"[1] had not been allowed so much as to put on his own boots. He was educated—on the days when his parents could not think of a reason for keeping their darling with them—in the home of a German neighbor whose teaching, despite its excellence, could not counteract the debilitating influence of Ilya's family. The schoolmaster had a son with whom Ilya developed a friendship which proved to be the one meaningful and lasting tie of his life. The young Stolz, with his half-German background, was the opposite of Ilya in temperament and inclination. After the conclusion of their schooling, they had few experiences in common, yet their friendship continued, for they shared happy memories of Oblomovka in addition to having a strong mutual trust and regard.

As a young man Ilya fulfilled his family's expectation by going into government service. This position had entailed the expenditure of a small amount of effort, the first he had ever been required to put forth, and Ilya had barely endured it for two years, by which time he had become completely distraught. Since then he had done nothing.

At the opening of the story Ilya Oblomov was, as usual, lying in bed.

> Lying down was not for Ilya Ilyitch either a necessity as it is for a sick or sleepy man, or an occasional need as it is for a person who is tired, or a pleasure as it is for a sluggard: it was his normal state. When he was at home—and he was almost always at home—he was lying down.

While he lay thus comfortably in bed, "his attitude and the very folds of his dressing gown expressed the same untroubled ease as his face." This dressing gown was his customary raiment,

[1] Translated by Natalie A. Duddington.

its soft folds reflecting its owner's indolence and love of comfort. Yet this morning Oblomov had wakened early (about eight o'clock), troubled by a disagreeable letter from the bailiff of his estate, who wrote that Oblomov must expect a curtailment of his income because things were not going well. As the morning progressed, Oblomov became convinced that he must rise and think about his perplexing affairs:

> One had to think of taking some measures. In justice to Ilya Ilyitch it must be said that, after receiving the Bailiff's first unpleasant letter . . . he had begun to think of various changes and improvements in the management of his estate. He proposed introducing fresh economic, administrative, and other measures. But the plan was not yet thoroughly thought out. . . .
>
> As soon as he woke up he made up his mind to get up and wash, and . . . to think matters over. . . . He lay for half an hour tormented by this decision; but afterwards he reflected that he would have time to think after breakfast, which he could have in bed as usual, especially since one can think just as well lying down.
>
> This was what he did. After his morning tea he sat up and very nearly got out of bed; looking at his slippers, he began lowering one foot down towards them, but at once drew it back again.

Oblomov's burdens became much heavier when his servant Zahar reminded him of the landlord's notification that they must change lodgings. Although the flat and furnishings were filthy and in a shocking state of disrepair, Oblomov was plunged into panic at the prospect of having to make a change. Confronted by this extra calamity, he could no longer decide which of his problems to think about first. Under these circumstances it was a strenuous morning for Ilya, even if he did not stir from his bed. "He was lost in the torment of worldly cares. . . . At times abrupt exclamations were heard in the room: 'Oh, dear, life doesn't leave one alone, it gets at one everywhere!' "

During the morning Oblomov had several callers. One or two came from habit, others because they could get a meal at Oblomov's, others to pick up money on various pretexts, and some because they could be sure of a willing listener. Whatever their reason for coming, the callers constituted Oblomov's one remaining tie with the world, for he had almost stopped going out. He was eager to tell each of them the story of his cares and to ask for advice, but only one, Tarantyev, would listen. The latter, expert at using Oblomov for his own ends, immediately saw in the predicament of the helpless man an opportunity to further his own designs. Of course, Oblomov never suspected Tarantyev of opportunism; he was too guileless to look for hidden motives or to suspect those who showed him attention.

Early in the afternoon Oblomov rose from his bed and walked to the table. He started to write a letter to the landlord, explaining that he could not possibly move. But he soon felt that the strain of writing was too much and tore up the attempted letter, hoping to solve the problem of moving by ignoring it. By three o'clock, exhausted and unnerved by what he had not accomplished, he went back to bed for a nap. He could not go to sleep immediately, however, for he was vaguely disturbed by the awareness of what he should have achieved. In such moments of introspection he blamed himself, but he was powerless to do anything about his weakness:

> His mind and will had been paralysed. . . . The events in his life had dwindled down to microscopic proportions, but even so they were more than he could cope with; he . . . was tossed to and fro by them as by waves; he had not the strength of will to oppose one course or to follow another rationally.

Oblomov was brought to full wakefulness by the unexpected arrival of his friend Stolz, in whose company he was always happy. In spite of his inertia he had a strong capacity for friendship, and the currents of his affection were pure and deep. Here at last was someone willing to listen. When Oblomov set his problems before his friend, they seemed almost to dissolve, for Stolz applied to them the same decisiveness that characterized all his conduct. Upon Ilya's lamenting the burdens by which he was weighed down, Stolz confronted him, "But what do you do?—You simply lie here like a piece of dough." Stolz urged Ilya to take hold of the management of his affairs: to go to his estate and put an end to the cheating and inefficiency of his bailiff, to open a school in his village, and even to make improvements—there were roads and bridges to be built and his house to be saved from the decay rapidly overtaking it.

Oblomov gave willing attention to his friend's urging, but he could find no attraction in the life of activity. He wanted only rest and peace and the privilege of sitting still. When Stolz objected that such a mode of existence wasn't life, Oblomov asked what it was.

> "It's—" Stolz broke off, trying to think of a word to describe this kind of existence—"it's a sort of . . . Oblomovism," he said at last.
>
> "Ob-lo-movism!" Ilya Ilyitch pronounced slowly, marvelling at the strange word and dividing it into syllables, "Ob-lo-movism!". . .
>
> "Your very Utopia is that of an Oblomov," Stolz retorted. . . .
>
> Oblomov listened, looking at him with anxious eyes. It was as though his friend were holding a mirror before him and he was frightened when he recognized himself.
>
> "Don't scold me, Andrey, better help me! . . . I suffer from it myself; had you seen me earlier in the day and heard the way I was bewailing my fate and digging my own grave you would not have had the heart to reproach me."

It was no accident that Goncharov took one-fifth of the novel to get his apostle of peace and rest out of bed. Oblomov was the embodiment of one dominant characteristic of the Russian gentry—their ineffectuality and sloth. Even though some of them were people of integrity and generous aspirations, and though occasionally, like Oblomov, they made plans, they were too bogged down in the quicksands of habit and passivity to bring dreams or plans to fruition. Oblomov and many of his kind saw that change was imminent, but they were unfitted by both temperament and training to do anything about it. They were, by nature and tradition, static and immobile.

Goncharov wrote his novel with almost as much attention to fullness of detail as a psychiatrist might give to a case study. To explain the adult Oblomov, he turned back to Oblomov's childhood and adolescence when he basked in the warm glow of peace. Oblomovka was like a land of contented Lotus Eaters. The days, each the same as every other, slipped by with gentle tranquillity. There was no distinct past, and the future was lost in the mist of unreality. The important time was the present—languorous, comfortable, and secure. The world did not stand out on either side. It ended with the boundaries of the estate. When masters and servants said their prayers, they gave thanks for having survived the day and asked the same blessing for tomorrow. Their world was small, but it was safe and friendly, and they wanted to keep it exactly as they had always known it.

As long as he remained in the sanctuary of the family estate, Oblomov was swaddled in love. But this love made him unfit for living, and the products of this love to which he had become attuned—the habits of ease, indolence, and self-absorption—were to be his undoing. By the time he reached maturity the dressing gown had become a symbol: it was soft and comfortable and adjusted itself to the wearer, and yet its silken folds were suffocating him. When the doctor warned Ilya that inactivity combined with rich food would bring him to an untimely end, he was literally reading the death warrant for Oblomov and for all his class.

On one occasion, when he was talking with one of the representatives of the rising middle class, a man who had learned how to get on by ingenuity, Oblomov made this confession:

> "I don't know anything about peasants' work, or agricultural labor. I don't know when peasants are considered rich and when poor; I don't know what a quarter of rye or oats means, what it costs, in which month they sow and reap and which crops, how and when they sell corn; I don't know if I am rich or poor, if in a

year's time I shall have enough to eat or be a beggar—I know nothing!—so you must talk to me and advise me as a child. . . ."

"Why, you ought to know: if you don't you can't reckon things out," Ivan Matveyitch said. . . . "A landowner should know his estate and what to do with it. . . ."

"Well, I don't. Teach me if you can."

But there was no one to teach the effete gentry such lessons as these, and those few who wanted to know had long before become unfitted for learning. Moreover, there was rapidly emerging a number of people—mostly in the growing middle class—who had plenty of ambition and energy and were ready to take the place of those lacking such qualities.

II.

The novel moves with dreadful inevitability. Oblomov's destiny, of course, lacked any alternative; it was inherent in his character and the times in which he lived.

Having tried to impress Oblomov with the realization that he must effect a change in his life "now or never," Stolz went abroad, but not without extracting from his friend the promise to join him soon. Before leaving, Stolz also introduced Ilya to Olga Ilyinsky, a charming young woman of intelligence and spirit, who made a great impression on Oblomov because of her talent for singing. Oblomov, of course, did not carry out his intention to join Stolz, but he did fall in love with Olga. His former experiences with women had been few "if only because intimacy with a woman involved a lot of exertion." To his intense joy Olga shared his feeling. For a time, under the inspiration of her singing and her love, Oblomov returned to something approximating normal life; his youthful ambitions stirred again, and in his dreams he saw a serene future with Olga. When she declared her willingness to be his wife, he could scarcely believe his good fortune. But he was increasingly haunted by the fear that he would not be good for her, that she was making a mistake. Her energy and forthrightness were strong enough to dispel his fears part of the time, yet the months passed without his being able to make the practical arrangements necessary to enable them to marry. He waited futilely for a letter from his bailiff, expecting it automatically to solve all his financial uncertainties. Meanwhile, he could not steel himself to make a formal request for her hand.

During the interval of waiting Oblomov supinely accepted Tarantyev's plan that he take lodging in the home of a widow with two children. Because of the gullibility of the trusting lodger, Tarantyev and his associate, the widow's brother, a dishonest schemer, saw a chance for selfish gain in the arrangement. The widow, passive and stupid, was an excellent cook and housekeeper, and without thinking about it at all, Oblomov gradually came to depend on her to make him comfortable. His love for Olga continued for a time to give meaning to his life, but his incapacity for solving difficulties made him more and more helpless. The summer idyl, Oblomov's one escape from inertia, had been a rose-colored moment in an otherwise gray life, but it soon ended. Olga recognized that since it was not within her power to change Oblomov, there could be no future for them. Still loving him and impressed by the sweetness and nobility of his character, she sorrowfully broke the unofficial engagement:

> She buried her face in her handkerchief, trying to choke her sobs.
>
> "Why has it all been wrecked?" she asked suddenly, raising her head. "Who put a curse on you, Ilya? What have you done? You are kind, intelligent, affectionate, noble . . . and . . . you are . . . doomed! What has ruined you? . . ."
>
> "Oblomovism!" he whispered.

Thus ended Oblomov's last chance. Thereafter he sank back into his previous condition of detachment and apathy, even lapsing again into the habitual wearing of the dressing gown, which had been stored away during the period of his happiness with Olga. Sucked inescapably into the marsh of inaction, he was the prey of the avaricious Tarantyev and his landlady's brother. At last he lost contact with the world, and he became once more "a piece of dough," not seeing beyond his comfort, his food, and the well-meaning, simple woman who supplied both. Several times Stolz appeared briefly to urge him to be active and to save himself, but without success. "You lost your ability for doing things when still a child at Oblomovka among your aunts and nurses. It began with your not knowing how to put your stockings on and ended by your not knowing how to live," Stolz said. To which Oblomov replied, "All this may be true, Andrey, but there is nothing for it, there is no retrieving it!" And he was right.

Stolz could do nothing for his friend except save him from the connivings of the scoundrels who had been battening on his ineffectuality. Eventually Stolz and Olga found happiness together, yet occasionally their sorrow at the death-in-life of Oblomov cast a shadow across their path, for they saw the good in him and could not become reconciled to his being useless. They gave up hope of saving him only when they learned that he had had a stroke and had sunk into a torpor in which they could not reach him. They could not bear to watch as "he settled down slowly and gradually in the plain and wide coffin he had made of his existence, like ancient hermits who, turning away from life, dig their own graves." When Stolz saw his friend for the last time, he thought sadly:

> "You are done for, Ilya! It is no use telling you that your Oblomovka is no longer in the backwoods, that its turn has come. . . . I won't tell you that in another four years there will be a station there, that your peasants will be working on the line and your corn will be carried by train to the river. . . . And then schools, education . . . and beyond that. . . . No, you will be alarmed at the dawn of the new happiness, it will hurt your eyes used to darkness."

It did not matter that Oblomov died shortly afterward, for he was dead already. His time had ended.

III.

Aside from Oblomov, the two characters of most significance in the novel are Olga and Stolz. Candid, energetic, and eager, Olga is an attractive personality, different in every way from the sheltered women of the gentry in old Russia. She had courage, insight, and an inquiring mind, was capable of decision and action, and was determined to live affirmatively. Yet she was in no sense a militant feminist. Her responsiveness to the best of Oblomov's qualities and her genuine grief at the recognition that he was unfitted for active participation in life reveal her integrity and capacity for appreciation. Life for her was not a routine; it was an adventure and a challenge.

Although Olga is not the first conspicuous representative of her type—that distinction belongs to Pushkin's Tatiana in *Eugene Onegin*—she is noteworthy because she served as model for many of the later heroines of Russian fiction. She set the tone, also, for the new woman of Russia. It is an interesting phenomenon that Russian women often appear (especially since the time of Catherine the Great) to have been more positive and aggressive than Russian men. Perhaps because they had everything to gain, they went forward toward the new day with remarkable energy and determination. This achievement is well illustrated in the heroines of Turgenev and later of Gorky, but Goncharov's Olga is in many respects the most attractive of all the new women who appeared in Russian literature.

Perhaps the best understanding of Oblomov comes from seeing him in relation to Olga and the widow. With her warm heart, alert mind, singing voice, and the branch of lilac in her hand, Olga is youth, resurrection, and spring. Oblomov loved her with all the love of which he was capable, but she asked of him what he could not give. In response to her assurance he could give only hesitation; in response to her joy in action and creation he could give only repose; in response to her gaiety he could give only sober withdrawal. She lived on the plane of ideas and the spirit.

Oblomov could worship from afar, but he could not find safety or peace in her world.

The widow was wholly different. She was without ideas and almost without words. She asked nothing except the chance to serve. She did not know there were other worlds besides the physical. Her ultimate concern was Oblomov's comfort. Without judgment or perspective she saw him as a creature to be lulled and satisfied and saved from strain. In her he found a link with Oblomovka which gave him security. Her household became for him a padded cell, but it was the life he knew and understood.

If there is much to suggest that Goncharov had a good deal in common with his character Oblomov, the same cannot be said of Stolz. Indeed, Stolz probably puzzled Goncharov and made him uneasy. The German's bristling efficiency could hardly have been intended satirically (satire is incompatible with Goncharov's placidity), but it is not made to appear attractive. Nevertheless, the author could not have failed to recognize in Stolz the qualities of the new men and to sense that such men and such qualities would create a new era. Stolz was fitted for action; he got things done. His self-reliance enabled him to organize and execute plans according to his own terms. He offered a preview of big business as the dominant force of the twentieth century; he belongs to the age of the adding machine and the bulldozer. In spite of their congeniality, Stolz and Oblomov were poles apart, one looking forward and the other backward. It is important to notice, however, that Goncharov did not intentionally present the one nostalgically and the other critically. His method was that of the assiduous reporter who observes and records the data. He simply used the two characters to show which way the wind was blowing.

Stolz seems to point ahead to Turgenev's Bazarov and Solomin and to some of Dostoevsky's "possessed." But there is a difference. Goncharov saw the past and the future as friends, not enemies. Stolz and Oblomov were opposites, but their unlikeness did not jeopardize their friendship. Neither really understood the other although the best in each man was brought out in relation to the other. Turgenev's new men still had some of the virtues of Stolz and Oblomov, but there were no virtues in the "possessed." The new man as he finally emerged was forged from harder metal.

It is, of course, fundamental in the characterization of Stolz that this man who had no doubts about the future came from the middle class. His energy and purposefulness are attributed to the fact that he was half-German. Goncharov apparently believed, however, that within Russia lay the possibility for the development of such men. His faith in the ability of Russia to produce them is clearly stated:

> Such a character, perhaps, could not be formed without the mixed elements of which Stolz was made up. Our men of action have always been of five or six stereotyped patterns; lazily looking round them with half closed eyes, they put their hand to the machine of the State, sleepily pushing it along the beaten track.... But, behold, their eyes are awakening from sleep, bold, lively footsteps can be heard, and there is a sound of animated voices.... Many Stolzes with Russian names are bound to come soon!

A minor character who should not go unnoticed is Oblomov's faithful servant, Zahar, a serf from the family estate, who had come with him to the city. As indolent as his master, Zahar never did any work that could be avoided. He would have been happy sitting on the stove all day or going with his cronies to the tavern where he liked to complain about how his master kept him toiling incessantly. But despite his being ignorant, lazy, filthy, quarrelsome, and untrustworthy, he loved his master and could think of no other life than serving him, confidently believing that no other master could be as good. When Oblomov died, Zahar lost his *raison d'etre* and had nowhere to go. Walking along the street one day, Stolz saw a beggar who looked familiar. It was Zahar. When Stolz inquired why he had not taken a new job, the old man replied:

> "I did try two posts, but I didn't suit. It's all different now, not as it used to be; it's much worse. A footman must be able to read and write, and fine gentlemen don't have their halls crammed full of servants as in the old days. . . . They take off their boots themselves: some sort of machine has been invented! . . . It's a shame and disgrace, there will soon be no gentry left!"

Master and servant alike had become anachronistic. Zahar had neither the skills nor the spirit to fit him for a role in the new society. However, the shame he mentions was not what he thought it. The shame was that Russia was full of Zahars, no longer needed and no longer useful, waste products of a system which had considered human life cheap and taken too little care of the individual.

Stolz, Zahar, and the prophetic Olga are of secondary concern, however, for Goncharov's book is the saga of Oblomovism. After its publication, "Oblomov" became a part of the vocabulary of Russia. The man and the thing he stood for and the relation of both to the national temper became symbols as significant as George F. Babbitt has since become in America. Oblomov was the epitome of hereditary privilege and, therefore, of ineptness and apathy. He was the absolute nonhero. As such, in spite of the ideality of his dreams and the inherent fineness of his character, he had to die. The Industrial Revolution was against him; also against him were the inscrutable reshaping of economic forces and the coming to political and social consciousness of the masses. Confronted by these pressures, neither Oblomov nor any other vestige of the past could hope to survive.

IV/ TURGENEV: THE NIHILISTS AND VIRGIN SOIL

IVAN TURGENEV was a devoted son of Mother Russia, yet he chose to spend half of his life away from his native land. But whether at home or abroad, he made a series of sensitive recordings of what was happening to the country he loved. Best known of these is his novel *Fathers and Sons*. Its chief character, Bazarov, is one of the major figures of Russian literature. Through Bazarov and several other characters Turgenev became both commentator and prophet.

The novels of Gogol and Goncharov were so unmistakable in purport that it is not difficult to visualize the part they played in shaping opinion in the nineteenth century. Whatever the intentions of their authors, they may be viewed as tracts of the times, which explain the causes for the ripening of the Russian grapes of wrath. The same cannot be said of Turgenev's novels, which present a panorama varied and paradoxical. They are full of innuendoes and contain contradictions. That this should be true of Turgenev's writing was inevitable since it was true of the man himself. He was adored and reviled, there being some excuse for the second and many reasons for the first. His liberalism was mixed with his conservatism in disconcerting forward and backward movements. He had the unhappy experience of bringing upon himself stormy abuse and high praise, both for exactly the same reasons. Turgenev's contradictions added to his insight and augmented his charm as a writer, but they decreased his stature as a man. In spite of its evasiveness, however, his writing is rich in connotation. In its totality it affords the most comprehensive literary survey of nineteenth-century Russia from the late forties through the seventies. These decades were marked by urgent—if often necessarily underground—stirrings on the part of the people, accented in 1861 by the legal emancipation of the slaves. More extensively than Gogol, Turgenev was an analyst and interpreter and, in a sense, the unwitting shaper of the history of Russia. Moreover, certain premonitions of the shape of things to come are clearly apparent in his works.

I.

Any understanding of what Turgenev wrote requires at least a rudimentary acquaintance with his personality and certain events in his experience, especially since he served as model for many of his male characters. Reading the novels of Turgenev is like attending an exhibition of self-portraits of the artist.

Haunted always by a sense of the imminence of death and the decay of his powers, Ivan Sergeyevitch Turgenev (1818–83) began in his early thirties to consider himself an old man. An aristocrat by birth, he spent his life trying to be a democrat but never succeeding. His father, a cavalry colonel, retired from a military career after he married a woman prodigiously wealthy in land and souls. This woman, violent of temperament and unloved in marriage, tyrannized over her serfs and her two sons. Turgenev found in her the personification of what he heartily condemned in the landowning classes. Born on his mother's estate at Spasskoye in the province of Oryol in central Russia, Turgenev began in early childhood to store up rich impressions of his native soil. Here he developed the warm affection for his country which was the fountainhead of his creative power during his entire career despite his spending much time abroad. That Turgenev was to the end of his days a man of defective will, irresolute like the heroes of his novels, is traceable to the unwholesome domination of his mother. Although intelligent and shrewd, she was so capricious, willful, and vindictive that her son early developed the technique of meeting difficult situations by nonresistance, a habit from which he was never able to recover.

Turgenev's facility in languages can be attributed to his education under an assortment of tutors of various nationalities. He was the only major Russian writer of the period adept in the use of English. At the age of nine Ivan accompanied the family on a move to Moscow; thereafter, he received more systematic education in private schools. At fifteen he entered Moscow University, transferring a year later to the University of St. Petersburg. It is of interest that he heard several of the lectures on history given by Gogol during the latter's brief professorial assay.

Turgenev's real intellectual experience, however, began after the completion of his Petersburg studies when he attended lectures at the University of Berlin. Here was opened to him an invigorating society of intense, dedicated young men worshiping at the shrine of Hegelian philosophy. Some of these adherents regarded philosophy as an end in itself; others were concerned with its political, social, and economic implications. The latter were consumed with zeal for the creation of a new world. At Petersburg and in Berlin, Turgenev made the acquaintance of a number of the fervent young Russians who later became leading figures in the cause of social revolution, among them Michael Bakunin and Alexander Herzen. Sharing many of their views and strongly influenced by them but lacking their fiery conviction, Turgenev never accompanied them beyond the role of passive supporter. From this role he partially withdrew after a time as some of them became too radical for him.

Back in Russia after the exhilarating experiences of Berlin, Turgenev half-heartedly carried out the work for a master's degree in philosophy, stopping just short of completing the requirements. Having outraged his mother by this indifference, he reluctantly accepted a post in the Ministry of the Interior to satisfy her demand that he enter a profession. Like Oblomov he spent two desultory years thus employed, apparently having no duties and wanting none. He "retired" from this incompatible position at the age of twenty-seven. His disinclination for regular and socially acceptable work widened the breach between Turgenev and his mother, who, especially after the death of her husband, had determined to mold her favorite son to the shape she desired. The impossibility of doing so wounded her pride; to this possessive woman motherhood was important only as a means of adding voltage to her egotism.

Meanwhile, Turgenev's literary activities were beginning to amount to something tangible. He had been writing lyric and narrative poetry for some years when in 1843 his first book of verse, *Parasha*, appeared. This was succeeded by other volumes of poetry which received favorable attention, although the critic Vissarion Belinsky (whose word was law in Russian letters) recognized limitations in Turgenev's poetic skills. Belinsky was one of the zealots who won the writer's affection and exerted a strong influence upon him. While a member of Belinsky's circle (Turgenev was by nature a devotee), he was exposed to diagnoses of the ills of Russia and to proposals for their improvement. At this time he devoted considerable attention to these questions, utilizing material from his childhood impressions of the serf as victim of such arrogant and despotic owners as his mother. Much of his later writing derived from his observations and from views developed in discussions during this period.

As ready as the critics to acknowledge his limitations as a poet, Turgenev soon turned entirely to the writing of prose. In later years he would scarcely acknowledge his youthful verse as his own. During the next seven or eight years after the publication of his poetry he wrote a few poor plays and a number of narratives. A collection of the latter, *A Sportsman's Sketches* (1852), made him famous. With these tales, simple and graceful, restrained and objective, he had found his genre. Thereafter Turgenev continued to write stories. In 1856 his first novel, *Rudin*, appeared. During the next twenty years he produced the series of novels which caused many to regard him contemporaneously as the foremost man of letters in Russia. To the end of his life he wrote short narratives of great charm and freshness, the last of them dictated from his deathbed. Thus persisted undiminished the imaginative vigor and creativity of one who, a prey to melancholy and hypochondria, passed most of his days convinced that the sources of his productivity had dried up, that all was futile, and that the only way to live was in a state of resignation.

One dominant design in Turgenev's experience demands special attention—his "friendship" with Pauline Viardot-García, one of the foremost singers and operatic stars in Europe in her time. Three years Turgenev's junior, Pauline García came from a Spanish family of outstanding musicians. Her rise to fame occurred while she was still in her teens. Before she was twenty she married Louis Viardot, director of the Italian opera in Paris, a handsome man twice her age, who gave up his own career to become her manager. Despite her having been brought up in a somewhat Bohemian environment, Mme Viardot apparently preferred a conventional pattern of domestic life, which she proceeded to maintain, the possible temptations in the life of a diva notwithstanding. Turgenev first heard her sing at her debut in St. Petersburg in 1843, when the Italian opera was restored after having been ruled out more than forty years before by Czar Paul I. He met her a short time later, four days after his twenty-fifth birthday.

At this meeting Turgenev's fate was sealed. From that day until he died in her house near Paris forty years later, Pauline Viardot was his religion and he her worshiper. The nature of this relationship has never been clear. During the author's lifetime his association with Mme Viardot gave rise to unbridled conjecture which has continued ever since, but there is no evidence that it was other than platonic.[1] That Turgenev longed for something more is beyond question, and the degree of his ardor—and also of his passivity—is indicated by his acceptance of the role of glorified uncle assigned him by his beloved. Of necessity he included in his esteem not only the singer, but also her husband and children. From the year 1847, Turgenev's home for long intervals

[1] Turgenev had a daughter whom he called Pauline, but her mother was a seamstress who worked briefly on the Turgenev estate. Efforts to prove that he was the father of any of Pauline Viardot's children have not been successful.

was wherever Mme Viardot happened to be. After living for several summer seasons with the singer and her family at her country home near Paris, he increasingly spent more of his time in western Europe until he became only an infrequent visitor to Russia. For several years he was a neighbor of the Viardots in Baden, and he later followed or accompanied them back and forth across Germany and France with long intervals in Paris. When he died in September, 1883, he was living close to them in Bougival.

The effect of Pauline Viardot upon Turgenev's artistic career is impossible to calculate. She was certainly his Beatrice, but since she continued to exist vigorously in the flesh, his feeling for her never passed through the refiner's fire into spirituality. The deprivation of what he most desired must have had a debilitating effect upon him creatively at the same time that the singer served as his most positive source of inspiration. It certainly accounts in part for the weakness of his heroes and their inability to take hold of love on the few occasions when it was within their grasp. Over all of Turgenev's writing hovers the intimation, not of immortality, but of a sigh.

His mother's frequent attempts to force her son to her will by curtailing the funds which should have been available to him prompted him to write out of sheer need of money. Her fury, both at his giving up his profession and at the fascination exerted upon him by the singer, was boundless. A rift between them was left unhealed at her death. Although her last thoughts seem to have been to cut her sons off from their inheritance, when she died in 1850, Ivan became the owner of nearly two thousand male souls, with land and other possessions in proportion. As a landlord he realized only a small portion of the profits he might have had from his holdings because of his prolonged absences from his estate and his incompetence in business affairs. Beneficent toward his serfs, he was not as progressive as the author of *A Sportsman's Sketches* might logically have been. Even if his intentions were the best, his interests were elsewhere. His role in the owner-serf relationship is reflected in his writings, especially in *Fathers and Sons.*

In 1852 a significant event in Turgenev's experience occurred. Although he knew Gogol only slightly, he had the highest esteem for the older author, at whose death he wrote a testimonial to the inspiration he had found in Gogol's writing. Since the author of *Dead Souls* was considered dangerous, the censor in St. Petersburg refused to sanction this obituary notice, whereupon Turgenev had it printed in Moscow. When this breach of respect for authority came to the attention of the Czar, he caused Turgenev to be arrested and imprisoned for a month and thereafter confined to his country estate for a year and a half. This taste of autocratic methods gave the author an increased awareness of the anachronism of the Russian political and social organization. This period of unwilling withdrawal from the centers of cultural activity was not without compensation, however. During his enforced rusticity he began his first novel.

Notwithstanding all his years abroad, Turgenev never felt completely at home away from Russia. Germany offered him relative congeniality, but France was always distasteful. Italy and England were not compatible to his temperament in spite of his many visits. He was thus the victim of an ambivalence, torn between love of a person and love of a country, the two separated by several kinds of distance. The person had the stronger appeal, yet Turgenev the artist was dependent upon his native land for the settings, characters, and topical issues of his books. His absence accounts for the objectivity of his analyses; he wrote as one looking on from afar. It also accounts, unfortunately, for a growing quality of unreality. But for the hypnotic attraction of Pauline Viardot, Turgenev probably would have kept his roots deep in the Russian soil and he might have created a grander gallery of characters with more positive responses to the problems of their times. Almost certainly if he had made his geographical home in the country from which he drew his material, his characters would have been less enervated and less dispossessed. But who knows? In Russia he might only have exchanged noncommitment for nervousness. He might have lost the beautiful precision and lyricism of style which make his books, even yet and even in translation, an artistic experience for any reader with ear attuned to the music of prose.

Estimates of Turgenev by his contemporaries vary from the excited superlatives of the American novelist Henry James (who on one occasion called him "adorable") to the vituperations of his sometime friends. The latter never forgave him for his growing conservatism, which they regarded as a betrayal of the cause of revolution. Wherever the truth may lie (probably somewhere between, for the author's nature was complex despite his seeming simplicity), there is no better vantage point than Turgenev's novels from which to view the changing scene in Russia after the middle of the last century.

II.

A Sportsman's Sketches has sometimes been called the *Uncle Tom's Cabin* of Russian literature, but this comparison, even though both were published in the same year, is misleading. Turgenev's sketches are for the most part reflective, their manner one of detached neutrality. Nothing could have been more foreign to Turgenev's personality and mode of expression than the exhortatory passion of Harriet Beecher Stowe. It is fascinating to speculate on how the aristocratic cosmopolite reacted to the great-souled lady from New England when they met in Paris not long after the publication of the two books. He probably felt no more kinship with her than he might have with one of the flaming evangels from a painting by William Blake if he had encountered such a celestial creature in a Paris salon. Turgenev was not capable of carrying the colors for anything. It is doubtful that he gave more sympathetic attention to the peasants who appeared in the sketches than to the magnificent vistas of woodland dear to the heart of the huntsman. The author was not in any sense an abolitionist. He was a gentleman of humane impulses, aware of the strength and courage of simple people and sincerely but objectively desirous that they might be relieved from oppression. That he hoped for a better life for the peasants is beyond question.

Although Turgenev never speaks against the landowning class, he shows the peasants suffering mutely from the caprice, the monstrous egotism, and the cruelty of their masters. There is, for example, in "The Peasant Proprietor Ovsyanikov" an account of a certain landowner ("He was an overbearing man; he oppressed us poorer folks"), who, seeing a choice bit of land which he coveted, took it away from its owner, a small farmer, by simple appropriation without paying a farthing. When the owner attempted to lay a petition before the court, the thief had him seized and flogged. The story is told by the son of the original owner to the grandson of the unscrupulous rich man:

> "What happened? They brought him to your house, and flogged him right under your windows. And your grandfather stands on the balcony and looks on; and your grandmother sits at the window and looks on too. My father cries out, 'Gracious lady . . . intercede for me! have mercy on me!' But her only answer was to keep getting up to have a look at him. So they exacted a promise from my father to give up the land, and bade him be thankful they let him go alive. . . . It's called 'The Cudgelled Land,' because it was gained by the cudgel. So you see from that, we poor folks can't bewail the old order very much."

In "Raspberry Spring," the peasant Vlass had been to Moscow to his master, "to ask him a favor . . . to lessen my rent, or to let me work it out in labor, or to put me on another piece of land, or something. . . . My son is dead—so I can't manage it now alone." And what of the master?

> "He drove me away! Says he, 'How dare you come straight to me; there is a bailiff for such things. You ought first . . . to apply to

the bailiff . . . and where am I to put you on other land? You first,' says he, 'bring the debt you owe.' He was angry altogether."

"What then—did you come back?"

"I came back. I wanted to find out if my son had not left any goods of his own, but I couldn't get a straight answer. I say to his employer, 'I am Phillip's father'; and he says, 'What do I know about that? And your son,' says he, 'left nothing; he was even in debt to me.' So I came away."

The peasant related all this with a smile, as though he were speaking of someone else; but tears were starting into his small, screwed-up eyes, and his lips were quivering.

Some peasants were "transported" to strange places, away from all their associations, for no reason except the whim of the master; some were refused permission to marry, one sadistic old curmudgeon not allowing a young man to "buy" a peasant girl whom he loved so that he could marry her and take her away. One proprietor who considered himself a cultivated man of the world never lifted his voice to reprove his serfs, preferring "a straight blow in the culprit's face." On one occasion he entertained a friend at breakfast. "He drank his tea, laughed, scrutinized his fingernails, propped himself up with cushions, and was altogether in an excellent humor." But when he discovered that the wine had not been warmed precisely to his satisfaction, he tranquilly sent the footman to be flogged by a bully he retained for such purposes. In the same tale, "The Agent," a variation on the usual forms of cruelty is revealed by the disclosure that the bailiff had outdone the inhumanity of the master. He had worked out a system by which he paid small debts for the peasants, thereafter squeezing from them without mercy what little they had. When nothing was left, he practically squeezed out their life's blood.

The sketches contain several descriptions of the crude, dark, smoky huts, almost bereft of furnishings, in which the peasants were forced to live. For the majority life was reduced to the most primitive conditions in comparison to which their masters' dogs lived in luxury. In one instance the narrator said to an owner:

> "The huts allotted to the peasants are wretched cramped little hovels; there isn't a tree to be seen near them; there's not a pond even; there's only one well, and that's no good. Could you really find no other place to settle them?"

To this the landlord replied:

> "I know my own business. I'm a plain man—I go on the old system. To my ideas, when a man's master—he's a master; and when he's peasant—he's a peasant."

Several of the serfs in *A Sportsman's Sketches* are shown destitute, ill, or suffering from accident, asking for and receiving nothing, waiting to die in quiet resignation. In one of the narratives, called "Death," the author records how death came to a number of poor people. "How wonderfully indeed," he says, "the Russian peasant dies! The temper in which he meets his end cannot be called indifference or stolidity; he dies as though he were performing a solemn rite, coolly and simply." These words are filled with unintentional irony. It was no doubt true that the Russian peasant died "coolly and simply," but why shouldn't he? All his life he had to live with death as the only certainty; often it was his close companion. He became familiar with it early and must have looked forward to it as offering better possibilities than anything he had been able to count on during his earthly experiences. Most of the peasants had no choice except to endure whatever came their way. After being schooled to the misery of living, they could hardly have been expected to have any qualms about dying.

It would be an error to give the impression that most of the tales in this volume are about serfdom. In truth, the peasant characters are only incidental to a slice-of-life treatment of rural life in which the pictorial and reportorial tones are dominant. The fact that this slender spark produced such a conflagration is indication that the fire was already laid, waiting only to be ignited. If one compares this volume with the militant *Uncle Tom's Cabin*, it is difficult to believe that the former played a part, as Czar Alexander II averred, in clinching his resolution to do away with serfdom. But it produced a strong impact upon Russian readers not accustomed to such material. For that reason, and perhaps involuntarily, Ivan Turgenev was destined to play in Russia a role more closely akin to that of Mrs. Stowe in America than on the surface appears possible.

A number of the longer later narratives (some long enough to be called novelettes), such as *Mumu*, *The Inn*, and *The Wolf*, supplement the treatment of the peasants in the *Sketches*. In most cases, no matter how free he was from intent to preach or incite, Turgenev presents the peasants as pitiable but strong in contrast to the weakness of their masters. Their strength contains some of the elements of the soil close to which they live. They are depicted as patient and enduring and also as having a native honesty and intelligence and potential for action which some day would make them a force to be recognized. He usually showed them undefiled by spiritual impoverishment, no matter how poor the physical condition. If in some cases Turgenev's view of the peasants was unduly rosy, it is important to notice that he was aware of the other side of the coin. He also saw the peasants' ignorance, irresponsibility, sloth, and shortsightedness. His view of them was not the result of a shallow spirit of romanticism or an urge to be philanthropic. It was dictated by the importunity of time, for Turgenev was writing at that moment in history which marked the emergence of the common man.

III.

Turgenev's first novel, *Rudin*, now appears to be a rather stuffy book about a man who talked too much and did nothing. Paradoxically, in the weakness of Rudin's character lay the power of the book. Like Oblomov, Rudin was a symbolic figure. Here, in the personality of a man of weak will and a nonheroic, divided nature, the thinking people of Russia could see themselves. If they were to do anything for their beloved country, they would have to cast off the infirmities of Rudinism. Rudin was, in short, the model of what they must not be. The novel thus served as a bell at whose ringing people were inspired to act.

Following his introduction to the wealthy Darya Mikhailovna, Dmitri Rudin became a regular member of the circle surrounding her in her summer home in the country. A conventional woman intrigued by the idea of appearing cultured, she was pleased by the attention of young men, especially if they were intellectuals, a requirement Rudin fulfilled. From the moment of his first appearance Rudin captivated most of the members of the group by the tumultuous exhibition of his oratory. Not all his listeners were as favorably impressed, however, as Darya and her daughter Natalya; the more thoughtful discerned his weakness. They realized that in spite of his noble-toned idealism he was a man unable to act.

Gradually Rudin began to fancy himself in love with Natalya, a quiet but combustible young woman who reciprocated his feeling with an intensity beyond anything of which the man was capable. Rudin had not foreseen this development; he had been playing with sentiment as one might sample a delectable flavor. The girl's headlong response precipitated a climax. With all the courage of Goncharov's Olga, and considerably more ardor, Natalya declared herself ready to abandon everything (for her mother would never have agreed to a marriage because of Rudin's lower social standing) in order to join her fate with his. Confronted by the necessity for action, Rudin could only crawl weakly away from the crisis, telling Natalya that they had no choice except to "submit." What Rudin had proposed to accomplish, what had endowed him with heroic dimensions in the eyes of Natalya, is never made clear beyond the fact that it was bound up with nebulous aspirations for the utopian future of Russia. When she discovered that the man to whom she had offered her love was a creature of straw, the young woman was chagrined and robbed of her illusions.

After this fiasco, Rudin wandered, dreamed, orated, and, as the years passed, continued to do nothing. Finally he became a pathetic figure, symbol of the gulf between dreams and deeds. At the end of the story, in a meaningless gesture of affirmation, he died on the barricades in Paris during the insurrection of 1848. It is noteworthy that this ending was appended to the book some years after it was written. Lacking it, Rudin would not have been accorded even the dubious distinction of a futile death, without identity, in a cause as confused in motivation as his own words had always been.

Even without a direction or a goal, Rudin gives evidence of a forward step in the development of the Russian social consciousness. A member of the middle class and university trained, he was at least aware of his country's needs and desired to do something about them. He had none of the vices of Gogol's landowning characters and none of the satisfaction with the status quo of Oblomov. But unfortunately he was another victim of Oblomovism, for in spite of his passionate eloquence and exalted dreams, as one of the characters of the book said, "Rudin's words seem to remain mere words, and never to pass into deeds." When she had caught the measure of the man by whose golden tongue she had been fascinated, Natalya said to him, "You have so often talked of self-sacrifice . . . but do you know . . . there's all the difference between word and deed." Rudin was aware of his own ineffectuality. Attempting to explain his weakness, he wrote to Natalya:

> "Alas! if I could really devote myself to these interests, if I could at last conquer my inertia. . . . But no! I shall remain to the end the incomplete creature I have always been. . . . The first obstacle . . . and I collapse entirely."

In a further effort at self-evaluation he said:

> "I am absolutely . . . a well-intentioned man. . . . I want to do the good that lies nearest, to be even a little use. But no! I never succeed. What does it mean? What hinders me from living and working like others? . . . I am only dreaming of it now."

What is most striking is that Rudin's inertia was not caused by the cushioned ease of upper-class life as Oblomov's had been. It was symptomatic of the inertia of the whole of Russia.

In an essay called "Hamlet and Don Quixote," Turgenev elaborated his theory that men are likely to fall into one or the other of two classifications, the Hamlets and the Don Quixotes. The former, thinkers and idealists, fail of achievement because of inadequate integration between what they propose and what they do. The latter are capable of concentrated, purposeful action. They may tilt at windmills, yet they keep on the offensive until they have accomplished their ends. This essay amplified the concept Turgenev had by that time already developed in at least two novels, the first being *Rudin.* Clearly, Rudin was the Hamlet type, able to inspire others but never really believing in himself. His path, like Hamlet's, was strewn with high resolutions unfulfilled. He was one of the long procession of "superfluous" men for whom Turgenev's story "The Diary of a Superfluous Man" supplied a fitting designation.

Rudin's character was probably patterned after that of one of the young students with whom Turgenev had been associated at the German university. It is generally assumed that the source may have been Michael Bakunin, who devoted his life to the cause of revolution. Even if Bakunin went farther in action than Rudin, he lived most intensely in words, plans, and dreams. The book also testifies to the patriotic enthusiasm and the passion for improvement of the students in the Russian universities. In one passage, Lazhnyov, who had been at college with Rudin, recalls the sense of mission of those young men who felt they were standing at the threshold of a door about to be opened on a better world. He mentions particularly one who lingers in his memory because he "breathed fire and strength into all of us . . . when he did stretch his wings—good heavens!—what a flight! up to the very height of the blue heavens!" Thus did the novelist record how the yeast, the leavening agent—students, intellectuals, dreamers and doers—began to act upon the great warm mass of dough that was Russia. At first the doers, handicapped by lack of a leader, were too few to accomplish anything tangible. Although Rudin was incapable of leadership, his significance resided in his ability to give focus to the dreams of others who, as Lazhnyov said, might some time develop the power to act.

From what has already been said about Natalya, it should be clear that she is the strong, unconventional woman of the new Russia, eager to give herself to a cause. A statement she makes represented a trend in the society of the times: "Believe me, a woman is not only able to value self-sacrifice; she can sacrifice herself." This quality did not belong to women alone, however. It was characteristic of many of the young radicals who became leaders of the revolutionary movements in western Europe and in Russia.

The sacrifices of which Natalya spoke were needed in a Russia where poverty of body and spirit were the millstones imposed by a despotic but ineffectual government. At the same time that the anemic irresolution of Rudin exasperated many zealous Russians who felt that Turgenev had not been fair to his countrymen in such a portrayal, his character and his failure served as a tocsin call to action. He heightened the consciousness of the need for leadership and for motivated, coordinated endeavor.

IV.

In the next novel, *A House of Gentlefolk* (or *Liza* in some English editions), Turgenev made no advance in exploring the problems of his country or in finding a leader. It is a love story in halftones. Granted that the unhappy developments of the narrative logically inhere in the circumstances, the author was unnecessarily disposed to submerge his characters in a somber sea. This is the voice of the Turgenev unfulfilled in love and beginning to feel old. The main character (Turgenev's novels do not have "heroes") is interesting because he is a further projection of the author himself and of his Hamlet theory.

The idealistic Fyodor Lavretsky loved and married a woman

who, unknown to him, was an irresponsible flirt completely absorbed in society. When he discovered her infidelity, he broke off his relationship with her. Returning to his home in the country, he devoted his efforts to the improvement of his estate. A distant relative who lived in the same vicinity had a daughter, Liza, to whom he became deeply, and he supposed hopelessly, attached. She was a modest girl of religious nature and habits, a complete contrast to his wife. Impressed by his simplicity and integrity, the girl returned his affection. After a period of resignation to the impasse caused by his marriage, Lavretsky was falsely informed of his wife's death. He had scarcely begun to savor the prospect of future happiness with Liza when his wife, alive and more calculating than before, reappeared to make heavy demands upon him. Powerless to avert this calamity, Lavretsky saw his hopes crash forever. Meanwhile, Liza, blaming herself for having aspired to what she considered a selfish happiness, became a nun. Lavretsky was left looking into an empty future of carrying out the duties of a conscientious landlord.

If Turgenev aimed in this novel to explore further the possibilities of leadership for Russia, his choice of primary character was inappropriate. Though "completely well intentioned" as Rudin had been, Lavretsky could only accept his destiny, not control it. There was much of Oblomov in him. Also, like Turgenev, Lavretsky was unduly and prematurely burdened with a sense of futility and old age. He differed from the author in one important respect, however: he went back to his native soil and there found peace, if only a sterile peace. Turgenev was prevented from doing the same by Pauline Viardot.

Liza continued Turgenev's parade of strong women, in this case strong-souled rather than strong-minded. Because of her otherworldliness, however, she is less appealing than several of the others. Indeed, heaven is so obviously her destination that she might as well get on with the journey. The biographer of Turgenev, Avrahm Yarmolinsky, speaks of her as "the Russian Gretchen . . . less a flesh-and-blood woman than a symbol of unattainable happiness and irrevocable youth."[2] Yet she can hardly be said to be *young*. Her submission belongs to *old* Russia. But her singleness of purpose and willing acceptance of authoritarianism link her to the new women who fill Russian literature after the middle of the nineteenth century.

More human, because more stubborn and passionate, is the heroine of Turgenev's next novel, *On the Eve*. Passing over an artist, a university student, and the stuffy "head secretary to the senate" whom her father had selected for his son-in-law, Elena was irresistibly attracted to Dmitri Insarov, a Bulgarian patriot. He had the ability to lose himself in the cause of the people, which she believed her Russian admirers lacked. She wrote in her diary that he not only talked but acted. Spellbound by the young man's fervor and the possibilities of his being useful on a grand scale, she cut off all her former ties in order to follow him. Even after her husband's melodramatic death, she would not be deflected from participation in his magnificent but mysterious program to emancipate the Bulgarians. Another of Turgenev's typical heroines, Elena further emphasizes his concept of the new Russian woman in her Spartan courtship of the hard way.

In this book Turgenev returned to his preoccupation with possibilities for leadership in his country, but with negative results. Insarov was a leader, but he was not Russian. Therefore, the search was not rewarded. The Hamlet qualities with which the author again endowed his male characters are analyzed by one of them:

> "We have no one yet, no men, look where you will. Everywhere—either small fry, nibblers, Hamlets on a small scale, self-absorbed, or darkness and subterranean chaos, or idle babblers and wooden sticks. Or else they are like this: they study themselves to the most shameful detail. . . . No, if we only had some sensible men among us, that girl . . . would not have run away from us, would not have slipped off like a fish to the water! What is the meaning of it. . . . When will our time come? When will men be born among us?"

[2] *Turgenev*, 164.

Turgenev's reasons for making his first strong man a foreigner are not clear. He may have been too disappointed, too disillusioned, or simply too tired to do otherwise. Or it may have been deliberate irony. Whatever his reasons, his intentions were unmistakable. They set off a barrage of rebuttals which would have intimidated a man of more substantial convictions than he.

Although Elena is a precursor of the new society, in many respects the most important thing about the book is its title. In 1860, when the book was published, Russia was "on the eve" of inevitable change. Indeed, the country had only a little more than a year to wait for the change basic to all others, the emancipation of the slaves. Furthermore, the title is prophetic with regard to Turgenev's career. His next book, *Fathers and Sons*, is not only his masterpiece but a novel of incalculable significance.

V.

After the publication of the three novels, *Rudin*, *A House of Gentlefolk*, and *On the Eve*, Turgenev's critics accused him of writing about a time and about character types already out of date. That this was at least in part true is attested by the repetitiousness of theme and character. Moreover, events in Russia were moving too fast to be chronicled accurately by one who spent most of his time on foreign soil. The same criticism could not be made, however, about *Fathers and Sons* (1862). This extraordinary document reveals many aspects of the evolutionary temper. Towering above everything else Turgenev wrote, it is distinguished by all his best qualities of style as well as by significance of content. Most striking, it frames a character, Bazarov, who looms like a giant above all other characters this author created. Studying the personality and career of Turgenev evokes the feeling again that when he conceived Bazarov he was an involuntary instrument. The author himself did not seem quite able to understand where Bazarov came from. This book reveals the Russia of the emancipation year (1861) and immediately afterward in a state of turbulence that demanded some kind of resolution. It records the emergence of a character and an attitude which were to serve as catalysts in producing a new element in the national consciousness.

The young doctor, Bazarov, trained in the tradition of the German universities, had become a disciple of the natural sciences. He called himself a Nihilist, one who believes in nothing. Turgenev did not coin this term, but he might well have done so. From the time of the publication of the book, it became a leading word in the Russian vocabulary and a major concept in the Russian mind.

The iconoclasm of Bazarov the scientist is especially pointed in contrast to the pastoral setting and the agreeable civility of the other characters of the novel. Bazarov came with his devoted school friend and follower, Arkady Kirsanov, to visit at the latter's country home. There he was thrown into relief first by the naïve indecisiveness of Arkady and then by the personalities of the country gentlemen and landowning aristocrats, Arkady's father Nikolai and his uncle Pavel. From the first Bazarov was antagonistic to these two men. They represented to him the conditions of privilege—idleness, softness, tradition, parasitism, and culture borrowed from the West—which he believed must be eliminated from Russia. Of Nikolai, Bazarov said to Arkady: "Your father's a nice chap . . . but he's behind the times; his day is done. . . . The day before yesterday, I saw him reading Pushkin. . . . Explain to him, please, that that's no earthly use. He's not a boy . . . it's time to throw up that rubbish." Even worse than that, Bazarov discovered, Nikolai sometimes played the cello, an activity Bazarov considered indicative of mental decay. To him the arts ("Raphael's not worth a brass farthing"), fine sentiments, good manners, the codes of gentlemanly behavior—all were decadent and diseased. He was a skeptic and a scientist. "A good chemist is twenty times as useful as any poet," he maintained. Arkady explained his friend's view of life thus:

"He's a nihilist," repeated Arkady.

"A nihilist," said Nikolai Petrovitch. "That's from the Latin *nihil, nothing*, as far as I can judge; the word must mean a man who . . . who accepts nothing?"

"Say 'who respects nothing,'" put in Pavel Petrovitch, and he set to work on the butter again.

"Who regards everything from the critical point of view," observed Arkady.

"Isn't it just the same thing?" inquired Pavel Petrovitch.

"No, it's not the same thing. A nihilist is a man who does not bow down before any authority, who does not take any principle on faith, whatever reverence the principle may be enshrined in."

Nikolai tried to understand the young man in spite of his vulgarity and rudeness, but Pavel could see him as nothing but a brash upstart. Every encounter between the two ended in mutual baiting. "You don't acknowledge art, then, I suppose?" Pavel once inquired, to which Bazarov replied, "The art of making money or of advertising pills!" And to the question, "Then you believe in science only?" he answered, "I have already explained to you that I don't believe in anything."

Bazarov would not permit himself the luxury of having positive reasons for negation. He explained his attitude as a matter of biology:

"Why, I, for instance, take up a negative attitude, by virtue of my sensations; I like to deny—my brain's made on that plan, and that's all about it! Why do I like chemistry? Why do you like apples?—by virtue of our sensations. It's all the same thing."

That the negation in which Bazarov found satisfaction was in fact prompted by constructive motives, even though the young idol breaker was not willing to acknowledge them, is illustrated by his response to a question as to what possible use there could be in Nihilists:

"We suspected that talk, perpetual talk, and nothing but talk, about our social diseases, was not worth while, that it all led to nothing but superficiality and pedantry; we saw that our leading men, so-called advanced people and reformers, are no good; that we busy ourselves over foolery, talk rubbish about art, unconscious creativeness, parliamentarism, trial by jury, and the deuce knows what all; while, all the while, it's a question of getting bread to eat, while we're stifling under the grossest superstition, while all our enterprises come to grief, simply because there aren't honest men enough to carry them on."

Bazarov's self-analysis was consistent, but he himself was not. The many and intricate contradictions of his character make impossible a formula that fits. Whereas he asserted that he believed in nothing, actually he believed passionately in disbelief—and in humanity. Although he pretended to distrust even science and would not admit to any particular curiosity, in truth he was a devotee of the scientific spirit, for which he died. He professed a hatred of people ("I felt such a hatred for this poorest peasant"), yet he knew how to get close to them, and many—especially simple people—were drawn to him. Despising sentiment, he fell in love abjectly, like the gawkiest schoolboy, being released from his turmoil only by the coldness of the woman. He scorned conventionality and was contemptuous of established concepts of propriety, but he fought a duel to satisfy another man's idea of honor, behaving toward him with whimsical magnanimity. He was vulgar, boorish and insulting. His treatment of his parents was an outrage. And yet behind all this behavior—prompted by sincerity on a grand scale and a hatred of pretense—his fundamental integrity was admirable.

His contradictions extended even to his egotism. In spite of almost insufferable arrogance, he recognized his own limitations. Determined not to appear other than what he was, paradoxically he appeared worse than he was. One is reminded of the young Cordelia at the court of King Lear, baited by her father to give an accounting of her love for him. This she could not and would not do, but her refusal in no way diminished that love. With strengths and weaknesses inextricably blended, Cordelia set the stage for her downfall. Likewise Bazarov, though he spoke in vehement rejection, lived by the faith he professed and died in majestic acquiescence. The man who did "protest too much" in life left in his dying a sense of real loss. He was a big man, not because he tried to be, but because he was. He supplied the answer to the artist's (Turgenev's) question in *On the Eve*: "When will men be born among us?"

Why did he have to die? Was it because Turgenev did not really believe in life, did not believe in anything but failure and resignation? Or did the author feel he had gone too far in the creation of Bazarov and must check the advance? Was he terrified by premonitions of what was to come? Did he fear to give offense? Or was he genuinely confused and unable to see the future of his country with such men as Bazarov in command? Perhaps Bazarov was stronger than his creator, and only by killing him could the creator retain his power. Whatever the reason, Bazarov's death was ironical. It was as if Turgenev wanted to say: "There *will* be men in Russia, but there will be no certain future for them. Their weaknesses will cancel their strengths. Because of their contradictions, their tragedy will be inherent within them."

The effect of *Fathers and Sons* was like a sudden storm. The excitement was intensified by the inability of almost everybody to understand Bazarov. The conservatives, especially those tenacious of the amenities, felt that Turgenev had created a monster to whom he had given his blessing. They were certain the monster would proceed to overthrow the strongholds of everything they held dear—manners, mores, and institutions based upon the system of aristocracy. On the other hand, the liberals, or more exactly the radicals, argued that Bazarov was but a caricature and that the recriminations he aroused would impede progress. Some objected to his cold rationality. Others declared he was deranged, a voice spouting words without meaning. If he had been a rascal, he would have pleased the reactionaries; and if a hero, he would have delighted the young revolutionaries. But as he was neither one extreme nor the other, he satisfied nobody. Turgenev was not prepared for the abuse his book and his character Bazarov provoked. This was the last blow needed to make him feel an alien in his own land. Never again did he feel as close as before to the beating heart of his country.

Other aspects of the book worthy of study cannot be considered here except in summary. For example, Turgenev's treatment of the gentry, although attended with the same politeness he always accorded them, still disclosed their clinging traits of Oblomovism along with a stuffy complacency. They were well bred, well mannered, well educated, well groomed, and well intentioned—but they did little. Pavel Kirsanov—with his polished fingernails, his starched linen, and his living in the past on memories of an unhappy love affair—came especially close to being a satirical portrait. Eager to bridge the gap between the old and the new, Nikolai is a more appealing character. Surprisingly, the cleavage between the "fathers" and the "sons" was not a matter of clear-cut division between the two generations. With his inclination to be a follower, Arkady was not as much a member of the "new" generation as his father. Loosed from the spell of Bazarov, Arkady returned to the shelter of traditionalism. Bazarov's father, on the other hand, trying pathetically to be worthy of his awe-inspiring son, made an effort to keep up with the times.

Another way in which the book is instructive is in what it says about the peasantry through the relations between Nikolai and his serfs. Three years before the emancipation, Nikolai had already freed his peasants, who continued to work the land but were expected to pay rent. In response to Bazarov's pointing out the ineffectiveness of these efforts, Nikolai said:

> "I thought I was doing everything to keep up with the times; I have started a model farm; I have done well by the peasants, so that I am positively called a 'Red Radical' all over the province; I read, I study, I try in every way to keep abreast with the requirements of the day—and they say my day's over. And, brother, I begin to think that it is."

Nikolai did not need to blame himself, but the situation certainly left much to be desired. With centuries-old habits of dependence, improvidence, and inefficiency behind them, the serfs could not quickly adjust to the challenges of their new freedom. Nikolai explained to his son: "I have had a lot of bother with the peasants this year. . . . They won't pay their rent. . . . They are being set against me . . . and they don't do their best. They spoil the tools. But they have tilled the land pretty fairly." Being extremely generous, Nikolai proposed to cut more timber so that the land might go to the peasants, who "were all in tatters and on the sorriest little nags."

In spite of Nikolai's efforts, the transition period was marked by continuing discouragements:

> Difficulties on the farm sprang up every day—hired laborers had become insupportable. Some asked for their wages to be settled, or for an increase of wages, while others made off with the wages they had received in advance: the horses fell sick; the harness fell to pieces as though it were burnt; the work was carelessly done. . . . The overseer suddenly turned lazy, and began to grow fat, as every Russian grows fat when he gets a snug berth. . . . The peasants who had been put on the rent system did not bring their money at the time due, and stole the forest timber. . . . To crown all, the peasants began quarrelling among themselves; brothers asked for a division of property, their wives could not get on together in one house. . . . There were not hands enough for the harvest; . . . and the corn meanwhile went to waste; and here they were not getting on with the mowing.

This passage gives only a small suggestion of the conditions which prevailed all over Russia. It will sound familiar to Americans because it recalls the post–Civil War period in the United States when the slaves, legally freed, were by no means free in all respects. In Russia, likewise, emancipation was little more than a legality not quickly accompanied by social or economic health. The transition period, filled with confusion, furnished fuel for the Nihilists' fire.

An unexpected detail in *Fathers and Sons* is a comment on a government official, which might have come out of the pages of Gogol. He was a governor "at once a progressive and a despot, as often happens with Russians":

> He had the highest opinion of himself; his vanity knew no bounds, but he behaved simply, looked affably, listened condescendingly and laughed so good-naturedly, that on first acquaintance he might even be taken for "a jolly good fellow." . . . He was an adroit courtier, a great hypocrite, and nothing more; he had no special aptitude for affairs, and no intellect, but he knew how to manage his own business successfully. . . .
>
> He was gracious to all, to some with a shade of disgust, to others with a shade of respect.

This ridicule is supplemented by several brief satirical sketches of representatives of the new intelligentsia. Sitnikov damned all authority in servile imitation of Bazarov, whom he admired without having Bazarov's capacity for independent thought or action. Mme Kukshin was fascinated in turn by chemistry, the woman question, Emerson, embryology, Macaulay, and anything else that came to her attention. These two offer a preview of the scathing attack upon pseudo-intellectualism found in the next novel, *Smoke*.

With his Nihilist, Turgenev joined Gogol and Goncharov in the creation of a type immediately a source of universal concern in Russia. It is worthy of note that although at first most of the young radicals felt they had been maligned by the book (they considered Bazarov something of a grotesque and certain of his views and actions unworthy of their own "enlightened" attitudes), some of them—led by the young critic Pisarev—tried to emulate or go beyond Bazarov. Bazarov's view of himself was as ambivalent as the reactions to him. "I was needed in Russia," he said as he was dying, and then, "No, it's clear, I wasn't needed." This was his final contradiction. But needed or not, he was there. Unhappily, the best of Bazarov died with him. What remained was too often the callow, vociferous, and disorganized zealotry of those who found stimulation in destruction. Almost all were earnest; some were honest—with a lopsided honesty; some were genuinely humanitarian; all were completely humorless. Rejecting everything intangible, aesthetic, or traditional, as disciples of the practical they worshiped at the shrine of science. Although idolizing science, they were not scientists, for they lacked objectivity. Although professing rationality, they were not rational. Dedicated they certainly were, but to what? They talked a great deal about solving social problems, and in truth the problems needed solution. But what were their real aims? What would be the inevitable result of their sterility of spirit? It is small wonder that Turgenev was disturbed by the implications of these questions—and not Turgenev alone. The answers were provided by Dostoevsky.

Fathers and Sons is a reminder that the Nihilists emerged when the autocrats still held the winning hand. The people, coming to consciousness, had at last begun to have hopes of ridding themselves of the incubus of aristocracy and autocracy. But their leaders and spokesmen—the Nihilists and revolutionaries—could not even begin to help them realize their hopes except as they acted in defiance of the existing order. The problem was where this defiance would end and what its real purpose was. Turgenev's Bazarov cast a long shadow before him. How long, the world does not know even yet.

VI.

Considering Turgenev's disinclination to participate actively in the conflicts of his time, the controversy precipitated by *Fathers and Sons* must have reverberated around him like a profane cacophany. As might have been expected, in the next novel he returned to passivity. The main character of *Smoke*, Litvinov, another "superfluous" man and a "Hamlet of Russia," offers nothing new. Still, *Smoke* is notable for two reasons. The first of these is the savage criticism of two groups, the pseudo-intellectuals and the shallow, snobbish aristocrats, both of whom regarded themselves as fundamental to the scheme of things in Russia. The author, however, saw them as manifestations of unwholesome artificiality.

There is a matchless chapter in which the devotees of a certain Gubaryov, just arrived in Baden from Heidelberg, are shown gathered at the feet of their master. Gubaryov moved about, an unctuous luminary, filling the role of leader and prophet:

> Remarkable—really remarkable—was the respect with which all these people treated Gubaryov as a preceptor or chief; they laid their ideas before him, and submitted them to his judgment; and he replied by muttering, plucking at his beard, averting his eyes, or by some disconnected, meaningless words, which were at once seized upon as the utterances of the loftiest wisdom. Gubaryov himself seldom interposed in the discussions; but the others strained their lungs to the utmost. . . . It happened more than once that three or four were shouting for ten minutes altogether. . . . Mme Suhantchikov talked about Garibaldi, about a certain Karl Ivanovitch, who had been flogged by the serfs of his own household, about Napoleon III, about women's work, about a merchant . . . who had designedly caused the death of twelve workwomen, and had received a medal for it with the inscription "for public services"; about the proletariat, about the Georgian Prince . . . who had shot his wife with a cannon, and about the future of Russia . . . There was an outburst all of a sudden from Vovoshilov; in a single breath, almost choking himself, he mentioned Draper, Virchow, Shelgunov, Bichat, Helmholtz, Star, St. Raymund, Johann Müller the psysiologist, and Johann Müller the historian—obviously confounding them—Taine, Renan, Shtchapov, and then Thomas Nash, Peele, Greene.

One of the most fatuous members of the circle was a woman whose eyes "were fairly leaping out of her head. But then they were always leaping, whatever she might be talking about." After telling an absurd yarn about how "Madame Beecher Stowe" slapped a man because "he presumed to be introduced to the author of *Uncle Tom*," the lady confided to Litvinov (the "Hamlet") that she never read novels:

"Because I have not the time now; I have no thought now but for one thing, sewing machines."

"What machines?" inquired Litvinov.

"Sewing, sewing; all women ought to provide themselves with sewing machines, and form societies; in that way they will all be enabled to earn their living, and will become independent at once. In no other way can they ever be emancipated. That is an important, most important social question."

Turgenev's disdain for these empty-headed poseurs was perhaps secondary to his contempt for the aristocrats who had both empty heads and empty souls. The moths fluttering about Gubaryov's flame were at least alive, filled with eagerness, enthusiasm, and desire. They prepared the way for a revolution urgently needed. But those others who had long enjoyed privilege and wished to remain within its sheltering arms were part of what made revolution necessary. One of them, a fat general, made their position clear:

"I am not hostile to so-called progress, but all these universities and seminaries, and popular schools, these students, priests' sons, and commoners, all these small fry . . . that's where one ought to draw the line, and make other people draw it too. . . . My dear friends, why should we curry favor with the multitude? You like democracy, it flatters you, and serves your ends . . . but you know it's a double weapon. It is better in the old way, as before . . . more secure. Don't deign to reason with the herd, trust in the aristocracy, in that alone is power."

These would-be aristocrats included Mme H., "once a celebrated beauty and wit, who had long ago become a repulsive old crone, with the odor of sanctity and evaporated sinfulness about her"; a young man "with a face as stony as a new doll's [who] remembered nothing of all his travels, and cared for nothing but Russian puns"; and Count H., "our incomparable dilettante [who] gave a little song of his own composition cribbed wholesale from Offenbach." Having nothing better to occupy their time, they were fascinated by a spiritualist's endeavors to hypnotize a crab. A small-scale, up-to-date rendition of "dead souls" was provided by the acid depiction of these "aristocrats."

Small wonder that as Litvinov, disappointed in love and generally disillusioned, looked out the train window, "suddenly it all seemed as smoke to him, everything, his own life, Russian life—everything human, especially everything Russian. All smoke and steam." Nevertheless, he set himself to the work of managing his land. Here he discovered that whereas the old economic and social order had been displaced, the new had begun badly. "Ignorance jostled up against dishonesty; the whole agrarian organization was shaken and unstable as a quagmire bog, and only one great word, 'freedom,' was wafted like the breath of God over the waters."

Litvinov's feeling of confusion and futility is a reflection of the widespread reaction which developed in Russia in the sixties. The emancipation had created as many problems as it solved, as Nikolai Kirsanov, the landowner of *Fathers and Sons*, discovered. There was no way to satisfy such disparate elements as the gentry and the peasantry. Moreover, freeing the slaves did not and could not mean providing them with the means or the know-how to achieve a satisfactory livelihood or raise their standards of living appreciably. By the time Turgenev was ready to write *Smoke* (published 1867), he saw that the public attitude toward the government reforms had settled into an antagonism far different from the comparatively co-operative and hopeful spirit of a decade previous. To the large number of those always indifferent had been added many who had become indifferent from disappointment. At the other extreme were those who had become increasingly determined to see conditions improved and who recognized that improvements could only follow a program of reform much more radical than the existing regime would undertake. In 1866 an attempt on the life of the Czar widened the breach between the government and the public. The temper of the country—compounded of inertia, disillusionment, grim determination, hostility, and a growing readiness to accept violence—was bad and growing worse.

The analysis of this temper is the second reason for the special import of *Smoke*. It was the work of a Turgenev who was weary, who was a little ashamed of his defection in leaving his native soil. But more important, it emphasizes Turgenev's conviction that Russia was at once backward and decadent—and sick of soul. He viewed his own future without anticipation and the future of his country with misgiving. He believed that if his country were to be saved or even improved, it must be saved or improved from without. In particular, he was distressed by the cultural poverty of Russia in contrast to the cultural richness of western Europe. The novelist Dostoevsky, an ardent patriot, could not forgive Turgenev for these views. Writing to his friend Apollon Maikov, Dostoevsky commented that he disliked Turgenev for several reasons:

> . . . but my bitterest complaint against him is his book "Smoke." He told me himself that the leading idea, the point at issue, in that book is this: "If Russia were destroyed by an earthquake and vanished from the globe, it would mean no loss to humanity—it would not even be noticed." He declared to me that that was his fundamental view of Russia.

VII.

Turgenev's last full-length novel, *Virgin Soil* (1876), was considered a failure, because, according to the critics (still railing at the author for spending so much time abroad), its treatment of events was unrealistic. Notwithstanding this dictum, the book contains a lucid account of an important phase in the revolutionary movement, that is, the effort on the part of certain intellectuals to join forces with "the people" in developing revolutionary sentiments and in carrying out reforms. The book suggests that this back-to-the-people effort was particularly enlightening for the intellectuals (many of them young university students and some the sons and daughters of the aristocracy), who discovered that they had much to learn about "the people" and that the peasants had much to learn about everything.

The central character of the novel, Alexei Nezhdanov, the son of a nobleman, had no secure place in society because of his illegitimacy. He became associated with a group of revolutionaries, who welcomed him enthusiastically. In order to earn a living, Nezhdanov left St. Petersburg to accept a position as tutor to the son of the wealthy landlord Sipiagin.

While striving to perform his duties faithfully, Nezhdanov was disturbed by the reactionary attitudes in the home of his employer. He was baited by a neighboring landowner, another in the gallery of Turgenev's unpalatable portraits of the gentry. When Nezhdanov defended his radical views, it was impossible to avoid scenes with his employer as well as the neighbor. Meanwhile, the young man had found a sympathetic listener in his employer's niece. Mariana secretly longed to share in the movement for freedom, having no respect for the parasites among whom she was a poor relation. Mariana's sympathy with his point of view was extremely welcome to the lonely Nezhdanov. Soon Mme Sipiagin began jealously to suspect their attachment and their "free" views. As the situation became intolerable, the two young idealists decided to go away together before a crisis occurred.

Nezhdanov had become acquainted with the manager of a factory who was known for his sane, well-balanced personality. Solomin believed in and sympathized with the new movements, but was not disposed to participate in radical activities; he did not consider them wise or necessary. Yet he had unusual insight into the problems of peasants and factory workers, relations between him and them being characterized by mutual respect. Nezhdanov and Mariana found a haven in the home of Solomin, where it was assumed that they would marry.

In the meantime they began to get acquainted with the laborers in the fields and factories and to learn how and where to be of use. Mariana's adjustment was immediate and complete.

Filled with earnest resolve, she welcomed an abundance of tasks —but not so Nezhdanov. At every attempt to make a contact with the people or to carry out some part of the program, his unfitness became more apparent. A man of scholarly inclination (he was ashamed of sometimes writing poetry in secret), nervous, brooding, and refined, he had no basis for compatibility with the masses. Like Rudin, he was a man of thoughts, not deeds. He soon came to doubt his sincerity as well as his ability. Although Mariana's loyalty was undeviating, Nezhdanov could not bring himself to marry her, knowing there could be no future for the relationship of two people only one of whom had genuine strength and conviction. Depressed by his own ineptitude and aware that Mariana had, unknowing, found security in Solomin, Nezhdanov decided to end his predicament by suicide. Shortly afterward, Solomin and Mariana married and left the factory to lose themselves in revolutionary activities elsewhere.

It is noteworthy that Turgenev finished his novels, as he began them, with an account of a Russian Hamlet.[3] Nezhdanov tried to speak the language of the masses, but he could not escape being an artist and an idealist. He struggled to develop an interest in politics and social issues, but when he discussed them, his words often rang false, for he could not make over his nature to fit the pattern of what he thought he should be. He believed in the cause he professed, and yet it was never really *his* cause. After a humiliating fiasco in his approach to the peasants, he faced himself sternly: "Don't at any rate mistake your sickly, nervous irritability and caprices for the manly wrath, the honest anger, of a man of convictions! O Hamlet! . . . How escape from the shadow of thy spirit?" In a letter to a friend he analyzed the artificiality of his position: "I am not one of those who regenerate themselves by contact with the people. . . . I feel that I am . . . a bad actor in a part that does not suit him."

[3] In 1873, three years before the publication of *Virgin Soil*, a lesser novel, *Freshets of Spring*, appeared. The main character, Sanin, another "Hamlet," was said by some critics to be a self-portrait of Turgenev. Sanin is not, however, any closer to the author than several similar characters from the other novels.

Nezhdanov's efforts to become simplified were defeated by his character, his tastes, and his training. Turgenev made this last of his Hamlets, like his Rudin of the forties, a well-intentioned but "superfluous" man. This failure of the intellectuals was of great symbolic importance. The leaders of Russia were not to be thinking men. The thinkers had been too long crippled in spirit or too long disinclined to act.

In contrast to Nezhdanov, Mariana joins Natalya (*Rudin*), Liza (*House of Gentlefolk*), and Elena (*On the Eve*) in the procession of Turgenev's strong women. "You are already," Solomin said to her, "all you Russian women, more capable and higher than we men." But in Solomin the novelist presented these women with a "straight-forward man" worthy of them; "one could rely on him as on a stone wall."

> Solomin did not believe that the Russian revolution was so near at hand, but . . . he did not intrude his opinions or hinder others from making attempts. . . . He himself belonged to the people, and fully realized that the great bulk of them, without whom one can do nothing, were still quite indifferent, that they must first be prepared, by quite different means and for entirely different ends than the upper classes. . . .
>
> The most unusually friendly relations existed between Solomin and his workpeople. They respected him as a superior, treated him as one of themselves, and considered him to be very learned. . . . And he really was theirs and one of them.

Solomin had been educated for his task; he worked hard and efficiently, and he understood, respected, and was willing to sacrifice for the people. He rejected the status quo but was able to wait for the realization of his hopes. His faith was not in violence but in systematic pursuit of goals. He had none of the inertia or ruthlessness of the gentry. Nor did he suffer from the irresponsibility of the government officials. ("The governor of S. was one of those good-natured, happy-go-lucky, worldly generals who, endowed with wonderfully clean, snow-white bodies and souls to match, of good breeding and education, are turned out of a mill where they are never ground down to becoming the 'Shepherds of the people.'") In Solomin, Turgenev at last found the answer to his quest; here was a leader for Russia, a worker who was an enlightened man.[4]

And leadership was needed. The reform enthusiasm of the young intellectuals was important for a number of reasons, but especially because, as Solomin understood, "The people are asleep." Nezhdanov was not the only one oppressed by the difficulty of doing anything with or for the peasantry.[5] The peasants suffered from more than ignorance, however. The emancipation had done little to lighten their load. On one occasion Nezhdanov said: "When our forefathers emancipated the serfs, do you think they could foresee that a whole class of money-lending landlords would spring up as a result? . . . Landlords . . . [who] drain the peasants to the last drop of blood!" Turgenev still attributed strength and dignity to the peasants though he depicted them more realistically than when he had paid homage to them in *A Sportsman's Sketches*. Now, however, he saw them and their plight as taxing the balance and vigor even of a Solomin. But he implied that Solomin would meet the challenge. One of the other characters said of Solomin:

> "His strength lies in the fact that he doesn't attempt to cure all the social ills with one blow. What a rum set we are to be sure, we Russians! We sit down quietly and wait for something or some one to come along and cure us all at once. . . . Solomin, on the other hand, is different; . . . he knows what he's about!
>
> "I tell you that people like him are the real men! . . . The future

[4] Unfortunately, Turgenev was not able to make Solomin a wholly convincing character despite his obvious desire to do so.

[5] If Nezhdanov could have seen a short way into the future, he would have realized that his failure was but a symptom of the failure of the whole movement, which did not long survive him. The adherents of the movement (*narodniki*) were defeated by their own unfitness as well as by the hostility of both the haves and the have-nots. The book *Hidden Springs of the Revolution*, by Katerina Breshkovskaya, is an extremely interesting account of the movement written by one of the participants.

is in their hands. They are not heroes . . . but they are robust, strong, dull men of the people. They are exactly what we want just now. You have only to look at Solomin. A head as clear as the day and a body as strong as an ox. . . . Why, think of it! here is a man with ideals, and no nonsense about him; educated and from the people, simple, yet all there."

If the simplicity, sanity, and integrity of Solomin could have prevailed, the history of Russia might well have been written in a different key. But the men who succeeded in cultivating the virgin soil were dominated by other characteristics.

The reigning literary critics in Russia from the late 1830's insisted that literature should have political, economic, and social significance. Turgenev conformed to this requirement. Although each of his books that dealt with contemporary issues provoked acidulous and outraged responses from reactionaries or radicals or both, the evidence of history has in large part substantiated what the novelist saw and set down. Turgenev recorded the whole shifting, tumultuous design of the time, with its many conflicting elements. There were the "superfluous" visionaries of the forties (and later), nourished on the rich fare of German philosophy and science but prevented by character and censorship from converting their eloquence into action. There were the enervated or arrogant gentry, complacently enjoying their follies and vices, and the intellectuals, often worshiping false gods and playing at heroics, pretending to be more than they were, but sustained by genuine enthusiasm which distinguished their pretensions from those of the passionless aristocrats. There were also the conscientious young intellectuals who yearned to set the spark to the cold embers of "the people" and who in their back-to-the-people movement planted the soil with the seeds of revolution. And there were the peasants—suffering, enduring, lethargic, and rebellious—often creatures of more character, compassion, and honor than their masters. There were the Nihilists, driven by an understandable urge to destroy but terrifying because they lacked a balancing urge to create, and also the strong women, courageous and idealistic. Among other conflicting elements were the need for strong men to be leaders and the emancipation that had to be but was not enough. Finally, there was the gathering and acceleration of forces dammed up for centuries, at last too powerful to be resisted. Of all these Turgenev has been proved the accurate though unofficial historian. The novelist also recognized one other development: the struggle between East and West (Slavophilism *versus* Westernism). Several of the leading actors in this latter conflict will receive consideration in the next chapter.

But it was in the creation of Bazarov, the Nihilist, that Turgenev's real stature as historian and prophet became evident —Bazarov—whom Turgenev himself admitted he did not know whether to love or to hate.

V/ Four Rebels in Search of a Revolution

In Turgenev's novel *Smoke* is a character, Potugin, who plays no part in the action of the story and has no function except to talk. What he says is all of a piece: he expresses the conviction that Russia is far behind western Europe in culture and in practical affairs as well. He insists that the only way to cure this backwardness is for Russia to become acquainted with and emulate the West. The views of Potugin are, in essence, the views of Turgenev. The novelist's admiration of the West was more than a matter of familiarity based on long residence abroad. It was a manifestation of one of the currents of thought prevailing in Russia by the middle of the nineteenth century. This approbation of the West was opposed by a strongly nationalistic view which emphasized the importance of everything Slavic, affirming that the seeds of Russia's greatness and the possibilities for her improvement were to be found in her own soil and in her own tradition and culture.

I.

The two divergent philosophies, Slavophilism and Westernism, have deep roots in Russian history and wide ramifications which reach outside the boundaries of this book. By the beginning of the nineteenth century both had commenced to have considerable influence in shaping the intellectual temper of the times. During the repressive reign of Nicholas I, the intellectuals longed increasingly to discover some means by which their country might be freed from the yoke of tyranny and enabled to realize the liberation of body and spirit in which they believed. Their zeal was not diminished by the autocratic and anachronistic system which made it impossible for them to be useful to their country—made them, in a sense, "superfluous" men. The fact that some of the intelligentsia had traveled outside Russia added to their awareness of the differences between their country and other parts of Europe. The strongest influence upon them was probably the German universities or, more specifically, certain German philosophers whom most of them studied in Moscow or St. Petersburg, if not in Germany.[1] Even Turgenev, whose political interests were never keen, was indoctrinated with the views of the German philosophers. Another strong influence upon them was the vogue of French utopian socialism, many references to which appear in Russian writings of the 1840's and 1850's.

At first the contrasts between Slavophiles and Westerners were not sharply defined, nor did the premises of one exclude all the premises of the other. This early similarity is to be explained by their common origins and the fact that both were indebted to non-Russian cultures, which offered a great wealth not available in their native culture. In the early stages of division, the Slavophiles agreed with the Westerners that a large cultural gap existed between Russia and western Europe, and that Russia should learn from the West and profit from its superior development. During the decade of the forties, however, their differences increasingly apparent, the two opposing systems became crystallized. Both sets of proponents grew passionate, often angry, in the defense and elaboration of their views and in the effort to win converts. Sometimes the controversy took a personal turn. The result was that in the salons, in the literary reviews, in every medium available to the intellectuals, the practice of mutual disparagement mounted.

Under Alexander II, the son of Nicholas, there was some mitigation of the severity of censorship. Activities that might have a political cast were not so closely watched as before. Thus opportunities for overt discussion became more numerous. In

[1] Kant, Fichte, Schelling, and—in particular—Hegel. The reader who expects to go below the surface in his study of Russian literature or history would do well to familiarize himself with the basic tenets of Hegelian philosophy, expecially with Hegel's treatise on *The Philosophy of History*.

the late fifties and in the decade in which the emancipation occurred, the cleavage between Slavophiles and Westerners was sharp. The controversy shifted from the drawing room declamations of the intelligentsia to the arena—still largely clandestine because of the strangle hold of autocracy—of political and social propaganda. In this later stage it was still often impossible to identify even the leaders of the opposing camps as belonging strictly to one classification or the other. There were not only differences among Slavophiles and differences among Westerners, but some of the most magnetic orators and influential thinkers of the time embraced certain tenets of each system. Changing events in western Europe produced shifting reactions in the Russians who observed and often participated—vicariously if not actively—in these events. In the over-all picture of the second half of the nineteenth century, however, the growing unification of the Slavophiles is one of the pronounced features.

The novelist Turgenev was an avowed Westerner, his temperament, education, and experience all leading him in that direction. From the moment he first became aware of the submission of the serfs on the family estate to the tyranny of his mother, he began to search for something better than the backwardness and brutality of the Russian system. His prestige enabled him to serve as unofficial spokesman for Westernism. For nearly two decades during the time of his highest productivity, he held a position at the center of that movement.

From the perspective of the present it appears that most of the leaders of progressive thought and action in Russia a century ago were Westerners. This assumption is invalid, however. Many of the Slavophile leaders wielded an enormous influence even though the less literate quality of much of their writing caused them to have smaller opportunity for survival than the Westerners with more powerful pens. Actually, the passing decades marked a diminishment in the authority of the Westerners and a corresponding increase in the power of the Slavophiles. This shift is reflected in the emerging eminence of Dostoevsky, who played for the Slavophiles the part Turgenev played for the Westerners.

Slavophilism differed from Westernism in not consistently proposing or advocating a political program. Its ideology was predicated on faith in Russia—Russian character, Russian history, the religion of Russia, the future of Russia, and the Russian national spirit. The Slavophiles were more concerned with the people than with the state. They had no particular faith in monarchy but considered that authoritarianism did not necessarily interfere with the natural development of the people. They deplored what they regarded as the sinister contagion of the West, whose rationality and rebellion they believed antipathetic to the faith native to Russia. This faith, they assumed, was largely a product of Eastern Orthodox Christianity, which had played a dominant part in the development of Russian character and mores. The chasm they saw between Russia and western Europe was, therefore, more a matter of religious differences, though they were repelled also by the academic and the critical aspects of Western culture and by the tendency to political upheaval. The Catholic and Protestant faiths of Europe were alike repugnant to them, based, as both seemed to them to be, upon an appeal to reason. Only the Orthodox creed, they believed, could have been divinely inspired; only the Orthodox creed was adequate to minister to the spiritual needs of the people. The Slavophiles declared that the leadership of the West would make spiritual paupers of the Russians as it had impoverished the souls of other Europeans. The antidote was the intuitive approach to faith. This would restore and maintain the wholeness of spirit that they idealistically associated with earlier periods in Russian history. The Slavophiles lived either in the past or in the dim future; in contrast, the Westerners lived in the present or in the near future. The former did not blind themselves to the symptoms of disease in Russia. Yet they maintained that not only the disease but also the curative agents resided in the same body. Improvement must come from within.

The Slavophile advocacy of nationalism, increasingly characteristic of Russian thought in the latter part of the century, appears to have much in common with the nationalistic bigotry which in more than one instance has developed to obsessive proportions in the twentieth century. This unquestioning patriotism of devoted Slavophiles was based on absolute acceptance of both the Orthodox faith and the commune as the basic unit in the structure of Russian society, especially agrarian society. Acceptance of the concept of communal organization led logically to the rejection of Western (Roman) property laws, which justified private ownership. To the true Slavophiles, the land was sacred, the possession of all, particularly of the peasants who worked it. They saw in Western capitalist society the selfish aggrandizement of the *bourgeoisie*, whereas they believed civilization to be dependent upon the land and the peasantry. Associating the emergence of the *bourgeoisie* with the dominance of materialism, they were convinced that both were symptoms of egotism and loss of faith—the prelude to disunity. Already the Slavophiles were threatening the West with the decay tirelessly prophesied by the Marxist-Leninist-Stalinist ideologies as the inevitable end of Western capitalism. They had faith in the possibility of maintaining national unity only if Russia was allowed to follow the star of her own destiny, freed from what they saw as the greedy, paralyzing sterility of western Europe and America.

One of the striking features of Slavophile thought has already been anticipated in the statement of Gogol in which he prophesied the great future of his country. This is the concept of the messianic mission of Russia. Many Slavophiles believed that Russia's destiny included saving not only herself but also the rest of Europe. The early and more modest Slavophiles conceded that Russia might gain something from the West at the same time that she gave more than she received, but the later Slavophiles considered the West lost unless she grasped the saving hand of her Russian neighbor. This and other Slavophile views expressed with conviction by Dostoevsky will be illustrated in the next two chapters, which deal with several of the novels by that most persuasive of all Slavophiles—indeed, of all Russians.[2]

In contrast to their Slavophile compatriots, the Westerners believed that the principal mission of Russia was to imitate and to catch up with the West. The extremists among them erred in the opposite direction from the extremists among the Slavophiles. They held that Russia had nothing to be really proud of, nothing original or significant in her history or culture, nothing that could not be enriched by the enlightenment of the West. The Westerners did not necessarily reject the Orthodox creed, but they had no hope that it could improve their country, believing that improvement could come only as a result of political reform, rather than the moral, mystic reform recommended by the Slavophiles. Their concern with politics was accompanied by a concern with economic problems. This led them to take an active interest in the emancipation of the serfs as essential to the economic as well as the social health of Russia. Because of their desire for outer as opposed to inner reforms, the Westerners opposed the monarchy and everything which helped preserve the status quo. The result was that large numbers of them were radical, even anarchistic, in their pronouncements and endeavors. They soon became, therefore, anathema to the government. Many were forced to suffer for their conviction by banishment to Siberia, exile in western Europe, imprisonment, or death. Although the Nihilists cannot be said to have derived specifically from either camp and although they exploited the revolutionary tendencies at first more noticeable among the

[2] It should be noted that Dostoevsky did not consider himself a Slavophile. He said that he was neither a Slavophile nor a Westerner, but that his position was somewhere between the two.

Westerners, their justification of their attitudes and deeds often involved a fierce nationalistic absorption having more in common with Slavophilism.

It would be inaccurate, however, to imply that the Westerners had no interest in nationality. Their love of country was no less warm because of their ability to see defects; their criticism was stimulated by fervent desire for improvement. Often their spiritual kinship with Russia was a sacred thing. Even when they contrasted her backwardness and subservience with the enlightenment and freedom of certain countries of western Europe, Russia held first place in their affection. In many cases, the better they came to know Europe, the more they loved Russia; they realized that her defects were but intensifications of the defects of all Europe. This was particularly true after the collapse of the revolutionary attempts in western Europe in 1848. Thereafter, few of the Westerners ever regained the buoyancy of their former hope, doomed to a death as premature and inglorious as that of Rudin on the barricades of Paris.

With reference to Rudin, it is interesting to notice a statement a former schoolmate made about him. In an effort to analyze the failure of Rudin, his friend concluded: "Rudin's misfortune is that he does not understand Russia, and that, certainly, is a great misfortune. Russia can do without every one of us, but not one of us can do without her." That statement seems hardly characteristic of Turgenev until one reflects that, in spite of the novelist's long residence abroad, he never felt completely at home in other countries or able to draw inspiration from any scenes outside his native land. It is important to remember this to balance against the vehemence of some of Turgenev's statements paying tribute to the West. Several of these passages will serve to clarify the views of the Westerners, especially in the period between 1850 and 1870.

In *A House of Gentlefolk*, one of the characters is a young upstart proud of his modernity. In spite of Turgenev's scant liking for the young man, he permitted him to say what the author and his friends among the Westerners must have said on many occasions:

> "Russia," he said, "has lagged behind Europe, and must be driven up along side of it. We are told that ours is a young country. That is all nonsense. Besides, we have no inventive power. Khomakov [a poet and a leading Slavophile] himself admits that we have never invented so much as a mouse-trap. Consequently, we are obliged to imitate others, whether we like it or no.
>
> " 'We are ill,' says Lermontof, and I agree with him. But we are ill because we have only half become Europeans. With that which has wounded us we must be cured."

Again, in *Smoke*, the aforementioned Potugin gives vivid expression to the views current among the Westerners:

> "In reality, there is nothing done, and Russia for ten whole centuries has created nothing of its own, either in government, in law, in science, in art, or even in handicraft. . . .
>
> "The humblest German flute-player, modestly blowing his part in the humblest German orchestra, has twenty times as many ideas as all our untaught geniuses; only the flute-player keeps his ideas to himself . . . while our friend the rough diamond has only to strum some little waltz or song, and at once you see him with his hands in his trouser pocket and a sneer of contempt on his lips: I'm a genius, he says. . . .
>
> "Russian art," he began again. "Russian art, indeed! . . . Russian impudence and conceit, I know, and Russian feebleness, too, but Russian art . . . I've never come across. . . .
>
> "If it were decreed that some nation or other should disappear from the face of the earth, and with it everything that nation had invented . . . our dear mother, Holy Russia, could go and hide herself in the lower regions . . . for even the samovar, the woven bast shoes, the yoke-bridge, and the knout—these are our famous products—were not invented by us. . . . Our older inventions came to us from the East, our later ones we've borrowed, and half spoiled, from the West, while we still persist in talking about the independence of Russian art!"

Bitter as they are, these indictments are likely to be misleading. The fact remains that in the majority of cases this glorification of the West was dictated, not by love of the West, but by love of Russia and a sense of shame that in contrast with other countries the "holy mother" fell short of the best. No matter how acid the denunciation, it usually came from a critic who acknowledged no deeper loyalty than the love of his native land.

II.

A number of individuals had a marked influence on Russian literature without being major contributors to it. Three such men, in particular, left their imprint upon much that was written and thought in nineteenth century Russia. Many of their utterances throw light upon the Slavophile-Western schools of thought and upon the attitudes and events which were to determine the shape of the future.

The first of these was Vissarion Belinsky (1811–48), sometimes called the father of the Russian intelligentsia and of Russian realism. He was not, like Turgenev, Herzen, and many other intellectuals, a privileged son of an aristocratic family; but he joined forces with these young liberals when he went to the University of Moscow. During this period he became convinced of the significance of Western culture. One of the noteworthy events of his university experience was the writing of a drama in protest against serfdom. It made the authorities suspect him, caused him to be threatened with banishment to Siberia, and was instrumental in his being dropped from the university.

In spite of insecurity, threats, and extreme poverty, however, Belinsky was not then or later deterred from his efforts or shaken in his convictions. By the age of thirty he was solidly established in his position as Russia's foremost literary critic. He developed remarkable authority, both because he recognized and encouraged the outstanding writers of his time (Pushkin, Lermontov, Gogol, Goncharov, and Dostoevsky were among those whose place in literature he helped make secure) and also because under the guise of literary criticism he was able to write what probably would not have passed the censor in any other form. Indeed, he was only secondarily a critic of letters; he was primarily a critic of life—of Russia and the Russians. But even though his first allegiance was to mankind, his efforts on behalf of literature —the soundness and vigor of his critical judgments and the enthusiasm of his sponsorship of the great writers—were of inestimable value to the "golden age" of Russian letters.

Along with other young radicals, Belinsky found in Hegel "the algebra of revolution." His liberalism was also colored by his sympathies with French socialism. But his liberalism, perhaps more fittingly called "revolutionary ardor," always bore the stamp of his own individuality. There was nothing static about his intellectual patterns, and he discarded all philosophical concepts (in the end, even Hegelianism) that might have served as boundaries to his passion for inquiry and justice. He proclaimed love for mankind and hatred of all forms of oppression with vociferous resolution. He was also unremitting in his attacks upon mysticism and superstition ("superstition" usually meant to him the religion of contemporary Russia) as well as upon the inertia of head and heart of the Russians. However, he also considered skepticism an abomination and could not condone negative acquiescence. He was above all a man who hated falsehood and hollow gesture and who was roused to righteous wrath by the never ending spectacle of human misery. Yet his rejection of the existing society was no more persistent and vehement than his championship of the new society which ought to be. His anger for the sake of others was balanced by warm loyalties and warm loves. He loved literature, he loved knowledge, and he loved freedom; but most of all he loved humanity in general and his country in particular. Almost everything he wrote and did was dictated by longing for the improvement of that country and refusal to stop short of trying to transform desire into reality. Belinsky was, in effect, the antithesis of Rudin and the other Hamlets of Russia.

In the closing years of his life the "Raging Vissarion" was recognized by the authorities as the pole star of the progressive (or radical, depending upon point of view) movement. Even to mention his name publicly finally became dangerous. Only his untimely death from tuberculosis at the age of thirty-seven and the fact that he had left Russia a year earlier in a vain effort to retard the course of the disease saved him from a cell in the Peter and Paul Fortress, where he would have added his name to the list of martyrs to the cause of Russian monarchy.

It is a strange irony that the pronouncement for which Belinsky is best known was written to censure the man whom only a few years earlier he had embraced as a savior of Russia. Gogol had been for some time in a state of religious mysticism amounting to aberration when in 1847 he published the book called *Selected Passages from Correspondence with Friends.* In this book he condoned, and at times championed, the institutions he had indignantly condemned in the works written at the height of his powers. Obviously the product of one who had become only a tragic reminder of his former self, the book had virtually no significance except in relation to the famous letter it elicited from Belinsky. The critic was horrified by what seemed the incredible defection of the author of *Dead Souls.* He reviewed the book in the only way he could, making no effort to excuse the apostasy of the writer. Thereupon Gogol, interpreting the review as a personal attack, wrote accusingly to Belinsky. Upon receipt of this letter, Belinsky composed his memorable reply, the "Letter to Gogol," which became the testament of the Russian intellectuals, especially of the Westerners.

Although the protests of Belinsky were keyed to the abuses of the reign of Nicholas I, they continued appropriate under the reduced absolutism of Alexander II, and the influence of Belinsky flamed like a burning brand through several decades. The letter is a remarkable affirmation by a man of understanding and integrity who believed in the future as much as he deplored the status quo:

. . . you have not observed [wrote Belinsky to Gogol] that Russia sees its salvation not in mysticism, not in asceticism, not in pietism, but in the successes of civilization, of enlightenment, of humanity. It is not preachments that Russia needs (she has heard them aplenty!) nor prayers (she has said them over and over . . .), but an awakening among her common folk of a sense of human dignity (for so many ages lost amid the mire and manure) and rights and laws, conforming not with the teaching of the Church but with common sense and justice, and as strict fulfillment of them as is possible. But instead of that Russia presents the horrible spectacle of a land where men traffic in men, not having therefor even that justification which the American plantation owners craftily avail themselves of, affirming that a Negro is not a man . . . where there are not only no guarantees whatsoever for one's individuality, honor, property, but where there is even no order maintained by police, instead of which there are only enormous corporations of various administrative thieves and robbers! . . .

You . . . do not understand the Russian public very well. Its character is determined by the condition of Russian society, in which fresh forces are seething and straining to burst forth but, crushed by severe oppression, finding no escape, induce only despondence, ennui, apathy. Only in literature alone, despite the Tatar censorship, is there still life and a forward movement. That is why the title of writer is held in such esteem among us. . . . And that is why among us any so-called liberal tendency is especially rewarded by universal attention, even if a talent seem poor, and that is why the popularity of great talents who give themselves up sincerely or insincerely to the service of Orthodoxy, autocracy, and nationalism declines so quickly. . . . The idea of becoming some sort of abstract paragon, of rising superior to all men through resignation, can only be the fruit either of pride or of feeblemindedness, and in both instances inevitably leads to hypocrisy, sanctimoniousness, Celestial quietism. . . .

. . . you ought now, with sincere resignation, repudiate your last book and to expiate the heavy sin of having brought it into the light of day.[3]

[3] From the translation by Bernard Guilbert Guerney.

This "Letter" would never, of course, have been sanctioned by the censor, and it was unthinkable that even such a liberal journal as the *Contemporary*, with which Belinsky's name was associated, should publish it. But passed from hand to hand, the subject of rapturous approval by hundreds, if not thousands, it unified, encouraged, and gave direction to Russian liberalism.

The views of Belinsky are important because of their relation to later developments in Russian thought. The problem he faced is, in essence, that with which Dostoevsky wrestled in *The Brothers Karamazov*. Ivan Karamazov was the spokesman for the difficulty of reconciling the idea of God (a good God) with the evil and suffering in the world. Likewise, Belinsky—a rebel against the misery and unfulfillment of mankind, and filled with desire for the good—rejected the concept of God, which seemed to him bound up with the mysticism, superstition, and inertia the church had nourished in "the people." A few clergymen representing the church, he wrote in the "Letter," were distinguished for "a chill ascetic consciousness. . . . But the majority of our clergy has always been distinguished solely for potbellies, scholastic pedantry, and savage ignorance." Belinsky did not stop with the Karamazov negation, however. He was repelled by any profession of idealism which did not seek to actualize the profession by making it reality. Paradoxically, he was so intent on improving the lot of mankind that he was willing to see violence used in order to achieve that end. The atheism Belinsky preached grew out of intense righteous indignation. The welfare of humanity was his religion, and he was a practicing zealot. His negation was a necessary weapon in the crusade to provide a good earth for all men.

In *The Origin of Russian Communism*, Nicholas Berdyaev pointed out a connection between the thought of Belinsky and that of Lenin. According to Berdyaev, Belinsky "more than any other, must be regarded as an intellectual ancestor of Russian communism." In him "may be studied the inward motives giving birth to the general outlook on life of the Russian revolutionary intelligentsia, which remained dominant for a long while and finally produced Russian communism, though in a different historical setting."[4] Whether or not this view exaggerates the influence of the critic, it is certain that he was an evangel of revolution, a warrior against the monarchy and the status quo and even against God. His humility and selflessness, however, made him a different kind of man from the unprincipled Nihilists who followed in his steps. Belinsky's anger was a form of love; his rebellion blossomed from benevolence.

III.

Another imposing figure who influenced practically everything written in Russia during the late 1840's, 1850's, and early 1860's was Alexander Herzen (1812–70). The illegitimate son of a wealthy aristocrat, Herzen was born the year Napoleon took Russia and lost it. Perhaps this fact accounts for the vibrant patriotism of his early years, which was intensified by the Decembrist uprisings. Stirred by the execution of the five Decembrist leaders, the young Herzen vowed to avenge their death if it were necessary to devote his entire life to the cause. In his *Memoirs* he recalls that, when they were boys in their early teens, he and his friend Nicholas Ogarev, looking down on Moscow from the hills outside the city,[5] swore lifelong fidelity to each other and to the cause of Russian freedom. And they kept their vow.

Like Turgenev, Herzen early learned the sordid truth about serfdom from observation of the way the peasants were treated on his father's estate. He soon began an effort to help the oppressed, which continued until the end of his life, and he developed an abiding antagonism against the pleasure-loving, complacent aristocracy and all who represented privilege—from priests to princes. At the University of Moscow he became associated with other young intellectuals and was introduced to the

[4] Page 44.
[5] This site is now the main campus of the University of Moscow.

German philosophers and French socialists. Like the others, he was fascinated by Hegelian philosophy, but he was not a slavish follower, and his mind was distinguished by a capacity for independent inquiry and conviction. Among his associates were Belinsky, Bakunin, and a young man named Stankevich, probably the most magnetic personality among the Russian intelligentsia of this period.

After he began to express his views in print, Herzen had a personal taste of the effects of despotism when he was twice banished to the provinces for short periods, for slight political "indiscretions." These violations of his freedom, symptomatic of the pall of tyranny which smothered the whole country, had an influence upon his thinking out of proportion to the degree of repression to which he was forced to submit. Although he was one of the most energetic and brilliant contributors to the intellectual scene in a decade marked by unusual brilliance, the forties, he felt increasingly uneasy and confined. Therefore, when it was possible for him to leave Russia in 1847 after he inherited a fortune on the death of his father and after long maneuvering with the authorities, he seized the opportunity to escape. When he went to live in western Europe, which beckoned like a veritable utopia, he did not know that he would never be able to return a free man to his native land.

For several years Herzen moved from country to country in search of the sun of freedom, which had an elusive way of disappearing behind clouds. He observed the Italian and French revolutions of 1848 and discovered with chagrin that Rudin's were not the only dreams that expired ignominiously. The collapse of these revolutionary endeavors was a blow from which Herzen and other political idealists never fully recovered. Meanwhile, after a tangled domestic tragedy he was left like one dispossessed, needing an outlet for his yearning to assist in the betterment of society. Indeed, he was able to recover from his personal despair only because of his power to lose himself in concern for humanity. In 1852, having received *in absentia* the sentence of permanent exile from his homeland, he settled in London. From this vantage point, an exile in a land he admired but could never cherish, Herzen made an impression upon Russian thought and action impossible to estimate except in a general way.

In London, Herzen was able to do what he could not have done in his own country. He established a free Russian press. Completely unaffected by the exigencies of czarist censorship, he gave to the Russian pen and spirit liberty such as it had never known before. Assisted by his friend Ogarev, he first published a review called *Polar Star*, which carried on its covers pictures of the Decembrist leaders whose execution had given substance to the youthful Herzen's hatred of autocracy. After a short time the two friends supplemented this journal with a publication, *The Bell* (*Kolokol*), intended to appeal to a more general public. When the latter became immediately popular and effective in the dissemination of news and propaganda, they concentrated their efforts upon it. By means of *The Bell,* Herzen became from a distance the director of the conscience of Russia, a feat with few if any parallels in history. Even his detractors and the Slavophiles who stood at a distance from him in ideology acknowledged the unprecedented scope of his influence.

The Bell continued for nearly ten years, during the first eight of which it maintained its unchallenged position in the forefront of Russian thought. Its circulation often went as high as five thousand copies, even though copies could only be taken into Russia by returning travelers and had to be passed about without benefit of the postal system. The journal became the unofficial organ of the forward-looking intelligentsia. Alexander II was reported to be a regular reader. This exercise must have had an exhilarating effect on a monarch who, despite liberal tendencies, can hardly be described as having been fascinated by the contemplation of freedom.

In 1864, at the urging of his friends Ogarev and Bakunin, Herzen permitted *The Bell* to declare its sympathy with Poland on the occasion of a Polish insurrection. This stand caused a decline in the prestige of the journal from which it was unable to recover. It was finally forced out of publication several years before the death of the editor in Paris in 1870. But it had already served its major purpose.

During the forties, while he was still in Moscow, Herzen was one of the leaders of the Westerners, though he had an emotional attachment to Slavism which was characteristically Russian. He was convinced that western European science and political structures offered the only hope for the solution of Russia's problems. His dreams of a better world were rooted in the socialist political theories and the philosophy of western Europe. After the collapse of the abortive revolutionary efforts of 1848, however, he began to fear that western Europe could not consummate a revolution because of that very culture which caused him to love the West. Lacking that culture, he thought, Russia might by reason of her backwardness be able to achieve what had become impossible to a people nourished on a more sophisticated pattern of thought.

This clinging to a fundamental faith in the people and the culture of his own country helps to explain Herzen's conviction that the maintenance of the peasant commune was essential to the best interests of the people and to the agricultural economy of Russia. He was certain that the commune (*mir*) represented what was soundest and most stable in the social and economic framework of Russia. The *mir* symbolized for him a form of freedom which the industrialization of western Europe was rapidly making impossible. In his thinking the communal plan of agrarian Russia stood apart from the issues which divided theorists into Western and Slavophile camps. It was as basic to his hopes for the future of Russia as the Orthodox church was to Dostoevsky's. Herzen shared with Dostoevsky the view that the security of Russia was based on the peasantry.

It is noteworthy that Herzen did not, like most of his fellow revolutionaries, advocate the use of force. Although he was not, like some Slavophiles, a sentimental advocate of "the people" per se, for he knew how backward and lethargic they were, he had few reservations about the potential of man. Consequently, he thought that democracy could be achieved by the growth of reasonableness on the part of men of good will. In his editorials in *The Bell*, he often held out the hope that Alexander II might be such a man. He implied that the failures of the government were not due to bad intentions on the part of the monarch but to the malevolence, ineptitude, and self-seeking of the ministers and to the evil inherent in the system. He never detached himself wholly from an idealized view of revolution, yet in his mature years he approached a middle ground position; consequently he was increasingly criticized on the one side by those who believed that reform could not be pushed and on the other by those who felt that issues should, if necessary, be forced to the point of explosion.

In a general sense Herzen became a co-worker with Proudhon, Garibaldi, Mazzini, and other well-known revolutionary figures. The part he played in shaping the affairs of his country was similar to their roles in their respective lands, in spite of the fact that Herzen never organized or participated in an insurrection or took any active part in the radical movements within Russia. As he was a philosopher without a system, so also was he a rebel without a barricade. Prevented from returning in person, he never really left his native country in spirit. His pen was one of the many which have proved mightier than the sword.

Herzen did not profess atheism in the sense in which Belinsky was an atheist, but he found his true religion in action to improve the welfare of humanity. This attitude is expressed in the dedication to his son of his famous treatise, *From the Other Shore*. "The man of today," he wrote, " . . . does no more than build the bridge which will be crossed by an unknown in the unknown future. . . . Do not stay on the old shore. . . . It is better to perish than to remain safe in the madhouse of reaction. The religion of the coming social reconstruction is the only religion I bequeath you." The cant and the piety which sometimes make religion a cruel and destructive weapon were abhorrent to Herzen. He thought that reliance on God often provides an excuse for complacency and sloth. There was no place in his program for waiting for God's good time. Herzen was, in fact, unresponsive to the concept of a God-centered universe. He responded to the needs and the irresistible potentials of man. Herzen's religion was deeper than ceremony and profession. It was the religion of benevolence and reverence for life. It was, likewise, the religion of responsibility—the responsibility of the strong for the weak, of the haves for the have-nots, and of the privileged for the oppressed.

Herzen has never been accorded the place he rightfully deserves in Russian literature, because, although he wrote some good fiction, he has been remembered almost exclusively for his journalistic and polemical writings. Certainly some of the best of the rich lode of revolutionary writing in the nineteenth century is to be found among his papers. But he was far more than a polemicist. That he was a scholar, an informal philosopher, and a practitioner of fine style is abundantly demonstrated by his letters and *Memoirs*, particularly the lengthy *My Past and Thoughts*. The latter is at once a full autobiography of Herzen (except for his last years) and a record of the intellectual currents and political issues of several decades. The following excerpts from the *Memoirs* suggest the quality of Herzen's thinking and will perhaps clarify his position. In the second volume, certain statements are of special interest in revealing the way the Westerners felt about their opponents, the Slavophiles:

> "The way out is with us," said the Slavophiles, "the way out lies . . . in going back to the people from whom we have been cut off by foreign education and foreign government; let us return to the old ways!" But history does not turn back. . . .
>
> Moreover, we have nothing to which to go back. The political life of Russia before Peter the Great was grotesque, poor, savage, yet it was to this that the Slavophiles wanted to return. . . .
>
> The mistake of the Slavophiles lies in their imagining that Rus-

sia once had an individual culture. . . . Russia never had this culture, never could have had it. . . .

Only the mighty thought of the West to which all its long history had led up is able to fertilize the seeds slumbering in the patriarchal mode of life of the Slavs. The workmen's guild and the village commune, the sharing of profits and the division of fields, the *mir* meeting and the union of villages into self-governing *volosts*, are all the cornerstones on which the temple of our future, freely communal existence will be built. But these corner stones are only stones . . . and without the thought of the West our future cathedral will not rise above its foundation. . . .

The receptive character of the Slavs, their femininity, their lack of initiative, and their great capacity for assimilation and adaptation, make them pre-eminently a people that stands in need of the other peoples. . . .

Both they [the Slavophiles] and we had been from earliest years possessed by one unaccountable, physiological, passionate feeling . . . a feeling of boundless, absorbing love for the Russian people, Russian manner of life, Russian mode of thought. . . . We looked in two different directions while one heart throbbed within us.

The following passage from Volume III shows some of the motivations of Herzen and many others whose purposes were similar to his:

Our classic ignorance of the western European will be productive of a good deal of harm; race hatred and bloody collisions will develop from it later on. . . .

. . . Young men, horror-stricken by the infamies of the life about them, surrounded by gloom and oppressive misery, gave up all and went in search of a way out. They sacrificed everything that others strive after . . . for the sake of their convictions, and they remained true to them.

Certain sections of Volume VI are of interest for what they say about Nihilism:

What has our generation bequeathed to the coming one? Nihilism?

> Somewhere about 1840 our life began to force its way out more vigorously. . . . Externally everything was deathlike under the ice of Nicholas' government, but something was stirring in the mind and the conscience. . . .
>
> The machine wound up by Nicholas had begun to give way. . . .
>
> Two batteries were quickly moved forward. Journalism became propaganda. . . . University lecture rooms were transformed into pulpits. . . .
>
> And the propaganda went on gathering strength . . . always unchanged; tears and laughter and books and speech and Hegel and history—all roused men to the consciousness of their position, to a feeling of horror for serfdom and for their own lack of rights, everything pointed them on to science and culture, to the purging of thought from all the litter of tradition, to the freeing of conscience and reason. That period saw the first dawn of Nihilism—that complete freedom from all established conceptions, from all the inherited obstructions and barriers. . . .
>
> Nihilism does not transform something into nothing, but shows that nothing which has been taken for something is an optical illusion.

As the years went by without bringing any appreciable fulfillment of his hopes, Herzen's anticipation and buoyancy were gradually replaced by disappointment. His last years were lonely, not only because of his enforced exile and because a succession of tragedies had cut his personal life to shreds, but even more because of the gap between the dream and the realization. Also, the younger exponents of reform and revolution began to look upon him as an anachronism. Lacking their intensity and precipitousness, he earned their indifference, if not their scorn. He had been dedicated to the principle of change, but he had never destroyed idols for the sake of destruction. The men who passed him in the race were idol breakers by choice. The time had come for an end to moderation. The Chernyshevskys, the Dobrolyubovs, and the Pisarevs[6] dominated the sixties and sev-

[6] Nikolai Chernyshevsky (1828–89) and Nikolai Dobrolyubov (1836–61) were journalists, critics, and political theorists of exceptional vigor and influence. Dmitri Pisarev (1830–68) was the most vocal spokesman for the Nihilists.

enties as Belinsky and Herzen had dominated the forties and fifties. These new leaders of the revolutionary spirit were to end by being among the "possessed"—possessed not by indignation and love, as Belinsky and Herzen had been, but by violence and hate.

IV.

Belinsky and Herzen were alike in that, though neither was primarily a creative artist, both were associated with the literature of their time and affected it persuasively. Both were powerful protagonists, one as critic, the other as editor. Each left an extensive body of writing valuable in tracing the evolution of modern Russia. The same cannot be said of Michael Bakunin, whose influence was almost entirely personal, generated by the impact of his flamboyant personality and the multiplicity of his activities. A man cast in a large mold physically, Bakunin figuratively made his weight felt everywhere in Europe. Compared to him and his cyclonic disturbances, the "Raging Vissarion" (Belinsky) and the rational, methodical Herzen were March winds. What Turgenev's Bazarov was in literature, Bakunin was in the flesh—a preparation for and a partial model for the revolutionaries who were to follow. Although he devoted his life to anarchical gestures and made a profession of anarchy, he was never convincing. His revolutionary activities were not only unflagging, they were also fantastic. He had too much enthusiasm and too little balance. Nevertheless, to attempt to trace the course of events in nineteenth-century Russia without acknowledging the influence of Bakunin is unthinkable.

The biography of Bakunin is full of incident, but it is enough here to suggest the outlines. Born in 1814 at Premukhino, a beautiful, pastoral region to which he retained a sentimental attachment, Bakunin was reared in a family of cultured tastes and habits. There was nothing about the father to explain his fiery rebel of a son. Yet in his young manhood Bakunin's father had shown some liberal tendencies, and his mother was related to one of the executed Decembrists. Michael was trained in an artillery school for a military career, to which he gave only desultory attention. After attaining the rank of officer and serving for a short time at a second-rate assignment, the young man discontinued a relationship he found distasteful. Going on to Moscow, he spent several years becoming acquainted with the works of German philosophers, and for a time he followed the familiar pattern of almost total immersion in the Hegelian concepts. He soon became associated with Stankevich, Belinsky, Herzen, and others of the "Moscow circle."

Later, in Berlin, Bakunin broadened the range of his philosophical, political, and social studies. Soon he began to write passionate declamations of belief, but at this early period, as later, his writing was characterized more by iconoclastic bombast than by intellectual consistency. One frequently quoted sentence from an early essay supplies the key to his whole career. "The passion for destruction," he wrote, "is at the same time a creative passion." His contacts with radical societies and the fervor of his writings brought a warning signal from Russia, and he was ordered to return. This command he ignored. After tasting the freedom of western Europe, he knew that the tyranny of Russia would be intolerable. More than that, he wanted to make a revolution, and western Europe appeared a more auspicious setting than Russia.

In Paris, Bakunin became associated with the French socialist Proudhon and got to know a group of Polish revolutionaries who paved the way for many of his later activities. There, too, he met Marx; but their relationship was conspicuously lacking in friendliness, then and later. Still, he admired Marx, not so much because he was impressed by Marxist theories as because Marx had a talent for success. Despite having been ordered to leave Paris after an inflammatory speech in behalf of the Polish efforts for liberation, Bakunin came back for the uprising of 1848, in which he played an exuberant but inconclusive part. After the collapse of this attempt he went on to Prague and then to Dresden to participate in the insurrectionary movements in both places. Following the debacle in Dresden he was arrested and sentenced to death, the sentence being subsequently changed to life imprisonment. He had been incarcerated for a number of months when he was passed on to Austria to go through the same procedure again. Finally, he was returned to Russia, the fate he dreaded above all others.

By this time Bakunin's activities had been extensive and dramatic enough for several countries to be glad when he was safely stowed away in the fortress of St. Peter and St. Paul. He spent three years there in circumstances so miserable that a less vigorous man would have been unable to survive. Then he was transferred to another prison where the unwholesome conditions were slightly mitigated by the efforts of his family. When he had been behind bars for eight years, most of the time chained in solitary confinement and with such bad diet that he had developed scurvy and lost all his teeth, he was permitted to exchange prison walls for exile in Siberia. Through a series of fortuitous circumstances—one being the fact that the governor-general of eastern Siberia was a distant relative of his, the others the result of his own ingenuity—he was finally able to carry through daring plans for escape. He went to Japan, across the Pacific to San Francisco, by way of Panama to New York, and thence across the Atlantic to London, where his friends Herzen and Ogarev were at the height of their success with *The Bell.*

In the first conversation with his friends after this reunion, Bakunin's personality and purposes were clearly revealed. Having inquired about political events, he was assured that there were no disturbances except for demonstrations in Poland. He was incredulous and disappointed when told that Italy, Austria, and Turkey were all quiet. "Then what are we to do?" he asked. "Must we go to Persia or India to stir things up? It's enough to drive one mad; I cannot sit and do nothing."[7]

Nor did he. Among other things he attempted to give aid to

[7] Edward H. Carr, *The Romantic Exiles*, 220.

certain Polish nationalists in a series of melodramatic maneuvers. He formed various secret societies of his own, usually involving elaborate organizations (with him at the center), codes, and programs. He rampaged about western Europe like a hungry tiger. After the establishment of the International made impossible his unchallenged domination of the revolutionary scene, he became a disgruntled member of that association. But he and Marx were truculent rivals, and he was finally ousted from the Marxist organization after four years of stormy participation. He was always inciting, always plotting. Bakunin loved conspiracy as some men love women.

Not until shortly before his death at Berne in 1876 did he relax somewhat from his machinations, and then only because the constantly changing ranks of his followers had dwindled to nothing. Irrepressible to the end, he died almost forgotten, a disappointed anarchist who had hatched a thousand plots without ever experiencing what would have been to him the joy of witnessing a revolution on a grand scale. His complete impracticality, his substitution of excitement for sustained effort, and his melodramatic plans impossible of fulfillment—these were some of the factors which prevented this would-be father of revolutions from realizing his dream of a world turned topsy-turvy.

Despite the fact that the career of Bakunin resembles a histrionic extravaganza, it is important to acknowledge his earnestness and some measure of integrity in his intentions. In any attempt to piece together impressions of Bakunin's nature and conduct, one is always confronted with the dualism familiar to all who are acquainted with the characters of Dostoevsky. There can be no doubt that he had something akin to nobility in his character and that he had extraordinary mental gifts, amazing energy, and an unquenchable ardor for reform—or at least revolution. But he was also disorganized, egocentric, indifferent to the rights and feelings of others, and careless about responsibilities entrusted to him. He used people without regard for consequences. He was highhanded and mercurial, generous with other people's money and with his own time and effort, and wholly indifferent to his comfort or security. In fact, security was to him the root of all evil. He was, paradoxically, unstable and persistent, childlike and complicated, warm in his attachments and yet incapable of love, irreverent and mystical. He created lies but told the truth. He was handsome and ugly, both of body and of spirit. His only consistency was his inconsistency, his only religion the worship of stormy change. He seems to have been a man whose nature was compounded of elements which would not harmonize, with a largeness and a smallness of soul always at odds.

Some of his friends who suffered most from his flamboyance, his arrogance, and his dominance still testified to his sincerity. Herzen, for example, continued to respect him, although Bakunin's tempestuous espousal of the Polish cause expressed in *The Bell* cost Herzen the popularity of his journal. In the fifth volume of the *Memoirs*, Herzen wrote:

> To a passion for propaganda, for agitation, for demagogy, to incessant activity in founding, organizing plots and conspiracies, and establishing relations, to a belief in their immense significance, Bakunin added a readiness to be the first to carry out his ideas, a readiness to risk his life, and reckless daring in facing all the consequences. . . .
>
> Bakunin, not too much given to weighing every circumstance, looked only toward the ultimate goal, and took the second month of pregnancy for the ninth. He carried us away not by arguments but by his hopes.

What were his hopes? What was the platform of the party of which he was leader and the only permanent member? First, although his original associates among the young radicals were almost all Westerners and he belonged originally in that camp, he moved sharply in the direction of Slavophilism, though without rejecting certain Western ideologies. His Slavophile sympathies soon became Pan-Slavic sympathy; he visualized a union of all Slavic peoples, undisturbed by foreign influence or national boundaries. He was suspicious of nationalism, but he was one more in the procession of nineteenth-century Russians who envisioned the messianic destiny of the Slavic people. Moreover, like many of the liberals schooled in German idealism, he distrusted the *bourgeoisie* (what Herzen contemptuously called "the interests of the countinghouse and bourgeois prosperity"). Like the liberals, too, he believed in the peasants, especially the Russian peasants. It was his conviction that real revolution—that is, the overthrow of all established authority—could be achieved only by the common people.

Bakunin believed that the state—the centralized government—should give way to a society based on the goodness of the people—on the justice and liberty he thought they desired to live by. He believed in human nature unperverted by the sordid institutions of society and government. The "noble savage" who had such an appeal for many of the romantic European intellectuals, particularly of the eighteenth century, was an object for whom Bakunin felt glowing, if vague, affection. The state appeared to him to be the strait jacket of society. He rejected all forms of organized government. Not only monarchical but also constitutional forms of government were anathema to him. He considered all legal machinery and laws suffocating and archaic. Since the church and organized religion seemed to him one of the most pernicious influences affecting mankind, he wanted to discard it along with other institutions. The existence of God means that man is a slave, he said; therefore, even the idea of God is cruel and unjust. He saw God and man not as partners, but as antipodal. He believed passionately in what he called "freedom" for all people, but freedom achieved by violence. He favored the use of the methods of dictatorship to enforce liberty.

It is obvious that Bakunin mistook anarchy for liberty. He was certainly the apostle of change, but he had no concept of what might be accomplished by revolution. That is to say, he did not so much seek certain ends as relish the process of destroying the status quo. If he had been permitted to enter heaven, he would have proceeded immediately to demand and plot a total renovation. He had as much horror of peace and quiet as Oblomov had need of them. Perhaps Bakunin was the inevitable antithesis of Oblomov.

Was Bakunin a true humanitarian? The answer must be both yes and no. More exactly, he was a warrior without a country and without a definitive cause. He was driven by a frenzy half-bestial and half-divine. Though he never saw any of his grandiose plans fulfilled, he persisted to the end in his self-appointed mission. And no matter how bizarre the man and his methods, his influence spread out of all proportion to the logic or sanity of his designs. Berdyaev saw him as one of the primary architects in the structure of communism. "He believed that the world-wide conflagration would be kindled by the Russian people and Slavdom," wrote Berdyaev. "And in this Russian revolutionary messianism he is a forerunner of communism. . . . He wants to destroy the old world; he believes that on the ruins of the old world . . . the new world will spontaneously arise. . . . Communism has made great use of his anarchism and spirit of rebellion."

V.

In 1869 in Geneva, where he was engaged in the usual process of agitation, Bakunin came into contact with a young Russian, Sergei Nechaev (1847–82), in whom the old master of conspiracy met for the first time not only his equal but his superior at machination. This unscrupulous young rascal, almost a genius at intrigue, worked his way into the good graces of Bakunin—not a difficult task considering the old man's guilelessness and his desire for disciples. Soon Bakunin was indulgently calling the young man "Boy" and treating him with paternal familiarity. The two became fellow conspirators, each stimulating the other in the playing of revolutionary games. Bakunin proceeded to set up the plans for yet another fabulous organization—this one, apparently, to be named the "World Revolutionary Alliance"—

and to commission Nechaev his representative to develop a Russian section of the alliance. Both men busied themselves for a time with writing pamphlets (one called *Catechism of a Revolutionary*) to furnish literature for the organization. Then they cast their eyes about for funds. Finally they were successful in wheedling out of Nicholas Ogarev his half of a large sum entrusted to him and Herzen for quite different purposes. Bakunin was, as usual, blindly in earnest. His naïveté made him a novice compared to the cunning Nechaev. With pockets full, Nechaev left Switzerland to return to Russia, there to create his alliance or do whatever else the supply of money at his disposal suggested to his inventive mind. But Bakunin never doubted that the undertaking would be blessed and would produce blessings.

Although specific details are not known, it appears that Nechaev did build up an organization called, among other things, The Society of the Axe. Its members were grouped in "cells" of five, all authority vested in Nechaev himself, the whole design heavily coated with mystery. He passed himself off as the mastermind of the organization, especially commissioned to perpetrate revolution. He enjoined upon his followers the necessity for absolute obedience and absolute secrecy. The latter injunction proved so successful that it is impossible to ascertain how far the organization developed, how many cells there were, or whether any serious activities were carried out. But one thing is certain: before long Nechaev decided to establish his authority once and for all. Declaring that one of the members of the group was "unfaithful," Nechaev decreed that he must die—presumably as an awful example of what would happen to anyone who failed to devote himself slavishly to the society and, more particularly, to its leader. On November 25, 1869, the body of the young student Ivanov was found in a pond near the Moscow Agricultural Academy, where he had been studying. He was the victim of Nechaev's schemes and his death the result of the inflammatory partnership between Bakunin and his dear "Boy."

Having conspired with his probably reluctant disciples to

carry out this crime, Nechaev blithely made his way back to western Europe, leaving his followers to be tried and punished in large numbers. It seems incredible that a blatant anarchist should have been able to escape unscathed from Russia, but such was the case.[8] Nechaev did not, however, return to Bakunin. He had by this time no use for the old man who could offer his own fertile villainy no further stimulation. It is none the less noteworthy that the personality of Bakunin was not absent from the trial following the death of Ivanov. During the investigation the *Catechism of a Revolutionary* came to light in the possession of one of the young men being tried. Thus the startled lawyers and judges were able to read the testament of anarchy. The revolutionist, according to this document, "is wholly absorbed in one exclusive interest, one thought, one passion: revolution. . . . Whatever promotes the triumph of the revolution is moral, whatever hinders it is immoral, is criminal. . . . Our business is passionate, complete, ubiquitous, ruthless destruction."

In fairness to Bakunin, it is necessary to admit that the *Catechism* was without doubt less his work than Nechaev's. There were limits beyond which Bakunin did not go, but limits meant nothing to Nechaev. Still, in altogether too many respects the behavior of Nechaev did demonstrate the philosophy of Bakunin in action. It was more Nechaev than Bakunin, however—Nechaev's concepts, his attitude, his murder of Ivanov—who furnished the seeds for Dostoevsky's embattled denunciation of Nihilism in *The Possessed*. Nechaev was the monster begotten from the best intentions of the liberals who started with the desire to make Russia a country where people might live in freedom. Ironically, the tyranny they were resolved to destroy was succeeded too often by an even more insidious tyranny. For Nechaev was both begotten and begetter. His descendants made destruction a profession and an art.

[8] Nechaev's immunity proved to be only temporary. Somewhat later he was turned over to Russia by the Swiss authorities. When he died in the fortress of St. Peter and St. Paul in 1882, he had served ten of his twenty-year sentence.

VI.

When Alexander II (1818–81) came to the throne in 1855 at the death of Nicholas I, he was well aware that his father's autocratic system had engendered hatred against the monarchy and produced little good to balance its evils. The tension and agitation within the country were bad enough even before the Crimean War. But when that conflict ended in the Treaty of Paris (1856), which took from Russia nearly all her hard-won gains in the Near East and severely damaged her prestige as a European power, it was necessary immediately to restore confidence in the monarchy to compensate for past errors in both internal and foreign policy. Alexander satisfied both these requirements by a reform program in dramatic contrast to his father's despotism.

At the beginning of his reign, Alexander acted with vigor and dispatch. On the day of his coronation he granted amnesty to surviving Decembrists in a manifesto containing a number of reassuring provisions. He introduced an era of reasonableness and tolerance such as Russia had not known before. One of his most noteworthy accomplishments was the sponsorship of judicial reforms based on those inaugurated earlier by Michael Speransky. Moreover, Alexander introduced order into the system of military service and reduced the period of compulsory service. However, the achievement which brought him the titles of "Liberator" and "Great Reformer" was the abolition of serfdom. This was a momentous event in the history of Russia.

When Alexander II became the Czar, 67 per cent of Russia's seventy million inhabitants were still serfs. The circumstances of some, especially the state serfs, had been improved by earlier enactment and by the process of redemption through state funds. To free them required little more than legal action which entailed relatively few complications. The difficulties came in handling the problem of the privately owned serfs, who constituted nearly one-third of the population. It was a tribute to

Alexander's diplomacy that in spite of resistance from a large section of the gentry and some highly conservative officials he was able to obtain widespread approval and support for the measure. After a lengthy period of planning and deliberation, the emancipation manifesto was issued on March 3, 1861, the sixth anniversary of Alexander's coming to power. On this day the Czar accomplished without bloodshed what caused in America a civil war and disunity not yet entirely healed.

Unfortunately, legal emancipation did not solve all the problems of the serfs. The transition between dependence and independence was long, painful, and uncertain, no matter what the circumstances. Agricultural peasants could continue to live on the land, but must either pay for its use or buy it. Since few of them had any capital, they became the victims of alarming exploitation and were often badly treated by landlords. Gradually, however, with state assistance a large proportion of the peasants managed to acquire small holdings. But in too many cases their former impoverishment was not diminished, because they did not have enough land, equipment, or knowledge to make more than a "Tobacco Road" livelihood. And they were not the only ones who suffered. The difficulties of Nikolai Kirsanov, in *Fathers and Sons*, were typical of the problems of well-meaning members of the gentry who tried to assist the peasants, only to discover that they were too ignorant, improvident, and shiftless to be able to benefit from assistance.

One extremely important aspect of the Russian emancipation is not widely known in the West. Even after the enactment giving the serfs personal freedom, the land which came into their possession was not actually their own property (in the Western sense of the word). Their land was usually owned by the commune (*mir*), which took on even more authority after the emancipation than it had previously held. The commune as the unit of organization was thus strengthened, whereas the individual who had to accept its regulation was, in effect, scarcely more free than before. His former subservience to his master was succeeded by his subjection to the commune. Historians and political theorists are in general agreement that the development of Russia would almost certainly have been different if an emancipation formula enabling the peasant to own his land independently could have been devised and administered. Such a system would have furnished the basis for a large increase in the middle class, which is the stabilizing element in any society. A larger middle class in Russia would have reduced the likelihood of revolt.

Next to granting freedom to the serfs, Alexander's liberal policies were most significantly expressed in his removal of a number of the restrictive measures Nicholas I had enforced in regard to education, censorship, and minority religious groups. In the first years of Alexander's reign there was unprecedented freedom of the press and of study and discussion in the universities.

Unfortunately, this period of tolerance did not last. Alexander was caught between two opposing forces. The reactionists believed he had gone too far. They resented the loss of privilege and were convinced that only severe repression would prevent the radicals from taking a mile if given an inch. The intelligentsia, on the other hand, were agitated by the gap between what they had hoped for and the improvements that had been forthcoming. Alexander's moderation had come too late. For too long they had dreamed, had been forced to plan and to work underground, and then to conspire. Now the flood was a mighty force not to be checked even by the sandbag defense of reform.

The liberals had come to a time for decision. They must either recede to conservative shores or sweep into the surging channels of radicalism. Ten years after the emancipation the reasonable liberalism of Herzen was archaic. The philosophical idealism of Belinsky gave way to the radical pronouncements of Chernyshevsky and of Dobrolyubov, who used the pages of the *Contemporary* to lash out against the government even in the early years of Alexander's regime. Their radicalism, in turn, took on a restrained tone by comparison with the iconoclastic thunder of

Pisarev, who in *The Russian Word* excoriated not only the government but the old liberals as well. It was inevitable that Pisarev and many of his ideational brothers should out-Bazarov Bazarov. When a student fired at the Czar in 1866 (the first of many attempts on the life of the Czar and his deputies), that shot was the overt signal that the days of the existing society were numbered.

Never a true liberal, Alexander had done only what it was necessary to do. After reaching the peak represented by the emancipation act and worrying through the innumerable readjustments required thereafter, he had no more energy for leadership. The glow of greatness which had surrounded him at the high moment of his career was soon clouded. The dissatisfaction of the gentry, the continuing problems of the peasants, the accelerating momentum of the radicals and the Bakunin-inspired insurrectionists, the humiliating losses by the Treaty of Paris, the depletion of the state treasury as a result of the Crimean War and the funds expended on assisting the peasants to purchase land—all these pressures made demands upon the Czar which a much greater man might not have been able to meet.

In 1867, Russia sold Alaska to the United States for $7,200,000. The money was used for railway construction, part of the extensive program of industrial expansion by which the country hoped to bolster her financial structure. The Franco-Prussian War in 1871–72 temporarily caused a lessening of internal agitation and gave Alexander's government the opportunity to pursue its policy of expansion in the Far East. All efforts at balancing the treasury and reconciling the conflicting tensions within Russia were cancelled, however, by a war with Turkey, which began in the spring of 1877. The Russians were the victors, but the victory meant little. Much of what they had gained by the Treaty of San Stefano in 1878 was lost through the diplomatic maneuverings of other European nations after the war. Neither Germany nor England was willing to see Russia acquire much new territory or power.

Thus the reign of Alexander had come full circle. It ended as it began, with prestige low, the state treasury drained, the populace disgruntled, the peasant problem still not solved, and the flood of radicalism sweeping on with frightening velocity. The bomb which put an end to Alexander's life in March, 1881, was thrown by an assassin who belonged to a society of anarchists called "The Will of the People." It was the final irony of Alexander's career that at the time of his death he had just accepted a constitution which would have changed the whole plan of Russian government. If Alexander's life had been spared, he would have been the father of constitutionalism in his country. The fatal bomb was in a sense fatal for Russia, too. It destroyed the last opportunity for a peaceful, evolutionary settlement of her governmental problems.

Both Alexander II and Abraham Lincoln (with whom he has sometimes extravagantly been compared) lost their lives in a period of upheaval connected with the issue of slavery. Perhaps the fact that the first volume of Marx's *Capital* had been translated into Russian nine years before Alexander's death (and translations of others of his works soon followed) helps to explain why the leadership Alexander attempted to give his country proved so much less significant than the leadership of Lincoln in America. After Lincoln's death his fellow countrymen could still read his "Gettysburg Address," as well as the Constitution. In Russia after Alexander's death, however, most of the thinkers among "the people" read *The Communist Manifesto.*

VI/ Dostoevsky and the Underground Man

In January, 1881, a man named Fyodor Dostoevsky, who lived in St. Petersburg, published the last installment of his *Diary of a Writer*, starting it with these words: "Such is my nature that I shall begin with the end, and not with the beginning, and straightway I shall set forth my idea."

When he wrote the words, he could not have known how fitting they were, but in a short time their appropriateness became clear. Before the month ended, Dostoevsky was dead. He had been hated and loved, reviled and revered as few other men have ever been. He was always driven—by passion, by illness, by events, by the volcano of creativity that burned within him, and perhaps most of all by the "idea."

What the "idea" was may be best suggested by words he spoke near the end of his life. In June, 1880, at the height of his career, he delivered an address of commemoration to honor the great poet Pushkin. The speech added to the stature of Pushkin and made Dostoevsky a hero of Russia. His words had a hypnotic effect upon his listeners, and no wonder, since they were born of the convictions of a lifetime. The following, from the conclusion of the address, contains the essence of what the novelist had spent his life preparing to say:

> To be a real Russian and to be wholly Russian means only this: to be a brother of all men, to be universally human. . . . to the true Russian, Europe and the affairs of the great Aryan race are as dear as the affairs of Russia herself and of his native country, because our affairs are the affairs of the whole world, and they are not to be obtained by the sword, but by the strength of fraternity and by our brotherly effort toward the universal union of mankind. . . . In the long run I am convinced that we, that is to say, not we, but the future generations of the Russian people, shall every

one of us, from the first to the last, understand that to be a real Russian must signify this: to strive towards bringing about a solution and an end to European conflicts; to show to Europe a way of escape from its anguish in the Russian soul, which is universal and all-embracing; to instill into her a brotherly love for all men's brothers, and in the end perhaps to utter the great and final word of universal harmony, the fraternal and lasting concord of all peoples according to the gospel of Christ.

In order to understand what lay behind this "idea," it is necessary to begin with what has been called "the novel of Dostoevsky's life."

I.

Fyodor Mikhailovich Dostoevsky was born in Moscow on October 30, 1821. His father was a physician in a hospital for the poor. In their small flat attached to the hospital,[1] the Dostoevsky family could not avoid contact with poverty, misery, and death. Patients came with all kinds of diseases, physical and mental, most of them not to be cured but to die. With ironic appropriateness this setting foreshadowed the suffering which pursued Dostoevsky throughout his life.

The environment was made even more grim by the irascible father, who ruled his children like a despot. He permitted them no outside companions, no recreation, and no spending money. In the *Diary* written in the last years of his life, Dostoevsky recalled the experiences of his childhood in softened outlines. He wrote of "my parents' affection for me." "We, in our family," he said, "have known the Gospel almost ever since our earliest childhood. I was only ten when I already knew virtually all the principal episodes in Russian history—from Karamzin, whom, in the evenings, father used to read aloud to us. Every visit to the Kremlin and the Moscow cathedrals was, to me, something solemn." Such visits must have been rare, for the family lived

[1] These rooms now serve as a museum where the visitor may see many things which belonged to Dostoevsky, including some of his manuscripts.

apart from the world. Fyodor was not even permitted to talk with the hospital patients as he would have liked to do. Obviously, however, part of his absorption in illness and abnormal mental states is traceable to his memories of their haunted faces.

The delicate boy was expected to occupy himself with books. No wonder he was always pale. Although the education supervised by the stern father was inadequate and ill planned, it provided the young Fyodor with the consuming interest in literature which determined the direction of his life. Without parental urging he read with a hunger that could not be satisfied.

Fyodor was fortunate in one respect. His older brother, Mikhail, was a real companion and as long as he lived remained the person dearest to Dostoevsky's heart. In Fyodor's tenth year the routines of family life became somewhat less restricted. The father purchased a farm some distance from Moscow, to which thereafter the mother and children went for the summers. Previously, the children's contacts with nature had been limited to the walks on which their father talked to them about "improving subjects." In the country there was more freedom. There Fyodor had an occasional contact with the peasants—"the people" he always idealized. But he never knew or understood the peasants. Unlike Turgenev and Tolstoy, who had roots in the soil, he was always a man of the city. When Fyodor was thirteen, his father sent him and Mikhail to a private boarding school in Moscow in the hope that their study might be better balanced. Here they remained for three years until the death of their mother brought about the dissolution of the Dostoevsky family life.

By this time the young Dostoevsky's character was already formed. He was nervous, intense, uncertain of himself, and undisciplined in practical affairs. His aloofness masked his yearning for the understanding he had never received, not even from the mother who had been dear to him.

Shortly before Fyodor's sixteenth birthday the two brothers were taken by their father to St. Petersburg to be prepared for entrance into the Military Engineering Academy. The farewell between father and sons was a final parting. Having given up his position after the death of his wife, the father withdrew to his farm. There his eccentricities apparently increased, his growing alcoholism adding to the explosiveness of his temper. In less than a year his brutal treatment of the serfs provoked them to kill him. The murder is known to have been done with all the bloody savagery of melodrama, but beyond that, nothing is certain. What the specific motivation may have been and who actually committed the deed were never discovered. There is no evidence that it made an abnormally deep or melancholy impression upon the young Fyodor, as certain psychological studies of the author have tried to prove.[2] In spite of some feeling of respect for his father and love for his mother, he could hardly have experienced any strong emotional response at their deaths. Nor could he have looked back on the circumstances of his childhood with marked nostalgia. The fact, however, that the novelist's father was a man so given to impatience and rage that his peasants could find relief only in killing him probably accounts in part for Dostoevsky's penetrating studies of violent men in some of his novels.

After his more robust brother had been rejected as physically unfit, it was a surprise when Fyodor passed the entrance examinations and entered the engineering academy. Mikhail went on to an academy in another city, leaving Fyodor alone for the first time to face a world for which he was poorly prepared. His years at the engineering school were important chiefly for the opportunity they gave him to read. He fulfilled his responsibilities as a student abstractedly, his mind always in a different world. As a boy he had become familiar with Pushkin and Walter Scott. Now he went on to Schiller, Goethe, Corneille, Balzac, Victor Hugo, George Sand, Lamartine, Paul de Kock, Hoffmann, Shakespeare, Dickens, and other popular authors. The writers of Gothic tales and the French romantics especially appealed to him, but later their influence proved secondary to that of Dickens and Gogol,

[2] Freudians have made the most of the opportunity to interpret every aspect of Dostoevsky's character and career.

both of whom visibly affected his early works. He did not stop with Pushkin and Gogol among Russian authors, but read avidly the history, poetry, and fiction of his own country. Dostoevsky never had the opportunity for the educational and cultural advantages that wealth had made available to Turgenev and Tolstoy. Yet during the lonely years of dull routine in a military school his intellectual eagerness enabled him to live an intense inner life of adventure.

The city of St. Petersburg, too, stimulated the young man. As he became acquainted with its huge contours, its "mean streets," the magnificence of public buildings, and arrogant displays of wealth in contrast to squalor, he began to see it, not as an impersonal metropolis, but as a scene of mystery. "White Nights" (one of his early stories) mitigated the harsh outlines of reality; the Neva was a river of enchantment. Even in the abjectness of most of the inhabitants he felt the city's beating heart. As Dickens drew upon his familiarity with London, so Dostoevsky depended for character and situation upon the residents of the city and upon their tortured neuroses, which their divorce from the soil had helped to aggravate.

In his associations with other students, Dostoevsky was shy and uncertain, never one of them. In company he usually sat alone, tormented by not knowing how to approach people. When he made the attempt, it often ended in shouting and insults. Then he would rush away to try to atone for his boorishness in contrite letters of apology. His inability to associate naturally with other people was part of the legacy imposed upon him by his father's unwillingness to permit the Dostoevsky children to have friends or acquaintances outside the family. The novelist never overcame this handicap. In spite of his genuine liking for people, he was cut off from them by a sense of unfamiliarity as well as by the extremes and diversity of his moods.

At the end of his course in the academy, Dostoevsky was given a commission and appointed to a post in the engineering department of the Ministry of War. But already he was wedded to literature. He hesitated only briefly before resigning the appointment to devote his life to writing. Thus he cut himself adrift from any possibility of financial security. From this time until the last decade of his life he was unable to meet his financial obligations.

In Dostoevsky's first book, *Poor Folk*, the influence of Gogol, especially of his story "The Cloak," was apparent. He wrote and revised it during the winter of 1844–45 with a care seldom lavished on his greater works. If the later life of Dostoevsky was battered by hardships beyond the capacity of most men to endure, he had at least the satisfaction of making his literary debut under the most favorable circumstances. Indeed, his emergence into the world of letters was heralded with blasts of approval.

Dostoevsky tells the story in his *Diary*. When he had painstakingly completed the manuscript to his satisfaction, he showed it to Grigorovich, a would-be writer like himself. His friend took it to Nekrasov, a poet and critic whose judgment was respected and who was in a position to serve as literary sponsor to the young author if he saw fit. Imagine the scene. Too nervous to sleep, Dostoevsky had spent most of the night talking to friends and returned to his room just before dawn. He was sitting before the open window when he heard a vehement pounding at the door. The two men, unable to put down the manuscript, had continued reading through the night. Now, almost as excited as the author, they had come to tell him he had written a masterpiece. Nekrasov immediately took the manuscript to Belinsky, at that time the final authority, whose commendation assured the publication and success of what now appears a modest first effort. When Dostoevsky was introduced to the great critic, Belinsky could hardly control his fervor. "Do you realize what you have done?" he shouted at the young writer. Understandably, Dostoevsky found it hard to believe his good fortune, but he soon accepted it with greedy abandon. In letters to his brother he wrote glowingly of his happiness and intimated that although at first he was surprised at the idea of being a "great" man, he did not find it difficult to accept the role and the adulation which for a time went with it.

It was unfortunate for Dostoevsky's self-assurance but fortunate for his development that his initial success was not soon repeated. His complacent acceptance of the attention heaped upon him after the publication of *Poor Folk* helped to turn commendation to censure. His next story, *The Double*, is still derivative in nature but more individual than the first and more mature. It suggests the remarkable psychological penetration which later proved to be Dostoevsky's most distinguishing asset as a writer. But since *The Double* was subjective and analytical, looking inward instead of at the poor people upon whom the liberals based their hopes for the future of Russia, Belinsky and other critics rejected it. Actually, it is interesting for the clues it furnishes to the personality of its author and also because it is the first of his many studies of the distorted, split personalities, the "doubles" who have become the increasing preoccupation of modern psychology. These first stories introduce the two main character types of his later works—on the one hand, the meek souls, lonely, poor, and unloved, who have to bear too much from life but still turn faces of patient endurance toward its blows, and on the other hand, the unhappy modern men, victims of the tensions between the primitive and the civilized, led astray by education, rebellious and insecure, alien to grace but wanting desperately to make their peace with God and society.

When the initial approbation of Belinsky and his associates turned to disfavor, Dostoevsky was humiliated, but he was mature enough to realize that some of their judgments were prejudiced and faulty. Fortunately, his disappointment did not diminish his creative urge. Even after the rift between him and his critics became complete, he continued to write and to appear in print. Following the publication of *The Double*, he produced a number of long stories, none of which added to his reputation. In the autumn of 1848 he began what was intended to be a full-length novel, *Netochka Nezvanova*, but that was a novel Dostoevsky never wrote. He was prevented by an event which changed the course of his life and interrupted his career for ten years.

Dostoevsky and his brother had been for some time members of a group of young intellectuals who met regularly for discussion. Known by the name of the man who had invited the group to meet at his home, the Petrashevsky circle was composed of earnest but naïve young theorists. They delighted especially in exploring the possibilities of French socialism and other utopian programs. Even though they did nothing but talk, smoke, talk, drink tea, and talk again, they aroused the misgivings of Nicholas I, who could scent danger where none existed. Alarmed by the uprisings of 1848 in western Europe, the Czar was determined to stamp out anything threatening the inviolability of his regime. He delegated an agent to insinuate himself into the Petrashevsky organization to report on every syllable the unsuspecting idealists spoke. About the same time some of the more ardent members of the society formed an inner circle, hoping to engage in definite action. Apparently none had any idea what the action might consist of beyond the possibility of installing a secret press on which they could print their own liberal articles. The Czar's spies did not penetrate into the inner group, but they suspected its existence and assumed it was treasonous. After a period during which they gave detailed reports of the meetings of the larger society, the trap was sprung.

On the night of April 23, 1849, Dostoevsky, along with thirty-three other members of the Petrashevsky circle, was arrested for "revolutionary activities" and sent to the notorious fortress of St. Peter and St. Paul.[3] For eight months he was kept in what was as nearly solitary confinement as existed in Russian prisons. During the first half of the imprisonment he was not allowed even

[3] The cell in which Dostoevsky was confined was located in a building which has been razed, but the visitor to Leningrad may still see the cell in which a later author, Gorky, was briefly imprisoned.

writing materials; as soon as they were permitted, he started with remarkable buoyancy to work on another story. The charge against Dostoevsky was that at a meeting of the society he had read aloud the famous letter from Belinsky to Gogol in which the critic had castigated the author of *Dead Souls* for his ignoble reactionary views.

In November the court, about whose proceedings the prisoners knew nothing, pronounced the death sentence upon twenty-one of the accused, Dostoevsky among them. Not one of them had lifted a hand against the government. Such a travesty on justice is a reminder that strict surveillance, political purges, witch-hunting, and death for political crimes, either real or imaginary, have not been introduced to Russia in the twentieth century. Within a short time the sentence was reduced to penal servitude in Siberia for periods varying from life to four years, but the prisoners were not told of the reprieve. There was too much drama inherent in the situation for the authorities to let it go unexploited.

Shortly before Christmas the prisoners were summarily informed that they were to be executed. They were conveyed to a public square where they saw a scaffold awaiting them. This was to be the dreadful object lesson for these fledgling revolutionaries, most of them no more dangerous than college boys dreaming of a "brave new world." Even during the days of witch trials in America the imagination of the most perverted Salemites never offered anything to equal this for diabolic torture. Dostoevsky described the fateful experience in a letter written to his brother later on that same day:

> We were taken to the Semenov Drill Ground. There the sentence of death was read to all of us, we were told to kiss the Cross, our swords were broken over our heads, and our last toilet was made (white shirts). Then three were tied to the pillar for execution. I was the sixth. Three at a time were called out; consequently, I was in the second batch and no more than a minute was left me to live. I remembered you, brother . . . during the last minute

> you, you alone, were in my mind. . . . I also managed to embrace Plescheyev and Durov who stood close to me and to say good-bye to them. Finally the retreat was sounded, and those tied to the pillar were led back, and it was announced to us that his Imperial Majesty granted us our lives.[4]

He then explained that he had been sentenced to four years' hard labor, after which he would be forced to go into military service as a private:

> But do not grieve . . . for me! Do believe that I am not downhearted, do remember that hope has not deserted me. . . . I was today in the grip of death for three-quarters of an hour; I have lived it through with that idea; I was at the last instant and now I live again!

Dostoevsky did not tell his brother that several of his associates had contracted pneumonia from their exposure to the cold in their white death shirts or that one had gone mad from the horror of the experience. He himself did not know how it would affect him. It is not strange that during the rest of his life all his sensibilities were heightened, his perceptions sharpened, and his concern for human suffering greatly increased. The ineffaceable impression of this moment in the life of the author helps to explain the peculiar intensity in the emotional life of his characters. In one of the most memorable passages of *The Idiot*, Dostoevsky gives an account of the experience, etching the details with stark clarity.

After these outrageous histrionics on the drill ground, the sentences of the accused were put into effect with dispatch. Two days later, on Christmas Eve, Dostoevsky was permitted to bid his brother a hasty farewell. Then he and one fellow "criminal" were put into chains and sent in an open sleigh to the wilderness

[4] Quotations from letters of Dostoevsky are taken from the following: Ethel C. Mayne (trans.), *Letters* (London, Chatto & Windus, 1917); S. S. Koteliansky and J. M. Murry (trans.), *Letters and Reminiscences* (New York, Knopf, 1923); and Elizabeth Hill and Doris Mudie (trans.), *Letters to His Wife* (London, Constable, 1930).

of Siberia. It is not hard to imagine the numbness of their hearts as they left the city, lighted in preparation for the celebration of Christmas, to face the blackness of an unknown future. The trip took more than three weeks, in temperatures as low as forty degrees below zero. During a pause at Tobolsk the prisoners were relieved to have their inadequate clothing supplemented by the efforts of the wives of some of the Decembrist conspirators, who had then been exiled for nearly twenty-five years. Finally, Dostoevsky and his fellow convict arrived at the prison in Omsk to which they had been assigned. There they were swallowed up in "the house of the dead." It was nearly ten years before Dostoevsky returned to St. Petersburg, a free man, one-sixth of his life having been sacrificed to monarchical absolutism. The amazing thing is that he never rebelled against this futile waste, but bore it all with humility.

To understand the conditions of Dostoevsky's four-year imprisonment, it is necessary to read his *House of the Dead.* This book paints an unforgettable though objective picture in black and grey of the life of criminals in penal servitude—a picture of brutality and bestiality, of strength and weakness, of cruelty and defiance, of kindness and strange fidelities, of loneliness in a crowd, of persecution, illness, deplorable physical circumstances, and of loss of hope. Here political "offenders" as innocent as Dostoevsky were herded together with the most practiced criminals, the former usually more harshly treated. Here the novelist was provided with a laboratory stocked with living corpses. Here he could study human nature reduced to basic ingredients as no novelist before or since has been able to do.

> I had made acquaintance with convicts in Tobolsk [he wrote to his brother a week after he had left the prison]; at Omsk I settled myself down to live four years with them. They are rough, angry, embittered men. . . .
>
> . . . I spent the whole four years behind dungeon walls, and only left the prison when I was taken on "hard labor." . . . Once I had to spend four hours at a piece of extra work, and in such frost that

> the quicksilver froze; it was perhaps forty degrees below zero. . . . We all lived together in one barrack-room. Imagine an old, crazy wooden building, that should long ago have been broken up as useless. In the summer it is unbearably hot, in the winter unbearably cold. All the boards are rotten. On the ground filth lies an inch thick; every instant one is in danger of slipping and coming down. The small windows are so frozen over that even by day one can hardly read. The ice on the panes is three inches thick. The ceilings drip, there are draughts everywhere. We are packed like herrings in a barrel. The stove is heated with six logs of wood, but the room is so cold that the ice never once thaws; the atmosphere is unbearable—and so through all the winter long. . . . All the prisoners stink like pigs; they say that they can't help it, for they must live, and are but men. We slept upon bare boards; each man was allowed one pillow only. We covered ourselves with short sheepskins, and our feet were outside the covering all the time. It was thus we froze night after night.

It was not, however, the physical conditions—cold, filth, heavy work, and near-starvation—that caused Dostoevsky the most suffering. The worst of the ordeal was the impossibility of being alone, even for one moment. Always being exposed, vulnerable, with no privacy, no chance for quiet—that was for him the real punishment. He suffered, also, from the scorn of the common prisoners. Their "hatred [for all who were superior to them in intelligence or social class] is boundless; they regard all of us . . . with hostility and enmity. They would have devoured us if they only could," he reported. Small wonder that under such conditions, although he spoke of having been in some ways "restored to health," his nervous disorders were aggravated until he began to have in severe form the epileptic seizures which tormented him for the remainder of his life. Small wonder that when he was "free" after ten years, he looked like a man who had lived a lifetime.

His spirit, however, was more vital than his body. Even in prison the magnificent creative power of the artist was at work.

He was himself aware of unexpected compensations. He wrote to Mikhail:

> I won't even try to tell you what transformations were undergone by my soul, my faith, my mind, and my heart in those four years. . . . Still, the eternal concentration, the escape into myself from bitter reality, did bear its fruit. . . .
>
> . . . Even among the robber-murderers in the prison I came to know some men in those four years. Believe me, there were among them deep, strong, beautiful natures, and it often gave me great joy to find gold under a rough exterior. . . . Decidedly I have not spent my time there in vain. I have learnt to know the Russian people as only a few know them.

After more than four years of the tribulations of prison life, Dostoevsky was sent as a private to a Siberian battalion stationed at Semipalatinsk. Here he was able to have other books in addition to the New Testament, to which he had been limited in prison, and was permitted to correspond with his relatives. Yet he felt at first almost more cut off from the world than before. It was frustrating to be neither a prisoner nor yet his own master. Gradually, however, he made a few friends and after a short time developed an attachment for the wife of an inept minor official. She was a capricious and irresponsible woman, unworthy of Dostoevsky in all respects, but irresistible to the man starved for affection and companionship. When she accompanied her husband to another post, Dostoevsky's devotion to her continued to grow. Separation from her proved among the most painful of all the trials he had had to face. When her husband died from alcoholism, Dostoevsky hastened to make her his wife although he could not expect and did not receive any more fidelity from her than she had accorded her previous husband.

Dostoevsky's first marriage had no chance of being a happy one. Unquestionably he used his wife as the model for some of his captious, violent female characters whose love was associated with hate. This woman added to the hardships Dostoevsky had already been forced to endure, with her ungovernable temper and her almost maniacal outbursts of jealousy and suspicion. She may have had a quality of fragile attractiveness, but she was sulky and absolutely selfish. She had no understanding or appreciation of Dostoevsky's talent or of the gnawing ambition that kept him restless and made his exile almost insupportable. Her rages did not diminish with the passing of time. When illness added to the complications of her disposition, she became practically impossible to live with. Only because of his power to live within himself was Dostoevsky able, during the relatively short period of their marriage, to avoid being psychologically broken by it.[5]

Not the least of the encumbrances forced upon the author by this marriage was a stepson, who combined the worst qualities of both his parents. A whining, weak boy, he was pampered by his mother when she gave him any attention at all. She did not expect him to do anything useful, and he grew up with the conviction that he was conferring a favor on society by merely existing.

In 1859, after his own prolonged efforts and those of his friends were at last heeded, Dostoevsky was permitted to end his exile and return to Russia. At first he was required to live in Tver, but the ban was soon lifted. His return to Petersburg was like coming back from death to life. There has been considerable speculation regarding how Dostoevsky felt about his imprisonment and exile, and the ten years lost from his active career. Specific evidence on this point is lacking, but there is no indication that his spirit was scarred by what would have been justifiable bitterness. In a letter written while he was still in Semipalatinsk he said: "I was guilty, and am very conscious of it. . . . I was lawfully and quite justly condemned; the hard and painful experiences of the ensuing years have sobered me, and altered my views in many respects." Even if these words were in part determined by his frantic desire

[5] The study of Dostoevsky's relation with women, *The Three Loves of Dostoevsky* by Marc Slonim, is extremely useful as an illumination of Dostoevsky's female characters and the male-female relationships in his writings.

to return to the world from which he had been cast out, they indicate the state of mind in which he picked up the pieces of his former life.

After the end of his exile there was never any doubt of his conservatism. He loved the Czar, and he loved Russia even more than before, despite the indignities to which he had been subjected. His faith in "the people" was increased by the sufferings he had borne at their hands and in their company. Now he was a real Slavophile—the most vocal and impassioned of them all.

Back in Petersburg and without any other means of livelihood, Dostoevsky began to write stories, the first of which had no particular significance. Soon he and his brother started a periodical, *Vremya* (*The Time*). This undertaking proved interesting chiefly because of its serial publication of his first full-length novel, *The Insulted and Injured*, and the book referred to earlier, *Memoirs of the House of the Dead*. The former contains intimations of the intensity and psychological acumen of the later great novels, but it is marred by sentimentality and the worst faults of Dostoevsky's style. *The House of the Dead*, on the other hand, is distinguished by repression and understatement, despite which —or perhaps because of which—it is a poignant book, a document having few equals in photographing the abysses of human experience.

A short visit, his first, to western Europe in the summer of 1862 solidified the writer's antipathy to Russia's neighbors on the west. When he met Herzen briefly in London, the two men must have realized what a chasm separated them. Herzen believed that Russia's salvation depended upon the culture of the West, and Dostoevsky was certain that the West would have to appeal to Russia to be saved.

Vremya was proving moderately successful, and the two brothers were beginning to have hopes of establishing reasonable financial security when the journal was suspended for the publication of an innocuous article touching on the Polish question, at that time a red-hot issue (the treatment of which had caused

Herzen's *The Bell* to lose popularity). Thereafter, instead of settling down to work in an effort to find a practical solution to his problems, Dostoevsky—always helpless before financial complications—borrowed money and went again to western Europe. He hoped to re-establish relations with a young woman with whom he had been madly in love since the previous winter. During this unhappy excursion he began the gambling which was to be the curse of his life for the next five years. It aggravated his other miseries and kept him always on the defensive. These years were filled with calamities sufficient to create a private inferno from which it is almost unbelievable that a man could come back to walk with Titan steps into literary immortality.

The young woman, Polina Suslova, although more intelligent than his wife, had many of the characteristics of that miserable woman, now dying of consumption. If Dostoevsky still had anything to learn about the anguish to which a man can be subjected by the capricious and willful cruelty of a woman, he learned it from Polina. Before Dostoevsky was able to rejoin her, she had fallen in love with someone else, who promptly abandoned her. Thereupon, she took out her vexation on Dostoevsky. He followed her meekly from one country to another while she treated him like a brother or a slave, depending on her moods. He would have done anything for her, but she would not show him even a little kindness. When at last he understood that he was nothing to her and that she was incapable of honesty or constancy, he went back to Petersburg to attempt to make easier the last months of his wife, from whom, feeling that he could endure no more, he had for some time been separated. In spite of her irritability and unreasonableness, accentuated by her illness, he stayed with her until she died after exacting from him the promise to take full responsibility for her wayward son. Thus even in death she imposed upon him a continuation of the burdens which had been her contribution to the marriage.

Dostoevsky and his brother had embarked, meanwhile, upon another journalistic venture, *Epokha* (*The Epoch*), which they managed to keep alive just long enough to bring out the challenging *Notes from Underground.* This book, written during the months when Dostoevsky's wife was slowly dying, bears the marks of the author's concentrated woes. Its principal character —it is the soliloquy of a doomed soul—has much in common with the author. Yet there are marked contrasts; for example, whereas Dostoevsky loved the world by which he had been mistreated, the Underground Man counteracted the despair of being ignored and misunderstood with malice and bitter cynicism.

It was already apparent that *Epokha* could not be saved from failure when perhaps the hardest blow he ever had to bear fell upon the luckless author—the death, after a short illness, of the person dearest to him, his brother Mikhail. His desolation of spirit was painful, but the practical consequences were almost insurmountable. Dostoevsky never questioned that he must assume all his brother's personal obligations. This meant not only the mountainous debts connected with the failure of the second periodical, but also the support of Mikhail's wife and her four children and of an illegitimate child and its mother. And always he was harried by the importunities of one of his younger brothers, a dipsomaniac, and by his shiftless stepson. The latter made no effort to provide for himself or, when he married, for his wife and children. In addition, the physical harassment of epilepsy and other disabilities, the haughty indifference of Polina Suslova, the spiritual ravages of loneliness and insecurity, and the inability to accomplish what he felt himself capable of doing filled out the pattern of Dostoevsky's distress.

After the death of his brother the battering of creditors became so imperious that Dostoevsky would almost certainly have ended in the debtors' prison if he had not been saved from financial ruin by a woman who gave him the only sustained serenity he ever knew. He had long managed to exist only by the practice of asking his publishers for payment in advance on books not yet written. At this time, when his affairs were most crucial, he entered upon a fantastic arrangement with a publisher who required his furnishing the manuscript of a new novel by a certain date. If it was late, he would receive substantially less payment; if more than a month late, the publisher would automatically acquire the rights to all his future work. One month before the date set, the stipulated novel had not even been started, though Dostoevsky knew that failure to meet the deadline would mean a mortgage upon his entire future. He was rescued from this impasse by a young stenographer, Anna Grigorievna Snitkina. Through her skillful handling of his dictation, the novel, *The Gambler,* was completed by the date specified. Shortly thereafter he turned over to her the management of his affairs.

Less than five months after their first meeting Dostoevsky married Anna, who was twenty-six years younger than he. Although the novelist appeared to bring to this marriage only an ill-starred past, poor health, frightening debts, and an uncontrolled passion for gambling, the young woman was wise enough to understand that he also brought a rare quality of genius. From that time on she devoted herself to providing an environment in which that genius might come to fruition. In order to write *The Gambler*, the novelist had to interrupt the composition of *Crime and Punishment*, with which he had been engrossed during the previous year of staggering indebtedness. It is not likely that Dostoevsky felt many passages he wrote as keenly as those relating to the predicaments of the "gambler" and the poverty-stricken Marmeladovs of *Crime and Punishment.*

Anna Dostoevsky saved her husband from the nagging of his relatives and the insistent demands of his creditors by persuading him that they should live abroad until they had achieved economic stability. As long as her husband's fever for gambling remained unsatisfied, her hopes were futile. With the illogicality of the gambler, he was positive each time he went to the gaming tables that he would win. Instead, he lost with grim, monotonous regularity. Advances on books, personal possessions, and even clothing were repeatedly gambled away until there was nothing more to stake. Dostoevsky hesitated before asking Anna to let him risk her cherished earrings, but when there was nothing else, she gave them up, as she had given up her shoes and coat, without reproach or complaint. Each time the devoted husband returned to her in despair, cursing himself for his folly. Each time his "good angel" received him with patient understanding. When at last the disease had burned itself out, the tormented man had completed another chapter in his experience with misery. He had also gained strength from the assurance that in his wife he had found a woman who really loved him.

The Dostoevskys remained abroad for four years. After they came back to Russia, the author still had ten years of life left to him, years of increasing security and mounting fame. His wife proved an astute businesswoman. Realizing that her husband had long been the victim of unscrupulous publishers who, although they had advanced payments, had never paid the novelist what his writings were worth, she decided to start her own business venture. Thereafter she was the publisher of her husband's books as well as of his journal, *Diary of a Writer*, which appeared intermittently during his last years. The astonishing energy and resilience of this woman enabled her not only to manage her husband's affairs, to assist him in the role of stenographer, to run a business, and finally to pay his debts, but also to bear four children (only two of whom lived past early childhood) and to be a wife upon whom her husband came to depend absolutely for comradeship and devotion. Even if the blessings of life came to Dostoevsky seldom, this one must have seemed to him bestowed by Providence.

The author's dislike of western Europe was not in any way mitigated by his stay abroad. After he had been in Germany for a short time with his young wife, he wrote to his friend Apollon Maikov of a meeting with Turgenev in which the latter's Westernism had clashed with his own Slavophile views. He had told Turgenev, he wrote, about "all the hatred that these three months have accumulated in me against the Germans." Dostoevsky called the Germans "swindlers and rogues" and believed that "the common people are much more evil and dishonest here than they are with us; and that they are stupider there can be no doubt." He could see few signs of the civilization of which Turgenev was "always talking." Nearly four years later, before returning to his own country, he wrote to another friend: "Men write and write, and overlook the principal point. In western Europe the peoples have lost Christ (Catholicism is to blame), and therefore western Europe is tottering to its fall." He saw in the West nothing but materialism, a shoddy affectation of superiority, and depravity of spirit. His deep capacity for appreciation simply did not extend beyond the boundaries of his native land. The death abroad of his first child, the "darling Sonia" whom he idolized, added personal bitterness to his dislike of Germany, Austria, and Italy which the birth of the second, in Dresden, did nothing to relieve.

The novels which have endowed Dostoevsky with immortality all belong to the last fifteen years of his life. *Crime and Punishment* was written in 1866, the dark year previous to his second marriage. This masterpiece was followed in 1869 by *The Idiot* (written abroad), in 1871–72 by *The Possessed,* in 1875 by *The Raw Youth,* and at last in 1879–80 by *The Brothers Karamazov,* the climax of the great procession. *The Eternal Husband,* a lesser work also written near the end of the novelist's career, is of extreme interest to psychologists. Somewhat lighter in tone than the other novels, it is none the less filled with irony.

Dostoevsky had for so long defied death in spite of growing physical weakness that neither he nor his admirers thought of his work as ever coming to an end. The burning eyes, the white face, the husky voice, and shaking hands all signified physical decay, but the spirit was luminously alive. When death from a lung hemorrhage ended his career on January 28, 1881, it was an incredible shock to multitudes of people. He had already planned enough books to fill the next ten years. His creative energy had not shown the slightest diminution even though the wiry body, which he had once described as having "the vitality of a cat," had been more and more beset by ills. Indeed, the circumstances of most of his life would have drained dry the springs of creativity if they had not proceeded from nearly inexhaustible sources.

To the end of his life Dostoevsky remained, as he had always been, frail of body but dynamic when he set himself to productive effort; at times lazy and dilatory, at other times unbelievably industrious; in company, shy, aloof, and argumentative, but on occasion magnetic and warmhearted; in human relationships, passionate and tempestuous yet capable of deep love and tenderness; sometimes gripped by harsh antagonisms but usually generous and disposed to see only the best in others; dependent in practical matters but self-sufficient in his creative genius; chaotic of spirit but filled with an understanding far beyond the range of ordinary men; disturbed by skepticism yet always yearning for the faith he sometimes grasped; of monumental intelligence but as simple as a child—a fascinating enigma, a genius in search of God.

The climax of Dostoevsky's career occurred on June 8, 1880, when on the occasion of the unveiling of a statue of Russia's poet, Pushkin, he delivered an address which resulted in a personal triumph of unprecedented magnitude. Other outstanding writers and public figures (including Turgenev, who was expected to be the "lion" of the occasion) had made impressive speeches, but it was the frail voice of Dostoevsky, rising in a crescendo of impassioned patriotism, which aroused adulation mounting to pandemonium. He appealed to the nationalistic sentiments of his fellow countrymen. On the resulting wave of popular enthusiasm Dostoevsky became a hero. From the ignominy and despair of a scaffold on a public square to the tumultuous ovation given to an idol—these were the extremes by which his career was bounded. When he died, all Russia mourned. As thousands followed his body to its burial place in the cemetery of the Alexander Nevsky monastery in St. Petersburg, the hearts of the people were filled with a numb desolation and at the same time with the exaltation of unity of spirit. The Russians he had loved were for the moment brought together in devotion to him and what he stood for.

Even in death, however, he was not spared the final irony. The wave of harmonious communion engendered by his Pushkin speech and heightened by the mourning at his bier was abruptly shattered less than two months later when an assassin's bomb took the life of the Czar. The reverberations of that event never subsided; indeed, they gathered momentum until they burst into the Revolution of 1917. That this explosion with all its lurid sequels was far from the consummation Dostoevsky fervently anticipated is made manifest in the following excerpt from one of his letters to Maikov:

> Our nature [the Russian] is infinitely higher than the European. And generally all our conceptions are more moral, and our Russian aims are higher than those of the European world. We have a more direct and noble belief in goodness . . . as Christianity, and not as a bourgeois solution of the problem of comfort. A great renewal is about to descend on the whole world, through European thought (which . . . is solidly welded with Orthodoxy), and this will be achieved in less than a hundred years,—this is my passionate belief.

II.

Several of Dostoevsky's minor works indicated the course his major novels would follow. In *Poor Folk*, Dostoevsky revealed once and for all with what class of human beings he was most in sympathy. This is a story of the poor, whose lives are simple from necessity but within whose hearts exist the same yearnings felt by people in more favorable circumstances. Although in writing this novel Dostoevsky was obviously influenced by Gogol's "The Cloak," his choice of characters from the same milieu as that of Gogol's clerk was not mere imitation. It was part of a tremendous social change, slow yet inevitable, namely, the emergence of the common man as a force to be reckoned with, not in Russia alone, but in all parts of the world. The twentieth century has been called "the century of the common man," but the phenomenon thus described had been long preparing.

The story of *Poor Folk* is told through the letters exchanged between two people, the middle-aged Makar Devushin and a young girl, Varvara. Their loneliness brings them together. Although Makar occasionally calls upon Varvara, the letters offer both of them a means for the expression of their true feelings, which they are too shy to express in person. Like Gogol's ill-fated purchaser of an overcoat, Makar is also a poor clerk, but he has something more substantial than the prospect of a new cloak to brighten his days. His pleasure in being able to supply Varvara with an occasional treat—anything to relieve the meagerness of her existence—makes him almost oblivious to his own poverty. For her he cheerfully endures the pawning of his overcoat and the tongue-lashings of a landlady to whom he cannot pay his rent. Because Varvara really needs assistance, though she tries desperately to support herself as a seamstress, she accepts Makar's gifts without realizing the extent of his sacrifices. Her letters or any other sign of affection keep him in a state of tremulous delight, yet he is harassed by fear that he will not be able to help her sufficiently in emergencies.

At length Makar's distress of mind causes him to make an error in copying, and he is summoned by his superior. Now his misery touches bottom; he assumes that he will be dismissed. As he stands trembling before the official, a button drops off his coat and rolls across the floor. It is the final ignominy, the symbol of his destitution. Unexpectedly, the official, sensing his despair, gives him a hundred rubles. Makar is transported with joy. He will pay his pressing obligations and—most important—give all the rest to Varvara. But his joy is abruptly ended. Varvara has made a decision. Knowing that Makar cannot provide for her no matter how strong his desire to do so, she has decided to marry the wealthy landowner from whose earlier importunities she had fled. Now that he proposes matrimony—though he admits his only purpose is to have an heir who will prevent his relatives from inheriting his property—she has no choice but to accept. As she sadly prepares for the wedding, she is well aware that she is exchanging the wretchedness of St. Petersburg for a different kind of wretchedness on a country estate. Dazed by the collapse of his hopes, Makar numbly tries to help her, ordering and purchasing baubles for the trousseau while his world falls to pieces. Only on the day of the wedding does he acknowledge his anguish in the last letter he writes to Varvara. It is again the old story: "From him that hath not shall be taken away even that he hath."

In *Poor Folk*, Dostoevsky expressed no indignation or rebellion. The book has none of the sentimentality or entreaty of the English reform novels of Dickens and his contemporaries, none of the denunciatory brashness of the proletarian novels of Europe and America. The story of Makar and Varvara is utterly simple, but it is heavy with compassion. Two people of no importance are suddenly important. Makar is a little ridiculous, perhaps, and ineffectual and poorly educated, but his abnegation and his love are genuine. No wonder Belinsky demanded of the young Dostoevsky whether he realized what he had done. For Belinsky, the passionate advocate of utopia in Russia, sensed in *Poor Folk* the spirit of "the people," rising and marching toward a better future.

This sympathy with the people is again apparent in *The House of the Dead*. Despite the mood of detachment, as if the narrator's experiences were not the author's own, it is clear from this account that Dostoevsky's years in prison provided him an opportunity to know intimately a representative cross section of the common people. Ironically, although Dostoevsky frequently criticized other writers, particularly Turgenev, for aloofness from the soil and the masses, he was as far removed as they were from what he regarded as the source of Russia's strength. Only in prison did he begin to discover who and what "the people" really were. There he learned to know the lowest of the low—the poor and the criminal. And from this close association Dostoevsky came away convinced that even among the dregs of humanity was the raw material for a great future for "Holy Russia." He discovered courage, unselfishness, loyalty, industry, and kindliness, where such qualities could not have been expected to exist. Though he lamented that many of the convicts held themselves apart from him, he never held this alienation against them. He felt it was his responsibility to bridge the gap and that he would be the loser if he failed to do so. He became convinced that the wise men had little to impart to the people, whereas the people could teach the "wise" a great deal. In the peasants, as he presents them, appear some of the same qualities which distinguish Turgenev's peasants in *A Sportsman's Sketches*. What is impressive is Dostoevsky's recognition of these elements among people branded as evildoers. He wrote in *The House of the Dead*:

> After a time the affability and good-will shown to me by certain convicts gave me a little courage, and restored my spirits. . . . I soon noticed some kind, good-natured faces in the dark and hateful crowd. Bad people are to be found everywhere, but even among the worst there may be something good. . . . These persons are perhaps not worse than others who are free.

Speaking of the criminals of the lowest class, he asserted:

> It is a great satisfaction to me to be able to say that among these dreadful sufferers, in a state of things so barbarous and abject, I found abundant proof that the elements of moral development were not wanting. In our convict establishment there were men whom. . . I looked upon as wild beasts and abhorred as such; well, all of a sudden, when I least expected it, these very men would exhibit such an abundance of feeling of the best kind, so keen a comprehension of the sufferings of others . . . that one might almost fancy scales had fallen from their eyes.

Without doubt Dostoevsky idealized the common people of Russia beyond reason. His faith in them as they were and in their potentials amounted almost to religious veneration. His compassion for the unfortunates had been expressed in *Poor Folk*, but his belief in them had its inception during his imprisonment. This faith was to Dostoevsky one of the compensations for his knowledge of death-in-life.

The Double, as mentioned earlier, was the first of Dostoevsky's studies of divided personality, a concept to which he repeatedly returned. Instead of looking into this early story, however, we may turn to *Notes from Underground* to see a more impressive example of a Dostoevskian "double" and at the same time to see the author as critic of certain developments in Russia which filled him with apprehension and which he was to discuss more fully in the later novels.

Actually, it has become inaccurate to classify *Notes from Underground* as a minor work. Its stature has loomed larger as the years pass, and appropriately so, for this small and obviously germinal book contains the essence of all Dostoevsky's later work. It was proved to be germinal in a larger sense, also; its shadow hovers over much of modern literature.

Notes from Underground is of interest, first, as a foretaste of many of the ambivalent characterizations in the novels which came later. It is a psychological analysis of an introspective man, torn apart by the conflict between what he is and what he wants to be. The key to his nature is that he is a creature trapped by contradictions. He has enormous vanity, but nothing to be vain about. He has looked at mankind and disliked what he has seen, and in brooding upon and expressing the causes of this disfavor, he has become spiteful and contemptuous. As his hatred for men grows, so also does his desire to be noticed and respected. Lacking humility, he feels driven to impress his personality and his importance upon others. The attempts to do so make him obnoxious and ridiculous, each failure turning him more bitterly inward. Because he suspects himself, it follows that he suspects everyone and everything else.

The time comes when the Underground Man is nourished only on the gall of his hatred. Alone, insignificant, and ignored by the world, he suffers terribly from his isolation and his sense of inferiority. He knows his predicament is primarily his own fault, yet he strikes out at mankind in scorn. Trying to raise himself in his own esteem by being rude and sadistic to others, he would bludgeon both man and God with mocking hauteur. His values are upside down. He rejects good if it is offered; he desires evil. He is determined to make others suffer and to suffer himself—to continue forever to pay off old scores against the intangible forces, within and without, that oppress him. He is at once despicable and pitiable, caught in the paradox of acute consciousness and of blindness of mind and heart.

The Underground Man calls himself a "sick" man ("to be too conscious is an illness"), and sick he is; but there is irrefutable logic in many of his perceptions and conclusions. He is in many respects extremely rational, but he does not like rationality, and he sees that men in general have a taste for irrationality. Man, he insists, does not do "nasty things because he does not know his own interests," but because he does not care about what is to his advantage. Exasperated by what he considers the illusory hopes of the socialists and meliorists who have faith in the principle that man's lot might be improved by reason, the Underground Man points out that man is not a reasonable creature. He does not desire or will to live by reason. "I . . . would not be in the least surprised," he said, "if . . . a gentleman with an ignoble, or rather with a reactionary and ironical countenance, were to arise and . . . say to us all: '. . . gentlemen, hadn't we better kick over the whole show and scatter rationalism to the winds, simply to—enable us to live once more at our own sweet foolish will!' " The whole book testifies to Dostoevsky's conviction that man is determined to go to any length to reject (sometimes to twist) rationality:

> And if he does not find means he will contrive destruction and chaos, will contrive sufferings of all sorts, only to gain his point! He will launch a curse upon the world. . . . If you say that all this, too, can be calculated and tabulated—chaos and darkness and curses, so that the mere possibility of calculating it all beforehand would stop it all, and reason would reassert itself—then man

would purposely go mad in order to be rid of reason and gain his point!

The Underground Man has observed that men are determined to exercise freedom of choice and to assert their wills "in order to prove that men still are men and not the keys of a piano" to be played upon by forces beyond their control. He sees that humanity is creative but also that it "loves chaos and destruction." He doubts whether civilization is advancing. Indeed, he says:

> The only gain of civilization for mankind is the greater capacity for variety of sensations. . . . And through the development of this many-sidedness man may come to finding enjoyment in bloodshed. In fact, this has already happened to him. . . . Civilization has made mankind if not more blood-thirsty, at least more vilely, more loathsomely blood-thirsty. In old days he saw justice in bloodshed. . . . Now we do think bloodshed abominable and yet we engage in this abomination, and with more energy than ever. Which is worse?

The rationality of the Underground Man becomes irrational morbidity. Finally it paralyzes his power to act. For the most part he is inert, but if he does act, the results are far from his intention, and he is thrown back into a state of unhealthy self-castigation and loathing of others. The entire book is an assault upon the creeping rationalism which Dostoevsky interpreted as a disease of his time, a disease Russia had caught from her western European neighbors. It was an answer to the widely expressed view that all the problems of Russia could be solved by reason. The one book to which it retorted most specifically was Chernyshevsky's *What Is to Be Done?* (a rather pompous exposition of a "new" society created by rational but self-centered men). But the vogue of rationalism was in the air, and it filled Dostoevsky with acute alarm. It seemed to him to threaten all that was best in Russian culture and personality. It left no place for the human heart, and, worst of all, it disturbed the balance between man and God, relegating God to a secondary position or no position at all.

Dostoevsky's distrust of rationality unmodified by feeling is most bitterly enunciated at the close of the book when the Underground Man attributes all his problems to his being a thinker, to the fact that he is obsessed with the idea:

> Leave us alone without books and we shall be lost and in confusion at once. We shall not know what to join to, what to cling to, what to love and what to hate, what to respect and what to despise. . . . We are still born, and for generations past have been begotten, not by living fathers. . . . Soon we shall contrive to be born somehow from an idea.

Some years later, in *Diary of a Writer*, Dostoevsky added a provocative postscript to his characterization of the Underground Man: "Everyone, as it were, wishes to revenge himself upon somebody for his nullity." This nullity and the alienation inseparable from it are the basic elements of the antiheroes who have become representative of twentieth-century man. Kafka's tortured "K" began here, as also did Camus' "stranger" and Ralph Ellison's "invisible man," to mention only a few. It is no accident that Walter Kaufmann called his book, which has become the standard fare of young readers, *Existentialism from Dostoevsky to Sartre.*

III.

There are excellent studies of Dostoevsky as a great creative artist, a psychologist, a philosopher of the human soul, and an apologist for Christianity (more specifically, Orthodoxy)—all of which he was. Our concern, however, will be limited to Dostoevsky as social critic and seer. He denounced and denounced again, with all the eloquence of his artistic power and moral conviction. And he saw into the future with certitude.

The novels of Turgenev in chronological order supply a running commentary on the times. They trace from 1850 to 1875 the major currents of Russian thought and a number of the movements—occasionally even events—precipitated by these currents. Turgenev thus filled the roles of reporter and of an omniscient editorial conscience, which saw and rendered judgment on the changing scene. With Dostoevsky it was different. He was in no sense a reporter. Dostoevsky was concerned primarily with the subjective experiences of individuals and secondarily with the forces serving as causal factors of these experiences. Furthermore, there is not the progression in his views of man and society which appears in Turgenev's books. The forces that influenced the spiritual history of Dostoevsky's characters did not change perceptibly between 1865, when he began *Crime and Punishment*, and 1880, when he completed *The Brothers Karamazov*. Dostoevsky hammers away at the same points until the relationship between certain of his views (as expressed by his characters) and what was happening in Russia becomes unmistakably clear.

The Underground Man is a key figure in the novels of Dostoevsky just as the "superfluous man" is the key figure in Turgenev's writings, but the methods they used in creating characters are quite different. Whereas Turgenev observed his characters externally, reporting upon them with the loving care of an artist, Dostoevsky forces his readers to accompany him into the recesses of personality. He makes us see and know more than we are accustomed to or feel we have a right to. With Dostoevsky the process of characterization involves an invasion of the soul. Even if it is not our purpose to deal with the subject irresistible to students of Dostoevsky—that is, the psychology of his characters, their motivations and errors, their spiritual tribulations, and their struggle from sin to salvation—it is necessary to approach the great novels knowing that at the center of each stands at least one character who embodies the essence of what Dostoevsky wrote the book to say. That character is either the Underground Man—a brooding intellectual, tortured by contradictions, sterile of spirit, a Faustian type but lacking Faust's humaneness—or his opposite, a man who, recognizing the limitations of reason, has elected to live by faith and to walk in the light of God's love. These two, poles apart, symbolize what Carlyle called "the Everlasting No" and "the Everlasting Yea." They are the antagonists in the great debate which constitutes the substance of all Dostoevsky's major works.

A reader with a predilection for modern detective fiction will find in *Crime and Punishment* a tantalizing variation to whet his appetite. But he will not proceed far without recognizing that in this novel there is a great deal more than an account of crime. Indeed, that "more" is the novel.

Since the plot of *Crime and Punishment* is the skeleton holding together the flesh of ideas, it is advisable to recall the bare outline. Rodion Raskolnikov, a university student of intelligence and fine feeling, has been driven by poverty to a condition of unhealthy introspection (the first stage in the making of an Underground Man), in which he dwells upon certain abstract ideas. In this condition he plans and carries through the murder of a repulsive, avaricious old pawnbroker for whose existence he can find no reason, and by accident also murders her stupid but well-meaning sister. He has intended to use whatever he might get from the old woman's hoarded treasures to meet his own pressing needs and those of his mother and sister, who have sacrificed to help him get an education. After committing the crime, however, he is too much disturbed to take advantage of the opportunity for theft. Although he is able by coincidence to make his way from the scene of the crime without leaving any clues, he begins immediately to be racked by an inner compulsion he had not foreseen, a shattering experience. The Greeks would have described him as a man haunted by the Furies of unavenged murder. The strain of this conflict, added to the frailty of body induced by long-continued undernourishment, makes him give way to a severe attack of fever accompanied by delirium.

Upon recovery he becomes so obsessed with his crime that his obsession determines his every word and act. At last he is impelled to confess, first to the prostitute Sonia and then to the authorities, who have in the meantime become suspicious of him because of his behavior and the views set forth in an article he had written. Sonia, daughter of the drunken Marmeladov, had become a prostitute in an effort to save from starvation the family of her weak-willed father. At the death of Marmeladov, the family descends into the lower depths of misery in which Raskolnikov, whose suffering makes him responsive to the sufferings of others, comes close to Sonia, the only human being able to understand and help him. When she finally persuades him to accept his penalty, he goes to Siberia, and she goes with him. Still unrepentant and unable to accept the necessity for punishment, Raskolnikov is eventually saved and regenerated by the two forces of suffering and love, in which Dostoevsky ardently believed. His rationality has been destructive, but the purity and faith of Sonia—the "amazing grace" available to those who desire it—is strong enough to bring him back from the lost world of those who are without love. The role of Sonia recalls the intercession of Margaret on behalf of Faust.

What is that "more" which was Dostoevsky's principal concern in the writing of *Crime and Punishment*? It is the answer to a question, Why did Raskolnikov, in no sense a criminal, with no violence in his nature, a faithful son and brother, sensitive to others' woes—why did he kill, kill not in anger or self-defense but with calculation? And having killed, why did he respond to the crime as he did?

To answer this question is not a simple matter, for Raskolnikov's motives were intricately blended. But Dostoevsky had no uncertainty about the basic premise he intended to set forth. He began to make his point clear in a conversation between the murderer and the examining magistrate, Porfiry Petrovich, who is almost certain that the young student is guilty, though he has no proof. He has read an article of Raskolnikov's published a couple of months earlier, in which, as Porfiry recalls, men are divided into two classifications:

> "Ordinary men have to live in submission, have no right to transgress the law, because . . . they are ordinary. But extraordi-

> nary men have a right to commit any crime and to transgress the law in any way, just because they are extraordinary. . . ."
>
> "That wasn't quite my contention," [Rodya] began. . . . "I don't contend that extraordinary people are always bound to commit breaches of morals. . . . I simply hinted that an 'extraordinary' man has the right— . . . an inner right to decide in his own conscience to overstep—certain obstacles . . . in case it is essential for the practical fulfilment of his idea. . . . I maintain that if the discoveries of Kepler and Newton could not have been made known except by sacrificing the lives of one, a dozen, a hundred, or more men, Newton would have had the right . . . to eliminate the dozen or the hundred men for the sake of making his discoveries known to the whole of humanity. . . . Then . . . I maintain in my article that . . . legislators and leaders of men, such as Lycurgus, Solon, Mahomet, Napoleon, and so on, were all without exception criminals, from the very fact that, making a new law, they transgressed the ancient one . . . and they did not stop short at bloodshed either, if that bloodshed . . . were of use to their cause. . . . I maintain that all great men or even men a little out of the common . . . must from their very nature be criminals. . . . Otherwise it's hard for them to get out of the common rut; . . . I only believe in my leading idea that men are *in general* divided by a law of nature into two categories, inferior [ordinary], that is . . . material that serves only to reproduce its kind, and men who have the gift or the talent to utter *a new word*. . . . The first category . . . are men conservative in temperament and law-abiding; they live to be controlled. . . . The second category all transgress the law; they are destroyers or disposed to destruction according to their capacities."

To all who are acquainted with the superman theory that Nietzsche developed in his *Zarathustra* and *The Will to Power*, these opinions of Raskolnikov's will sound familiar. They were not new when the novel was written, as Raskolnikov pointed out to his friend Razumihin, but Raskolnikov was the first to enunciate them with such clarity. Razumihin realized at once that there was something startling, terrible, about Raskolnikov's pronouncement. "What is really *original* in all this," he said, "and is exclusively your own, to my horror, is that you sanction bloodshed in the name of conscience, and . . . with such fanaticism." Whether readers are familiar with Nietzsche or not, the idea of bloodshed with fanaticism is no stranger to the twentieth century. It requires little imagination to visualize the incarnation of Raskolnikov's theories. Such "extraordinary" men as Lenin, Stalin, Hitler, and Mussolini have recently been "destroyers or disposed to destruction according to their capacities."

Having read Raskolnikov's article and listened to the author's exposition of it, Porfiry Petrovich begins to understand how the parts of the puzzle fit together. "When you were writing your article," he asks, "surely you couldn't have helped . . . fancying yourself . . . just a little, an 'extraordinary' man, uttering a *new word* in your sense?" Raskolnikov "answers drily," "Allow me to observe that I don't consider myself a Mahomet or a Napoleon, nor any personage of that kind."

Was he sincere in his denial? Rodya himself did not know, even at that excruciating moment when, his burden having become too heavy to bear alone, he went to Sonia to make his confession. When the "terrible idea" of the murder overwhelmed her, she asked him how he could have brought himself to commit such a deed. It must have been, she said, because he wanted to help his mother or because he was hungry. But Rodya is forced to admit that neither of these was his motive:

> "What if it were really that?" he said, as though reaching a conclusion. "Yes, that's what it was! I wanted to become a Napoleon, that is why I killed her. . . . Do you understand now? . . .
>
> "It was like this: I asked myself . . . what if Napoleon, for instance, had happened to be in my place, and if he had not had Toulon or Egypt nor the passage of Mont Blanc to begin his career with, but instead . . . there had simply been some ridiculous old hag . . . who had to be murdered too to get money from her trunk (for his career, you understand). Well, would he have brought himself to that, if there had been no other means? . . . I guessed at last . . . that it would not have given him the least pang. . . . Well,

> I too . . . left off thinking about it . . . murdered her, following his example. And that's exactly how it was!"

He tells Sonia he had come to the realization that wealth, power, and authority belong to the men who seize them. "There is only one thing, one thing needful: one has only to dare. . . . I . . . wanted to have the daring . . . and I killed her." It was not to gain money or power or to help mankind that he committed the murder. An altogether different idea had taken possession of his mind, and at last he explains to Sonia exactly what that idea was: "I wanted to find out then and quickly whether I was a louse like everybody else or a man. Whether I can step over barriers or not, whether I am a trembling creature or whether I have the *right.*"

Thus Dostoevsky explained the reason behind the crime—not poverty and hunger, not the desire to help his mother and sister or to finish his education (though all of these had an influence upon Rodya)—but the determination to discover whether or not he is "extraordinary." This is the motive which made Rodya a murderer.

As Dostoevsky has developed his parable, there is an unbreakable connection between the cause of the crime and one reason (not the only reason, to be sure, but a very important one, nonetheless) Rodya suffers so terribly after committing the act. This reason is not, as the moralists would like to suggest, because good, being stronger, gained the ascendancy over evil in his soul by a process of inevitable magnetism. On the contrary, Rodya suffers because he is forced to recognize that he is not a Napoleon and that he does not have "the *right.*" He has gambled everything in the effort to prove to himself that he is an extraordinary man, and he has lost. Even in the heart-breaking scene just before he goes to make his official confession, when he explains to his sister Dounia what he has done, he still cannot accept the view that his deed was evil:

> "Crime? What crime?" he cried in sudden fury. "That I killed a

> vile noxious insect, an old pawnbroker woman, of use to no one! . . . Killing her was atonement for forty sins. . . . Only now I see clearly the imbecility of my cowardice, now that I have decided to face this superfluous disgrace. . . . I couldn't carry out even the first step, because I am contemptible, that's what's the matter!"

He hates himself for his weakness, for what he called "the vulgarity" and "abjectness." He killed for a principle, and in his failure he killed the principle itself ("The old woman . . . is not what matters") and precipitated himself into a vacuum. Rodion Raskolnikov has to bear the discovery that he is not a superman. He is only Hamlet aspiring to be Napoleon but forever prevented from realizing his hopes because he is "an aesthetic louse."

What is behind all this confusion and error, this crime and suffering and needless waste? Why does Rodion Raskolnikov commit this crime and sentence himself to the desolation of Siberia, the physical counterpart of the desolation within his soul? Because he is a member of the intelligentsia, said Dostoevsky. Because he thinks too much. Because he attempts to live by reason alone. Because, being a thinker, he cuts himself off from the primary sources: the soil, the people, the Orthodox creed, the Russian God! Because—perhaps worst of all—he has been infected by the noxious poison of western European thought. He is the victim of books and theories, of the German idealists, the French socialists, the German and English romanticists, and all the intellectual impedimenta which get in the way of faith. In April, 1878, Dostoevsky wrote a letter to a group of Moscow students, in which he graphically summarized his views:

> The younger generation has broken with *the people* . . . and with society. . . . The younger generation lives in dreams, follows foreign teaching, cares to know nothing that concerns Russia, aspires, rather, to instruct the fatherland. Consequently it is today *beyond all doubt* that our younger generation is become the prey of one or other of those political parties which influence it wholly from outside.

Dostoevsky believed that Raskolnikov sold his soul to the devil as certainly as Faust did, his reward being not the beautiful and virtuous Margaret but the phantom of rationality, an alluring but hollow ghost. Led astray by this empty spirit, he dared, like Clytemnestra, to play at being God. The Greeks considered that the most deadly sin, one the gods could not excuse, was *hubris*, the arrogance of the man or woman who appropriated for himself too much power or too many rights. So Clytemnestra *presumed*, when she took the life of Agamemnon, a decision which belonged to the Fates. So Creon *presumed* when he abrogated the celestial laws and punished Antigone for fidelity to the dictates of the gods. So Raskolnikov *presumed* when, having been turned to atheism by intellectuality and the fatal contagion from the West, he took upon himself the power of decision and action beyond the rights of man.

Dostoevsky was tireless in his attacks upon the intelligentsia, because he was convinced that belonging to that group precluded having any remnant of religious faith. Rationality and atheism were to him inseparable. The intelligentsia, moreover, meant to him Nihilism, a scourge from which Russia must be cleansed. He made no secret of the fact that *Crime and Punishment* was written as an antidote and a solemn warning. This is what our Holy Russia will come to, he said over and over again, if the Nihilists are not held in check. These young men, without feelings, all head and no heart, nourished on foreign philosophy and science, will become Frankensteins to destroy us. And they will not stop with smashing the skulls of greedy women.

Dostoevsky was much excited, and probably gratified in a grim way, when just before the appearance of the first installment of *Crime and Punishment*, he read in the newspapers an account of the murder of a moneylender by a young Moscow student under circumstances astonishingly like those he had depicted in his novel. Then he knew he was justified in his worst presentiments. These godless monsters would start by destroying old women and proceed on an ascending scale of violence. Some would fire upon the Czar (as one student did in April, 1866). They would not stop until they had demolished the most sacred of Russia's institutions and traditions; nothing would be inviolate. Although he had already expressed the essence of his convictions in *Notes from Underground* and was to give them further embodiment in *The Possessed* and in the character Ivan Karamazov, Dostoevsky used Raskolnikov as his first dramatic retort to Turgenev's *Fathers and Sons*. You do not know what to think of Bazarov? he shouted. Then look at young Raskolnikov! Here is your Bazarov in action. Bazarov's scalpel has become an axe, a sinister blade, with which to kill.

As if unable to bring himself to conclude the book without adding a postscript of warning and prophecy, Dostoevsky included in the epilogue one final warning to accent all the earlier ones. At this point, Raskolnikov, having taken upon himself the burden of paying for the murder he had committed, is in prison, but not yet repentant. The conflict still persisting between his intellect and his better feelings coupled with the privations of his former life have again made him ill. When he begins to recover, he still remembers the nightmares he had while he was delirious. In particular, he remembers a frightful dream about a plague which swept over the whole earth. Some strange new microbes were causing the disease, microbes which had intelligence and will. With a few exceptions, all mankind was to be wiped out; when the microbes attacked, men "became at once mad and furious":

> But never had men considered themselves so intellectual and so completely in possession of the truth as these sufferers, never had they considered their decisions, their scientific conclusions, their moral convictions so infallible. Whole villages, whole towns and people went mad from the infection. All were excited and did not understand one another. Each thought that he alone had the truth and was wretched looking at the others, beat himself on the breast, wept, and wrung his hands. They did not know how to judge and could not agree what to consider evil and what good: they did not

> know whom to blame, whom to justify. Men killed each other in a sort of senseless spite. They gathered together in armies against one another, but even on the march the armies would begin attacking each other. . . . All men and all things were involved in destruction.

Dostoevsky has here written the prologue to the half-mad world of Franz Kafka, the plague-ridden city of Albert Camus, the nightmare monstrosities of George Orwell's *1984*, and Arthur Koestler's *Darkness at Noon*; the prologue to the gas chambers at Buchenwald, the death march at Bataan, the holocaust at Hiroshima, the cold war, and the deaths that come too soon to too many. Here is anticipated what Archibald MacLeish called "the terrors that lurk by night" in the lands where the people create their own oppressors. Dostoevsky had no difficulty deciding "what to consider evil and what good." Excessive rationalism and Nihilism were the plague, and the presumption they engendered was the crime.

Why did Rodya react as he did after he committed the crime? One reason has already been explained—his melancholy recognition that he was a "louse" and not an "extraordinary" man. But there is another, more important reason, one which is absolutely basic to Dostoevsky's view of human nature. Almost immediately after the murder, Rodya begins to feel that he has cut himself off from humanity. "A gloomy sensation of agonizing, everlasting solitude and remoteness, took conscious form in his soul." He becomes isolated by the recognition of what he has done, not to the two old women, but to himself. At times it is imperative for him to be alone, for only thus can external conditions match the condition of his spirit. And yet in the midst of isolation he often feels a desperate need to establish some kind of contact with others. Although he is slow to feel remorse for his crime or even to acknowledge that it was a crime, he quickly becomes aware that he cannot live with the solitary knowledge of it eating away at his consciousness. As Dostoevsky himself in prison and in Siberia had felt "like a slice cut from the loaf," so Raskolnikov feels as a result of his crime like a man shut in behind a wall of ice. He cannot get through the wall even to his mother and sister. When he tries to talk to them: "Again that awful sensation he had known of late passed with deadly chill over his soul. Again it became suddenly plain and perceptible to him that . . . he would never again be able to *speak* of anything to anyone." When his mother tries to ask him about the events of his recent past, he realizes that those events no longer have reality for him. "I seem to be looking at you from a thousand miles away," he says. He almost hates his mother and sister because of the guilty secret he dares not share. At one point he longs to tell his sister Dounia the truth: "There was an instant when he had longed to take her in his arms and *say good-bye* to her, and even to *tell* her, but he had not dared even to touch her hand," for he feared that "afterwards she may shudder when she remembers that I embraced her." This sense of the unendurability of spiritual solitude is one of Dostoevsky's recurrent theories. And this condition of being excluded from the human race is the cost to Rodya of his crime; this is the absolute punishment.

It is not so much the fact that he has committed a crime which cuts Rodya off from others as the fact that it was a crime of the intellect. It was committed because of a theory, and as a result Rodya finds himself in a separate category from other criminals. Even in prison, where he would have least of all expected to find himself isolated, the wall is impenetrable.

> What surprised him most of all was the terrible impossible gulf that lay between him and all the rest. . . . He was disliked and avoided by everyone; they even began to hate him at last. . . .
>
> The second week in Lent, his turn came to take the sacrament with his gang. He went to church and prayed with the others. A quarrel broke out one day, he did not know how. All fell on him at once in a fury.
>
> "You're an infidel! You don't believe in God," they shouted. "You ought to be killed."

The convicts, however, are mistaken about Rodya and his belief in God. They do not know that when he talked with Sonia's little sister, Polenka, he asked her to pray for him, identifying himself when he told Polenka to say on his behalf, "'And Thy servant Rodion,' nothing more." They do not know that when Porfiry was probing into his theories and asked whether he believed in God, Rodya replied with a firm "I do." This affirmation, however, is integral to Rodya's character and to Dostoevsky's argument in *Crime and Punishment*.

In his isolation Raskolnikov is able to establish contact with only two people, both of whom are in a sense extensions of his own personality and both of whom are essential to the rounding out of the parable. One is the evil man Svidrigailov, and the other the good woman (though a prostitute) Sonia. Here again are the personifications of the Everlasting No and the Everlasting Yea.

Svidrigailov is calculation and self-will carried to the extreme. He is not an intellectual, and yet he is intelligent and smart in a conniving way. Acknowledging no restraints and no law, he has lived entirely for his own gratification. Recognizing no obligations, he has devoted himself to the satisfaction of his own desires. But unfortunately for his comfort, after having lived by a hedonistic code, having indulged in lust, and having tried both good and evil (between which he can make no distinction), he discovers that he actually has no desires. And to be without desire is to be dead. Life is hollow for him. He moves about in a vacuum, trying in vain to find something to titillate his senses, swaying with the wind, doing and feeling nothing. Bereft of passion, even of hope, he is a limb lopped off the body of life. Like the suicides in Dante's *Inferno*, he has turned into a petrified stump which can put forth neither branches nor any but poisoned fruit. In his dream the child he has rescued from the cold changes until her face is that of a harlot. The man is literally worn out with boredom. Even the concept of eternity presents him with nothing more than an image of black spiders. He is beyond redemption.

Svidrigailov is Dostoevsky's strongest statement in *Crime and Punishment* about the danger of willfulness, lack of feeling, and sterile rationality. He is incapable of the enthusiasm of the young liberals (whom Dostoevsky called "dullards . . . half-animate abortions, conceited, half-educated coxcombs") or of the Nihilists who found a sadistic satisfaction in destruction. He is the total Nihilist, the man who cares for nothing and is destroyed by his noncommitment, the man lost to both humanity and God. Dostoevsky was positive that man cannot survive in a vacuum. Therefore Svidrigailov cannot live, having lost touch with the essence of life. When he kills himself—and he approaches even his suicide with mockery—he does not really change his condition, for he is already dead. From this fate Raskolnikov is saved (though Svidrigailov rightly felt that the two of them had something in common), because he is still capable of feeling—of experiencing need, desire, and hope; because, as he learned in the wilderness of Siberia, he is still capable of loving and being loved. In short, because he believes in God.

The element in Raskolnikov's character which enables him to be regenerated is personified in Sonia, who stands at the opposite extreme from Svidrigailov. Driven by the necessity of providing some livelihood for her drunken father and his destitute family, she had given herself up to prostitution. But the unselfish profanation of her body has left no stain upon her soul. Raskolnikov recognizes in her one who will be able to understand and strengthen him, because she has experienced evil but has remained pure. Sonia is one of the meek who make no demands upon life but somehow manage to survive its blows by clinging to a transcendent faith. It is enough for her to know—and she does know—that a God who is good exists. When Raskolnikov tries to think what her probable end will be, he wonders whether she expects a miracle to save her. To his surprise he discovers that she prays "to God a great deal." But he does not see how God can help her and says as much. "What should I be without God?" she replies in alarm. "And what does God do for you?"

he asks. Then comes her answer, spoken with the conviction of her total being: "God does everything."

Critics of Dostoevsky who condemn him for having chosen a prostitute as the noblest woman character he was ever to create are evidently forgetful of the New Testament words: "This is my body which I have given for you." Sonia's whole life is a sacrifice and at the same time a sacrament. The father who had made it necessary for her to fulfill his responsibilities is cradled in her arms when he dies. She can never think of sparing herself as long as there are children to be fed. When she reads the story of Lazarus to Rodya at his bidding, she reads as one transfigured, for she believes with all her soul in the promise of which Lazarus had received an intimation. When Rodya is impelled to make his awful confession to her, she thinks of nothing but his suffering. He does not need to ask her forgiveness, for she neither feels nor utters any condemnation. But she is none the less determined that he should begin to work his way up from the abyss of evil into which he has fallen. When Raskolnikov is in prison, when she is living her promise of eternal fidelity to him, he notices with surprise the way Sonia affects others. Even the most hardened criminals accept her visits to the prison as if they are a benediction. When she smiles at them, the smile goes like the sun into their hearts. They ask for her advice and seek her help when they are ill. "Little mother Sofya," they say, "you are our dear, good, little mother." And never once does Sonia ask anything for herself.

Sonia incarnates the qualities lacking in the haughty intellectuals, "the young people carried away by their own wit," as the novelist called them. Here is none of the ruthlessness of the Nihilists, no will to destroy and no violent rejection of old values. Humility, sympathy, unselfishness, and belief in the goodness of man and the goodness of God—these are the links with which she forges her soul. She gives her body, but her mind and her heart are her own, and she makes them into shining armor. Her soul with all the warmth which radiates from it is the instrument by which Raskolnikov can be saved. When he first seeks her out to ease the loneliness imposed by his evil deed, he drops to the ground and kisses her foot, thus bowing down, as he says, "to all the suffering of humanity." Later, because her influence is a power too strong for him to resist, he follows her command to "stand at the crossroads, first kiss the earth which you have defiled and then bow down to all the world" to confess. However, not until she has followed him to Siberia, until she is ill and alone but continues to think only of him, not until he knows for all time that she will give everything and asks nothing from him in return—only then does he fully understand her spirit. Then the miracle occurs: "How it happened he did not know. But all at once something seemed to seize him and fling him at her feet. He wept and threw his arms around her knees. . . . She knew . . . that at last the moment had come." Later, as Raskolnikov thinks of the past and the future, "he could not have analyzed anything consciously; he was simply feeling. Life had stepped into the place of theory."

This Rodya who can at last feel the love of God through the intercession of human love is the same Rodya who, when he was trying to nerve himself to commit murder, had had nightmare dreams of a horse being beaten to death by its master. This is the Rodya who gave the few kopecks he had to the Marmeladovs when he was starving and who instantaneously recognized Sonia for what she truly was. This is the Rodya who did in fact have something in common with Svidrigailov, but much more in common with Sonia. He is a man whose heart is finally stronger than his rationality.

One of the most memorable achievements of the novel is the depiction of poverty and its effects. "And do you know, Sonia, that low ceilings and tiny rooms cramp the soul and the mind?" Raskolnikov said. Nowhere else in the literature dealing with "poor folk" has the unrelieved desolation of the have-nots been more poignantly etched than in the funeral feast after the death of Marmeladov or in the scene of the dying Katerina, his wife. Even in her last moments Katerina goes out into the street with her children to dance and beg. This is injustice that demands relief. These are the people, the novelist was certain, whom God loves best, because none of the material goods of life get in the way of their need of Him. These are the people whose sufferings had created a revolution in France and would have to be relieved in Russia, for the grapes of wrath were growing for the harvest.

But Dostoevsky was not primarily concerned with poverty of body or the revolution of the poor. *Crime and Punishment* is an arraignment of that poverty of spirit which makes men who see themselves as supermen dare to challenge God. It is a prophecy of the revolution the Nihilists proposed, to destroy everything. The crime is intellectual arrogance, the "will to power." The cause is the divorce of reason from feeling. And the punishment? Dostoevsky presented it in the suffering of Raskolnikov and the death of Svidrigailov. The twentieth century has seen it in the suffering of all mankind.

IV.

In many ways the most fascinating and certainly the most intangible of Dostoevsky's works is his novel *The Idiot*. Although this novel contributes little to the author's interpretation of events and attitudes in his beloved country, certain details within it throw further light upon some of the arguments advanced in *Crime and Punishment*. These details have small relation either to the main character or the main plot, but were obviously planted in the novel for propaganda purposes. *The Idiot* has been called, among other things, the "noblest" of all the literature of the Slavophiles. But many of the Slavophile tenets expressed in the book are out of place. They mar the artistic unity of the novel and furnish a disappointing indication of the limits to which Dostoevsky was willing to go to discredit those whose view of Russia differed from his. In *The Idiot* are to be found some of the most blatant of the author's denunciatory statements; here he is anti-rational, anti-liberal, anti-socialist, anti-Catholic, anti-foreign, and anti-western European. This vitriolic brew keeps seething over and disfiguring the main substance of the novel.

It is unlikely that in writing *The Idiot* Dostoevsky had any idea of suggesting that he had found a leader for Russia, because he knew from the outset that the type of character he wanted to portray came too close to perfection to be convincing or finally useful. He stated his purpose for the book in a letter to his favorite niece: "The basic idea is the representation of a truly perfect and noble man. And this is more difficult than anything else in the world, particularly nowadays. All writers, not ours alone but foreigners also, who have sought to represent Absolute Beauty, were unequal to the task." He mentioned that he had set himself a difficult problem because of the nature and circumstances of his hero. In spite of difficulties, however, it was his aim in *The Idiot* to make a study of goodness which should serve as a complement and a contrast to the brilliant exposition of evil in *Crime and Punishment.*

The "idiot" is Prince Myshkin, a young man of noble lineage, who has been afflicted all his life by epilepsy, which has damaged his health and, to an extent, his mental faculties. At the beginning of the novel, having undergone a cure, he comes back from Switzerland to Russia to live on a small inheritance. He is not like other men; he is as simple as a child, and his nature is the essence of the meekness and the sweet, gentle dignity of the Christian ideal. To the hardness of the world, its vanity, mockery, and cruelty, he offers a naïve humility and an unwavering expectation of good.

Because of his open heart, within a short time after his return he becomes intimately involved in the lives of a number of people he had not known before. Even when his purity amazes them and provokes them to ridicule, it is too strong for them; he calls forth respect mingled with affection from even the most cynical and dissolute. Two passionate women fall in love with him. Aglaia Epanchin is the capricious young daughter of a general, and Nastasya Filipovna, having been the unwilling mistress of a man she hated, is tortured by self-pity and the loss of her ideal of chastity. Both women love tumultuously and with the ambivalence of many Dostoevsky characters. Although the gentle prince loves both of them, he decides that Nastasya has the greater need of him and prepares to marry her. At the last moment she turns aside from the marriage, perhaps because she cannot endure the goodness of Myshkin, perhaps because she knows she will destroy him. She surrenders, instead, to another suitor, the evil Rogozhin, a somewhat humanized Svidrigailov. Maddened by jealousy and knowing he can possess her in no other way, Rogozhin murders Nastasya, as both she and Myshkin had foreseen that he would. The book ends with the two men keeping vigil by the body of the dead woman, Myshkin attempting to comfort the savage Rogozhin whose passions have destroyed his sanity. But the prince, also, has had too much to bear; he has returned to a state of mental and physical collapse. The good man appears once more to be only an "idiot."

This outline does not begin to suggest the multiplicity of incidents and characters with which the novel is crowded. One group of ill-assorted and bad-mannered young men move through its scenes with no other function than to highlight the character of Prince Myshkin and to enable Dostoevsky to make protest after protest against Nihilism. These tag ends of humanity are given to noisy expounding of what they regard as idealism, but Dostoevsky revealed them as so disorganized, shabby, and boisterous, so sniveling and mean that their "idealism," which deserves better treatment, appears disgusting and false. As Ernest Simmons aptly says, "Like some prince out of a fairy tale, Myshkin waves his spiritual wand, and these youthful devils of revolutionary destruction are transformed into docile creatures, confounded by his moral perfection."[6] But even though Myshkin vanquishes these young Nihilists, he does not do so until Dostoevsky has had plentiful opportunities to lash out at them. For ex-

[6] *Dostoevsky*, 175.

ample, speaking through one of the minor characters, Dostoevsky called them: "Lunatics! Vain creatures! They don't believe in God, they don't believe in Christ! Why, you are so eaten up with pride and vanity that you'll end by eating up one another." Another character, Yevgeny Pavlovitch, also speaks for the author:

> "I am attacking Russian Liberalism, and I repeat again I attack it just for the reason that the Russian Liberal is not a Russian Liberal, but an un-Russian Liberal. . . .
>
> ". . . everything they have done and are doing is absolutely non-national." . . .
>
> "What is Liberalism . . . but an attack . . . on the established order of things? . . . Well, the fact is that Russian Liberalism is not an attack on the existing order of things, but is an attack on the very essence of things . . . not on the Russian regime, but on Russia itself. My Liberal goes so far as to deny even Russia itself, that is, he hates and beats his own mother."

So much, Dostoevsky protested, for the Westerners! So much for the socialists; "Proudhon arrived at the right of might." So much for the coming of "progress": "I should say [our age] of steamers and railways, but I say vices and railways." So much for anyone who dares criticize Holy Russia!

In the final consideration, however, it is not the scraggly young Nihilists who provoke the major blast of the novel. On the contrary, the saintly "idiot" himself suddenly forgets his mildness and leaps on the soapbox, with a screech in his voice and a fanatic light in his eye. It is ironic that Dostoevsky, who should have been above the violation of his magnificent creative power, used his "perfect and noble man" as spokesman for one of the most virulent invectives to be found anywhere in his writings—his attack on Catholicism, which he reviled above everything else in western European civilization:

> "Catholicism is as good as an unchristian religion!" . . . Myshkin began. . . .

"And . . . Roman Catholicism is even worse than atheism itself, in my opinion! . . . Atheism only preaches a negation, but Catholicism goes further: it preaches a distorted Christ, a Christ calumniated and defamed by themselves, the opposite of Christ! It preaches the Anti-christ. . . . To my thinking Roman Catholicism is not even a religion, but simply the continuation of the Western Roman Empire. . . . Atheism has sprung from Roman Catholicism itself. . . .

"Why, socialism too springs from Catholicism and the Catholic idea! Like its brother atheism, it comes from despair in opposition to Catholicism on the moral side, to replace the lost moral power of religion, to quench the spiritual thirst of parched humanity, and to save them not by Christ but also by violence. . . . Our Christ whom we have kept and they have never known must shine forth and vanquish the West. Not letting ourselves be slavishly caught by the wiles of the Jesuits, but carrying our Russian civilization to them, we ought to stand before them."

It is something of a shock to discover that Dostoevsky's concept of the "perfect man" includes the imperative that he must be as passionate and vocal in his Slavophilism as the author was. Or perhaps the real shock comes with the recognition that Dostoevsky, who seemed at times in his later writings to have been illuminated by a divine fire, was not above scorching the rapturous evocation of faith with the flame of ugly diatribe.

Truly, Dostoevsky believed in Russian Orthodoxy as holding the key to the future harmony and well-being, not only of "Holy Mother" Russia, but of all the world. Yet he was also aware of a quality in the Russian character which offered a hazard to the realization of that dream of universal concord. A statement placed at the conclusion of Myshkin's scalding outburst against Roman Catholicism is of special interest to modern readers who cannot understand what is to them the incredible phenomenon of the devotion to Communism of a segment of the Russian people:

If one of us . . . becomes an atheist, he's sure to clamor for the

> extirpation of belief in God by force, that is, by the sword. . . . It's easier for a Russian to become an atheist than for anyone else in the world. And Russians do not merely become atheists, but they invariably BELIEVE in atheism, as though it were a new religion, without noticing that they are putting faith in a negation. So great is our craving!

Important as the polemical passages of *The Idiot* obviously were to Dostoevsky, they are the least impressive part of the novel. The real interest lies in the characters whose souls are the battleground for good and evil and also in the impression the book conveys that in writing it Dostoevsky was pursuing his private quest for the Grail. The book is delicately touched with wistfulness, an evanescent sense of loss, and a reluctant recognition that paradise is beyond the reach of man. *The Idiot* has more variety in character types than is customary in Dostoevsky's novels. Madame Epanchin, for instance, is a rarity among Dostoevsky characters, a woman with a loud bark but a warm heart, whose actions are better than her pronouncements, and who often amuses the reader. Her two older daughters are well-balanced young women, neither neurotic nor introspective, good humored, competent, and altogether sensible. It is pleasant to discover that Dostoevsky could portray women who do not lurch from one emotional crisis to another. Their younger sister, Aglaia, is more what one expects. Selfish, fickle, and introvertive, she does not understand herself and causes confusion if not calamity. But she is so spontaneous and gay that people cannot avoid loving her, and her youthfulness—a matter of spirit rather than years (a characteristic she shares with her mother)—makes her attractive. The members of the Ivolgin family, with the exception of the buffoon husband and father who lives in a nonexistent world where he is always the only important actor, are ordinary people, free from the usual Dostoevskian complications. Kolya—the merry, high-spirited boy who is also kind and honest—is probably the most appealing adolescent in all of Dostoevsky's novels.

Nastasya is, of all the women created by Dostoevsky, the one who comes closest to being a tragic figure. Her beautiful face is a mask which scarcely hides a soul ravaged by disappointment and self-laceration. She is lacerated by the conflict between her own essential purity and the impurities of the world she has been forced to live in. Goaded as she is by this conflict, she has taken on the tinge of evil, and she no longer knows who or what she really is. Myshkin senses her need to have her faith in herself and others restored, and he offers her the beatitude of a Christ-like love. But the wounds are too deep and they have become infected. Nastasya cannot be saved.

The house Dostoevsky had in mind as the home of Rogozhin still stands on a street in Leningrad. It has been diminished by the encroachment of other buildings, but it still has the closed, dark appearance which made it the perfect background for a man whose soul was as closed and dark as his house. It is easy to imagine Rogozhin coming stealthily through its doors to lose himself in the crowd on the street. Occasionally the crowd opens, and there are his eyes with the malignant stare—eyes impossible to escape. Not even Myshkin can escape. An epileptic seizure saves his body from Rogozhin's knife, and the shield of his innocence protects Myshkin's soul. But Rogozhin and the evil he represents are too much for Myshkin's mind to cope with.

Some of the most vividly pictorial scenes Dostoevsky ever drew involve Nastasya, Myshkin, and Rogozhin. The moment when Nastasya throws into the fire the huge pile of ruble notes with which Rogozhin has just bought her and taunts one of her other suitors to take the notes out with his bare hand is one of these unforgettable scenes. The scene of Rogozhin emerging from the stairway niche with his gleaming blade ready to plunge into the body of the approaching Myshkin is also unforgettable. And perhaps most memorable of all is the scene in which the ubiquity of Rogozhin's eyes at last compels Nastasya, in her wedding finery, to join him for a fatal Walpurgis Night.

The Idiot is finally, of course, only a variegated frame for the character of the "idiot" himself, and for the study of his relation to others. There is a luminosity about him which sets him apart from other idealized characters in literature. Don Quixote, for example, no matter how firmly his eyes may be fixed on the stars, has his feet in the mud. This is not so with Prince Myshkin. The mud of life never touches him. The sordidness and misery in the book fall away from the prince—and from the reader, too, as he is carried along by the power of Myshkin's purity. This purity is not so much an armor standing between Myshkin and the world as it is a light which radiates from within. A link, no doubt, exists between the "idiot" and the "holy fool" of Russian folk tales, but there is a significant difference. The holy fool is good because he is a child in mind—an incomplete personality. Myshkin's goodness, however, is the essence of his personality. Whereas the innocence of the one is probably a result of biological accident, the innocence of the other is the primary factor in his identity.

Myshkin's qualities are shown in contrast to the vanity and pride of the Epanchins, the Babbittry of Ganya Ivolgin, the impotent fury of the dying young rebel Ippolit, the cruel caprice of Nastasya, the black passion of Rogozhin, and also in contrast to the sullenness of the Underground Men and the raucous iconoclasm of the Nihilists. It would not be accurate to say that the prince is the antithesis of Rodya in *Crime and Punishment*, for kindness, generosity, and humility are basic elements in Rodya's character, too. Dostoevsky saw Rodya as one whose personality has been twisted by too much thought. Myshkin, on the other hand, is the man of feeling. In place of Rodya's analytical bent Myshkin has intuition, and in place of Rodya's intellectual arrogance Myshkin has compassion. Myshkin has the same simplicity which Dostoevsky attributed to "the people." His heart is bound to essential things—nature, children, and the poor and wretched. His hand and his heart reach out in love.

The Idiot is a parable with blurred outlines. It is prevented from being a great work of art by its prolixity and by the failure of its amorphous and disparate elements to fuse harmoniously.

But it is an eloquent and tragic drama of the human spirit. When it ends with the sheet-covered body of Nastasya spread out on the black sofa, with only the raven cloud of her hair still somehow alive, we see that the blazing eyes of Rogozhin have become dull and the fair face of Myshkin is now specter white. Good and evil have joined forces. Neither has won. What did Dostoevsky mean to tell us? That goodness is defeated by its own nature? That human society is not ready, and perhaps never will be ready, for goodness? We cannot be sure, and probably he did not himself quite know. But when he wrote *The Idiot*, he was convinced of one thing—that travail and anguish are the lot of mankind and there is no sure or easy triumph for the human soul.

VII/ THE POSSESSED AND THE SAVIORS

IN NOVEMBER, 1869, the weighted body of a young man was found in a pond on the grounds of the Moscow Agricultural Academy. His murderer was subsequently discovered to be the anarchist Nechaev. This event supplied Dostoevsky with the spark which kindled to flame his feverish distrust and fear of the radicals who would, he was sure, bring incalculable harm to his country. For years this fire within him had been almost ready to ignite. It caused him to analyze the Underground Man, a product of rationality in opposition to feeling. Then it led him to Raskolnikov (*Crime and Punishment*), who tried to prove himself a superman so that he might use the superman's "right" to make his own rules. Raskolnikov failed in his attempt because he had a heart capable of being saved. But Svidrigailov, all head and no heart, stood outside both good and evil. Dostoevsky was convinced that this was the position of all revolutionaries.

In 1867, Dostoevsky was in Geneva when the Congress of the League of Peace and Freedom convened there. His observations of Bakunin and some of his cohorts in action at the Congress fanned the smouldering flames of the author's distrust. With the corpse of young Ivanov as proof of the violence resulting from the spirit of anarchy, Dostoevsky no longer hesitated to say what he felt he must say on the subject of revolution. In his *Diary of a Writer* several years later he stated what his purpose had been: "I meant to put this question and to answer it as clearly as possible in the form of a novel: how, in our contemporaneous, transitional and peculiar society, are the Nechaevs, not Nechaev himself, made possible? And how does it happen that these Nechaevs eventually manage to enlist followers?"

The answers are to be found in that chaotic outpouring, *The Possessed*, a book too often passed over because of its massive proportions and diffuse subject matter. In this book the views which animated Raskolnikov, causing him to commit murder, are shown on a broader scale. As E. H. Carr has observed: "The ethical theory which, individually, produced the crime of Raskolnikov, leads socially to revolution. The Raskolnikov of private life is the Nihilist of politics."[1] Such, at least, was Dostoevsky's conviction.

I.

The novelist always maintained that he knew nothing about the Nechaev case beyond what he read in the newspapers and that his portrayal of Nechaev in the character of the "possessed" Pyotr Verkhovensky was entirely his own creation. But he had more intimate information than this. Shortly before the details of the case appeared in the Russian press, the Dostoevskys, staying in Dresden, were visited by the novelist's brother-in-law, a young man who had been a fellow student in the same academy with Ivanov. The author must have learned a good deal from this young man about the personalities and attitudes of the students in the academy. When the crime was publicized, it confirmed his gloomiest expectations regarding the Nihilists. It provided the climax for a novel intended to expose and denounce the activities of the revolutionaries. A decade earlier, in *Fathers and Sons*, Turgenev had introduced the Nihilists in the person of Bazarov, to whom he gave at times a somewhat grudging admiration. However, Dostoevsky, incapable of Turgenev's objectivity and seeing only the evils of Nihilism, was determined in *The Possessed* to show it up for what he believed it to be. He saw it as a threat to everything he held most dear in Russia and to everything he dreamed that Russia might some day become.

To find any reasoned, consistent political theory in *The Possessed* is impossible. In his approach to the issues of the novel, Dostoevsky exhibits the same dualism frequently manifest in his characterizations. But his complexity may be one of the marks

[1] *Dostoevsky*, 218.

of his genius. Out of the indignation and apprehension which supplied the material for *The Possessed* he compounded a remarkable mixture, adding the bitterness of satire and the pungency of prophecy. He made a number of false assumptions and errors in deduction, but the most striking thing about many of his seeming errors is that the passing of time has proved them not to have been erroneous at all.

When Dostoevsky wrote *The Possessed* he considered it "a historical study." In this appraisal, however, he was wide of the mark. The Nechaev case was not typical of radical activities in his time; in fact, it produced a nearly universal sense of outrage. The offenders—except for Nechaev himself, too much a professional criminal to get caught—were summarily brought to justice.[2] The book was, in truth, a prophetic study. It was necessary to wait until after the Revolution to perceive the extent of Dostoevsky's almost clairvoyant vision.

In *The Possessed,* Dostoevsky used three characters to hold up the main framework of the argument. Each of the three is clearly individualized, but each is also a basic symbol. The elderly Stepan Verkhovensky represents the liberalism of the West, which Dostoevsky regarded as confused and effete, and he was cursed with Rudinism, that is, he was all hollow theory with no substance. Stepan's son, Pyotr Verkhovensky, stands for Nechaev, or Nihilism carried to the extreme form Dostoevsky believed it would assume. The third character, Nikolay Stavrogin, is the pupil of the first and the idol of the second. He is another—but far more imposing—Svidrigailov, contaminated by the influence of the West and enervated by separation from the Russian people and the Russian God. He is the atheist Dostoevsky feared the Russian intellectual would become. All are "possessed"—Stepan by liberalism (or, more exactly, his idea of liberalism), Pyotr by Nihilism, and Stavrogin by skepticism and negation.

The novel begins with an attack upon the idealists of the 1840's —that is, the period dominated by Belinsky and Herzen and also

[2] Nechaev was apprehended and imprisoned some time later.

the period during which the novelist himself had belonged to the Petrashevsky circle. Since most of the thinkers and idealists of this period drew their inspiration from the West, the novelist now associated them with the materialism, the bourgeois morality, the atheism, and the political unrest—everything he detested about western Europe. It has been pointed out earlier that Dostoevsky felt guilty in later life because he had participated even passively in the liberal movements of his youth. He did not resent his arrest and the harrowing experiences of the ten years of imprisonment and exile, and he blamed himself rather than the system by which he had been victimized. It is not strange, therefore, that he considered the revolutionary activities two decades later, including the monstrous Nechaev affair, the product of what he conceived to be the folly of the radical idealists who were making their influence felt when he was a young man. The idealists of the forties, he insisted, were both literally and figuratively the parents of the terrifying Nihilists of the sixties. To illustrate this relationship, he presented in *The Possessed* the liberal Stepan Verkhovensky and his son Pyotr, leader of the "possessed."

Dostoevsky made no effort to disguise the fact that the prototype for Stepan Verkhovensky was a man named Granovsky, a former professor of history at the University of Moscow. Granovsky had been admired by Herzen and other Westerners as a dedicated exponent of enlightenment. From the perspective of 1869, however, Dostoevsky saw Granovsky as an entirely different figure. Stepan (Granovsky) is depicted as a sentimental liberal. His Europeanization was only superficial, yet he lacked any meaningful contacts with his native land. Always making grandiose plans, he never executed them; as he frequently said, "I seem to be ready for work, my materials are collected, yet the work doesn't get done!" He had an uncontrollable urge for theorizing or at least moralizing, the irony being that he had no wisdom upon which to draw. Although most of his historical studies (such as they were) had dealt with the Arabs, the period of knighthood, or other remote subjects, he had on one occasion written what he called "a cruel and skillful thrust at the Slavophiles of the day." Thus he had established, he thought, his place among the liberals and the intelligentsia.

Stepan was always bemoaning the fact that the Russian intellectuals could not bring themselves to work, with the result that "our opinions will be formed for us by those who have hitherto done this work . . . that is, as always, Europe." He delighted in explaining that he had done everything he could to sound "the summons," but in truth his only labor was writing pompous letters. " 'The higher liberalism' and the 'higher liberal,' " Dostoevsky said acidly in reference to Stepan, "that is, a liberal without any definite aim, is only possible in Russia."

Stepan had come to depend upon the patronage of the wealthy Varvara Petrovna, whose only son he had tutored years before. As helpless as a child in practical matters, he had never once recognized that for a long time he had not given any service in return for the benefactions he received. He had, in short, become a parasite, though he behaved as if he were conferring a favor upon Varvara Petrovna by accepting her patronage.

In spite of being irresponsible, ridiculous, and anachronistic, Stepan is goodhearted. There is about him a suggestion of Don Quixote in a dissonant key. This fact made it possible for Dostoevsky to end the characterization of Stepan on a somewhat sympathetic note. The reason for this apparent inconsistency is not hard to find. Part way through the novel another liberal is introduced. This is the author Karmazinov, who is Turgenev under a thin disguise. The impression is inescapable that, without having initially intended to do so, Dostoevsky shifted his attack on the liberals from Stepan to Karmazinov.

Upon Karmazinov-Turgenev, Dostoevsky loosed the full measure of his wrath, a wrath which had been accumulating for years. On the personal plane Dostoevsky resented everything about his fellow novelist: that he had been born to privilege, that he had had the advantages of the best education, that he had ample wealth to cushion his writing career against hardships, that he had leisure for creative activity, that he liked western Europe (had even chosen to live there), that he had close friends among the liberals, and that he did not share Dostoevsky's febrile patriotism. Dostoevsky further condemned Turgenev because he was easygoing and yet capable of the arrogance of aristocracy; because he was—as Dostoevsky conceived it—without aims; and, not the least, because he had been apathetic about heeding Dostoevsky's requests for financial assistance, especially during the period of the latter's mania for gambling. Unfortunately, this personal dislike was largely a product of envy. But the vituperative assault upon Karmazinov-Turgenev was dictated by something more. Turgenev had become for Dostoevsky a symbolic figure, representing all the qualities he hated in the West, the attitudes he believed menacing to Russia. The author of *Fathers and Sons* appeared to his fellow novelist not only an apostate, but, in effect, a traitor to his country. In the light of all this, it is small wonder that the portrait of Karmazinov is splenetic and malicious.

Dostoevsky's vindictiveness expresses itself in every detail of the characterization. The most concentrated venom appears in relation to Turgenev's Westernism, pilloried and caricatured outrageously. The following passage gives some idea of the treatment Dostoevsky meted out to his fellow novelist:

> "The Russian peasantry [said Karmazinov] is still held together somehow by the Russian God; but according to the latest accounts the Russian God is not to be relied upon, and scarcely survived the emancipation; it certainly gave him a severe shock. . . . Everybody has been rolling downhill, and everyone has known for ages that they have nothing to clutch at. . . . I understand only too well why wealthy Russians all flock abroad, and more and more so every year. . . . If the ship is sinking, the rats are the first to leave it. . . . Holy Russia is a country of wood, of poverty . . . and of danger."

This unjustified spite reaches its climax when Dostoevsky makes Karmazinov assert that he is more interested in the laying of new water pipes in Karlsruhe than in all the questions which are engrossing his fellow Russians "in this period of so-called reform."

Dostoevsky assumed without reason that liberals and terroristic anarchists were identical, because they were "possessed"—possessed by materialism and possessed by atheism. In fact, many of the liberals were reasonable, civilized men, often of gentle disposition. Despite their atheism, when it existed, most of them were animated by sincerely humanitarian impulses. The terrorist activities of the Nechaev group distressed almost all of the liberals as much as they distressed Dostoevsky. He could not and would not understand that when the liberals considered or proposed the use of violence, they did so, not because they relished violence for its own sake, but because the existing regime gave them no other choice if anything was to be done beyond hoping and dreaming.

Although Stepan Verkhovensky is physically the father of the character who stands for Nechaev, in mind and spirit Pyotr Verkhovensky is almost more the child of Karmazinov. This is the final thrust, the most devastating charge Dostoevsky could have made against Turgenev and the Western liberals.

The aggressive attack upon the Nihilists in *The Possessed* begins with the return of Pyotr Verkhovensky, after long residence abroad, to the provincial town where his father was vegetating under the sponsorship of Varvara Petrovna. At once he set about forming a unit of five men who would work for a mysterious cause, interpreted differently by each one but in reality nonexistent. The "quintet" was to be one of many, part of a vast conspiratorial network, all answerable to a central authority. The plan can easily be recognized as that proposed by Bakunin's "Catechism of a Revolutionary," and it was in all important respects the one Nechaev had followed.

> "All that you have to do [Verkhovensky instructed his followers] is to bring about the downfall of everything—both the government and its moral standards. None will be left but us, who have

prepared ourselves to take over the government. . . . We shall organize to control public opinion."

As far as purpose was concerned, there was none. A vague humanitarian impulse had caused Bakunin to justify violence in his revolutionary schemes, because violence would probably lead to some rosy, distant dawn. But Nechaev, with his cold egocentricity, had no illusions; he needed no excuses. Likewise, Verkhovensky had a predilection for violence because of the exhilaration it offered him. The urge to destroy was irresistible and intoxicating.

Verkhovensky had no difficulty in finding disciples. There was Virginsky, "a universal humanity man"; Liputin, "a Fourierist with a marked inclination for police work"; and Shigalov, "that fellow with the long ears," who had a system of his own all ready, waiting only for the organizational energy of a leader. These eccentrics and half-mad zealots supplied the grist for Verkhovensky's mill. Only one of the quintet, Shatov, was a man of integrity. Shatov, like Ivanov whom he represented, had to die for his integrity and for daring to wonder whether he had made a mistake in becoming associated with this crew of fools and fanatics.

Verkhovensky has some kinship with Bazarov, but what was only suggested in the latter became explicit and terrible in Dostoevsky's creation. Verkhovensky is Nihilism unmitigated. He is the walking theory not so much of revolution as of destruction. It was appropriate that Verkhovensky's (Nechaev's) secret society should adopt the axe as its emblem. He spoke to his followers with all the appetite of a man ready to gobble up the whole world:

> "Listen, [Verkhovensky said] we are going to make a revolution. . . . We are going to make such an upheaval that everything will be uprooted from its foundation. . . .
>
> "First of all we'll make an upheaval. . . . Do you know that we are tremendously powerful already? . . . The lawyer who defends an educated murderer because he is more cultured than his victims and could not help murdering them to get money is one of us.

> The schoolboys who murder a peasant for the sake of sensation are ours. The juries who acquit every criminal are ours. . . . Russia will be overwhelmed with darkness, the earth will weep for its old gods."

This statement of intention was not an idle boast. Verkhovensky played with people as children play with toys. He made murder and arson his weapons, and also thievery, lying, and setting friend against friend and child against parent. He came to the town for the express purpose of turning everything upside down and did not leave until he had succeeded in doing so. His grotesque deeds were not a matter of impulse. He was deliberate, cunning, and ruthless. With savage vanity and assurance he appropriated for himself "the right" to do anything that pleased his fancy, the right Raskolnikov longed for in vain. Moreover, his taste for evil was insatiable, and his keenest satisfaction was not the evil he did himself, but what he incited others to undertake. He was a specialist in vice and depravity. In him Svidrigailov's dead moral sense was replaced by a lusty artistry in crime. When he decided that the deluge of violence he had precipitated was likely to engulf him, he made a neat getaway, leaving behind a stage strewn with the bodies of his victims. After Verkhovensky's flight one of the quintet who was left tried to run away, but he did not have enough courage; then he tried to commit suicide, but did not succeed. In a panic, he then sought out the officials, hoping to relieve his mind by confession:

> When asked what was the object of so many murders and scandals and dastardly outrages, he answered . . . that "it was with the idea of systematically destroying society and all principles; with the idea of nonplussing every one and making hay of everything, and then, when society was tottering, sick and out of joint, cynical and skeptical . . . suddenly to seize it in their hands, raising the standard of revolt."

Unfortunately, not only death and destruction were left behind, but suspicion, fear, and malignant hatred. The title of the book as it commonly appears in English translations, *The Possessed*, is appropriate enough, but a more literal translation, "the devils," is even more appropriate. No wonder the liberals joined in protest against Dostoevsky's assumption that all believers in socialism, all sympathizers with the ideas or institutions of western Europe, and all those opposed to the existing order in Russia were demons, debauched and brazenly iconoclastic.

In developing the character of Pyotr Verkhovensky, Dostoevsky worked from the premise, previously brilliantly demonstrated in *Crime and Punishment*, that no man—even the most ruthless destroyer—can continue to function without an object of devotion. Therefore, in spite of being incapable of either fear or remorse and in spite of making his own laws and treating his fellows contemptuously, forcing them to execute shameful enormities in the name of revolution, Verkhovensky proved to be not entirely adequate, not able to stand alone. Paradoxically, in view of his refusal to acknowledge God, he needed someone before whom he might bow down, someone to look to as master. This idol he found in Nikolay Stavrogin, son of his father's patroness.

Stavrogin is the third of the characters Dostoevsky used as the framework upon which to build his case in *The Possessed.* Nikolay Stavrogin has probably confused more readers than any other of Dostoevsky's complicated and inscrutable personalities (with the possible exception of Kirillov in the same novel). He is one more in the procession beginning with the Underground Man, including Raskolnikov and Svidrigailov and reaching a climax in Ivan Karamazov—though because of his greater complexity, Ivan is at once similar to and different from the others. Dostoevsky used all of them to prove his thesis that man cut off from God and "the people" cannot preserve his spiritual wholeness. Verkhovensky had chosen Stavrogin to be, not the leader of the upheaval—that was his own prerogative—but its inspiration, in a sense its deity. Stavrogin's fitness for this role lay in his extraordinary strength and his enormous capacity for evil. Verkhovensky was fascinated by Stavrogin's imperviousness; it was the quality he most admired. Thinking ahead to the time when "Russia will be overwhelmed with darkness," Verkhovensky told Stavrogin that "then we shall bring forward . . . Ivan the Tsarevitch." Stavrogin was utterly incredulous when he realized that Verkhovensky was referring to him—had chosen him to be the center of "the legend." Verkhovensky assured Stavrogin that to have a "legend" would be essential; and moreover, "You'll conquer them . . . and the whole gimcrack show will fall to the ground, and then we shall consider how to build up an edifice of stone."

Even with all his hysterical enthusiasm, Verkhovensky was not able to enlist the interest or co-operation of his idol, who responded to his proposal by calling it "madness." And it was mad—the same kind of madness which, since the Russian Revolution, has appealed to more ambitious Stavrogins and enabled them and the Verkhovenskys to perpetrate heinous crimes through the instrumentality of other "legends."

Stavrogin was obviously suggested to Dostoevsky by some of the radicals who were appearing in Russia. It is likely, also, that the concept of his character was influenced by some of the criminals the author had known during his imprisonment in Siberia. However, Stavrogin is primarily to be explained as the embodiment of the self-will which horrified Dostoevsky more than any other defect in human character. It was the same self-will which gripped Raskolnikov, but from which the latter was able to recover, and the self-will which led Svidrigailov to a vacuum admitting escape only through death. Stavrogin is in many ways like Svidrigailov, but he is a man of larger dimensions. He is utterly fearless, with an inflexible will and a personality that makes an ineradicable impact upon everyone who meets him. Yet his strength is weakness, because he does not believe in anything and therefore has no use for his strength. He does not, in fact, even believe in disbelief.

In an effort to escape the boredom which poisoned his existence he tried many experiments of submerging himself in vice, only to discover that none produced satisfaction, exhilaration, or remorse. He did not so much disdain morality as deny its existence. He associates himself with Verkhovensky's rebel crew without either conviction or desire, but only as one more attempt at diversion. Like all the other attempts, however, this one is also futile. Verkhovensky's unquenchable taste for destruction is incomprehensible to Stavrogin, because Stavrogin has no taste for anything. He is like a gloomy Lucifer sentenced to live among men, unable to enjoy defying man because he disdains mankind or to enjoy defying God because he is certain there is no God.

Stavrogin wished he could believe in something, anything, even suicide. Yet when there was no other experiment left, he hesitated to take his own life lest doing so would be another deception, the last of many; he was weary of making gestures. There was, however, nothing else left to be done. A letter Stavrogin wrote before making the final gesture is one of Dostoevsky's most eloquent analyses of the spirit of negation. Stavrogin explained that he had tried everything, including debauchery at its worst, but his desires were so weak that he had got no satisfaction from any of his attempts to find satisfaction. He said he had often wished he could be one of "our iconoclasts," for they have hope. However, his own life—everything about it—had been small and unspirited. He was not interested in ideas or able to feel indignation or shame or despair: "On a log one may cross a river, but not on a chip."

Some of Dostoevsky's implications regarding Stavrogin are confusing, but there is no question about what caused the predicament of this eagle with clipped wings, perched on the brink of the abyss. "I have no ties in Russia—everything is as alien to me there as everywhere," said Stavrogin. Furthermore, "the man who loses connection with his country loses his gods, that is, all his aims." To Dostoevsky, failure to love Russia and failure to love God were inseparable, twin calamities fostered by Nihilism and leading irrevocably to catastrophe. Stavrogin is Dostoevsky's solemn warning to those skeptics who do not believe in country and in God.

Oddly enough, neither Verkhovensky nor Stavrogin is used as the spokesman to express the political and social theories Dostoevsky believed the Nihilists would put into practice if their views and activities were not brought under control. Verkhovensky did not bother with plans, and he was too impatient to concern himself with theories; but he found that Shigalov, of the "long ears," had worked out a system that needed just such a leader as himself. Having an inexhaustible hunger for leadership, Verkhovensky seized on the system and launched his campaign. He was interested solely in destroying the existing standards and institutions of society but pretended that he would eventually set up something new, as the proposed program suggested.

For modern readers the most significant thing in *The Possessed* is Shigalov's plan. It carries a powerful impact, both because of the shocking premises upon which it is based and because it sounds familiar. Views as monstrous as those of Shigalov have been propounded and acted upon in the twentieth century. The theory of Shigalovism begins with the proposition that mankind is to be divided into two parts. The largest part, at least nine-tenths, is to be a herd without individuality or any rights except the right to be led. The select one-tenth, the masters, have complete freedom, even the freedom to do whatever they like with the herd men. The means by which Shigalov proposes to bring about this goal are revealed when Verkhovensky confides to Stavrogin his plans for the future and appeals to him to become the center of the legend which will assist the idol-breakers in creating the new society:

> "He [Shigalov] suggests a system of spying. Every member of the society spies on the others, and it's his duty to inform against them. . . . All are slaves and equal in their slavery. . . . To begin with, the level of education, science, and talents is lowered. . . . Great intellects . . . will be banished or put to death. . . .

> "Down with culture. . . . The thirst for culture is an aristocratic thirst. The moment you have family ties or love you get the desire for property. We will destroy that desire: . . . we'll make use of incredible corruption: we'll stifle every genius in its infancy. We'll reduce all to a common denominator! . . . Slaves must have directors. Absolute submission, absolute loss of individuality."

It is obvious that the views set forth in the article written by Rodion Raskolnikov anticipated much of what is central to "Shigalovism." The main difference is that Rodya's views did not go so far as to advocate corruption and bestiality for their own sake. Rodya's "extraordinary" man was to exert his "right" because by doing so he could accomplish something which would benefit humanity. Passages much closer to the system advocated by Shigalov are to be found scattered through the pages of *Mein Kampf*. Even a cursory survey of the latter document makes clear the fact that with Hitler, as with Shigalov-Verkhovensky, the fundamental concepts were force, destruction, and submission (though the dicta of Hitler, at least on paper, pale into dullness against the brilliance of Dostoevsky at his most impassioned). It would almost seem as if Dostoevsky had a foreknowledge that the flames which were ignited in Russia in 1917 would burn far on into the century. This is his vision of the future as Verkhovensky zestfully described it:

> ". . . one or two generations of vice are essential now: monstrous, abject vice by which a man is transformed into a loathsome, cruel, egoistic reptile. . . . And what's more, a little 'fresh blood' that we may get accustomed to it. . . .
>
> "We will proclaim destruction. . . . We'll set fires going. . . . We'll set legends going . . . and there will be an upheaval! There's going to be such an upset as the world has never seen before."

The murder of the student, Ivanov, supplied Dostoevsky with the incident he needed to give focus to the unwieldy polemics of the novel. The ostensibly fictitious situation is almost an exact replica of what occurred in the Nechaev case. Fearful lest his authority was not as absolute as he desired, or wishing to test the extent to which he had become master of his fantastic brood, Verkhovensky decided that his followers must be cemented into unquestioning subservience by the sharing of a dire secret. Knowing that the shedding of blood would unnerve them, he looked for a scapegoat, and he did not have far to seek. Earlier Shatov had been one of them in spirit, but he was not as single-minded as the others. He had traveled to America and elsewhere and had begun to have ideas that might lead him to freedom of thought and action. He might even infect the others, Verkhovensky conjectured, though that seemed unlikely considering their submissiveness. At any rate, it would be no loss to have him out of the way, and then Verkhovensky's mastery would be supreme. The reader knows long ahead of time that Shatov has been marked for death. As he goes unaware toward the fatal moment, the suspense is worthy of the storytelling art of the author of *Crime and Punishment.* As Verkhovensky incites the others to set upon the hapless victim and throw his body into the pond, the preface is being written to the tale told after 1917 in a crescendo of purges, blood baths, gas chambers, and mass exterminations.

Shatov was needed in the novel, also, for another purpose than that of victim. Dostoevsky used him to declaim a theory, the author's idea of the antidote to all the horrors produced by allegiance to Verkhovensky-Shigalovism (or Nihilism-anarchy). Shatov is surprisingly close to the author even in personality, and there are indications that Dostoevsky felt considerable warmth toward him. Although dwarfed by the malignant characters, Shatov carries a heavy share of the ideology with which the book is loaded. As a result of his trip abroad, we are told, he had completely changed some of his "former socialistic convictions" and had gone to the opposite extreme. "He was one of those idealistic beings common in Russia," Dostoevsky said, "who are suddenly struck by some overmastering idea" in which they "put passionate faith." Shatov's "overmastering idea" is belief in and love of the Russian people.

By way of Shatov, also, Dostoevsky took a characteristic dig at Belinsky and other liberals now anathema to the author. Shatov said that liberals such as they did not love or suffer or sacrifice for "the people." "You can't love what you don't know and they have no conception of the Russian people." Shatov had a cynical explanation for the zeal of the reformers—both the genuine ones and the Shigalovs:

> "They'd be the first to be terribly unhappy if Russia should suddenly be transformed, even to suit their own ideas, and become extraordinarily prosperous and happy. They'd have no one to hate then, no one to curse, nothing to find fault with. . . . An immense animal hatred for Russia . . . has eaten into their organism."

Thus Dostoevsky tossed aside any possible claim to sincerity on the part of those who believed that Russia needed improvement other than the renewal of spiritual faith which he advocated.

In a powerful scene between Shatov and Stavrogin, the former tries to explain the gospel of which he has become a disciple. Unexpectedly, he gives credit to Stavrogin as the source of his original inspiration. The following statement sounds like an echo of Prince Myshkin's (the "idiot's") declaration on the same theme:

> "Do you remember [Shatov asks] your expression that 'an atheist can't be a Russian,' that 'an atheist at once ceases to be a Russian'? . . .
>
> ". . . you said then that 'a man who was not orthodox could not be a Russian.' . . .
>
> ". . . you believed that Roman Catholicism was not Christianity. . . . You pointed out that if France is in agonies now, it's simply the fault of Catholicism. . . .
>
> "Socialism is from its very nature bound to be atheism."

This is the prelude to Shatov's assertion of militant nationalism which is only a thin cover for the voice of Dostoevsky:

> "Every people is only a people so long as it has its own god and excludes all other gods; . . . so long as it believes that by its god it

> will conquer and drive out of the world all other gods. . . . A nation which loses this belief ceases to be a nation. . . . There is only one truth, and therefore only a single one out of the nations can have the true God. . . . Only one nation is 'god-bearing,' that's the Russian people. "

There was no question in the mind of Dostoevsky about the identity of the "chosen" people; he never doubted the messianic function of his country. His faith in Russia was firmer than his belief in God. Shatov gives evidence of what Dostoevsky often acknowledged—that his *will* to believe in God was stronger than his actual belief. When Stavrogin asked Shatov the question which appears in every major Dostoevsky novel, that is, whether he believed in God, Shatov stumbled around the answer, making a positive affirmation only when he was forced to answer "yes" or "no." Thus Shatov reflects the wavering nature of Dostoevsky's own faith throughout most of his mature life. On the other hand, Shatov's impassioned love for the common people and for God through the people caused him to accuse Stavrogin, whom he had formerly idolized, of being an atheist. Stavrogin, Shatov asserted, could not distinguish between good and evil, because he had lost touch with his own people. He begs Stavrogin to reestablish that tie in any way possible and particularly to "attain to God by work." When Stavrogin in astonishment asks what Shatov means by "work," the reply is: "Peasants' work! Go, give up all your wealth."

Peasants' work! This was the theme exalted by Tolstoy. It is the final indication of Dostoevsky's Slavophilism that he, knowing nothing of peasants, should select them and their lowly toil as the road by which to approach the Russian God.

It would be inaccurate to suggest that the "devils" of *The Possessed* are limited to the Verkhovensky-Nechaev group. Dostoevsky was also concerned because Stavrogin was "possessed" by spiritual paralysis, his arrogance offering no palliative against the ache of a heart turned to stone. He was concerned, too, with the obsession of the strange character, Kirillov, who believed he must commit suicide in order "to manifest my self-will . . . the highest point of my self-will is to kill myself with my own hands." Kirillov's theory was essentially the same as that of the young consumptive, Ippolit, in *The Idiot*; but Ippolit's expostulations were his effort to hit back at his undeserved fate. Kirillov, on the other hand, is a mature man, sober and sincere, though perhaps half-mad. The striking fact about Kirillov's death, however, is that it was caused by Verkhovensky and not by Kirillov's fidelity to his own "self-will."

In the personalities of Stavrogin and Kirillov, the novelist explored again the menace of the superman, who discounts God and tries to set himself in place of God. Dostoevsky saw a relationship between the rejection of the existing social and political order and what he believed to be the inevitable concomitant, the rejection of God and the ways of God. In other words, he was convinced that if the Russians did not accept monarchy, they could not accept Orthodoxy either; and if they rejected Orthodoxy, all was lost. When the book was published, this assumption provoked protest and was generally regarded as invalid. It is interesting that the phenomena associated with modern changes in the social order supply some substantiation for the likelihood that social and political upheaval may be symptoms of, or at least accompanied by, loss of reverence for the established religious faith. That this loss might in some instances be beneficial is a possibility completely outside Dostoevsky's consideration.

In the final analysis, however, Dostoevsky wrote *The Possessed* to attack the liberalism he deplored, because he believed that Western liberalism (Stepan Verkhovensky-Karmazinov) was the father of Nihilism (Pyotr Verkhovensky-Shigalov) and tutor to skepticism-atheism (Nikolay Stavrogin). Lest the reader fail to understand this attack, with all its attendant warnings, the author placed a curious scene near the end of the book. The sentimental old Stepan Verkhovensky, father of the scoundrel modeled after Nechaev, had become agitated by the disasters his son had precipitated. He decided to go on a pilgrimage, "holding aloft the 'standard of a great idea, and going to die for it on the open road.'" The "great idea" was as vague as his earlier enthusiasms had always been, but he was resolved to do something. He was not physically adequate to such an undertaking and soon became ill and died, but not without having made a contact with "the people," which enabled him to feel he had touched reality. Shortly before his death he asked a wandering "gospel woman" to read the Biblical passage about the devils that entered into the swine: "Then went the devils out of the man and entered into the swine: and the herd ran violently down a steep place into the lake, and were choked." As Stepan listened, he became excited, for he saw a comparison between the implications of the biblical story and the condition of Russia. The devils, he said:

> ". . . are all the sores, all the foul contagions, all the impurities, all the devils great and small that have multiplied in that great invalid, our beloved Russia. . . . But . . . all those devils will come forth, all the impurity, all the rottenness that was putrefying on the surface. . . . They are we, we, and those . . . and Petrusha and *les autres avec lui*—and I perhaps at the head of them, and we shall cast ourselves down, possessed and raving, from the rocks into the sea, and we shall all be drowned—and a good thing, too, for that is all we are fit for."

Thus did Dostoevsky enunciate his epitaph for liberalism.

II.

Written between *The Possessed* and *The Brothers Karamazov*, *A Raw Youth* is a valley between mountain peaks.[3] After the tornadic polemics and prophecies of *The Possessed*, it is anticlimactic. The absence of more than superficial concern with political, social, or ethical issues makes it unlike the greater novels;

[3] *The Eternal Husband*, with its painful probing of marital disharmony, is of particular interest as an example of Dostoevsky's mature handling of the "double." Dostoevsky's magnificent and tantalizing "doubles" have probably received more attention than any other single aspect of his writing.

only the intensity and intricacy of characterization reveal the master hand. His relatively passive mood may have been caused by Dostoevsky's realizing that he had gone too far in the earlier work, or perhaps he had been wearied by his own vehemence. More likely, it may be traced to the fact that the novel was published in a journal, *National Notes*, well known for liberalism. The editor of this journal was the same Nekrasov who thirty years earlier had taken the manuscript of *Poor Folk* to Belinsky, proclaiming it the work of another Gogol. He and Dostoevsky now led opposing camps of thought, Nekrasov being as devoted a radical as Dostoevsky was now a reactionary. When a series of circumstances caused Dostoevsky to accept the handsome terms Nekrasov offered him for the serial rights to his next novel, he was to some extent committed to avoid flagrant violation of the policies of Nekrasov's journal. Consequently, the characters of the novel are burdened with impulses but lacking in ideas. When an occasional serious comment is tossed in, it has no relevance to any ideological framework, for none exists.

A Raw Youth recounts the incidents and emotional experiences crowded into less than a year in the life of young Arkady Dolgoruky. An illegitimate son of a landowner, Arkady had had a sensitive and lonely childhood in a Moscow boarding school. He had always admired his father and yearned to be accepted and given the affection due a son, but he had not had any opportunity to become acquainted with either of his parents until at the age of twenty he was summoned by his father to St. Petersburg. The wary approach to each other of father and son, the emotional entanglements in which they and other members of the family become involved, and the distracting ambivalence of the father's personality form the substance of the novel.

Dostoevsky treated a group of radical intellectuals (or so they considered themselves) in *A Raw Youth* more like lambs than like the raging lions who compose the "quintet" in *The Possessed*. When Dolgoruky feels compelled to oppose their arguments, he can advance only pallid rebuttals. After one appearance during which their earnestness, lucidity, and humaneness are unmistakable, all but one of the members of the group simply vanish. Apparently Dostoevsky had no heart for depicting radicals except as degenerate scoundrels. When that interpretation was denied him, he preferred to overlook them as far as possible.

In spite of its oddly noncommittal tone, even this book occasionally reveals the author's true thoughts. For example, a statement made by the father of the "raw youth" is one of Dostoevsky's most positive messianic prophecies:

> "Among us has been created by the ages a type of the highest culture never seen before. . . . It is a Russian type. . . .
>
> "Only Russia lives not for herself, but for an idea . . . for almost the last hundred years Russia has lived absolutely not for herself, but only for the other states of Europe! And what of them? Oh, they are doomed to pass through fearful agonies before they attain the Kingdom of God."

After the completion of *The Possessed,* Dostoevsky entered upon a period of journalistic activity. His editorship of *The Citizen* proved distasteful, however, because of the stupid interference of the nobleman who owned it. Before severing his connection with the periodical, Dostoevsky had begun a feature called *Diary of a Writer*, which was so popular that he resolved to continue publishing it on an independent basis. This he did, issuing monthly installments during 1876 and 1877, with an additional installment in 1880 and the last one in January, 1881, the month of his death. The *Diary* is an odd mixture of editorial comments, discussions of current issues, statements of personal conviction, heated nationalistic affirmations, and occasional bits of narrative. Unfortunately, it has little of the charm or power of Dostoevsky's best work. It is repetitious and filled with the abusive attacks familiar to the reader of the Dostoevsky novels. Here the novelist reveals himself as opinionated in political outlook, his everlasting glorification of Russia proving a bitter dose for even the sympathetic reader to swallow. This is

Dostoevsky at his least appealing level. The *Diary* affords, however, a compendium of the author's mature views on many topics. It summarizes the contentions of all the novels except the last.

As would be expected, the *Diary* abounds with vituperative thrusts at the Westerners, Belinsky in particular, but all Westerners in general—"people with extraordinary malignancy."[4] Even the Russians who respected and were influenced by European civilization were caustically stigmatized. Worst of all, he said, some of these latter had even changed their religion to Roman Catholicism. That meant, of course, that in Dostoevsky's view they had become traitors positively bent on the destruction of Russia. Dostoevsky insisted that Catholicism had put the Pope in place of Christ and even stated on several occasions that the papacy was a threat to world peace. Particularly in Catholic France, but also in other parts of Europe, he said, the people are irreligious and have no familiarity with the Bible. What difference does this make to us? he asked. "Well, it is our concern because Europe will be knocking at our door, crying for help and urging us to save her when the last hour of her 'present order of things' strikes." These and the multitude of related blasts need no further commentary here; however, the *Diary* does elucidate some Dostoevskian views not previously discussed.

Dostoevsky was exhilarated into a state of patriotic fanaticism by the war with Turkey, which Russia began in the middle 1870's with considerable optimism. There were complex motivations behind this struggle, but Dostoevsky saw it only as a sacred cause. The most important reason Russia must win the war, he contended, was that the preservation and spread of Orthodoxy depended upon it. Orthodoxy alone was in possession of the truth. With another typical promise of messianic destiny he assured readers of the *Diary* that a "new word" would be uttered from the East (specifically Russia), and that this word would be able to save all of Europe.

The author went so far as to associate the Czar with Ortho-

[4] Translated by Boris Brasol.

doxy. The people perceive, he asserted, "the beloved title of the Czar in the word 'Orthodox.'" He was apprehensive because some of the people of the East, having been corrupted by the West, had lost sight of the fact that Orthodoxy was the only hope for the "regeneration and resurrection" of both East and West. But he was sure that in the mass of common people there still resided enough faith, unpolluted by the intelligentsia and Western culture, to bring about the victory of the true religion. This glorious consummation would be accomplished, he announced, by "the czars of the people in sublime communion with the latter." As Dostoevsky saw him, the Czar had a surprising resemblance to an Old Testament prophet!

Dostoevsky was positive that nothing could be "purer and more sacred" than the war with Turkey, for it obviously had no other aim than that of liberating the peoples who had been enslaved by alien conquerors and ideologies. He could even see reasons why Russia had a right to Constantinople. Among other things, if Constantinople could be reunited with her Slavic neighbors to the north, that union would be a first step in the harmonious relationship of all "Orthodox peoples." Russia, he said, "is their guardian," but not their sovereign unless sometime in the future they should elect to join themselves with her. Such a union would, of course, assure the preservation of the independent spirit of each of the parts. He looked forward with confident delight to the time "when even the Slavic nations will comprehend the whole truth of Russian disinterest" and be influenced by the "irresistible witchery of the great and mighty Russian spirit."

This hope for the unification of all Slavic people was the second reason Dostoevsky believed it was imperative for Russia to win the war with Turkey. Pan-Slavism had long been a matter for rapturous contemplation to the Slavophiles, and Dostoevsky's excitement was second to none. In the reconciliation of Russia with the other Slavs he saw "the beginning of that active application of our treasure of Orthodoxy—to the universal service of man." Moreover:

> We . . . will now begin . . . with becoming servants to all nations, for the sake of general pacification. . . . Therein is our grandeur because this leads to the ultimate unity of mankind. . . . This is how I understand the Russian mission *in its ideal*. . . . The first step . . . had to consist in the unification of the whole Slavdom . . . under Russia's wing. And this communion is to be effected not for the sake of usurpation, not for the sake of violence, nor for the purpose of the annihilation of the Slavic individualities . . . but with the object of their own regeneration, so that they may be placed in a proper relation to Europe and to mankind.

Although reverence for the peasants was expressed more eloquently by Tolstoy than by any other Russian writer, Dostoevsky did not come far behind. With regard to the peasants' religion, he wrote that the Russian peasants are firm in their convictions and cannot be misled to relinquish their faith in God. He pondered whether or not there was anything the educated Russians could teach "the people" and concluded that the process was more likely to occur in reverse. If the intellectually sophisticated could get close to the people, he thought, they could come to understand many things which their sophistication hid from them.

A sour note which sounds much too often in the *Diary* is Dostoevsky's contemptuous disrespect for the Jews. Intimations of this regrettable prejudice appear in several of the novels, and the condemnation blares forth boldly from the *Diary*. The author pointed out how remarkable it was that in Russia the people had not forgotten their "great idea"—Orthodoxy—even though they had heavy burdens to contend with. The burdens were "their two-hundred-year slavery, dark ignorance," and, more recently, "despicable debauch [by which he probably meant Nihilism], materialism, Jewry, and alcohol."

Dostoevsky's anti-Semitism was so outspoken that he received letters of remonstrance. To these he made such withering retorts as, "I am unable fully to believe in the screams of the Jews that they are so downtrodden, oppressed, and humiliated." And in response to one suggestion that he would be less prejudiced if he were more familiar with the history of the race, he replied acidly, "I do not know the 'forty-century-old' history of these chaste angels." The following comment in the *Diary* has special interest for American readers:

> I have just read in the March issue of *The Messenger of Europe* a news item to the effect that in America, in the Southern States, [the Jews] have already leaped *en masse* upon the millions of liberated Negroes, and have already taken a grip upon them in their, the Jews' own way, by means of their sempiternal "gold pursuit" and by taking advantage of the inexperience and the vices of the exploited tribe. Imagine, when I read this, I immediately recalled that the same thing came to my mind five years ago, specifically, that the Negroes have now been liberated from the slave-owners, but that they will not last because the Jews, of whom there are so many in the world, will jump at this new little victim.

Dostoevsky maintained that the Jew, instead of raising the educational level or "generating economic fitness in the native population," always, "wherever he has settled, has still more humiliated and debauched the people." Of course the logical conclusion to this distortion of history was his contention that the Jews were largely responsible for the despicable bourgeois materialism of western Europe. However, he voiced this theory only when he was not intent on damning the socialists.

Dostoevsky's attacks upon the Poles, although less numerous than his attacks on the Jews, betray a shocking inability to sympathize with any form of nationalism not Russian and suggest that he, like many other ardent patriots, believed in freedom only when it pertained to his own country. He accentuated his hatred of Europe by frequent reiteration that Europe hated Russia. This hatred would not be eliminated, he said, until Europe became convinced that Russia "has no intention of annexing anything." Even then, he added, the hostility would continue, because Europe feared Russia and would naturally hate the object of her fears. This resentment of western Europe rises to a whining, "Europe has always extraordinarily disliked us; . . . always has viewed us as disagreeable strangers."

Whatever the criticism or the protest, however, Dostoevsky always came back to exuberant statements of faith in Russia. In 1876 he went so far as to proclaim that Russia had established a degree of political unity beyond any precedents in human history. Even England and America would do well to look upon it with awe. It was all an inevitable part of the emergence of a "god-fearing" people whose destiny was as certain as movements of the stars. Her western neighbors did not properly appreciate Russia:

> Much of what we have taken from Europe and transplanted to Russia, we did not copy like slaves from their masters, as the Potugins invariably insist, but we have inoculated it into our organism, into our flesh and blood. . . . Europeans emphatically refuse to believe it; they do not know us. . . . All the more imperceptibly and quietly will the necessary process take place—a process which will subsequently astound the whole world.

It is astonishing, the above passage notwithstanding, to be told "that every European poet, thinker, humanitarian" is understood better in Russia than in any other country except his native land. "Shakespeare, Byron, Walter Scott, Dickens are more akin and intelligible to Russians" than, say, to Germans, even though (How could Dostoevsky have brought himself to acknowledge the fact?) "in Russia not even one-tenth of the number of copies of these authors, in translation, are being sold."

Dostoevsky always urged his countrymen to be and to remain Russians. Only if the Russians respected themselves and their nation strongly enough could they hope to see the coming of a golden day when Europeans would respect them appropriately.

> We should acquire the appearance of free men, and not that of slaves, lackeys, of Potugin. . . . We . . . should then understand that much of what we used to despise in our people is not darkness

> but precisely light; not stupidity but reason. And having grasped this . . . we should utter in Europe such a word as has never been heard before. We should then become convinced that the genuine social truth resides in no one else but our people; that their idea, their spirit contains the living urge of universal communion of men.

After this paean of Slavophile ardor, it is no surprise that Dostoevsky demands: "Is it not . . . clear that the Russian people bear within themselves the organic embryo of an idea which differs from any idea in the world? And this idea comprises in Russia so mighty a force that it will naturally exercise an influence upon our whole future history."

It is another of the lengthy series of paradoxes demonstrated by his life and work that Dostoevsky should have written the *Diary*—which shrinks his size as man and as artist—at the very time he was planning and creating the novel that crowned his achievements, his masterpiece, *The Brothers Karamazov*.

III.

The *Diary* is a sorry contrast to the creative achievements of Dostoevsky as they are best revealed in a series of magnificent characterizations in the novels. In spite of his genius, his profile is disfigured by weaknesses and flaws. He was an overzealous patriot, so desirous of substantiating his insecure religious faith that he made outlandish claims for Orthodoxy. That he was emotional, inconsistent, sometimes petty, and capable of violent hate as well as violent love, there can be no doubt. He said of himself—and it has been often repeated—that he "felt ideas," the result being, of course, conflict between his emotions and his ideas. It is difficult to excuse him for violating the integrity of art by using the great novels as vehicles for propaganda. Seen against the majestic beauty of his final novel, however, none of the earlier blemishes seem finally to matter. In the crucible of his mature genius Dostoevsky at last fused disparate elements into an almost perfect union. Whereas in some of the earlier works, as Avrahm Yarmolinsky has pointed out, he "smothers a curse in a shout of hallelujah," in *The Brothers Karamazov*, Dostoevsky created one of the great symphonies of literature, the "shout of hallelujah" having developed into a complete, resounding orchestration.

Everything from the earlier books is to be found in *The Brothers Karamazov*: the poor folk, the gambler, the profligate, the priest, the man poisoned by intellectuality, the men and women tormented by love and hate, the unjustified suffering, the skepticism, the brutality and tenderness, the contest between doubt and faith, the sin, the search, and, in the end, the way of salvation. This novel is Dostoevsky's synthesis after a lifetime of searching. The doubts are still there and the questions not categorically answered, but the resolution gives substance again to the contention that "there is more faith in honest doubt" than in unquestioning acquiescence.

Years earlier, after his release from prison, Dostoevsky had written to the wife of one of the Decembrists who had befriended him on his way to prison and during his imprisonment: "If anyone could prove to me that Christ is outside the truth, and if the truth really did exclude Christ, I should prefer to stay with Christ and not with truth." Fortunately, the novelist did not have to make a choice; *The Brothers Karamazov* shows him finally satisfied that Christ and the truth are one. The truth apprehended by Dostoevsky sets *The Brothers Karamazov* apart from his other novels and makes it the most meaningful and beautiful of them all. It also tells what is most important to know about Russia and the Russians—indeed, in larger context, about all mankind.

The novel is ostensibly the book of the Karamazovs—father and four sons, one illegitimate—but it is much more than that. It is a debate in which these men are the spokesmen of denial and affirmation. Without sacrificing their lifelikeness, Dostoevsky made the Karamazovs symbols.

Certain critics have attempted to prove that the genesis of the novel can be traced to the author's lifelong brooding over the murder of his father, for which he felt subconsciously guilty because he had resented his father's arbitrary behavior. The evidence, however, is not adequate to support this Freudian hypothesis. There were in Dostoevsky and his Underground Men some elements of the Byronic hero dwelling moodily upon his dark past, but they were not strong enough to justify pushing the resemblance too far. At the same time, it can hardly be an exaggeration to suggest that within his own experience Dostoevsky found the model for strained relations between a father and his sons.

The action of the novel is based on the rivalry between Fyodor Karamazov and his oldest son, Dmitri, over the woman Grushenka, a "prostitute" more sinned against than sinning, like Nastasya in *The Idiot.* Dmitri's hatred of his father is shared by the second son, Ivan, another of Dostoevsky's coldly rational young men tainted by Nihilism. When Fyodor is found murdered, suspicion falls upon Dmitri, who is tried, found guilty, and sentenced to Siberia. The actual murderer, however, is the illegitimate Smerdyakov, a slavish admirer of Ivan, whose precepts he had put into practice by taking the father's life. Following the principle that the thought is father to the deed, Ivan is regarded both by himself and by the author as the guilty one, for without the stimulus of his skepticism Smerdyakov would not have acted. In spite of his innocence of the murder, Dmitri acknowledges his past errors and wishes to expiate his sins by suffering. Ivan, meanwhile, is so burdened by a sense of guilt that he gives way to brain fever. Smerdyakov hangs himself when he realizes that his idol is not what Raskolnikov called an "extraordinary man." In contrast to this maelstrom of passion and rejection, the youngest son, Alyosha, reared in a monastery under the loving supervision of the Elder Zossima and other monks, exemplifies the Christian virtues of humility and brotherly love. He is the only "whole" man among the Karamazovs.

This framework exists only as a backdrop against which the real drama is played. The central conflict of the novel is a debate in which Alyosha and Ivan are the principal speakers for the affirmative and the negative. The debate is introduced near the beginning of the book when the lecherous old buffoon, Fyodor, turns his maudlin thoughts, as he occasionally does after too much liquor, to a subject that tantalizes him because he is no longer young. He addresses Ivan first:

> "Speak . . . is there a God, or not? Only, be serious. I want you to be serious now."
> "No, there is no God."
> "Alyosha, is there a God?"
> "There is."
> "Ivan, and is there immortality of some sort, just a little, just a tiny bit?"
> "There is no immortality either."
> "None at all?"
> "None at all."
> "There's absolute nothingness then. Perhaps there is just something? Anything is better than nothing!"
> "Absolute nothingness."
> "Alyosha, is there immortality?"
> "There is."
> "God and immortality?"
> "God and immortality. In God is immortality."

It is hard to decide which of the characters of the novel was intended to hold the central place. Probably the nearest to real flesh and blood is Dmitri, whose spirit is endlessly struggling with base desires, tempestuous passions, yet yearning for the good. Ivan has often been said to represent Dostoevsky himself, but Dostoevsky was no more Ivan than he was Dmitri. As a matter of fact, each of the Karamazovs except Smerdyakov is imprinted with some aspect of the author's complicated personality. In total perspective, however, Ivan is the most memorable character. A mature and hardened Raskolnikov, he is the one tragic figure among the "possessed." The war between doubt and belief that ravages his spirit is a microcosm of the everlasting war within the human soul. The part assigned to Ivan is best explained by Dostoevsky in a letter he wrote after he had completed the first half of the book:

> The denial now is finished and sent off, but the refutation will come only in the June number. The denial I described just as I felt it myself and realized it strongest, that is, just as it is now taking place in our Russia in nearly the *whole* upper stratum of society, and above all with the younger generation. I mean, the scientific and philosophical refutation of the existence of God has been given up, it no longer occupies at all the *socialists* of today; . . . instead men are denying with all their might and main the divine creation, the world of God and *its meaning.*

The debate pervades the entire book, carried on by deeds as well as by words. The climax for the negative side is to be found in the remarkable section called "Pro and Contra" in which Ivan attempts to explain to his brother Alyosha his views with regard to "the eternal questions, of the existence of God and immortality." This discussion, which takes place in a tavern, with the bustling of waiters, the clinking of dishes and glasses, and occasional bursts of raucous laughter in the background, is one of Dostoevsky's most impressive feats in the use of dramatic contrast.

Ivan is the last and the greatest of Dostoevsky's portraits of men at odds with God. He is not, like Svidrigailov and Stavrogin, as much attracted to evil as to good. Although he shares with the earlier characters the inability to obtain satisfaction from negation, he is unlike them in that he cannot remain indifferent to good and is not passive about morality. Well educated and with a high degree of intellectual honesty, he cannot reconcile what he would like to believe with what he does believe. It is appropriate that the Book of Job was Dostoevsky's favorite book of the Bible. Ivan's problem, however, was more devastating than Job's. Whereas Job's faith was *tested* by the problem of suffering, Ivan's faith was *prevented* by the problems of suffering and sin. Still, Ivan suffers from his spiritual predicament and makes a persistent effort to find a solution. Of necessity, however, according to Dostoevsky's interpretation, Ivan is defeated before he begins the struggle by the fact that the only weapons at his disposal are intellectual ones. He bears a striking resemblance to Raskolnikov in that he is a man of theories. He, too, had written articles, and he had asserted:

> . . . that there was nothing in the whole world to make men love their neighbours. That there was no law of nature that man should love mankind, and that, if there had been any love on earth hitherto, it was . . . simply because men have believed in immortality. . . . If you were to destroy in mankind the belief in immortality, not only love but every living force maintaining the life of the world would at once be dried up. Moreover, nothing then would be immoral, everything would be lawful. . . .
>
> "Yes" [Ivan agreed]. "That was my contention. There is no virtue if there is no immortality."

In his explanation to Alyosha, Ivan does not wholly reject God. He says he is willing to "accept God simply," although "I've long resolved not to think whether man created God or God man." But as for God's world, he does not and will not accept it. There are several reasons why he cannot cross this hurdle. First, he sees no reason why he should be "his brother's keeper." Moreover, he says, "I could never understand how one can love one's neighbours." This reaction to humanity is based on the senseless and horrifying suffering men inflict upon each other and, worst of all, upon innocent children.[5] "A beast," he says, "can never be so cruel as a man, so artistically cruel." He knows that "there is suffering and that none are held guilty":

> "I know that, but I can't consent to live by it! . . . I must have justice or I will destroy myself. . . . Listen! if all must suffer to pay for the eternal harmony, what have children to do with it? . . . And

[5] It is extremely ironic that Ivan hates mankind because of the senseless cruelty men inflict upon one another but does nothing to ameliorate the suffering of others. He is a humanitarian in theory only.

> if it is really true that they must share responsibility for all their fathers' crimes, such a truth is . . . beyond my comprehension. . . . Those tears . . . must be atoned for, or there can be no harmony. But how? How are you going to atone for them? . . . Besides, too high a price is asked for harmony; it's beyond our means to pay so much to enter on it. And so I hasten to give back my entrance ticket. . . . It's not God that I don't accept, Alyosha, only I most respectfully return Him His ticket."

Ivan's *saying* he is willing to accept God is an example of what George Orwell calls "doublethink." Dostoevsky may have chosen to mitigate Ivan's atheism because of his own fidelity to Orthodoxy, or he may have thought that Ivan would want to soften his negation out of respect for Alyosha. Nevertheless, the essential fact about the tormented Ivan is that he does not believe in God or immortality, and therefore he concludes that "everything is lawful."

To Ivan's assertion that he must "give back [his] entrance ticket," Alyosha replies, "That's rebellion." And that is precisely what Dostoevsky intended it to be. In rejecting the existing order, Ivan rejects not only the social and political, but also the moral order. He is a rebel in the spiritual realm as Verkhovensky is in the material. This meant to the novelist that the young man was "possessed" by the will to destroy, that he had assumed, like a tyrant from Greek drama, the right to defy God's laws. It meant that he *thought* too much.

As the climax to his analysis of his position, Ivan recites to Alyosha a prose poem called "The Grand Inquisitor," in many respects the most unforgettable chapter Dostoevsky ever wrote. Ivan tells how during the Inquisition, Christ returns to sixteenth-century Seville, where, though "He came softly," the people, recognizing Him, flock about him joyously, many yearning to be healed. As He performs several miracles, the Grand Inquisitor passes by, sees everything, and looks at Christ with malice. When he orders the guards to take Christ, there is no remonstrance from the people. They are so accustomed to submission that they obediently stand aside.

That night the Inquisitor goes to the prison cell to confront Christ. He accuses Him of having come to interfere with the church and states that on the morrow he will have Him burned at the stake. He then charges Christ with having made His first mistake when He resisted the temptations in the wilderness, thereafter offering men, not an object of worship, but absolute freedom. This freedom, the Inquisitor says, does not bring men happiness; it brings them misery. He taunts Christ with having ignored the basic fact of human nature, the desire for physical satisfaction. To be happy, he says, men must bow down before gods and idols, and they must have bread. "I tell Thee," he insists, "that man is tormented by no greater anxiety than to find some one quickly to whom he can hand over that gift of freedom with which the ill-fated creature is born."

To satisfy this anxiety, says the Inquisitor, the church has taken freedom from man, knowing that he prefers slavery, and men have willingly accepted subservience in order to have bread. The church will feed men as if in the name of Christ, and "they will marvel at us and look on us as gods, because we are ready to endure the freedom which they have found so dreadful." The Inquisitor asks Christ, "Didst Thou forget that man prefers peace, and even death, to freedom of choice in the knowledge of good and evil?" He assumes that Christ must have known that eventually men would reject Him rather than accept the responsibility of freedom of choice. Christ is guilty, continues the Inquisitor, for "Thou didst Thyself lay the foundation for the destruction of Thy Kingdom." In contrast, the church has improved upon the way of Christ and has established itself upon "miracle, mystery, and authority." And men rejoiced that they could lay down their freedom—the "terrible gift that had brought them such suffering"—and depend wholly upon the church.

Throughout this disquisition Christ remained silent. At last the Inquisitor, disturbed by this magnetic silence, wished that Christ would offer some argument in opposition. Instead, Christ went silently to the old man and kissed him, and this kiss had such power that the Inquisitor released Christ as if he were being moved by a force beyond his control. Although "the kiss glows in his heart," Ivan concludes, still the Inquisitor's views have not been altered. All the evidence of his long experience prompts him to see man as a paltry and unworthy creature.

Obviously, the legend was intended to substantiate Ivan's views and to serve as another denunciation of Roman Catholicism and socialism, that is, both the religious and the social institutions of western Europe. More important is the obvious indication of the author's own problem regarding belief. Like Ivan, Dostoevsky had never been able to justify suffering or to reconcile the concept of a just and loving God with a world of creatures who are "weak and vile." Dostoevsky could not find logical answers, since none exist. He discovered that this dilemma can be resolved, or at least made less painful, only by instruments other than logic.

The most impressive thing about the legend is the argument that man prefers slavery to freedom. With few exceptions, the entire history of mankind supports the position of Ivan and the Grand Inquisitor. In spite of his hatred for Potugin (Turgenev's eloquent Westerner), Dostoevsky must have been struck by one of Potugin's assertions in *Smoke*: "The habits of slavery are too deeply ingrained in us; we cannot easily be rid of them. We want a master in everything and everywhere; as a rule this master is a living person, sometimes it is some so-called tendency which gains authority over us." Potugin was speaking particularly about the Slavs, but, unfortunately, the Slavs are not the only people who "want a master." Clearly, if Ivan must lose the debate—and Dostoevsky never questioned that he must—it is not for lack of evidence on his side.

Dostoevsky was convinced that material evidence, no matter how logical, is not enough to live by. Therefore, despite the honesty, the unanswerableness, and the rationality of his propositions, Ivan reaps nothing but anguish from his position, for—and it was the last time Dostoevsky had the opportunity to say it—

men cannot live by reason alone. Ivan is always uneasy, filled with doubt and malice, a subtle infection, a continuous slow poison that destroys his mental health. He is a dispossessed soul unable to escape from the inferno in his own mind.

And how terrible were the results of his negation and disbelief. When Smerdyakov confronted Ivan with his reasons for murdering their father, he concluded, "It was only with you, with your help, I killed him." This blow completely unnerved Ivan. He was immediately staggered by the truth of the accusation, but he could not take it in. He wondered whether Smerdyakov was a bad dream or a phantom. He cried out in alarm, asking what "third person" was there with them, and Smerdyakov grimly replied that it was God: "Only don't look for him, you won't find him."

Thus, at the moment of his greatest need Ivan's atheism is thrown in his face by his alter ego. As he really sees Smerdyakov for the first time, he sees himself—a poseur, conceited, presumptuous, and counterfeit. He had always recognized Smerdyakov as despicable and degenerate. Now he becomes conscious that he had made Smerdyakov after his own image—except that the image, like a shadow, was taller, more threatening, and concentratedly darker. This was what all his fine theories had amounted to. "And so," said Smerdyakov, "I want to prove to your face—that you are the only real murderer in the whole affair, and I am not the real murderer, though I did kill him."

Ivan is not the only one uprooted by the crime. To Smerdyakov, as to Raskolnikov after he had sunk the axe into the skull of the old pawnbroker, something entirely unexpected happens. He had taken the money old Fyodor had put aside for Grushenka, but now he doesn't want it. Even if "all things are lawful," he knows that now it is futile to think of going to Moscow or of beginning a new life. Time stood still for him and for Ivan. Ivan had thought he was seeing the truth, but now he understands the enormity of his misconception. Now he has found the truth at last: he *is* his brother's keeper. In the pride of his intellect he had presumed, but something had eluded his grasp. Now it is too late. Ivan recognizes that he is in fact guilty. What he had created was evil, and evil must contrive its own end. Whereas the noose was quick for Smerdyakov, Ivan, like Lear, must suffer mentally, on the same plane on which he had sinned: "O, that way madness lies."

Having heard and acknowledged the truth of Smerdyakov's indictment, "as [Ivan] entered his own room he felt something like a touch of ice on his heart, like a recollection or, more exactly, a reminder of something agonising and revolting, that was in that room now . . . and had been there before." That "something" is Ivan's double, the devil, dressed in a rather shabby jacket. Ivan has not even the satisfaction of being hounded by a well-tailored devil. This pedestrian fellow lacks the suavity of Mephistopheles. He needles Ivan and taunts him with his own theories shorn of all eloquence, making the most exalted and convincing of them appear ignoble. No wonder Ivan "cried with a sort of fury":

> "You are a lie, you are my illness. . . . You are my hallucination. You are the incarnation of myself, but only of one side of me . . . of my thoughts and feelings, but only the nastiest and stupidest of them. . . .
>
> "You are myself, only with a different face. You just say what I am thinking . . . and are incapable of saying anything new!"

The devil reminds Ivan of his motives, better forgotten, as well as his deeds. From him come echoes of "The Grand Inquisitor." He recalls Ivan's view that "we only need to destroy the idea of God in man," after which "all things are lawful." Ivan attempts to defend himself by announcing his intention to testify at Dmitri's trial, but the devil assures him that his willingness to do so springs from base motives. With his sniggering gentility the devil makes everything about Ivan paltry and contemptible. After his doubles, Smerdyakov and the devil, finish with him, Ivan has shrunk to such a degree that, like Raskolnikov, he might describe himself as a "louse." As the full "anguish of a proud determination" closes around him, he sinks into brain fever. He has fought the fight of man *versus* God, and he has lost. What the outcome of the conflict of irreconcilables will be, Dostoevsky does not tell us. He makes Alyosha his interpreter only to a certain point. Watching the sick man tossing in delirium—

> He [Alyosha] began to understand Ivan's illness. "The anguish of a proud determination. An earnest conscience!" God, in Whom he disbelieved, and His truth were gaining mastery over his heart, which still refused to submit. . . . Alyosha smiled softly. "God will conquer!" he thought. "He [Ivan] will either rise up in the light of truth, or . . . he'll perish in hate, revenging on himself and on every one his having served the cause he does not believe in."

Svidrigailov, Stavrogin, and Smerdyakov—would Ivan stay with them and die, or would he choose to live in the affirmative? When God enters the lists against him, Ivan cannot compete with the adversary. Notwithstanding his defeat, he is still impressive, a dark and lonely creature, a fallen angel.

Dostoevsky made every effort to deal out the advantages to the affirmative side of the debate. If the arguments of the three affirmative spokesmen are less convincing than those of Ivan for the negative, it is not because of lack of eloquence or conviction. The first speaker, the Elder Zossima, carries the burden of the argument. He is like the Old Testament prophets in his singleness of purpose and certitude of belief, but in place of their harshness he has the kindliness and joy of David the Psalmist. Like David he looks upon the world and sees that it is good. "The mountains declare the glory of God," and man can be part of this universal harmony if he really desires. The requirements are not easy, yet not unreasonably difficult. Man must enjoy life, must be filled with love and appreciation; he must be willing to serve rather than to be served; he must pray, not for himself alone, but for all; he must "work without ceasing"; he must understand that no man can or should judge another; and he must "have no fear of men's sin":

> There is only one means of salvation, then take yourself and make yourself responsible for all men's sins . . . for as soon as you sincerely make yourself responsible for everything and for all men, you will see at once that it is really so. . . .
>
> If the evil doing of men moves you to indignation and overwhelming distress . . . Go at once and seek suffering for yourself, as though you were yourself guilty of that wrong. Accept that suffering and bear it and your heart will find comfort, and you will understand that you too are guilty. . . . Water the earth with the tears of your joy and love those tears.

"Heaven," the Elder declares, "lies hidden within all of us," waiting to be revealed at whatever moment we will. "We are all responsible to all for all. . . . So soon as men understand that, the Kingdom of Heaven will be for them not a dream, but a living reality." Hell, on the other hand, is "the suffering of being unable to love."

Zossima makes no effort to answer or deny Ivan's queries or arraignments.[6] He lives in a different world—a world of radiant goodness of his own creating. He does not deny sin and suffering; he sees them as instruments of the divine will. The important thing for man, he believes, is not to be saved from sin and suffering, but to know how to use them to climb toward salvation. Sin—recognition—repentance—humility—suffering—atonement—forgiveness—good works—love—salvation: these are the ascending rungs of the ladder leading to the throne of God. Since the way is easier for him "who has freed himself from the tyranny of material things and habits," the meek, the humble, and the poor will be most certain to desire and to receive the grace of God. Therefore, "the people," says Zossima (and Dostoevsky), will be the salvation of Russia.

The gospel of Zossima is the gospel of unselfish service. "Verily, verily, I say unto you, except a corn of wheat fall into the ground and die, it abideth alone: but if it die, it bringeth forth much

[6] He does assert, however, that if the debate cannot be decided for the affirmative, at least it will never be decided for the negative.

fruit." For that reason he sends Alyosha out from the safety of the monastery into the world. His last message to Alyosha is to seek happiness in sorrow, and above all, to work.

Although some readers of the novel have called Zossima a wraith-like figure too fleshless to bear the weight of life, Alyosha undeniably has the blood and sinew of the fullness of life. Capable in his youthful vigor of knowing temptation, still he has the rare understanding which springs from mature compassion. His recognition of the essential nature of Grushenka is immediate and unerring. He alone is able to see that the outrageous histrionics of the crippled girl Lise are caused by a nervous ailment which has twisted her soul out of shape as surely as it is twisting her limbs. When he is pelted by rocks thrown by the tortured Illusha, he asks at once, "What have I done to you?" Moreover, his humility is not superficial. He readily admits that, although his brothers have already ascended a number of rungs on the ladder of the "Karamazov baseness," he himself has stepped up onto at least the first rung. His sympathy brings healing, his humility is genuine, and his love of the good makes his spirit glow. Dostoevsky conceived of Alyosha as the man of pure feeling (intelligent, too, although his intelligence did not cause him to theorize). Dostoevsky shows him clearly by contrasting him with another student, one of Alyosha's acquaintances, the small-minded, scheming, niggardly Rakitin, one more of the novelist's stream of empty-souled intellectuals who have flirted with Nihilism.

The most appealing of the four affirmants is Dmitri. His turbulent passions are always waging war in his heart, but his impulses for good transfigure his vile deeds. In him, sinner and saint are both strong and forever at variance. His sins, however, are the sins of the flesh, unpremeditated and impulsive. Even when he is in Sodom, he is always aware of the vision of the Madonna. Dostoevsky would have assigned him before his repentance to one of the upper circles of Dante's Hell, among the carnal sinners. He would have been separated by a great gulf from Ivan, whose calculation and malice would plunge him into the dark abyss near the colossal, brooding, three-faced figure of the Devil encased in ice.

Dmitri's real character is demonstrated by his relation to two women. He understands Katerina for what she is ("she loves her own virtue, not me"), but he treats her with respect as long as respect is possible.[7] Early in their acquaintance he felt humble before her, as though being in his presence might becloud her purity. When he realizes that she is not pure, he tries to forgive her. Even when she lashes out at him in the courtroom, shaping his fate by the false accusations hurled from her arrogant spirit, he does not curse her as most men would. His reaction is a numb incredulity in the face of such vileness that he can scarcely believe it exists.

Dmitri's love of Grushenka is at first a love of the flesh, but as their love develops, it becomes clear that Grushenka has always been for Dmitri more than an object of passion. Perhaps she offers him a fleeting intimation of the "Madonna" he loves with his whole soul. As they are caught together in the web of suffering, their mutual recognition of the best in each other is like a star shining upon the world of darkness which Ivan cannot accept. If Dmitri depends upon Grushenka to give him courage in adversity, Grushenka depends upon Dmitri to give her the unwavering assurance that he is a man of honorable character, in whom she is justified in having faith.

There is grandeur in Dmitri's desire to make his peace with God and man. He finds it "impossible to die a scoundrel. . . . No, gentlemen, one must die honest." He has certainly sinned, but what was important to Dostoevsky was that Dmitri recognizes and repents of his sin. Then, after his dream about the starving babe, he goes a step further and embraces the fundamental concept of Christianity, that a man must lose his life in order to save it. "I want to suffer," he says, "and by suffering I shall be purified. . . . I accept my punishment, not because I killed him, but

[7] Katerina is in many respects the feminine counterpart of Ivan. She is less intellectual and more vindictive. Both censure others but are unable to love.

because . . . I really might have killed him." This is the suffering that chastens and teaches, that creates new men. Probably Dmitri's finest characteristic is his rigorous honesty. He always judges himself, not others.

Sometimes, of course, Dmitri worries about the existence of God. Rakitin's theories disturb Dmitri. He does not understand how man can love humanity if, as Rakitin says, God does not exist. Despite all the pressures upon him, however, Dmitri always returns to faith in the existence of God. In the court, when the jury is ready to decide his fate, these are his significant last words to them: "But spare me, do not rob me of my God! I know myself, I shall rebel." Dmitri, like his creator, "felt ideas"; and after he has come through the refiner's fire of sin and suffering to humility, he *feels* the goodness of God. That is all he needs. For the new Dmitri, as for Faust, "feeling is all in all." Thus once more Dostoevsky glorifies the human heart at the expense of the intellect.

Grushenka's testimony for the good and true is almost as eloquent as Dmitri's. She starts with only an onion, but she ends with a garden full of flowers. When she recognizes in Alyosha the kindliness, the compassion, and the purity of heart which she has looked for all her life, she is clothed with new aspiration. She casts aside her capricious willfulness, which has always been only an outer garment, and begins to move with sure steps toward grace. Like Nastasya in *The Idiot*, she has been wounded by the role and the label imposed upon her by society, and she has retaliated by playing her part with grim relish. However, she is different from Nastasya—more flexible, more resilient. Neither woman has ever found anything or anyone deserving of her fidelity, and the heart shrivels in the absence of loyalties. Grushenka has compensated for the ugliness of reality by putting her faith in an illusion. For five years she has carried in her heart an idealized image of the Pole and of her responsibility to him. When she sees him, in contrast to Dmitri, for the spurious creature he is, her faith is still alive. When she tells Dmitri that she believes in him, she is speaking out of the fullness of a soul that has been nourished on morsels, but nourished nevertheless. Her loyalty to Dmitri is for life, and it is strong enough to sustain both of them. When Dmitri is accused of the crime he did not really commit, she takes the guilt upon herself. And when Dmitri is being tried by almost unbearable pressures, she supports him with her love and her moral courage as surely as Sonia supported Rodya.

Grushenka is far more flesh and blood than Sonia, and she is more convincing, because she reaches out for the good in the midst of her fallibility. She practices the kindness that Ivan demands but fails to offer. Her generosity in giving old Maximov a sofa on which to sleep, her forgiveness of the Pole, and her insight into the needs of the family of the poor captain and her efforts to supply those needs—these are the acts which demonstrate that Grushenka is richly capable of love, not only the love of woman for man, but the love of one of God's creatures for all the others.

If ever there has been a victorious witness for the truth as revealed in Christianity, that witness is *The Brothers Karamazov*. The wayward heart of Dmitri, groping for the strength to go to Siberia if need be and to erect a tower of faith on the weak foundations of his indecisive and erring humanity, is a challenging attestation. The beautiful flowering of Grushenka's nature is another. And the experience of Alyosha at the moment when he passes from spiritual boyhood to manhood is another. Alyosha throws himself on the earth in despair when the corruption of the body of his beloved Zossima proves the failure of miracle. But the miracle does not fail after all, for he rises up knowing "that something firm and unshakable . . . had entered into his soul. It was as though some idea had seized the sovereignty of his mind. . . . He had fallen on the earth a weak boy, but he rose up a resolute champion."

To Alyosha is entrusted the opportunity to make the final affirmation. In the moving scene which concludes the book, Alyosha meets a group of boys after the funeral of little Illusha, who has died a luckless victim of "man's inhumanity to man." It is no coincidence that Alyosha is the last spokesman. There could be no other ending, according to Dostoevsky, for he believed that in the moral universe, as much as in the physical, the law of the survival of the fittest prevails. Old Karamazov has been murdered, Smerdyakov has hanged himself, Ivan is deranged by brain fever, and Dmitri is waiting for the sentence that may send him to Siberia, whither Grushenka, acknowledging her share in his guilt, is willing to accompany him. Even the saintly Zossima has fallen before the ravages of time. Only Alyosha is left—young, vigorous, pure, and buoyant in the faith. When the boys ask him whether it is true that "we shall all rise from the dead and shall live," he answers without hesitation, "Certainly we shall all rise again, certainly we shall see each other and shall tell each other with joy and gladness all that has happened!" He says to the boys: "Well, let us go! And now we go hand in hand." In his care they are safe. The arrogant young Kolya will be saved from being another Ivan, for the fittest has survived—not Ivan, but Alyosha, who will go out into the world to bring forth fruit in the vineyard of God.

It may be that Dostoevsky did not *prove* anything, but he did something better. He concluded his saga of the human spirit by answering—without any loophole for contradiction—the question old Fyodor addressed to his sons, answering with a profound and transcendent faith in the immortal soul of man. At the conclusion of *The Brothers Karamazov*, Christ and the truth are, for Dostoevsky, at last one. Is there a God? Is there immortality? There is! "In GOD IS IMMORTALITY."

Critics of Dostoevsky have no difficulty picking flaws in his consistency or his logic. He made mistakes in deduction and prediction. The earnestness of his own faith-seeking led him to make preposterous claims regarding Orthodoxy. Western readers can scarcely avoid being irritated by his passionate Russianism. But Dostoevsky's view of life is lighted by a remarkable vision of the truth. His finest contribution to humanity was his knowledge that the basic problem of Russia, and of civilized man, is a spiritual problem. He knew that the fate of Russia hinged upon the degree of her spiritual soundness and vitality. Dostoevsky's fear and suspicion of the materialism of the West came from an uneasy sense of impending danger. His rejection of science was motivated by awareness that the spirit is likely to suffer from an abundance of *things*. He knew that "enlightenment" means not so much the accumulation of information as the illumination of the spirit.

Dostoevsky was acutely aware that to hold fast to an anchoring faith in the good is a rare achievement, and he was convinced that without such a faith there is no possibility of health of spirit or of creative fulfillment. He could not resolve his own struggle for faith as he resolved Dmitri Karamazov's, but with all the "anguish of a proud determination" he kept up the good fight, and his books are the sensitive recordings of an earnest soul struggling toward understanding and peace.

VIII/ Tolstoy: Not Peace, But War

Most ironic among the many ironies of Russian literature is the fact that Leo Tolstoy's preaching of the gospel of peace inspired the spirit of revolution in his countrymen. During the last thirty years of his life he begged his fellow Russians to put on the armor of God and march forth to create heaven on earth. These words (from "Carthago Delenda Est," 1899) serve appropriately as the text of his message:

> . . . It is only necessary for you to awake in order to realize all the horror and insanity of that which you have been and are doing, and, having realized this, to cease that evil which you yourselves abhor, and which is ruining you. If only you were to refrain from the evil which you . . . detest, those ruling imposters, who first corrupt and then oppress you, would disappear like owls before the daylight, and then those new, human, brotherly conditions of life would be established for which Christendom—weary of suffering, exhausted by deceit, and lost in insolvable contradictions—is longing.

This and others of his utterances created a giant paradox. He who preached peace was answered—not by peace, but the sword. This was the bitter fruit of the long travail of his spirit.

I.

On August 28, 1828, Leo Nikolayevich Tolstoy was born at Yasnaya Polyana ("beautiful glade"), not far from the city of Tula and about 130 miles south of Moscow. Tolstoy's father and mother were both members of famous Russian families whose lineage can be traced back for generations. Many of his ancestors had played important political and cultural roles in the development of Russia. His father had already retired from the civil service at the time of Leo's birth. It is generally understood that the elder Tolstoy was the model for the character of Nicholas

Rostov in *War and Peace*. The author's mother was the model for Princess Marya in the same book. Leo had three older brothers. His only sister was born when he was a year and a half old. A few months after the birth of this child, Tolstoy's mother died.

Tolstoy's father supervised the affairs of his estate and carried on the activities typical of a country gentleman. He remained distant from all political affairs, particularly as he became more disturbed by the autocratic rule of Nicholas I. Tolstoy was fond of his father, but there is no evidence that the latter had any appreciable influence upon his son. A strong influence was that of the boy's dead mother, whom he idolized. Some impression of the place she held in her son's imagination may be gained from the chapters of *Childhood* which relate the poignant details of a boy's parting from his mother when he goes to the city to be educated and the final parting when she dies shortly afterward. Although modern readers seldom find Princess Marya (*War and Peace*) appealing, there can be no doubt that Tolstoy lavished upon her his utmost devotion as an author.

Tolstoy was nine years old when his father died. The family was then living in Moscow, the older boys being prepared for the university. The father's death occurred under circumstances which aroused the suspicion that despite his benevolence as a landlord he might have been murdered by the two serfs who had accompanied him on a business trip. Less than a year later, the children's grandmother Tolstoy, who had supervised their upbringing, also died. These two experiences of loss in close succession probably started what remained all through Tolstoy's life an abnormal awareness and fear of death. Even in the midst of robust health and at the height of his vigor, he was often gripped by terror at the inevitability of extinction.

"Auntie" Tatyana Yergolskaya, a distant relative of his father, influenced Tolstoy even more than his grandmother and aunts. This warmhearted woman gave her life to caring for the Tolstoy children, whose father she had loved and lost to the wealthy Princess Volskonski, their mother. Tolstoy leaned heavily upon her devotion and had a deep affection for "Auntie" Tatyana to the end of her long life. This woman, who was everything a mother might have been, was the inspiration for the character Sonia in *War and Peace*.

In spite of the loss of his parents, Tolstoy had a happy, active childhood in the company of his three older brothers. They were fortunate in having become acquainted with nature in the rich serenity of Yasnaya Polyana. From his earliest years Tolstoy was responsive to the ever changing power and beauty of nature. The leader among the brothers was the oldest, Nikolai. His qualities of unselfishness, modesty, and responsibility, and his imagination and creative faculties were well developed even in childhood. Tolstoy had a special feeling for Nikolai, as he had for his dead mother, whom Nikolai resembled in many ways. Led by Nikolai, the boys played a game they called "Ant Brothers." Nikolai had told them he knew a secret which could make all men happy and enable them to live harmoniously in a universal brotherhood. If men became "Ant Brothers," the strife and misery of human life would be replaced by peace and love. The secret, he said, was written on a green stick buried at a certain place in a forest at Yasnaya Polyana. The boys joined with zest in this and others of Nikolai's fancies, to which Tolstoy traced the beginning of his own ideals of brotherly love and purity. When the author was eighty years old, still cherishing memories of those early experiences, he asked to be buried "at the place of the green stick."

As was customary in the families of the Russian gentry, the education of the Tolstoy children was entrusted to tutors, who emphasized facility in the use of languages above everything else. Until the young Leo was nine years old, this training was anything but systematic. He learned more from his observation of nature, his long talks with the family servants, and his haphazard reading in the wake of his older brothers than from his formal lessons. Even as a young boy he began to exhibit the characteristics which marked his maturity. He was high spirited and fond of enjoyment, but his capacity for pleasure alternated with moods of earnest preoccupation when he was intent upon looking inward. He was volatile, tender, gay, and kind, his natural liveliness occasionally counteracted by shyness—probably a manifestation of his introversive tendencies and of self-consciousness springing from his belief that he was ugly in appearance. He always sought both affection and attention, but his pride and his habit of analysis stood in the way of friendship. While still a child he spent hours considering such abstractions as the relation of suffering to happiness, the possibility of the existence of God and immortality, and the problem of how to lead a good life. No wonder his lessons took second place in his interests.

For several years after the death of his father, Leo lived sometimes in Moscow but more often at Yasnaya Polyana. In his thirteenth year the first decisive change in his life took place. His father's older sister, the children's legal guardian, died. Thereafter they were entrusted to the guardianship of a younger aunt who lived in Kazan. She decreed that the young Tolstoys should join her in Kazan and proceeded to have her decision carried out. For the children the parting from "Auntie" Tatyana was painful. For Leo this change also meant something else; it was his formal introduction to the world.

In Kazan young Leo's immediate problem was to prepare for the entrance examinations at the university. Because his record as a student bore no signs of diligence, this process was not easy. But he applied himself to the task, and with the help of tutors and extra courses at the gymnasium he was ready to attempt the examinations shortly before his sixteenth birthday. After an unsuccessful first effort, he tried again, successfully, a few months later. When he matriculated, he expected to prepare for a diplomatic career. His failure in the first midterm examinations caused a change in his plans, and he decided to shift to the easier Faculty of Jurisprudence. But already his inclination to seek pleasure, combined with the worldly advice of his guardian aunt, had determined the direction of his interests. He began to specialize in being a man about town instead of a student, with unfortunate results academically.

Tolstoy's ineffectual performance as a student, however, was not the result of intellectual apathy. Even in the midst of social activity he read widely, was much interested in literature and philosophy, and was always ready to undertake independent research in a subject that attracted him. But he found the university routines crippling rather than stimulating. When he was eighteen years old, he received his inheritance, which included the beloved Yasnaya Polyana, the estate his mother had brought to the Tolstoy family. A short time later he made his decision: he would leave the university, return to his birthplace, and assume the responsibilities of a landowner.

He did not intend, however, to give up his intellectual development. After his return to his estate he outlined a plan of study of staggering proportions. He also began what proved to be a lifelong habit, the formulation of strict rules for his own conduct. Furthermore, he resolved to set about the improvement of the welfare of his serfs. His attitude toward them in this early stage was that of a paternalistic Santa Claus, who thought that by filling the peasants' Christmas stockings he would be able to change their misery to well-being and to inaugurate a new era of beneficence. This was the beginning of the never ending discrepancy between Tolstoy's theories and the unsatisfactory results of those theories. Neither he nor anyone else could have learned all he expected to master in the first year after he freed himself from academic restraints. Moreover, being Count Leo Tolstoy and not Saint Francis, he could not live up to the severe moral injunctions he imposed upon himself. He soon found that his peasants did not believe in Santa Claus or in the well-meaning but poorly planned efforts of their master to treat them honestly.

Tolstoy's initial enthusiasm quickly gave way to disillusionment, and the quiet of the country palled on the young reformer.

For several years thereafter he tried recklessly to lose himself in enjoyment. Moscow was most often his headquarters, but he also made a frontal attack upon Petersburg society, which dazzled him for a time. He occupied a nominal post in the Tula assembly, made several halfhearted attempts to gain readmission to the university, and retreated to Yasnaya Polyana when his debts forced him to economize. He also studied piano and did some miscellaneous writing. A dozen times he made a decision about his future, and each time shifted quickly to something else. In Moscow and Petersburg he followed the pattern prescribed for idle and dissipated young rakes. He drank, flirted—women were irresistible to him—gambled, wasted his time and substance, followed a meaningless routine of social activities, and pushed his way into the highest society. But Tolstoy was different from the other dilettantes and profligates. He lived a double life. Externally he was like the others, yet he waged unceasing war within himself. His diary is a monotonous but unrelenting record of his lapses from moral rectitude. He could not follow his rules, but he persevered in making them. He looked everlastingly inward, and every inward glance was followed by self-excoriation. He kept going in a circle: levity and excess, self-criticism and remorse.

The second major change in Tolstoy's life occurred when he was not quite twenty-three. When his oldest brother, Nikolai, came home on furlough from the Caucasus, Leo decided to accompany him when he returned to his battery. In the four years since Leo had left the university without completing his course, he had accomplished nothing tangible, but he had begun to store up material upon which he would draw all the rest of his life. Although he did not know it, he was at last ready to begin his career.

The long trip across Russia to the Cossack village where his brother was quartered made an unforgettable impression upon Tolstoy. In the village and among the Cossacks, he was impressed by the people themselves. He admired their simplicity, naturalness, and strength and yearned to be like them. But by this time it no longer surprised him that nothing was simple for him. He made no progress in conforming to his ideals. His periods of appreciation of the beauties of nature and of something akin to religious fervor were invariably succeeded, as before, by lapses into dissipation. Finally, resolved to put an end to his feeling of being useless, he applied for entrance into the army. He received his appointment and took part in several expeditions to put down the rebellion of frontier tribes. From the first he distinguished himself for courageous conduct in action, sometimes behaving as if unconcerned in the midst of danger. Nevertheless, he soon began to be aware of the brutality and futility of war, this awareness being the first stage in what gradually developed into an uncompromising rejection of war and everything related to it.

After he had been in the Caucasus for a year or more, Tolstoy finished a manuscript on which he had worked in his free intervals for some months. He sent it to the poet Nekrasov, editor of the *Contemporary*, who published it in his journal. This was the same poet-editor to whom Grigorovich had taken Dostoevsky's *Poor Folk* six years earlier. Tolstoy was now twenty-four years old, the same age Dostoevsky had been when *Poor Folk* was published. This first of Tolstoy's published works, *Childhood*, brought him approbation and the beginning of fame. From this time the stories that he wrote with increasing frequency were welcomed by publishers and readers. He was spared the unhappy experience of being buffeted by unfavorable reviews. In writing *Childhood*, he drew richly upon autobiographical sources. The narrative is a subjective record of the late childhood of a boy such as Tolstoy must have been, with emphasis upon feelings rather than events. It is a sensitive treatment, marred occasionally by sentimentality but stamped with absolute genuineness.

Tolstoy remained in the Caucasus for two and a half years. During that time he continued to swing back and forth between reckless abandonment to pleasure—especially the pleasures of women and gambling—and the severest self-examination, in a struggle to attain a degree of control and inward peace. Although military exploits at first afforded a tantalizing outlet for his energies, he soon recognized that an army camp was not a place where he could learn to control his passions. When his request for a transfer and furlough was granted and he returned briefly to Yasnaya Polyana after nearly three years' absence, he had already become an established writer. In addition to a number of short stories he had also completed *Boyhood*, which continued *Childhood* and added to his reputation. It has much of the same charm as the earlier narrative, though perhaps less freshness.

In 1853, Russia became involved in a conflict with Turkey, ostensibly caused by Russia's determination to protect all Orthodox Christians in the Ottoman Empire. Nicholas I welcomed the strife. He believed, as the Russian Czars of the nineteenth century had believed on more than one occasion, that conflict abroad would reduce antagonism to the reactionary government at home. The Russian forces occupied two Turkish provinces, and Russia declared war on Turkey, confident that she would receive aid from England and France. However, the reverse happened. In the spring of 1854, England and France declared war on Russia. After a short furlough Tolstoy was assigned to an artillery brigade near Bucharest, and he participated in the siege on Silistria. On the retreat of the Russian Danubian forces, he asked for a transfer to more active service. When the allies landed in the Crimea and the siege of Sevastopol began, he was given the opportunity he had requested. For several months he was stationed near the besieged city. Then his battery was ordered to Sevastopol, where he participated in that famous siege until the city collapsed. As commander of a gun battery he frequently took part in heavy firing.

In the prolonged engagement at Sevastopol, Tolstoy was completely repelled by what had increasingly become disturbing to him—the horror of violence, the futility of bravery, and the waste and meaningless slaughter of war. As he watched the city burn on his twenty-seventh birthday, his heart was heavy at Russia's loss of the war, but far heavier at the fact of war. He saw that no matter how devastating the physical destruction, it could not compare with the spiritual destruction. He could scarcely wait to resign his commission and turn his full attention to what he had at last decided were to be his two primary pursuits, literature and the tempering of his soul.

The degree to which literature had become his mistress is indicated by the fact that even during the most strenuous military activities at Sevastopol he was using every possible moment for writing. At this time he wrote two of the *Sevastopol Sketches*, "Sevastopol in December" and "Sevastopol in May." The first, composed during the early months of the siege and warmly patriotic, aroused a fervor of national feeling throughout the country. Alexander II, who had succeeded his father, Nicholas I, and hoped to see the war through to a favorable conclusion, read it with emotion, had it translated into French, and gave orders that the life of the young author should not be unnecessarily endangered. But between the first and second sketches a radical change had taken place in Tolstoy's reactions. The earlier patriotic theme was supplanted by a merciless unmasking of the uselessness and horror of carnage. Naturally, the second sketch aroused the editors' misgivings, but they went ahead with publication. When the censors finished with it, however, it was dismembered almost beyond recognition. Tolstoy also began work on *The Story of a Russian Landowner* and completed a number of other short narratives. During all this period, although he continued his intermittent dissipations, for which he sharply censured himself, his habit of looking inward increased. The fact that he broke all the rules he set for himself did not diminish his earnestness.

A few months before the collapse of Sevastopol an entry perhaps more significant than anything else up to that time appeared in his diary:

> Yesterday a conversation about Divinity and Faith suggested to me a great, a stupendous, idea to the realisation of which I feel capable of devoting my life. That idea is the founding of a new religion corresponding to the present development of mankind: the religion of Christ but purged of dogmas and mysticism—a practical religion, not promising future bliss but giving bliss on earth.

Somewhat earlier he had stated: "The aim of my life is known: it is goodness, the duty I owe to my serfs and fellow-countrymen." When he was near the end of his military experience, he wrote, "To-day I returned to my former view of life, the aim of which is welfare and the ideal—virtue." Tolstoy had at last begun to feel his way toward the mission which was to be a dominating motivation.

Yet when he returned to St. Petersburg, he seemed for a time less interested in virtue than in being lionized. Turgenev and Nekrasov took the lead in presenting him to literary circles. Here his indifference to social graces became manifest; he made few efforts to please. He gained the reputation of being difficult and developed more enmities than friendships in his association with writers. Turgenev's initial enthusiasm soon changed to open antagonism, which lasted as long as he lived. Tolstoy's fame was not injured, however, by his argumentativeness and rudeness in the salons. The publication of "Sevastopol in August" and *Youth*, the last of the three sections of his saga of growing up, strengthened his now impressive reputation. But he soon became bored by everything connected with his superficial way of life and turned his back upon it.

The death at this time of the brother just older than Tolstoy made a deep impression on him though he appeared to pay scant attention. This brother and the woman he had taken from a brothel and regarded as his wife were to appear nearly twenty years later as Nikolay Levin and his faithful Marya in *Anna Karenina*.

When Tolstoy realized that emancipation of the serfs was not far distant, he proposed to his peasants a plan to free them and enable them to pay for small land allotments over a period of time. This was his first positive attempt to improve the condition of his serfs and to rationalize his position as a landowner. With their customary distrust, the peasants refused his offer, much to Tolstoy's regret. His disappointment aggravated the recurring feeling of not having found his place in the world. He knew that he must write, yet he was harassed by a sense of urgency to make a positive contribution to the welfare of his fellow men. He had thought for some time that marriage would help him settle down, but repeated efforts to find a woman both congenial and attractive had met with no results. His frequent amorous adventures and his habits of dissipation had made it almost impossible for him to give up his freedom. He tried a grand tour of Europe, but his restlessness accompanied him, and extensive gambling losses forced him to cut the trip short. Before his return from abroad a new idea occurred to him, however. His decision to open a school for the peasant children of his village was the beginning of a new period in his development.

At this point Tolstoy was disinterested in the practice of literature. He broke off his connection with the literary men of his time, retaining a real friendship only with the second-rate writer, Fet. He was impatient with what seemed to him the alienation of literature from life and resented an assumption of superiority in his fellow writers. His vanity and pride made it difficult for him to acknowledge that others might have a talent superior to his, yet his talent no longer meant much to him. His almost morbid introspection continued, along with a deep interest in religion, but by this time he had given up hope of finding satisfaction in the Orthodox church. His correspondence with his cousin, the Countess Alexandra Tolstoy, is most revealing. In a letter to her in 1859 he clearly defined his position with regard to religion:

> I love and esteem religion; according to my lights man can

> never be good nor happy without it. Rather than all things in the world should I have loved to possess religion. . . . I have hopes still: I have for moments a gleam of faith, but I neither have religion nor dogma. Further, with me religion is the outcome of life and not the reverse. . . . Just now . . . I feel such a cad, and there is such a void in my heart that I am overcome with horror and abomination, and the urgency of religion becomes very prominent. May God grant it to me![1]

A few months later Tolstoy opened his school for peasant children at Yasnaya Polyana. His teaching was one of the most rewarding experiences of his entire life; he was intensely gratified by the alertness and responsiveness of the children. The school was conducted on the principles now associated with so-called progressive education. Tolstoy believed that all learning should be voluntary, that the students' interests should determine the subjects to be studied, that all forms of rigid discipline were a hindrance rather than an asset to learning, and that relations between teacher and pupil should be informal. He met the children on their own level, inspired their confidence and affection, and was rewarded by having pupils so eager for education that their thirst was an exhilarating challenge. The project was completely successful.

All thoughts of writing remained buried while Tolstoy concentrated upon his educational experiments. Not satisfied with his own theories, he made an extensive European tour for the purpose of observing pedagogical methods in other countries. In general he was repelled by the authoritarianism of the systems he studied. In addition to lavish giving of his own time and energy as a teacher, he also trained other teachers, for the school quickly expanded beyond his power to handle alone. He paid the teachers' salaries and paid the cost of an additional building, published a magazine for the discussion of his own and other educational theories, and made many efforts to sell the idea of

[1] From *Letters of Tolstoy and His Cousin, Countess Alexandra Tolstoy, 1857–1903* (London, Methuen, 1929).

peasant education throughout Russia. At last he had the satisfaction of knowing that he was doing something useful which needed to be done, something, moreover, which he could do excellently. During all his teaching experience he maintained one of his lifelong convictions: that the intellectuals could learn more from the peasants than the peasants could learn from the intellectuals.

One melancholy event saddened Tolstoy even during this period of escape from the disorganization and dissipation of his earlier years. A second brother, this time the beloved Nikolai, died from tuberculosis. The loss of the individual dearest to him drove his thoughts inward again to the preoccupation with death which shadowed so much of his life.

After the emancipation of the serfs Tolstoy was appointed to the position of Arbiter of the Peace for his district. The duties of the arbiters were to supervise the enforcement of regulations legalized by the Emancipation Act and to attempt to bring about amicable settlements between landlords and the peasants, who now were permitted to purchase land. Tolstoy served judiciously in this capacity but aroused the ire of landlords who knew that his sympathies were with "the people." After one term he was glad to be freed from this responsibility. His impatience with the reactionary czarist regime was changed to hostility by an event which occurred during one of his frequent absences from home. His house was ransacked by police searching for documents which might incriminate him by showing him in collusion with the revolutionary forces now steadily gaining ground. Naturally, the search yielded none of the expected evidence, but Tolstoy never recovered from the indignity of being submitted to this violation of his privacy. Thereafter he understood as never before the enormities of which the czarist regime was capable.

During the period of Tolstoy's concentration upon education, some of his friends and many of the thoughtful writers of the day were distressed by his desertion of literature. He had nearly ceased to be read, and some who had looked upon him as a literary rival whispered that his talent had burned itself out. In spite of the enmity between them, Turgenev was particularly disappointed, believing that Tolstoy was prostituting his talent by occupying himself with so prosaic a matter as education. But Tolstoy's attention still did not return to writing even after his interest in the school waned and he handed over the responsibility to others.

In the early autumn of 1862, Tolstoy was thirty-four years old, still unsettled, and convinced that if he did not marry at once he never would. He began to feel old, called himself ugly, and could not believe that any woman would be attracted to him. In this state of mind he was drawn to the daughters of a Moscow family with whom he had for some time been on intimate terms. The father, Dr. A. E. Behrs, had married a woman, only slightly older than Tolstoy, whom the author had known in childhood. They had three daughters. Liza, the oldest, was a grave, unsociable girl with a strong intellectual bent; Tanya, the youngest, was a vivacious, mercurial child, warm hearted and talented. Between the two was Sonya—beautiful, sentimental, and domestic in her interests, her liveliness frequently countered by a tendency to vague dissatisfaction with what came her way. When Tolstoy's determination to marry became unmistakable, it was assumed that he would choose the oldest of the sisters. However, her aloofness disturbed him, and he chose the second, Sonya, who was only slightly more than half his age.

After debating at length the eligibility of every woman he had met for the past ten years, Tolstoy at last reached a decision and was married not more than two or three months later. Although it would be inaccurate to suggest that he fell in love—it was a case of his making up his mind to marry—he behaved for a month or so like the greenest schoolboy, unable to bring himself to declare his "passion," afraid he would be rejected. The story of the courtship is outlined in *Anna Karenina*, except that there was no Vronsky to embitter Tolstoy and, despite her youth, Sonya had little of the complaisance of Kitty. Tolstoy proposed, as Levin did, by using only the initial letters of words in whole sentences, which the responsive girl delighted him by being able to read. Like Levin, he showed his prospective bride his diary containing a record of his earlier excesses, and Sonya forgave him with many tears. In October, 1862, when Tolstoy took his wife back to Yasnaya Polyana, he entered upon the next-to-the-last stage of his career. This was the stage of great creative achievement. It produced his immortal novels, *War and Peace* and *Anna Karenina.*

The marriage of Leo Tolstoy has probably been the target of more scrutiny than that of any other literary figure in history. Every detail of the marital relation that could be exposed has been laid open, and the frequent expression of varying views on the subject has worn it threadbare. Perhaps the best summary of the whole matter was made by Alexandra Tolstoy, the youngest daughter of the ill-joined couple, in her book *Tolstoy, A Life of My Father*: "Most writers have unconsciously taken the side of the one or the other, blaming either Tolstoy or his wife for the drama of their . . . life together. I believe that to write about it with impartiality is a task no one could fulfill."[2] Although it is tantalizing to conjecture what might have been if the novelist had married a different woman, such guesses are obviously futile. Let it suffice to say that Tolstoy accomplished his purpose of winning a wife—but not the kind of wife he had hoped for. During every one of the remaining forty-seven years of his life, the burden of his marriage became heavier until it drove Tolstoy to his grave.

The marriage started serenely enough, except for the misunderstandings and quarrels to be expected of two people of disparate ages and no real congeniality of temperament. The young wife was distressed by, but yielding in, her wifely duties. From the first, however, she evinced qualities of moodiness and determination that Tolstoy had not foreseen. The abrupt change from life in the city, where she had been in the center of family affection and social activity, to an isolated existence in the country,

[2] Page 158.

where she was dependent upon the company of her introversive husband and his elderly relatives and servants, would, of course, have been difficult for any girl. The birth of the first child after less than a year of marriage brought Tolstoy to a pitch of exaltation quickly reduced during the wearisome period of the child's infancy. As one child followed another and Sonya's attention was perforce concentrated on the nursery, she was unable to understand why her husband's concern was not centered there also, nor could she forgive him for what she considered his indifference to his children. The young wife quickly became a devoted mother and a competent housewife; the family was her world. This absorption was to be one of the major causes of conflict between husband and wife.

Tolstoy had hoped to find stability and completeness in family life. He needed to escape from his inner struggles to something satisfying, immediate, and wholesome. Family life, he had thought, would consume his energies and cause him to put aside his youthful excesses and false starts, the morbid fears, the sense of alienation, and the women he had trifled with and left behind (including the peasant Aksinia, probably the only woman he ever really loved). At first his hopes seemed to be realized. He was happy and relieved that the role of husband enabled him to hold his sensual nature within bounds. Moreover, he was kept busy by the responsibilities of the management of the estate. When these were not enough, he found outlets for his tremendous physical energy in hunting and other sports. To infer, however, that he became vegetative and absorbed by married bliss would be a mistake, a failure to recognize the essential quality of Tolstoy's temperament. Even in the first years with Sonya his moods of unrestrained felicity alternated with periods of deepening misgiving, not about the external circumstances of his life, but about the circumstances of his spirit. He continued to make rules for himself—sterner rules now—and he blamed himself for not living up to them. He was still trying to find some justification for his life.

Despite the intermittent spiritual strivings and failings, during the early and comparatively idyllic years of his marriage Tolstoy's creative power, kindled anew, rose to a white flame unlike anything it had known before or was to know later. The first work to appear, however, did not represent the attitude of Tolstoy at the time. *The Cossacks* (1863) had been written long before, most of it while Tolstoy was in the Caucasus. By the time of its publication, though it had been revised in the intervening years, Tolstoy had lost interest in it and considered it unsatisfactory. Obviously a lesser production in comparison with his great books, it still deserves more attention than it receives, both for the powerful evocation of the background scenes and, even more, for the characters, particularly the Cossacks. The story is plainly autobiographical. The main character, Dmitri Olenin, a fashionable young Moscow aristocrat disturbed by the emptiness of his existence, resolves to seek a new life. Living among the Cossacks, he is impressed by their simplicity and naturalness. He falls in love with a Cossack girl, Maryanna. When she decides in favor of another suitor from among her own people, Olenin is again oppressed by a sense of futility and returns to the artificial society of Moscow, still restless and without anchorage. This book was the last work of the youthful Tolstoy.

When he returned to writing, after the long interruption caused by his experiments in education and by his marriage, Tolstoy began to think about a novel which would deal with the Decembrist movement. Although the men who in 1825 had been martyrs to the cause of freedom were now nearly forgotten, the cause for which they had worked and been exiled was rapidly gaining momentum. Tolstoy collected great amounts of information, began to write, and even published a few chapters. In the process, however, he discovered that he needed to go back to the reign of Alexander I to understand the Decembrist uprising. Soon he dropped his original plan in favor of a study of the Napoleonic period and the French invasion of Russia. This project became the novel *War and Peace*, which engrossed Tolstoy's attention for five years. When *War and Peace* was published in 1869, it became a landmark in the progress of fiction.

Tolstoy next planned to move backward in history to the period of Peter the Great, but after making several false starts, he was drawn instead to his own time. In 1873 he began to write *Anna Karenina*. Although the novel was four years in the making, it brought Tolstoy little of the satisfaction he had felt in the creation of *War and Peace*. Changes taking place in his thinking made him impatient with what seemed to him the unimportance of all the subject matter except the spiritual history of the hero, Levin. When he had completed this novel, Tolstoy stood on the threshold of the last major development in his experience.

Even though Sonya's tastes and wishes conflicted increasingly with her husband's, it should be said to her credit that she always had a genuine interest in his writing. She was never so well satisfied as when he would lose himself in the composition of a book she thought would add to his fame. In the intervals between his creative periods she grew fearful lest Tolstoy might be forever distracted from the thing he could do supremely well. Beginning as his amanuensis, she later became his editor. Her patience in the copying of his manuscripts was virtually inexhaustible. She copied all of *War and Peace* five or six times, parts of it more than that. The time and effort she thus expended are particularly impressive when the extent of her domestic duties is considered, to say nothing of her function as a mother. In twenty-six years Sonya Tolstoy bore thirteen children, five of whom died in infancy or early childhood. In the second half of this period, childbearing and child rearing were extremely onerous to her, but Tolstoy was firm in his belief that women were destined primarily for wifehood and motherhood. At the same time that Sonya rebelled against the restraints imposed upon her by the ever increasing size of the family, she became more resentful of her husband's detachment from the children and his refusal to make their material welfare his primary concern.

When Tolstoy buried himself in his study, as he did for long intervals of research and reading, the whole household was under a cloud. In contrast to his youthful impatience at academic routines, his mature capacity for prolonged and intense intellectual discipline was phenomenal. He studied and read everything voraciously. When he did participate in the family activities, however, he charged them with vitality and gaiety. He could enjoy and appreciate and cause others to share his enjoyment and appreciation. Yet there was always something aloof about him, as if he were made on a bigger scale than ordinary people and could not quite blend his spirit with theirs.

As the older Tolstoy children began to grow up, their mother was inflexible in her determination to give them the advantages of city life. Consequently, she insisted that the family spend their winters in Moscow. These intervals away from the country proved a heavy burden to the novelist, but he bowed to his wife's will to the limit of his endurance. Frequent flights to Yasnaya Polyana or visits to friends or relatives helped him face intervals of city life although he could no longer reconcile himself to its pressures or artificiality.

By the time Tolstoy completed *Anna Karenina*, he was rapidly approaching a crisis in his spiritual development. This crisis was compounded of many elements. One of the most important was the sense of the imminence of death which had haunted him since childhood and which drove him to try to justify his existence. Another was the repugnance he felt for the false and useless life of his own social class and, in contrast, his admiration for the hard-working, uncomplicated, and (as he believed) noble peasantry. He went even further: he was repelled by all the trappings of what is called civilization. Another element of the crisis was his yearning for religion coupled with a rationalistic quality of mind which prevented him from accepting the supernatural and doctrinaire elements of Christianity. In one of Tolstoy's letters to the Countess Alexandra Tolstoy (1876) he asserted, "I not only hate and despise atheism, but I can see no possibility of living, and still less of dying, without faith." Yet he did not have a satisfying faith. He described his own beliefs thus:

> Those beliefs are neither very determined nor very consoling. Whenever questioned by the brain they answer all right, but when the heart suffers and seeks response there is neither help nor consolation. As to the exigencies of my brain and the answers of the Christian faith, I find myself in the position of two hands wanting to clasp each other, but whose fingers resist the uniting.

It is customary to speak of Tolstoy's "conversion" as having occurred in 1879. To draw an arbitrary line, however, is misleading, for Tolstoy's philosophy after that date was implicit in his earlier attitudes. The change led to a new solidification and consistency, as well as a clarification. This conversion meant the final rejection of the conventions of his earlier life—the rejection of the aristocratic society in which he had passed his youth, of the attempt to escape into enjoyment and material preoccupation during the first decade or more of his marriage, and the rejection of mysticism in religion. Thereafter, Tolstoy the artist was too often lost in Tolstoy the moralist. In this role he became not only the most famous man in Russia, but the center of a cult which spread far beyond the limits of his own country. It is hard to tell how much the prestige of Tolstoy the moral teacher was dependent upon his having written such magnificent novels as *War and Peace* and *Anna Karenina*, but it is unlikely that as author alone he could have achieved the position he held during the last twenty years of his life.

After 1880, Tolstoy's writings were different from his earlier works, both in quality (which suffered markedly) and in emphasis. He no longer wished to contribute to literature, but wrote for didactic and reform purposes. Moreover, he regarded all the books which had made him famous as unworthy of him, if not actually evil. They were cursed, he believed, with secularism, excessive realism, and lack of moral purpose. He rejected them as the old monks in Browning's poem rejected the paintings of young Fra Lippo Lippi, saying:

> *Make them forget there's such a thing as flesh.*
> *Your business is to paint the souls of men—*

During the next thirty years Tolstoy wrote not for art but for his soul. Or perhaps it would be more accurate to say that he adopted a new philosophy of art. In a labored exposition of this view, *What Is Art?* (1897), he set forth his theory that true art "infects" with sympathetic and right responses. In 1896 he had stated in his journal: "The aesthetic pleasure leaves one unsatisfied. . . . Only moral good gives full satisfaction." And two years later he wrote:

> I say that art is an infectious activity and that the more infectious art is, the better it is. But that this activity be good or bad . . . [depends] on how much it satisfies the demands of the religious consciousness, *i.e.*, morality, conscience.

There can be no doubt that this view of art made Tolstoy unreasonably, even ridiculously, intolerant. He did not hesitate, for instance, to toss aside Homer and Shakespeare as bad writers, because they did not conform to his requirements for art. Moreover, his theory of art introduced a new aridity into his own conceptions. Although zeal is not a substitute for creativity in literature, it is not altogether true, as many critics contend, that Tolstoy produced nothing but stuffy moralizing after his "conversion." Granted, much of his later expository writing is tiresome exhortation. Yet *A Confession* (1882) and *What I Believe* (1883) are among the great statements of faith and may without apology be classed with *The Meditations* of Marcus Aurelius and *The Confessions* of St. Augustine. Almost all his letters and articles are lifted by their masterful style into a class apart from ordinary polemical treatises. And everything Tolstoy wrote, no matter how dogmatic or abstract, has intensity and vigor that is unmistakably his.

The same can be said for the later fiction. Although many of the stories are marred by didacticism and some suffer from the author's determination to be simple and comprehensible to all people, others have a subtle power and are brightened by flashes of the old narrative insight and skill. One of the best of these is *The Death of Ivan Ilyich.* On the surface a record of morbid preoccupation with death, it actually goes deep into the recesses of the lonely soul searching for comfort before the fact of annihilation. *The Memoirs of a Madman* and *Master and Man* are two other distinguished stories in which Tolstoy powerfully set forth the travail of the human spirit. *The Kreutzer Sonata* is the most controversial of the later works of fiction. In this account of a jealous husband, the novelist denounced the artificial marriage codes of his time and, probably involuntarily, laid bare his own resentment against marriage, showing how far it falls short of expectation. A less well-known but more significant story is *The Devil,* in which the analysis of the sexual passion has autobiographical overtones. The best known of Tolstoy's later fiction is, of course, *Resurrection* (1899), which made a tremendous impression, probably more by reason of bulk than of quality. It is not the best of the later Tolstoy, yet it is an extremely important document because it summarizes many of the views for which he became universally known. In this last period Tolstoy also wrote a number of plays, the most familiar of which is *The Power of Darkness.* Even the best of his dramas, however, is not so good as the poorer stories.

Tolstoy's mature religion, as illustrated by many of the later writings, may be described as the morality of the Christian faith without the mysticism. Tolstoy believed in deeds, not dogma. Three of his deepest convictions attracted widespread attention. The first was the rejection of the material goods of life, even the ownership of private property. This view brought Tolstoy into conflict with his family—his wife and sons—and was the major cause of the domestic unhappiness of his declining years. The second was the rejection of violence in any form. This conviction included a condemnation of military service and inevitably brought the author under fire from the government. The third was the rejection of authority, particularly the authority of church and state. The only law, Tolstoy believed, was the moral law within man. That inner law was Tolstoy's God. It is no wonder that the Holy Synod of the Orthodox church finally excommunicated the great rebel in 1901, for he represented the most effective challenge to the power of the church in all Russia.[3] Only his fame and prestige saved him from the clutches of the government he opposed with increasing vehemence. A lesser man would have been banished to a dungeon in the Peter and Paul fortress. But the power of the Romanovs was no match for the prophet of Yasnaya Polyana, who wore a peasant's blouse and made his own boots or walked barefoot across the fields he yearned to give away.

The Countess Tolstoy was never able to understand why, if her husband were living for others, he should not live for his family first. From her point of view a father was obligated to satisfy every material desire of his family. It was impossible to reconcile their views. Time after time relations between the two were strained almost to the point of breaking. Tolstoy knew he could never have any peace of spirit or make his conduct harmonize with his teachings as long as he remained in the luxury of Yasnaya Polyana, but he could not bring himself to disrupt the family by following the directive of his conscience. He lived for years stretched on the rack of unwilling infidelity to his deepest beliefs. When he decided he had no right even to the income from his writings, the frenzied protests of the Countess were quieted only by his handing over to her the copyright of his early works and conferring on her and the children the ownership of all his property, which she would not hear of his giving away. This move slightly mitigated but did not eliminate the

[3] The Soviet government has made good use of this action by the Orthodox church, even to the point of showing the writ of excommunication and many related documents in the anti-religion museum now located in the Kazan Cathedral in Leningrad.

criticism Tolstoy had received from both admirers and detractors because he had continued to "enjoy" the riches against which he preached.

In the last twenty-five years of his life Tolstoy attracted a large number of disciples, people of all types, the famous and the humble. Chief among these was V. G. Chertkov, about whom opinions are as divergent as about the Countess Tolstoy. There is little question that he worked his way into Tolstoy's confidence and exercised much influence over him. Chertkov supplied overt opposition to the Countess, who suspected and reviled him with unceasing fury. Tolstoy was severely buffeted by the two of them, especially in the determination of each to have possession of his literary remains. He attempted to appease both, with no success as far as his wife was concerned. Whatever the motives of Chertkov, however, Tolstoy found in him—or thought he found—the sympathy and understanding needed by a person forced by conscience to live in opposition to the desires of most of his family.

Finally, in his eighty-second year, Tolstoy came to the end of his ability to endure the falsity of his position and the neurotic ragings of his wife. Accompanied by his physician, he did what he had wanted to do for a quarter of a century. He fled by night, going first to the convent where his sister, who had become a nun, was living. There he was joined by his youngest daughter, Alexandra, a true disciple. The trio went on with no destination in mind, urged by the old man's need to put his past life completely away from him. It did not matter that they did not know where they were going, for Tolstoy's strength soon failed. He became ill and was forced to stop at the little junction of Astopovo. There, in the home of an unknown stationmaster, the greatest man in Russia died on November 7, 1910.

The dying Tolstoy was still the victim of contradiction. He had tried to escape from fortune and fame, but from the beginning of his illness people all around the world waited anxiously for news, and even in the obscurity of a wayside junction he was the focus of universal attention. In death, however, he was spared the remorse and reproaches of his wife, though she had come with all their family to the scene where he lay dying. In his last hours he did not know that his wife still could not accept his need to escape. She had finally been restrained and was permitted only to peer in at him through the window.

It is paradoxical that Tolstoy, who did not believe in creeds, became the center of a cult and a creed. Although the number of his close followers was not large, some were completely dedicated, and uncounted numbers were attracted to the philosophy of a man who disdained riches and preached humility. Tolstoy would not have been human if he had not been gratified by the enthusiastic response to his views, but it should be said to his credit that he never permitted himself to exploit his influence. The statement in his journal in December, 1897, is a sincere expression of his position:

> There is no Tolstoyanism and has never been, nor any teaching of mine; there is only one eternal, general, universal teaching of the truth, which for me, for us, is especially clearly expressed in the Gospels. This teaching calls man to recognition of his filiality to God and therefore of his freedom or his slavery (call it what you want): of his freedom from the influence of the world, of his slavery to God, His will. And as soon as man understands this teaching, he enters freely into direct communication with God and he has nothing and no one to ask.

The final paradox concerning Tolstoy is the fact that he, who preached humility, was not a humble man. His spirit was wracked, but did not bow down. To the end he hurled his thunderbolts against the universe—an egocentric but sincere genius, bigger than other men, but not quite big enough to create a new design in human history.

Tolstoy's request that he be buried "at the place of the green stick" was fulfilled. Perhaps in death his "spirit sore from marching" achieved the peace it had never known in life.

II.

War and Peace is not only the prose epic of Russia, it is the prose epic of humanity. If it be heresy to suggest that certain of its characters and battle scenes may be compared only with those of the great epics of all times, let the heresy still be spoken. It towers above other works of fiction, for fiction is a representation of life, but *War and Peace* is life.

The novel continues some of the themes which had appeared earlier in Tolstoy's writing. The second and third *Sevastopol Sketches* depicted war realistically, and *The Cossacks* attributed rare qualities of virtue and heroism to simple people. *Childhood, Boyhood, Youth,* and *The Cossacks* reflected Tolstoy's introspective tendencies. But *War and Peace* does all this and more. Here for the first time Tolstoy stepped outside autobiographical limitations into an experience of creativity such as appears only in the rarest achievements of man.

The complexity of *War and Peace* makes impossible in this brief study anything more than a surface comment. It may be said of the novel that the action centers upon the activities of Pierre Bezukhov and of two families, the Rostovs and Bolkonskys. But in fact *War and Peace* surveys the whole life of the upper class in Russia during the period beginning with the uneasy alliance between Russia and France in 1805 and ending after the collapse of the Napoleonic invasion in 1812. The historical panorama serves as background for the detailed accounts of family life in a blend that has the exuberant vitality of real experience. The war is treated with a fidelity to historical fact which bears testimony to Tolstoy's capacity for research, but the obligation to be literally accurate never interferes with the irresistible flow of the narrative. Actually, the novel is, in a sense, unhistorical, for despite basic accuracy in fact, its interpretation of history is uniquely Tolstoyan. But historicity does not matter. This novel deals with more important things; it tells how Paradise may be regained by human beings.

In the brilliant accounts of battles in *War and Peace* it is difficult to see the man who in a few years was to condemn war without reservation. The details of the fighting are related with vividness that borders on gusto. One sees the bright colors of the standards carried proudly at the head of the charge. Beautiful horses bear their splendidly uniformed riders in formations of impressive precision. When Pierre lumbers about on the battlefield at Borodino, he is fascinated, as if the whizzing shells were the music of a calliope reaching the ears of a small boy on circus day. No one could have written such scenes without having experienced the exultation of battle.

The war scenes are not a matter of color and action only. Fear is there, too, and the wounds, the pain, and the death. If Tolstoy did not confine his accounts solely to the slaughter, it was because war as he knew it was not limited to gray and black and to the white faces of the dead. He depicted war realistically, but he did not glorify it. The shells not only whiz, they also burst and rip bodies to shreds. The proud colors are vanquished and lie tattered and trampled in the mud. Horses whinny in terror, lose their riders, and go down themselves, their forlorn carcasses multiplying on the battlefield. Dying lips call in vain for water. The arrogant general looks indifferently past the mangled corpses, disdainful of the "creatures that once were men." Ravaged fields stretch out to the horizon, and the people flee in desolation from their homes, away from the red flood of carnage. All this is *war*.

Tolstoy's mature views are foreshadowed in one significant passage. Prince Andrew, a soldier as Tolstoy had been, denounces war absolutely:

> The aim of war is murder; the methods of war are spying, treachery, and their encouragement, the ruin of a country's inhabitants, robbing them or stealing to provision the army, and fraud and falsehood termed military craft. The habits of the military class are the absence of freedom, that is, discipline, idleness,

> ignorance, cruelty, debauchery, and drunkenness. . . . He who kills most people receives the highest rewards.
>
> They meet . . . to murder one another; they kill and maim tens of thousands, and then have thanksgiving services for having killed so many people.[4]

The use of war as a theme of the novel gave Tolstoy an opportunity to stage a parade of historic personages. Napoleon dominates the group, but dominates by smallness rather than bigness. In this characterization the novelist was not bound by objectivity; most readers will chuckle with satisfaction at the treatment Napoleon gets. He is a pomaded and impertinent bantam, determined to grab the world in his fat fingers. His voice is unpleasantly shrill; it is easy to see that he does not know how to ride a horse well; he has neither the demeanor nor the understanding for true leadership. But he is buoyed up by his fatuous assumption of infallibility. A typical scene illustrates this characteristic. When Napoleon and Alexander were allies, the "undersized" Napoleon on one occasion took it into his head to present the Legion of Honor to a Russian soldier as a token of his esteem. He made the presentation with his customary arrogance: "It was as if Napoleon knew that it was only necessary for his hand to deign to touch that soldier's breast for the soldier to be forever happy, rewarded, and distinguished from everyone else in the world."

With all his conceit and ambition, Napoleon was not strong enough—indeed, Tolstoy maintained no man is strong enough—to make his will prevail. When he stepped on the raft at Tilsit, he seemed to be in control of the situation. When he entered Moscow, he reflected that though the city was his for the taking, he would prove his greatness by behavior which would make him appear merciful and magnanimous. But by the time he left Moscow "the laws which guide events" had proved too much for him. All his decisions had been wrong, the victory was in reality

[4] From the translation by Louise and Aylmer Maude.

a defeat, and he was confronted by the collapse of the edifice he had built on scheming and violence. Tolstoy condemns him, because he was never able to "understand goodness, beauty, or truth," and because, although he imagined that he had willed the war with Russia, "the horrors that occurred did not stagger his soul." With devastating strokes the novelist transforms Napoleon from giant to pygmy:

> To study the . . . tactics and aims of Napoleon and his army from the time it entered Moscow till it was destroyed is like studying the dying leaps and shudders of a mortally wounded animal. . . .
>
> During the whole of that period Napoleon, who seems to us to have been the leader of all these movements . . . acted like a child who, holding a couple of strings inside a carriage, thinks he is driving it.

In contrast to his contempt for Napoleon is Tolstoy's admiration for the Russian general and commander, Kutuzov. This admiration proceeds principally from the fact that Kutuzov's actions harmonized with Tolstoy's views of history. According to Tolstoy, the great men are not those who try to direct history, but those who have the patience to wait while "moment by moment the event is imperceptibly shaping itself." He further asserted, "The will of the historic hero does not control the actions of the mass but is itself continually controlled." Kutuzov exemplifies this circumstance. In consultations with his staff, even on the battlefield, he seemed not so much to give the "go" signals as to be waiting for the signals to be received from some unseen source. His lumbering gait was anything but commanding; he spent little time devising strategy; sometimes at critical moments he might be caught dozing or reading a French novel. But Tolstoy attributed to him a keen perception with regard to events. More than once "he alone understood the significance of what had happened." He was also, Tolstoy believed, a reverent man. When he heard that the French had evacuated Moscow, he turned at once to the icons and fell, weeping, on his knees to give thanks that Russia had been saved.

Tolstoy could not become reconciled to what he considered the false assessment of greatness. He believed that Kutuzov, who did not try to mold events to conform to his own will, had never received the credit he deserved, not even from his own countrymen.

> For Russian historians, strange and terrible to say, Napoleon—that most insignificant tool of history who never anywhere, even in exile, showed human dignity—Napoleon is the object of adulation and enthusiasm; he is grand. But Kutuzov—the man who from the beginning to the end of his activity in 1812, never once swerving by word or deed from Borodino to Vilna, presented an example exceptional in history of self-sacrifice and a present consciousness of the future importance of what was happening—Kutuzov seems to them something indefinite and pitiful. . . .
>
> And yet it is difficult to imagine an historical character whose activity was so unswervingly directed to a single aim; and it would be difficult to imagine any aim more worthy or more consonant with the will of the whole people.

The fact that he was in every sense Russian and that he was alert to the will of the whole nation was in Tolstoy's eyes Kutuzov's unique claim to excellence. Through his simplicity and modesty—the proof of his true greatness—the "will of the whole people" was able to make itself manifest. He was blamed by his contemporaries for not taking an aggressive stand against Napoleon, but in refusing to do so he was obeying what the novelist called the "law of necessity."

The third historical figure who receives full treatment in *War and Peace* is Alexander I, the monarch who raised high hopes in the Russian people after the dark days of the reign of his father, Paul I. Particularly effective is the suggestion of the confidence and affection Alexander inspired in the early years of his reign. When Young Nicholas Rostov saw the Czar for the first time, "he experienced a feeling of tenderness and ecstasy such as he had never known before. He thought that if the Czar should happen to speak to him, he would certainly die of happiness." An interesting detail, however, is the fact that, in spite of his youth and exaltation, Nicholas noticed a quality of indecision about the Czar which made him wonder momentarily, "But then even this indecision appeared to him majestic and enchanting, like everything else the Czar did." This uncertainty was the quality which caused Alexander to fall short of fulfilling the hopes of his people—caused him to submit to the influence of the wrong advisers and in the end to fall into conservative and arbitrary patterns of thought.

The mixture of authority and benevolence in the young Alexander presented a sharp contrast to the pomposity of Napoleon. Alexander could be inflexible, however. When the French entered Russia, he declared that he would not make peace while even one French soldier remained on Russian soil. And he kept his word. Like Kutuzov, he was able to sense and interpret the will of "the people," and as long as the war lasted, he kept their devotion. From little Petya, struggling to pick up one of the biscuits Alexander threw down on the crowd as he stood on the palace balcony, to the Moscow nobles listening while "the pleasantly human voice" urged them to provide money and men to carry on the war—all responded in the same way. Alexander was beloved for himself and as a symbol.

Tolstoy was particularly impressed by the fact that even after having achieved a dominant position in European affairs, Alexander realized that power brought few satisfactions. He is represented as turning his attention almost wholly to spiritual matters in the last years of his reign. In the satisfaction Tolstoy expresses at this development of other-worldliness on the part of the Czar, he anticipates his own spiritual development of later years.

Two of the individuals who played leading parts in the reign of Alexander are given some attention in the novel. Count Michael Speransky, who represented the rational and enlightened side of Alexander's reign, suffers unduly at Tolstoy's hand.

Speransky deserves credit for bringing order out of chaos in the legal system of Russia. In the novel, however, he is seen only through the eyes of Prince Andrew, who at first thought he had found in Speransky his "ideal of a perfectly rational and virtuous man." But Andrew finally discovered that Speransky was human and therefore ceased to admire him. This discovery is more a reflection of Andrew's attitudes than an account of the character of Speransky. Tolstoy's treatment of Count Alexey Arakcheev, on the other hand, harmonizes with the evidence of history, which attributes to him a baleful influence upon Alexander. He was harsh and despotic, and he inspired fear in almost all who were forced to deal with him.

Another character—a compound of fact and fiction—provides the occasion for one of the most unforgettable scenes in the novel, a scene which takes place in Moscow immediately before the entry of the French. Count Rostopchin had been appointed military governor of the city. It was his responsibility to supervise the evacuation of the civilian population and to prepare for the fall of the city into enemy hands. He was not an efficient administrator, and forces too strong for him soon caused him to lose control of the situation. When he recognized that he could no longer impose his authority, he decided on flight, furious at his own impotence. Then, "as often happens with passionate people, he was mastered by anger, but was still seeking an object on which to vent it." Suddenly the thought occurred to him that the mob gathered in the street below wanted a victim, and the thought was soothing to him because he himself felt the need of a victim. Without hesitation he made up his mind. When his attention was by chance called to an unfortunate young political prisoner, he literally threw the young man to the mob. "He has betrayed his Tsar and his country," he said. "He has caused Moscow to perish. I hand him over to you." Though the young man was helpless and not guilty of any crime, the mob proceeded to beat him to death with the bestial fury of human beings who desire to find a scapegoat. The Count derived satisfaction from the spectacle as the lords of Rome were gratified by the sight of Christians thrown before the lions. Later, "he even found cause for self-satisfaction in having so successfully contrived to avail himself of a convenient opportunity to punish a criminal and at the same time pacify the mob." This horrifying episode enabled Tolstoy to show how susceptible a mob is to the direction of unscrupulous maniacs driven by hunger for power. This is war within war—the epitome of humanity at war with itself.

If Tolstoy's insistence upon interlarding the novel with expositions of his theory of history (the "sum of human wills") is somewhat exasperating, all exasperation melts away when the reader is transported back into the company of that large and varied group of people whose emotions and experiences make *War and Peace* enthralling. In some of these characterizations Tolstoy transcends the limitations of fiction. Natasha at her first ball, her face "prepared either for despair or rapture"; Nicholas, Natasha, and Petya at the hunt; the Christmas celebrations, with Natasha singing and the coming of the mummers; Sonya going to the barn to learn her fortune, the prelude to the ebbing of her hopes; the death of the Little Princess in the bleak winter of Bald Hills; old Bolkonsky, goading the pale-faced Marya with his hatred and his love; Natasha, prevented from eloping with the rascal Anatole, learning of his baseness; Natasha's reunion with the wounded Andrew and Andrew's death; Pierre's involuntary non-proposal to the basilisk Helene; the carousing young men and the predatory old women; the companionship of Pierre and Platon in captivity—these characters and episodes are fiction at its best.

There is grandeur in the sweep of the novel, but its size is not the key to its magic. Perhaps the magic is best explained by the vitality which surges through it. That a work so massive could be so animated is remarkable. Tolstoy was nearly forty years old when he completed this masterpiece, but it is his testament of youth. Death and war are here, but in impact they are secondary to life and peace. The spontaneous laughter that rises above the sound of weeping is refreshing, for in Russian literature the infrequent laughter is almost always weighted with mockery. Even the beautifully attired figures moving about the drawing rooms of Moscow and St. Petersburg have a certain grace and dignity, though their hearts may be hollow. Tolstoy was never again to repeat the buoyant affirmation of this salute to life, for the sunlight which infuses it was soon to be transmuted into shadow, and the *joie de vivre* ended forever.

The most dynamic of the characters in *War and Peace* is Natasha Rostova. From the moment she appears—"this black-eyed, wide-mouthed girl, not pretty but full of life—with . . . black curls tossed backward"—she dominates the book. No other novelist in all of literature has surpassed Tolstoy in the evocation of female characters. Natasha's nearest rival is the quieter, more beautiful, more mature Anna Karenina. Both women were made to be loved. Natasha is the essence of woman—the everlasting Eve. In creating her, Tolstoy had in mind his wife's younger sister, Tanya Behrs. Natasha has the same irrepressible gaiety and resilience as her living model. Yet the softness and sweetness are deceptive, for when she makes up her mind, she has a will like granite. She is sometimes selfish, too. It never occurs to her that her pleasure and satisfaction are not the most important things in the world. However, she does not want to hurt anybody, and her kindness is genuine. The quick rush of her tenderness makes her irresistible. Part of her charm lies in her youthful vitality and her capacity for enjoyment. When she dances, her spirit has winged feet, and when she sings, she sings with her eyes and her soul. When she looks out her window at the moonlit night, she is so enraptured by the beauty that even the world-weary Andrew feels an answering lilt in his heart. She is both foolish and wise, but her foolishness can always be forgiven because it makes her suffer more than anyone else does; and although she plays with falsehood, she knows what is true. Natasha laughing and walking in the forest in her yellow dress, Natasha confiding in her mother in the intimacy of their bedtime chats, her fierce suffering after she learns of the treachery of Anatole, and her loving nature rarefied with its new wisdom as she cares for the dying Andrew—these designs in the fabric of her character stand out in vibrant colors. Only at the end of the book is Natasha disappointing. When she becomes dull, complacently absorbed in maternity, the reader can hardly believe she is Natasha at all. Indeed, she is not Natasha, but only an epilogue better left unwritten, deliberately manipulated to illustrate Tolstoy's formula for motherhood. With all his genius, Tolstoy could not make characters live when he forced them to prove a point.

Because of the special glow which surrounds Natasha, there is danger of failing to give adequate attention to some of the other female characters. Natasha's cousin Sonia is a pathetic testimonial to the rigid social system of the time, which made it inevitable for some women to be leftovers. The poor relative in an aristocratic family with social pretensions, she had no right to expect anything from life beyond the role of maiden aunt. To read her story is to be filled with a sense of outrage at the inequities of life and the blindness of those who are bound by social patterns both meaningless and ugly. The most striking of the women is the evil Helene—striking, not because of her beauty, but because she is so perfectly adjusted to evil. She is as inscrutable and uncaring as Mona Lisa and as vicious as the Lucrezia Borgia of the legends. As Dostoevsky's "idiot" emanated goodness, Helene emanates wickedness. Her beautifully chiselled face is a mask from hell. She is, ironically, far more convincing than the noble-spirited Princess Marya, about whom Tolstoy certainly intended to cast the aura of sainthood. However, as Marya emerges from the cocoon of religious resignation in which her father's harshness has caused her to take refuge, it becomes apparent that she has enough spitefulness in her nature to make her quite human, even though she is not appealing.

Marya's father, the old Prince Bolkonsky, is one of Tolstoy's greatest achievements. As he works at his whirling lathe, the flying chips of wood represent the vital energy of the man who is a craftsman as well as an aristocrat. He is caught between two worlds. He has no patience with and cannot understand the ennui of a son who does not find any satisfaction in being the child of tradition and of class. Yet the old man knows that the summer of privilege has ended and his way of life is becoming an anachronism. This knowledge, combined with his genuine love of his country, the future of which appears to him to be shrouded in uncertainty, and with the restrictions of old age, which have removed him from the opportunity to play a significant role in the events of his time and even from the society of men, has driven him to an accumulation of bitterness and frustration often near the point of explosion. The meek femininity of his daughter brings out his irascible despotism, but this severity is only the cloak of the exterior man. To know the real Bolkonsky, one must look into his eyes during the rare moments when his impulse to express his tenderness for his son is held in leash by the rigidity of his pride.

Prince Bolkonsky is more than an embittered aristocrat. He is proof that the Russian landowning class was not composed exclusively of "dead souls," Oblomovs, or "superfluous" men. Tolstoy himself was a member of that class, and he knew better. Bolkonsky is evidence that strength, intelligence, and even integrity could be found among the landed gentry. If there is too fierce a pride, there is also justification for pride. His handsome face, with its look of granite even in repose, is the face of distinction. His fine clothes are the appropriate apparel of a cultivated man. His preoccupation with mathematics reveals a sinewy mind. He is not a parasite or an idler. He has always known his responsibilities as a man of privilege, and he has always fulfilled them. There are order and industry at Bald Hills, both in the home of the master and in the life of his peasants. And there is mutual respect. This view of the aristocrat is so rare in Russian literature that but for Tolstoy it might not have been expressed at all, and it is fitting that we should hear it. Tolstoy himself never repeated it. Some of his other landowners are admirable men, but none other has the will, fortitude, and mental vigor of old Bolkonsky.

Perhaps the fact that *War and Peace* was set in the first two decades of the nineteenth century—a time to which Tolstoy looked with a degree of nostalgia—whereas most of his famous narratives belonged to the point in time when they were being written, accounts for this difference.

The two most important male characters in *War and Peace* (important from the standpoint of being interpreters of what Tolstoy wanted principally to say), Andrew Bolkonsky and Pierre Bezukov, are foils for each other. Tolstoy used the two to carry on a debate, with the intention of weighing man *thinking* against man *feeling*. It is noteworthy that while Tolstoy was working out this debate in *War and Peace*, sheltered in his quiet study at Yasnaya Polyana, Dostoevsky turned the electric energy of his creative power to the same question in *Crime and Punishment*. But Dostoevsky, harassed by creditors and tormented by other pressures, had little time for reflection or for the subtle refinements of the artistry of Tolstoy. The two writers were not in communication with each other. It is fascinating to note that despite the disparity of their circumstances and mental processes and though they approached the debate from different premises, they arrived at almost the same conclusions.

Actually, of course, Tolstoy had reached a decision before he began the novel; the *thinking* Andrew never really has a chance against the *feeling* Pierre. The men are alike in being idealists, but Tolstoy makes Andrew act as if he were not an idealist at all. His intellectuality, his habit of analysis, and the superficiality of the social codes which determine his conduct have clogged the receptors of his soul. He is bored with his "little princess" wife (and who can blame him, though she is a pitiful creature), bored with his official duties, and bored with his social milieu. He has developed a spiritual isolation which cripples his spirit and petrifies his hopes. He admits that the more he thinks, the less he finds life worth living. Obviously, the character of Andrew bears marked similarity to that of the self-willed, introspective type which appears many times in the novels of Dostoevsky (the

Underground Man or a modification of the type). Moreover, there is much of Tolstoy in Andrew—the self-searching, the sense of imperfection, the doubts, the ennui, and the scorn of what others consider important. Also, like Tolstoy, Andrew is forceful and efficient when his interests are channeled. But the force is impotent without affirmative belief, and belief is what Andrew lacks. "I only know two very real evils in life," he says to Pierre, "remorse and illness. The only good is the absence of those evils. To live for myself avoiding those two evils is my whole philosophy now."

Yet Andrew's deeds are better than his words. He maintains that he can see no point in doing anything to better the welfare of the serf or to "raise him from his animal condition and awaken in him spiritual needs," for "it seems to me that animal happiness is the only happiness possible." Yet he goes ahead to emancipate his peasants, bringing about the transformation without friction or confusion. Andrew frequently dwells on thoughts of death, as Tolstoy did, and he cannot find the satisfaction of belief in immortality or even sure belief in God. He does believe in honesty and mercy, and he hates violence and hypocrisy. He comes to see war for what it is. He deplores the fact that the "chivalry" of war—what he calls playing at "magnanimity"—has made mankind blind to the real causes and the real aims of war.

Only twice does Andrew reach out to life, sensing its beauty and power and the riches it holds for him. The first time is when he loves Natasha. His pride is larger than his love, however, and he does not love her enough to forgive her defection. "It takes life to love life," and Andrew's sterile spirit is touched by decay. Thus, he loses the opportunity to be strengthened by Natasha's freshness, her vitality and naturalness, and her firm hold on the life force. The second time he reaches out to life is when he is wounded and dying. Then suddenly he understands what has always eluded him:

> Yes, a new happiness was revealed to me of which man cannot

> be deprived . . . a happiness lying beyond material forces, outside the material influences that act on man—a happiness of the soul alone, the happiness of loving. . . .
>
> . . . But not love which loves for something . . . but the love which I . . . first experienced when I saw my enemy and yet loved him. I experienced that feeling of love which is the very essence of the soul and does not require an object.

Andrew must die in order to be ready to live. That is the ultimate irony of his experience, and Tolstoy often wondered whether all mankind was not cursed by the same irony. The only ones who might escape it, he thought, were those who had simple faith, for whom "feeling is all in all." Pierre Bezukov is one of these. Pierre represents other aspects of Tolstoy's character—the enthusiasm, the humanitarianism, and the love of life. He, too, is a seeker, but from the beginning he has faith. Even if his search brings disappointment, he can always try again. Pierre is the "natural" man, with the receptiveness and humility Tolstoy often found in the peasants—natural, because he cannot be confined by civilization.

Pierre is a bungler. The things Andrew does with superb efficiency, Pierre cannot do at all. He is hopelessly out of place in a drawing room. On the battlefield he is clumsy and foolish. When he tries to use his benevolence for the welfare of his peasants, he is the dupe of an unscrupulous bailiff. But Pierre can do what is impossible for Andrew: he can feel compassion, he can love, he can forgive, he can repent, and he can believe. He is absolutely sure that "in this world there is truth." Also, he is convinced: "There is the future life. The Someone is—God." Yet he is too honest to accept solutions when he perceives that they are false, and he is too honest to shut his eyes to the evil in the world. He has seen evil in many forms and still kept his faith. Finally, however, evil appears in a form which provides a crisis in his spiritual development. When, as a captive of the French, he witnesses the shooting of some of his fellow prisoners, the shocking, useless brutality is too much for him to accept:

> From the moment Pierre had witnessed those terrible murders committed by men who did not wish to commit them, it was as if the mainspring of his life . . . had suddenly been wrenched out and everything had collapsed into a heap of meaningless rubbish. Though he did not acknowledge it to himself, his faith in the right ordering of the universe, in humanity, in his own soul, and in God, had been destroyed. . . . When similar doubts had assailed him before, they had been the result of his own wrongdoing. . . . But now he felt that the universe had crumbled before his eyes. . . . He felt that it was not in his power to regain faith in the meaning of life.

Yet even in despair Pierre is responsive and warm of heart, and these qualities enable him to be saved. He meets Platon Karataev, the man of simple but invincible faith. The wholeness of Platon's soul is infectious, and Pierre develops wholeness in his presence. Almost from their first meeting, Pierre "felt that the world that had been shattered was once more stirring in his soul with a new beauty and on new and unshakable foundations."

There is no hero in *War and Peace*, but several of the characters were very dear to Tolstoy. Among them, the one he probably loved most was Platon. Certain readers may resent the obviousness of the purpose to which Platon is put, but to regard his role in the novel as an intrusion is to fail to understand what Tolstoy intended to say. In Platon, the novelist presented his view (which erred on the side of glorification but was none the less sincere) of the peasantry. In the relationship between Platon and Pierre, Tolstoy demonstrated his conviction that the aristocrats and privileged classes could hope for mental and spiritual health only if they strove to adopt the simplicity and brotherliness of the peasants. For all the rest of his life, Pierre remembered his humble friend as "an unfathomable, rounded, eternal personification of the spirit of simplicity and truth."

The weeks of Pierre's captivity were a period of regeneration. He attained a state of well-being he had never known before. It was more than good health; he also developed resoluteness and energy. Moreover, he learned patience: "He endured his position not only lightly but joyfully."

> At this time he obtained the tranquillity and ease of mind he had formerly striven in vain to reach. He had long sought . . . that tranquillity of mind, that inner harmony. . . . He had sought it in philosophy, in Freemasonry, in the dissipations of town life, in wine, in heroic feats of self-sacrifice, and in romantic love for Natasha; he had sought it by reasoning—and all these quests and experiments had failed him. And now . . . he had found that peace and inner harmony only through the horror of death, through privation, and through what he recognized in [Platon] Karataev.

In prison Pierre was judged in terms of what he really was, not in terms of his social position. The latter counted for nothing with his fellow prisoners. Nothing else in all his experience gave him greater satisfaction than the high opinion these men formed of him. He felt that their esteem imposed responsibilities upon him, and he tried earnestly to justify their esteem. Like many men before him and after, Pierre discovered that in prison he became for the first time completely free. He learned that happiness is positive, not negative, as Andrew had maintained. "Life is everything. . . . And while there is life there is joy in consciousness of the divine. To love life is to love God." He learned not to worry about the future, but to accept the present. He learned to forget himself. This was the end of his search. This was the *peace*.

War and Peace is a splendid affirmation. The simple life is the best. The real heroes are the little men who think of others before themselves. To live well is to enjoy and to create. No man is born free, but every man may achieve freedom. Life cannot be understood with the intellect, but it withholds nothing from those who embrace it with full devotion. The proud will fall, but the meek shall inherit the earth. He who loves and is humble will find that paradise is here, now.

Tolstoy knew all these things, but he was not able to live by them. He wanted to be like Pierre, but he was much nearer to being Andrew. After having spent all his life searching for God, he was still too proud to bow before any authority except that of the god he believed is in man himself. He did not proclaim the gospel of compassion and of love, but of charity and virtue. In his own soul the "war" had only begun. Still, he had found a direction. The Pierre-Platon design points the way to all his future work. He glorified the peasants, because he believed them capable of bringing about a spiritual revolution for all mankind. When Tolstoy unfurled the banner of "the people," he unwittingly accelerated the momentum of social revolution. In the end he gave to the land he loved, not a plowshare, but a battle cry.

IX/ After Resurrection, the Revolution

Although *War and Peace* is Tolstoy's masterpiece, *Anna Karenina* is also a superlative novel. If it seems to assume a secondary position, it does so only when measured against its predecessor. It may not take the reader's breath away by its sweep and magnificence, but its artistry and impact make it one of the most distinguished works of fiction. In many sections of the novel, Tolstoy is at his best as an interpreter of human experience. The machinery is more compact—and more obvious—than in *War and Peace*. On dispassionate analysis the novel appears contrived. The main character, Levin—not Anna—is at times a puppet whom the author manipulates for his own purposes. As one reads, however, these defects do not matter, for Tolstoy's sense of drama is so intense and the lives of the characters are so absorbing that the reader almost feels he is looking through a window at real people.

Dolly and Stiva, Anna and Vronsky, and even Karenin—all are distinct and three-dimensional. If Levin and Kitty are less convincing, Tolstoy is not the first great novelist unable to make readers respond wholeheartedly to his hero and not the first to find difficulty in preventing a "good" woman from being vapid. Tolstoy never understood what Dostoevsky learned from looking into his own heart—as well as from the death house, from the gaming table, and from the slums of Russian cities—that goodness which is simply not "badness" is neither compelling nor important. Tolstoy's characters are often representational as Dostoevsky's never are, but the best are those not easily classified as types. Natasha, for example, escapes the flatness which throttles Kitty, because even though she sings with the angels, she sometimes gambols with the devil. And Anna is thrillingly alive—dominating the ball by her beauty, watching in breathless agitation as Vronsky races, facing her husband with the icy avowal of her hatred, feverishly bent on reconciliation with Karenin at the birth of Vronsky's child, desolated by her alienation from her social set and the growing independence of her lover, going by stealth to see her son in the home now closed to her, lacerated by jealousy and loneliness, and lost in nightmare meditation on the train. Anna is perhaps most alive when she is about to die. Every reading of the scene in which she throws herself beneath the train brings a fresh pang. It moves one to the verge of tears—tears for all women, and all men, too.

Anna Karenina, as surely as *War and Peace*, proves Tolstoy's skill in the creation of vivid and unforgettable episodes. Vronsky is nowhere else so vital as at the race, and when his beautiful mare goes down under him and tries pitifully to rise in response to his kick, the animal's anguish carries the impact of all anguish. It is preparation for the destruction of Anna, who is broken by forces that once formed a harmonious background for her beauty and vivacity. Levin, working with the reapers, draws strength from the earth. He becomes elemental and grand. The wrinkles are ironed out of his soul by the swing of his powerful arm lending itself to the rhythm of the scythe. Surely few other accounts of birth equal in power the story of the birth of Kitty and Levin's child. And the terrible scenes in which Levin's brother, Nickolay, is shown being drawn irresistibly to his death have the imprint of decay in every word and gesture. When at last the moment comes, the taste and the touch of death are almost too real to be borne. Sharpest of all is the picture of Anna in search of release; it is etched forever in the beholder's mind. Anna's white face frames her dark eyes, their gaze concentrating on the blackness of the train. As the monster hovers above her, she lifts her face one last time, pale as a flower in the moonlight, and then the darkness becomes a shroud. These scenes represent Tolstoy the painter, working with the sureness and perfection of a Raphael or a Leonardo.

I.

It is usually assumed—and critics frequently assert—that *Anna Karenina* follows *War and Peace* in a natural sequence, but that is a false assumption. *Anna Karenina* is transitional. It is the bridge between the youthful Tolstoy and the Tolstoy starting to grow old. Its author was a man who had tasted deeply of love and life, who knew that fulfillment is rarely achieved and satisfaction is ephemeral. The irrepressible Natasha never doubted that the world was hers for the taking, and she took more than her share with joyous abandon. In contrast, in spite of her charms the mature Anna knew she would have to pay dearly for daring to reach toward the joy of life. Tolstoy had been calm and almost satisfied when he showed Pierre as a seeker who found an answer. Levin's search, however, is one in which satisfaction alternates with disappointment and misgiving. The answer rings loud in Levin's ears, but there is no indication that it will heal his spirit. *War and Peace* is a young book done in strong colors. *Anna Karenina* employs autumnal hues.

The latter novel is saturated with indications of Tolstoy's growing dissatisfaction with the life he has lived and the society to which he has belonged. If he had had serious doubts during the writing of *War and Peace*, now the doubts were confirmed. He still wrote of his own class, but the relaxed and indulgent mood of the earlier portrayal had now become taut. He no longer saw the life of the privileged as a splendid spectacle. That was only an illusion. The parties, balls, at-homes, social routines, the gaiety, luxury, ease, the culture, the elegance—all these, he knew now, were but a glittering exterior, covering something ugly and deadly. The laughter of gay women now sounded to him like mockery; their words conformed to the social proprieties, but they came from the lips, not the heart. Anna's husband became acutely aware of this derision after the birth of Anna's child made her infidelity a public matter. He had been noticing for some time that his acquaintances, particularly the women, were showing unusual interest in him and his wife. Then he realized that they were laughing behind their decorous mask-faces, laughing at him, the husband openly betrayed. He was appalled by his discovery of their malevolent delight.

In *Anna Karenina* every detail in the Tolstoyan tapestry of aristocratic life is marked by the same brittleness, falsity. In the presence of society women the reader seems to be looking on at a revel of witches. The worst of the lot is the leader, Princess Betsy. A malicious woman, she responds only to evil and enjoys nothing else. Even the kindhearted Anna says of Betsy: "*Au fond, c'est la femme la plus depravée qui existe.*" Although she and the Princess Myaky and the soulful Lidia Ivanova are briefly drawn, their portraits are clear and consistent. They are bad women. That Vronsky's mother is spoken of contemptuously even by Stepan Oblonsky—whose primary characteristic is indulgence of himself and everyone else—suggests the degree of her depravity. Anna is never really one of these women, and her being different makes her destruction all the more inevitable. Even if she cannot be true to her husband, she does try to be true to herself; and there is no room for truth in that society.

More alarming, though no more despicable, are the men behind the women—the government officials and military officers whose irresponsibility, greed, and uncontrolled ambition determine the destiny of their country. Among the officials, the power seekers and the luxury-loving irresponsibles dominate. Like the others, Karenin sees everything in terms of his own advancement. He has a degree of ability and a capacity for hard work, but he is a cold-hearted automaton. His response to Anna's relations with Vronsky is not based upon the moral principles involved or upon the human elements, but almost solely upon their effect upon his position. He cannot forgive the affront to his dignity. When Karenin is finally convinced that his wife has fallen in love with another man, "he experienced a feeling akin to that of a man who, while calmly crossing a precipice by a bridge, should suddenly discover that the bridge is broken, and that there is a chasm below. The chasm was life itself, the bridge that artificial life in which Alexey Alexandrovitch had lived." Objectionable though Karenin is, however, he is less objectionable than most of the other men of his class.

Stepan Oblonsky epitomizes irresponsibility among the Russian officials. Generous and warmhearted but without scruples, he cares for nothing except his own enjoyment and—if it does not interfere with his—the enjoyment of his associates. His friends are "the distributors of earthly blessings in the shape of places, rents, shares, and such," and he takes care that they remain his friends. He has won the respect and friendship of his fellow officials, subordinates, and superiors, both because he is indulgent toward others and because he is utterly indifferent to his official responsibilities. According to him, the aim of civilization is to make everything a source of pleasure. That is not only the *summum bonum*, as he sees it, but the reason for existence for him and his whole social class. As far as his political and social attitudes are concerned—

> . . . he firmly held those views . . . which were held by the majority and by his paper, and he only changed them when the majority changed them. . . .
>
> Stepan Arkadyevitch had not chosen his political opinions or his views . . . just as he did not choose the shapes of his hat and coat, but simply took those that were being worn. . . . If there was a reason for his preferring liberal to conservative views . . . it arose not from his considering liberalism more rational, but from its being in closer accordance with his manner of life. The liberal party said that in Russia everything is wrong, and certainly Stepan Arkadyevitch had many debts and was decidedly short of money. . . . And so liberalism had become a habit of [his], and he liked his newspaper, as he did his cigar after dinner, for the slight fog it diffused in his brain.

Stepan is completely at home in what one of the lesser worshipers calls "The Temple of Indolence." If George F. Babbitt can be imagined in an upper-class rather than a middle-class setting, he might easily take the form of Stepan Oblonsky. The essential difference is that Babbitt was still vigorously engaged in making his fortune, whereas Stepan was languidly engaged in losing his.

Tolstoy's attitude toward Vronsky—who represents the military elite—was almost as bitter, though he maintained more objectivity in the characterization of Vronsky than of Stepan and his friends. There is an undercurrent of scorn in Tolstoy's treatment of Vronsky, however, especially in the thumbnail sketches which suggest the whole character. For example:

> Vronsky's life was particularly happy in that he had a code of principles which defined with unfailing certitude what he ought and what he ought not to do. . . . These principles laid down as invariable rules: that one must pay a cardsharper, but need not pay a tailor; that one must never tell a lie to a man, but one may to a woman; that one must never cheat any one, but one may a husband; that one must never pardon an insult, but one may give one. . . . These principles were possibly not reasonable and not good, but they were of unfailing certainty, and so long as he adhered to them, Vronsky felt that his heart was at peace and he could hold his head up.

Vronsky is aware that his pursuit of Anna not only has the sanction of his social set, but that he becomes more interesting because of it. He knows that—

> . . . in their eyes the position of an unsuccessful lover of a girl, or of any woman free to marry, might be ridiculous. But the position of a man pursuing a married woman, and . . . staking his life on drawing her into adultery, has something fine and grand about it, and can never be ridiculous.

Compared with many of the members of his circle, Vronsky has admirable qualities. But these qualities cannot develop beyond a certain point because of the limitations of his world:

> In his Petersburg world all people were divided into utterly opposed classes. One, the lower class, vulgar, stupid, and, above all, ridiculous people, who believe that one husband ought to live

> with the one wife whom he has lawfully married; that a girl should be innocent, a woman modest, and a man manly, self-controlled, and strong; that one ought to bring up one's children, earn one's bread, and pay one's debts; and various similar absurdities. This was the class of old-fashioned and ridiculous people. But there was another class of people, the real people. To this class they all belonged, and in it the great thing was to be elegant, generous, plucky, gay, to abandon oneself without a blush to every passion, and to laugh at everything else.

Actually, Vronsky is superior in character to what his environment could have been expected to produce. He is not a rake or a thoughtless hedonist. Earlier affairs have left him untouched; he has played his part with the agility and superficiality expected of a man in his set. But his affair with Anna is different. He loves her and attempts to be honest with her. That he cannot live up to her expectations or maintain a satisfying relationship with her is due, according to Tolstoy, not alone to the fact that they have violated a moral principle but also that they have violated the code of their society. The patterns of conventional behavior are so precisely prescribed that the individual has no flexibility. After they have begun living together, Vronsky quickly becomes aware that, although he is still considered a highly attractive member of his social group, Anna no longer has any place in it at all. This situation presents him with an ambivalence which a stronger man than he could not have reconciled. Vronsky feels deeply and is grieved by the difficulty of Anna's position—more exactly, her lack of position, which he describes without exaggeration as "hell." The result of the lopsided code is that Anna's love for Vronsky improves his standing, but Vronsky's love for Anna destroys her.

Tolstoy was acid in his denunciation of the whole social system which was based on the double standard in sexual behavior. Men might be as licentious as they wished as long as they remained suave, dashing, and imperturbable. They need not bow to any restraint except the restraint of an outraged husband's dueling pistol. To engage in a duel, even to die in a duel, was entirely *comme il faut*. Most husbands did not become outraged, however, because they were busy with their own profligacies. The women also might be libertines, but they must go through the motions of graceful deceit. They were expected to avoid predicaments they could not handle according to the rules. It was taken for granted that they would be untrue to their husbands, but they were not expected to acknowledge their infidelities. Everyone might know what a particular woman was doing, but she must act as if no one knew. In simple words, the whole structure was built on falsehood. Lying and scandal were its essentials. Its culture was pseudo culture; its morality, pseudo morality. Cold-hearted egotism and debauchery were the fact; gay, sophisticated charm, the appearance. The spirit and deed did not matter as long as the appearance conformed to the pattern.

It was inevitable that in such a society Anna's virtues contributed to her undoing. If she had expected less from life, she would have suffered less. If she had been less honest, she could have used subterfuge to her advantage. When her heart becomes involved, however, she is at once the victim of her society, which allows no place for genuine feeling. The mixture of her genuineness and her rejection of the customary subterfuges makes her fall from virtue all the more tantalizing to her sadistic friends. Typically, soon everyone knows about Vronsky's "love" and guesses more or less accurately about the nature of his relationship with Anna:

> The greater number of the young women, who envied Anna and had long been weary of hearing her called virtuous, rejoiced at the fulfillment of their predictions, and were only waiting for a decisive turn in public opinion to fall upon her with all the weight of their scorn. They were already making ready their handfuls of mud to fling at her when the right moment arrived.

The individuals who find malicious pleasure in Vronsky's pursuit and whose admiration of him is heightened by it are the first to slam their doors in Anna's face. They desire that she sin, but will not excuse her. Even in her hysterical state of mind she appraises her situation accurately when she concludes that death is the only way out. If Vronsky were rejected with her, circumstances would be easier for her. It is impossible for an individual to live in a vacuum, and Anna has become a woman without a social milieu.

Tolstoy's scorn of his own society was boundless. To the greed and opportunism of Gogol's gentry, the do-nothing attitude of Goncharov's, and the Hamlet qualities of Turgenev's, Tolstoy added the synthetic charm and fake morality by which he was appalled. Although the settings in which Tolstoy placed his aristocrats were the ultimate in refinement and elegance—and no one has ever been able to surpass Tolstoy in the creation of colorful vignettes of the drawing room—the people themselves and the system in which they operated were decadent and rotten. No wonder Tolstoy was convinced of the necessity of change—and that the change must be inspirited by other classes in the social structure than the one to which he belonged.

Reprehensible though his social class was, however, Tolstoy knew that the guilt in Anna's case did not lie with society alone. She too was guilty. He pitied her—pitied her deeply—but he could not spare her, for even in *Anna Karenina* Tolstoy had begun to be a severe moralist. He did not blame her for loving Vronsky. No one knew better than Tolstoy (and he hated himself for the knowledge) that it is not always possible to master passion. He did not even blame her for not loving her husband. Indeed, he had begun to doubt whether he loved his own wife, and he knew that if it was hard for him to love the Countess Tolstoy, it would be much harder for the beautiful Anna to love Karenin, with his large ears, his awkward gait, and his habit of cracking his knuckles. If she cannot fulfill the responsibilities of wifehood except as an automaton, so be it; that cannot be helped. But the responsibilities of motherhood are another matter. When she permits herself to choose Vronsky rather than her own son, the mistake is fatal. That is her real offense. Tolstoy could not forgive her for that. She has been a good woman but not good enough. She knows what she must do, but she has neither the will nor the strength to do it. The only solution to her problem lies in renunciation, and she cannot renounce "what made up for her the whole meaning of life."

The latter part of the characterization suggests that Tolstoy was eager to have done with Anna, though she is certainly the one of his characters whom he loved most after Natasha in *War and Peace*. She has sinned and she must pay. It was time for Tolstoy to get on with what was absorbing him more and more—his imperative need to discover the meaning of life. There is irony in his punishing Anna for not being able to renounce, for that was exactly his own spiritual predicament. He also was tortured by the ambivalence of knowing what he should do and not doing it. Yet the longer he lived in the luxury of Yasnaya Polyana, the more determined he was to find relief for his spiritual pain. He wanted a character he could use as the instrument for his own self-searching and self-justification, and Levin was the answer.

By the time he wrote *Anna Karenina*, it had become clear to Tolstoy that the only group among the privileged from whom he might hope for something constructive was the small number of landowners who lived upon and took an interest in the land. Their closeness to the soil and their relationship to the peasants enabled them, he believed, to transcend the limitations which normally hedged in the life of the wealthy. He had tested this formula himself and was convinced that it offered people of his position the only opportunity for the achievement of a good life. Levin can date the beginning of his coming to terms with himself from the moment he recognizes the joy of honest toil. To his brother's remonstrance that mowing is not "gentleman's work" and that the peasants will not approve of their master's doing it, Levin replies that it gives him more satisfaction than anything he has ever done before. So Tolstoy had found in manual labor

—particularly in making his own boots—a means by which he could rationalize his continuing to live the life his wife demanded when his soul demanded something different.

Tolstoy's interpretation of the peasants is the climax of the attitude expressed in Turgenev's *Sportsman's Sketches*, in which emphasis was placed upon their simplicity, humility, and dignity. Later on, however, in *Virgin Soil*, Turgenev presented the peasants as simple creatures, almost doltish, waiting to be taught by the intellectuals and far below the latter in mental capacity as well as in social development. With Tolstoy this concept was changed. He saw the peasants as the teachers, the wealthy and the privileged as those needing to learn. He was certain that the artificial life of the Oblonskys, Karenins, Vronskys, and Schtcherbatskys could produce no other result than degeneration. In contrast, he believed that the simple life and hard outdoor labor of the peasants developed vigor, honesty, alertness, and a wholesome standard of values. After a day of reaping with the peasants, Levin concludes that he has found the long-sought clue. To attain real satisfaction, he thinks, he will have to renounce his old life and the education which now seems useless to him. This renunciation appears to him as the only path to contentment and peace.

Levin, speaking for Tolstoy, regards what he calls "the Russian peasant with his instincts" as a special being with "a quite special view of the land." Tolstoy was convinced that the peasant had an instinctive sense of the meaning of life and an appreciation of life which the sophisticated individual could not grasp unless he was willing to simplify his existence. This is what Levin proceeds in a degree to do (and what Tolstoy wanted to do). The result is that Levin becomes the ideal landlord of Russian literature, at the farthest extreme from the dead-souled gentry of Gogol, from Oblomov, and from the heedless absentee landlords who filled the Moscow and Petersburg salons in *War and Peace* and *Anna Karenina*.

Levin recognizes that the peasants often do shoddy work, are unreliable, cheat their masters, and live in a condition little above that of animals. But he realizes that they are not to blame. Their way of life, he decides, is the fault of the masters who take the profits and do none of the work, who hold the peasants down and blame them for being down. A conversation he has with the parasitic Stepan Oblonsky fortifies his conviction. Levin asserts that "all profit that is out of proportion to the labor expended is dishonest." Stepan agrees but reminds Levin that he is receiving more profit than his laborers receive and is therefore participating in the same dishonesty:

> "You say," Levin went on, "that it's unjust for me to receive five thousand, while the peasant has fifty; that's true; it is unfair, and I feel it, but. . . ."
>
> "Yes, you feel it, but you don't give him your property," said Stepan. . . . "If you consider this inequality is unjust, why is it you don't act accordingly?"

This is a challenge which Levin tries to meet, as Tolstoy also had tried, but the novelist had to wait for Nekhludov in *Resurrection* to meet the challenge squarely. Levin, however, decides that the only way to remedy this injustice is to work with the peasants on a partnership basis. Although he has difficulty in overcoming their conviction that a landowner can have no other object than to get everything he can out of them, Levin finally has the satisfaction of seeing his system begin to work. Certain that he has taken a step of great importance, he ruminates that the relation of landlord and peasant is no longer a private matter but involves the public welfare. The whole culture must be changed. There must be general prosperity rather than the prosperity of one class; there must be general harmony instead of a division of interests. This rearrangement of the economy would amount in the end to a rearrangement of society, but Levin-Tolstoy became convinced that such a rearrangement was absolutely necessary.

Levin's idealization of the peasants is not the only way in

which he interprets Tolstoy. Even more important is his representation of the unending Tolstoyan search for answers to the insistent questions life propounds. Like Tolstoy, Levin has always been aware of an incompleteness in his life—as if there were something he must discover, something elusive but essential—but he does not know what it is or where to look for it. This mystery has been deepened by his brother's death. Ever since that time Levin "had been stricken with horror, not so much of death, as of life, without any knowledge of whence, and why, and how, and what it was." He has never been able to find satisfaction in the answers Christianity gives, yet he does not know where else to turn. "He was in the position of a man seeking food in the toy-shops and tool shops." He has tried to find the solution by reading the works of philosophers whose explanation of life is nonmaterialistic, but they do not satisfy him. The discrepancy between the harmonious external circumstances of his life and his inner turmoil only deepens the turmoil. He has everything a man could ask for, and it is all nothing. When Levin tries to understand his true identity and the reason for living, he can find no answers to the questions. His resulting despair is like Tolstoy's despair. On at least one occasion Levin seriously considers whether suicide is not the only escape from his spiritual vacuum. In Tolstoy's case the possibility of suicide was often present in his mind. He often pondered whether the death he felt in life could not be best relieved by death in actuality.

Like Tolstoy, too, Levin attempts to escape from his inner confusion by action. He makes a series of attempts to become absorbed in externals, to lose himself in extrovertive responsibilities. The first and most satisfying of these experiences is love and marriage. Levin's courtship of Kitty is carried on in a condition of dedication. The almost mystic ecstasy of his feeling for her is strong enough to make him forget his spiritual craving for many months. But as the hunger of the flesh is appeased, the hunger of the soul returns. As Kitty changes from inaccessible ideal to daily companion, she ceases to be able to satisfy his deepest needs. The relationship of Levin and Kitty is, of course, an echo of the experience of Tolstoy in relation to his wife.

Levin makes other attempts at escape, too. It has already been pointed out that he tries hard physical labor, which gives him a sense of closeness to the earth and of physical well-being such as he has not previously known. But he soon feels there is something artificial in his efforts to identify himself with the peasants. A day of toil insures a night of peaceful sleep, but sleep is not fullness of life. He tries, also, to assume the burden of social responsibility by serving as arbiter for his district in the period of post-emancipation adjustment. But as Tolstoy had learned, Levin learns that there can be no satisfaction in working within a system which has tried to cure one form of rottenness by substituting another scarcely less rotten. Also, he feels smothered by falsity when he tries to help others solve their problems while his own problems remain unsolved.

The failure of one after another of his efforts to find the true meaning of life leaves Levin in a state of desolation. He is whole without but feels hollow within. So he resigns himself to being a tenant in the wasteland of the spirit. Much of Levin's difficulty, as it was much of Tolstoy's, is the fact that he has always approached his search rationally. He assumes that he should be capable of finding his way out of the maze of his spiritual confusion through his own efforts. He hungers for God, but he does not recognize the nature of his hunger. Instead of seeking God, he seeks satisfaction. Levin would have been a much more attractive character if he had blundered and fallen and then had reached up to beg for God's mercy and help as Dmitri Karamazov did. But Levin does not blunder, and he does not reach up. He is a good man and in some respects a humble man, but he lacks the humility which comes from bigness of heart. Although he is in certain respects a better man than Andrew Bolkonsky, he has something of the same self-containment and sterility of spirit.

The end of Levin's search is not, at first consideration, logically convincing. It comes suddenly, as if it had been thrust upon him

—and thrust upon the reader, too. It is as if Tolstoy had set out to follow Levin to the conclusion of his quest and was determined to make his point thereby. The reader finds it difficult to accept the sense of satisfaction and beneficence with which Levin recognizes the answer—in simple words spoken by a peasant—as the one for which he has long yearned. The solution is too obviously oversimplified, too obviously a formula.

Still, sudden changes do occur in human experience, and perhaps there is more preparation than at first appears. Ever since his brother's death some force has been at work in Levin, urging him to *live*. Until he is confronted by the finality of death, he is not able to understand that only to be alive is compensation for the predicament of being human. He does not quickly manifest this new sense of the value of life, but the seed is within him, waiting to germinate. Moreover, even if his relationship to Kitty has not proved to be the fulfillment he has hoped for, he discovers, when he turns away from the dead body of his brother to the living woman he loves and who loves him, that love, though it be taken for granted, has the power to survive and to give strength. Then, in the birth of his child, he discovers the meaning of the promise of resurrection. At this point he is able, at least for a time, to turn away from theories and feel the intimation of the fullness of life. Fortunately for Levin, it is not necessary for him, as it is for Andrew in *War and Peace*, to die in order to live.

In the light of the changes we have just mentioned, Levin's responsiveness to the answer is not necessarily unconvincing. His heart, at least, is ready for the message:

> At the peasant's words that Fokanitch lived for his soul . . . undefined but significant ideas seemed to burst out as though they had been locked up, and all . . . thronged whirling through his head, blinding him with their light. . . .
>
> He was aware of something new in his soul, and joyfully tested this new thing, not yet knowing what it was.
>
> "Not living for his own wants, but for God? . . . He said that

> one must not live for one's own wants . . . but . . . for something incomprehensible, for God. . . .
>
> ". . . I and all men have only one firm, incontestable, clear knowledge, and that knowledge cannot be explained by the reason—it is outside it, and has no causes and can have no effects."

Like the Elder Zossima and Alyosha, and echoing the experience of Pierre Bezukhov, Levin-Tolstoy learns that the truth means "to love God, for my soul." Moreover, truth cannot be known by reason but only by the heart. The chief thing is faith—"faith in God, in goodness, as the one goal of man's destiny."

But these words from Tolstoy in the great house at Yasnaya Polyana do not have the ring of conviction. He was still the man trying to make his own rules, the man trying to prove to himself that he was (as Levin put it) "not to blame." He was the gloomy Titan, struggling to master the universe. How different from the wracked spirit of Dostoevsky, who did not hesitate to fall on his knees before the awful power or to cry out as Job did, "Lord, I am vile!"

The result was that, although *Anna Karenina* was intended to be the book of Levin, Tolstoy could not make it so. Levin, the conformist, works in the fields to try to absorb their strength, says and does and loves the right things, but to no avail. Like Nekhludov who is to undergo "resurrection," he is not kindled by the spark of life. *Anna Karenina* is, rather, the book of nonconformists—of Nikolay, who dies in anguish of spirit, never having found any answer at all but knowing that he cannot accept the universe, knowing that humanity everywhere is in need and that he must try to help. And it is most of all the book of Anna, beautiful, inherently virtuous, but resentful of being cheated of life—reaching out her small, white, ring-covered hands in her understandable yearning for the *joie de vivre*. One can forget Levin, but not Anna. Like Nikolay, she rebels, and she loses the gamble. Yet she is not entirely extinguished. Though the wheels crush "the blood-stained body so lately full of life," she is careful to drop the little red bag on the station platform before she jumps. That is the symbol of the imperishable woman.

One reason for the greatness of Tolstoy's two famous novels is the fact that they have no endings. They suggest that life goes on. But there is also something disconcerting about the lack of a conclusion in *Anna Karenina.* It is as if the author simply could not see the way ahead. Not long after he ended the novel, Tolstoy wrote to the Countess Alexandra: "For two years now I see religion to be a chance of salvation. . . . But it is a fact that every time I hold on to this plank of salvation I am drowned with it." No wonder he could not bring *Anna Karenina* to a satisfying conclusion. He did not then know what the next step was—for Levin, for himself, or for any other honest seeker.

II.

By the time Tolstoy stopped working on *Anna Karenina* he was in the midst of the spiritual struggle which absorbed his almost complete attention for several years. When he had arrived at the period of what is usually called his "conversion" and had begun writing *A Confession,* it might have been assumed that his spirit would have been lightened so that his creative energies could have continued to glow with undiminished brightness. But the wrestling of the spirit was related by many intricate threads to what proved in terms of quality a diminution of those energies. Still the fire continued, and if at times it produced more smoke than flame, often the flame of his genius still burned. Indeed, a profile of Tolstoy the man and the artist can not be completed without considering some of the later works. It is obvious that the unifying motif of the later writing is the emphasis on ethical behavior and spiritual regeneration, but there is extraordinary variety in the design. In sheer volume, Tolstoy's output during the decades of the eighties and nineties was almost incredible, particularly in view of the age of the author. Quite apart from the restrictions imposed by moralistic considerations, it is no wonder that much of the writing is chaff. The remarkable thing is that so much is of the highest quality.

Most of Tolstoy's late fiction (the short story was the genre he most often practiced during the decades under consideration) falls into three general divisions. The first of these is the intensely introversive studies of the human personality lashed by the vicissitudes of the soul and suffering especially before the irrevocability of solitude and death. They are imbued with the anguish of the lost mariner looking for a light. They demonstrate that, even after he had ostensibly passed the crisis in his search for meaning, Tolstoy was still often in the clutch of misgiving, if not of actual fear. The second type, like the first, is strongly autobiographical. It includes several narratives in which the force of sensuality is brilliantly analyzed. These two types clearly illustrate the two elements in Tolstoy's nature which had not been reconciled by all his effort to find God and to follow His way. The third type, varying from simplicity to sophistication, includes the many stories which served as vehicles for the attempt to explain and persuade others to follow the religion Tolstoy had arrived at after such a lengthy period of trial and error. The fact that many of these stories were intended for readers of modest intelligence explains the existence of what in some of them can only be called preaching.

One of the most impressive stories of the first group is *The Memoirs of a Madman*, not published until after the author's death but apparently written in 1884. This story having been left unfinished, we may find an even more impressive example of this type in *The Death of Ivan Ilyich* (1886), an account of death in life. This narrative is proof of the recurring black periods in Tolstoy's experience, for it is written as if from the depth of darkness, except for a brief and perhaps incongruous streak of light at the end.

The only significant thing about Ivan Ilyich is his death. His life, Tolstoy said, "had been most simple and most ordinary and therefore most terrible."[1] Why is it terrible? Because it has been —as his death is—without true sense or meaning. Ivan Ilyich does not discover the truth about his life until it is too late to change. In fact, only his dying makes that discovery possible.

Occasionally, Ivan Ilyich is troubled by memories of vile things he has done, but he has always brushed these memories aside because his conventionality gives him security. His relations with his wife had deteriorated soon after marriage, but this problem, too, has been a minor one. He has simply taken up residence on his own island and left her and her querulous nagging on another. Sometimes he has felt that his abilities have not been fittingly recognized, but in good time he receives an appointment which promises everything he has wanted from life. Thereafter, he settles into a groove of complacent enjoyment of his drawing room, furnished like the drawing rooms of all other successful men, and enjoyment of his associates in the legal profession and of his friends in the social scheme which is perfectly adapted to his taste. He thinks his life is just as he wishes it to be until the most ordinary event precipitates him into the blackness from which there is no escape.

After the small and futile accident which starts his long dying, Ivan Ilyich realizes that his life—though he has been successful and has always done the proper thing—is all false. He cannot understand why he must die, but the nightmare unreality is not so dreadful as what he perceives in the midst of his bafflement. As he looks back upon "all that for which he had lived—[he] saw clearly that it was not real at all, but a terrible and huge deception which had hidden both life and death." In addition, there is something else that fills him with despair and a sense of alienation. When death becomes the only certainty, he has to face it alone, for no one has any idea of his suffering and desolation or gives him the pity he craves. Everything else goes on as always; nothing changes except him. He yearns for consolation, but it seems to him that no one really cares for him. He is engulfed in

[1] From the translation by Louise and Aylmer Maude.

a loneliness that "could not have been more complete anywhere —either at the bottom of the sea or under the earth." Indeed, his wife and daughter continue to buy dresses, to engage in the social whirl, and to act as if nothing strange or awful were occurring—to act, he thinks, annoyed because he is bothering them by the fact of his illness. When he looks back to childhood, his memories have a tinge of happiness; but when he considers his adult life and everything that has seemed most important to him, he sees that it has all been senseless and disgusting.

Only one person is capable of understanding his misery or, at least, of trying to relieve his pain. That is—as the reader of Tolstoy would expect—the peasant youth Gerasim. But even this small comfort cannot ameliorate the absolute desolation. Finally, Ivan Ilyich weeps at the cruelty of man and of God. He spends most of his last days lying with his face to the wall. This is more than a physical thing; it is symbolic of his spiritual isolation. The pain, the loneliness, and the terror are so intense that "he struggled as a man condemned to death struggles in the hands of the executioner, knowing that he cannot save himself." He feels as if he were being squeezed down into a black hole. Even before he dies, his friends are considering how they will benefit from his going; and his family is waiting and hoping for a return to normal.

The story is told with the utmost simplicity but with the clarity and insight of which Tolstoy at his best was capable. It stabs the reader's mind and heart, for he feels in it the essence of death —even his own. It does not help that in his last moment of consciousness, as the disfigurements of life fall away from him, Ivan Ilyich has an awareness of reconciliation and illumination as if cleansing waters have bathed his soul. Whether or not he intended to do so, Tolstoy created the impression that Ivan Ilyich —Everyman—has to pay too much for that intimation of peace.

An example of the second type among the late stories is *The Kreutzer Sonata*, in which Tolstoy gave the ugliest of his accounts of the war between the sexes. The narrator-husband tells the story of his murder of his wife with complete *sang froid.* In him the sensual passion has taken the form not so much of lust as of jealousy, and his almost casual disclosure of his response to marriage and his treatment of his wife adds to the generally repellent effect of his character. Another narrative belonging to the same year (1889), but not published until after Tolstoy's death, is in every respect a finer achievement. The main character of *The Devil* is a wealthy young man of the landowning class who, like Tolstoy, resolves to put his licentious habits behind him and to use marriage as a shield against temptation. He loves his wife—there is a compatibility between them which had never existed between Tolstoy and Sonya—but his love for her does not suffice to protect him. Tolstoy was sixty-one years old when he wrote this story, but he had never presented the combustible force of sensuality with more impact. The "devil" is the young peasant woman who has attracted the landowner before his marriage and from whose flashing eyes he cannot escape. As he unwillingly succumbs to her again after his marriage, he comes almost to believe that there is witchery about her. The crimson scarf with which she binds up her lustrous black hair is like a signal from hell. The distinguishing element in this narrative is the earnestness and yet the futility of the young man's effort to save himself. He is not like the lustful in the *Inferno*, who were gently and unwittingly wafted into carnality. He is driven as if by the Furies of his flesh. Much of the power of the story resides in its irrevocability. The most eloquent of puritans could not have made a stronger case for the helplessness of man before the fact of his own nature. Tolstoy wrote two endings: in one the young man kills the "devil," and in the other he kills himself. Either will do. What Tolstoy meant to say is equally clear in both cases.

When he wrote *Master and Man* in 1895, the blackness had lifted from Tolstoy's heart and mind. This, too, is a story of death, but of life in death. Vasili Andreevich has lived with even less probity than Ivan Ilyich. He has lived for the body only and for material things. When he looks back on his life, he thinks only of what he has already acquired, and when he looks to the future, he relishes the image of what he will yet acquire. But in his dying he sees the truth, sees what the "real thing" is. He "responded gladly" to the voice that calls him; as he dies, he is transported by a sense of joy. And the joy is justified, for his death is useful. The servant Nikita has always been to him only a piece of goods, but when they are alone in the blizzard, the master lies with his warm-coated body on top of the servant, and Nikita sleeps safely through the night, protected by his slowly freezing master. In this parable—and the last shall be first—Tolstoy proclaims with a resounding voice one of the basic tenets of his religion.

This story, representative of the third type among the late narratives, has some of the luminosity that marks certain of the simpler, shorter tales, such as "Where Love Is, God Is." The best of them speak to the heart almost as directly as the parables of the New Testament. As long as he avoided overt didacticism, Tolstoy's words carried their own magic. To the end of his life he could create characters as few other writers have been able to do. And the forces of nature which he so deeply loved surge and sing through the pages of his books, from first to last.

III.

In his journal for the year 1899, Tolstoy made the following entry in December: "Finished *Resurrection.* Not good, uncorrected, hurried; but it has fallen from me and I am no longer interested." With this terse comment he marked the end of an effort which had absorbed him for years—the effort to summarize his mature convictions in a work of fiction. More than four years earlier he had asserted in his diary that he couldn't "make *Resurrection* go better" because "it was begun falsely." He accused himself of having been trivial when he started to write it. The completed *Resurrection* has been criticized for many reasons, but not for triviality. In this book Tolstoy worked within the strait jacket of his own definition of art. Into it he crowded the essence of his best didactic writings: *A Confession, What I Believe, The*

Slavery of Our Times, and *What, Then, Shall We Do? Resurrection* is not one of the great books of Russia, but it is significant historically as a record of the continuing abuses and oppressions which were bringing Russia at the end of the nineteenth century ever closer to revolution.

Tolstoy did not intend *Resurrection* to be a work of fiction so much as a sociologist's report, a reformer's protest, and a prophet's denunciation. As with *Anna Karenina,* the germ of this narrative may be traced to an incident, of which Tolstoy had heard, in which a woman suffered "all for love." After he had subjected the incident to the process of identification with his ethical precepts, however, much of the writing became polemical instead of the mysterious blend of reality and art which constitutes literature.

After the splendors of *War and Peace* and *Anna Karenina, Resurrection* offers little stimulation or delight. There is no irresistible Natasha, no Anna pausing like a goddess in the doorway of the ballroom. Instead, squint-eyed little Maslova plods along the road to Siberia toward an uncertain future that will test her newly forged soul. As usual, the old master is the central character and writes mostly about himself. He is Nekhludov as certainly as he was Olenin in *The Cossacks,* Pierre Bezukhov and Andrew Bolkonsky in *War and Peace,* and Levin in *Anna Karenina.* Nekhludov is the last link in the chain. But the change that had occurred in Tolstoy between the writing of the two earlier novels and this one diminished his effectiveness as a subject for a self-portrait. Whereas the earlier disguises revealed his charm and humanity, Nekhludov reveals his priggishness and moralizing —and, at the end, even a surprising escape into mysticism.

Resurrection is the story of Prince Dmitri Ivanovitch Nekhludov, a landowner who has taken up the pursuits of a country squire after some years' service in the army. By coincidence he is summoned for jury duty in the case of a prostitute, Katusha Maslova, charged with a murder she has not committed. The jury resolves that she shall be acquitted, but as a result of a stupid error of the presiding officials the young woman is sentenced to four years of hard labor in Siberia.

For Nekhludov, however, the important fact is that he recognizes the hapless young woman as one he had known, seduced, and forgotten years before. After having borne his child, which soon died, she was finally driven by one misfortune after another to the house of prostitution where she had become the unwitting pawn for the murderers for whose crime she was tried. From the moment he recognizes her, Nekhludov is stricken with a sense of guilt. He knows he is responsible for having wrecked the woman's life, and he feels the more responsible when faced by the miscarriage of justice that makes her an exile. He determines to follow Katusha to Siberia and, as soon as possible, to marry her and spend his life making restitution. To complete the rupture with his old life, he arranges to give his property to his peasants, having long believed that he had no right to benefit from the labor of others. Thus Nekhludov sets about the "resurrection" of his soul.

From the time Nekhludov seeks out Katusha in prison, acknowledges his part in her downfall, and tells her of his plans, the relation between them is strained. Katusha soon realizes that his conduct is motivated more by his need to redeem himself than by genuine concern for her. On one occasion she accuses him: "You want me to be the instrument of your salvation. . . . I have served you in this life, and now you expect me to serve you as a means for getting to heaven!" Gradually, however, Katusha's old love for him is renewed, though she knows Nekhludov does not love her and the gap between them cannot be bridged. He has already ruined her life; it will give her no satisfaction to ruin his. At last, word comes that Nekhludov's efforts to have Katusha's case reviewed have been to some extent successful: Katusha must remain in Siberia for the period of her sentence, but she is relieved of hard labor and may live where she chooses. She makes her decision at once. She will marry her fellow prisoner, Simonson, and thus set Nekhludov free. Nekhludov accepts Katusha's decision blandly. Then, feeling no further obligation to her, he turns to what he calls "the business of my life": to "seek . . . first the Kingdom of God and His righteousness."

Tolstoy obviously made an earnest effort, but he did not succeed in providing convincing evidence of the redemption of Nekhludov's soul. Nekhludov is not so much a character with whom a reader can identify as a device to make it possible for Tolstoy to broadcast his views. The contrast between Nekhludov and the characters of Dostoevsky strengthens the impression that the former is a straw man. He goes briskly about the process of regeneration without inner conflict or humility. His earlier determination to follow and marry Katusha was his way of making a pact with the Almighty. That was the price he was willing to pay for an entrance ticket to heaven. It adds nothing to his moral stature that after Katusha frees him he spends the next night with his New Testament. That scene brings to mind the magnificent episode in *Crime and Punishment* in which Sonia reads to Raskolnikov the story of the raising of Lazarus. But everything moving and human in the latter incident is absent when Nekhludov resorts to the Gospel. If Nekhludov is the best argument Tolstoy could advance to make "Tolstoyism" convincing, one wonders how he gained so many followers.

Actually, a better argument is found in Katusha. In the hands of Dostoevsky she would have been a great character, but Tolstoy was not really interested in her. He approached her externally and obliquely. Like Nekhludov, Tolstoy was incapable of feeling for her or loving her. Yet she is truly redeemed. Her love, like Sonia's, puts the happiness of her beloved before her own. When Nekhludov turns away from "her pathetic smile," it was Tolstoy the aristocrat who turned away, unaware that he was discarding his best opportunity to create a victorious witness of his belief.

Resurrection is not what the author intended, that is, a chronicle of salvation. But even though Tolstoy failed in what he hoped primarily to accomplish, he succeeded in his secondary aims. His protests against what he called "the slavery of our times" are as powerfully presented in this novel as in any of the numerous tracts and letters by which he tried to waken the drugged consciousness of his compatriots. These protests take the form of indictments against four symbols of authority which Tolstoy held responsible for the poverty of flesh and spirit and for the tyranny and injustice from which the masses of Russian people suffered. These indictments were leveled against four corrupt institutions: the Orthodox church, the privileges of the aristocracy based upon ownership of land, the court system and the penal program culminating in the abuses of Siberian exile, and the government as represented by the corrupt monarch and the corrupt machinery which supported him. Not even Gorky with his avowed belief in revolution was able to deal heavier blows against existing institutions than Tolstoy did in *Resurrection.* If he could not awaken a spiritual consciousness, he managed to electrify the social consciousness. Thus the book partially succeeded in spite of partial failure.

The first of the four indictments—against the Orthodox church, especially its external trappings—inheres in the whole argument of the book. It finds particular expression in one episode which describes a service the prisoners are forced to attend. The prison church, the gift of a rich merchant, "glistened with gold and bright colors," its brilliance only slightly dimmed by the shaved heads and clanking chains of the worshipers. The service proceeds from incantation to incantation. The lighted candles, the icons, the sumptuously robed priests, and the gold cross with enameled medallions form a radiant pattern, but it is bereft of meaning.

> And not one among those . . . present . . . seemed to be aware that this same Jesus whom the priest had lauded with so many queer words . . . had expressly forbidden all that had been going on here; not only the senseless volubility and the blasphemous incantations of the priest . . . but had most positively forbidden

> one man to call another master, had forbidden all worship in temples . . . had forbidden the very temples themselves . . . but above all . . . had he forbidden human judgments and the imprisonment of men, or their subjection to the shame, torture, or death which was visited on them in this place. . . .
>
> . . . The Chief Warden and his assistants, although they had never known or understood what the dogmas of this faith really were . . . all thought that a man ought to believe that creed. . . . Moreover, they felt . . . that this creed justified their cruel duties. If there had been no such creed it would have been . . . impossible to use all their energy in tormenting men, as they were doing now, with an easy conscience.

This attitude toward the Orthodox faith indicates Tolstoy's rejection of what Dostoevsky considered the only hope for Russia. Tolstoy was as bitter about the Orthodox church as Dostoevsky was about Roman Catholicism. It is striking that the two greatest masters of Russian literature took impassioned positions on the opposing sides of the question as to what place the national church should occupy in their country.

The second indictment is pronounced against the property-owning classes, who accept and perpetuate their privileges on a foundation built on the toil and suffering of the peasants. When Nekhludov decides to go to Siberia with Katusha, he realizes that he must make a change in the management of his estate. Upon investigation he discovers that the existing rental arrangements for the peasants are grossly unfair. When he negotiates with the peasants, he still feels guilty despite his intention to allocate the land to them for 30 per cent less than other peasants in the district are paying. Nekhludov cannot understand why he feels so ashamed, but Tolstoy knew the reason. It was, he said, because the land the peasants had worked for centuries was theirs by right and not Nekhludov's at all. Tolstoy had suffered from the same sense of guilt.

Later Nekhludov proposes to rent the land to the peasants and to use the money he receives for the people's welfare. The peasants, of course, do not believe a landowner capable of a gesture of benevolence. They finally agree to accept the land on Nekhludov's terms when an old woman says "that the master had begun to be anxious about his soul and was doing this in order to save it." She has divined the real motive of Nekhludov, as it had been, in a sense, that of Tolstoy. Whatever the reason, Tolstoy was sincere in his conviction that the miseries of the Russian people could not be remedied until the gentry relinquished the right to profit exorbitantly from the labor of others.

The sharpest and most poignant of the several indictments in *Resurrection* was directed against the legal and penal systems of Russia. When Nekhludov considers the impressions he has received from observing the convicts as they marched from the prison and boarded the train to begin their doleful journey to Siberia, he realizes that every step was inhumane and horrible. He remembers particularly the face of the second convict who had died from weakness, fatigue, and the heat: "And the most appalling part of all this was that the man was murdered, and no one knew who did the deed."

This motif—death, not life—distinguishes all the court and prison scenes in the book. From the moment Katusha Maslova is apprehended, there is no opportunity for her to obtain just treatment. Like uncounted others, she cannot buy "justice." Except for Nekhludov's help she would have to pay to the limit for a crime she has not committed. In fact, "the people" did not even expect justice. They assumed it was a commodity beyond their reach, reserved for their "betters." The prison scenes are notable, not so much for their revelation of the crowding, filth, ill-treatment, and hopelessness of the convicts, as for their illustration of the convicts' capacity for stoic accommodation. Therein is offered one of the most convincing proofs in Russian literature of the dead weight of misery which the masses of Russian people had long been forced to bear.

Tolstoy was never able to throw off the incredulity that his study of the courts and penal institutions left with him. All he had observed and learned about the penal system was like a nightmare. Especially distressing was the unfeelingness and lack of concern of the officials. Their incompetence was bad enough, and their indifference was worse. Tolstoy was at a loss to understand their behavior unless he accepted them as beings of a special order, set apart by their work from the normal responses of humanity. The best of the officials, from the judges in the highest courts to the keepers of the vilest prisons, were Oblomovs and "superfluous men." The typical and more numerous officials were, at best, nincompoops and egotists, frequently tyrants and brutes. "And this," Tolstoy said in *Resurrection*, "is the condition upon which we who control the wealth of Russia and call ourselves Christian turn our backs, while we concentrate upon amusement and self-indulgence!"

What disturbed Nekhludov-Tolstoy most was his recognition that the majority of those in prison were not evil, were no more guilty than those at large, and certainly not as dangerous as their jailers. Still, the prisoners were degraded and robbed of self-respect, haunted by terror, and driven like rats into a trap. Worst of all, the innocent were subjected to the contagion of the guilty.

The last of the indictments which blaze forth from the pages of *Resurrection* is a scorching rebuke of the existing government. Tolstoy did not attack the regime as such—unless by his denunciation of the political and legal machinery—except through the views of some of the political prisoners with whom Nekhludov comes into contact. These "politicals" form a large proportion of the prisoners, as they did in any jail or convict gang in Russia. Among them are some types already familiar in Russian literature and others soon to become familiar. One of the latter is the young woman Marya Pavlovna, a spiritual sister both to the female revolutionists of Andreyev's *The Seven That Were Hanged*[2] and to a number of the characters of Gorky and of other writers during and after the Revolution. She is a general's daughter, but she acts like a working woman, wears only the simplest clothing,

[2] See Chapter XI.

and loses herself in revolutionary activity. She has decided on this course because from childhood she has been repelled by the useless lives of the members of the upper class. She has voluntarily taken up factory work and has helped operate a secret printing press.

Three of the political prisoners are of particular interest. Kryltzov had been a university student with no concern for revolutionary activities. After his arrest, a matter of sheer coincidence, he went to prison still having no sympathy with the revolutionaries, but what he saw and experienced in prison had made a revolutionist of him. He became a member of a group "whose object was to terrorize the Government until it abdicated its authority of its own accord." Although he has contracted tuberculosis in prison and has only a short time to live, he has no regrets. If he could live his life over, he says, he would use it to work for the destruction of the government that causes the hideous injustices he has witnessed.

Nabatov is a peasant, a brilliant young man who has had some opportunities for education but did not go to the university because he felt compelled to return as a teacher to the members of his own class. His "dangerous activities" consisted of reading books to the peasants and trying to educate them and of starting an industrial co-operative league. He has spent many years in prison and exile but has not flagged in his efforts or become bitter. When he was free,

> . . . he worked for the . . . civilization and the union of the working men. . . . And even when he was in prison he behaved with the same practical common sense and energy. . . . He seemed to want nothing for himself . . . but for his comrades he demanded much. . . . When he thought and spoke of what a revolution would do to benefit the people, he had always in mind the class from which he himself sprang. . . . He did not believe that the revolution for which he was working ought to destroy the main framework, but only to make certain changes in . . . this noble and permanent old structure.

The third "political," Kondratief, a factory hand, has suffered since childhood from a sense of oppression. When a famous revolutionist noticed him, she recognized in him a man of unusual ability and began to lend him books and to explain to him the causes of the predicaments of the underprivileged. He began to yearn not only for the freedom of the oppressed, but also for vengeance against the oppressors. He became a passionate student, read revolutionary books, organized a strike, and devoted himself wholly to the cause; and—Tolstoy emphasizes this point—"realizing the absurdity of the religion in which he was reared he abandoned it . . . and ever after . . . he bitterly ridiculed priests and religious dogmas."

Nekhludov learns to respect and love these three political prisoners. Earlier he had been contemptuous of the revolutionaries, but acquaintance with them brings a change in his attitude. He soon learns that their actions are not prompted by a love of violence for its own sake, but that they have been forced to adopt violence as the only means by which they can dent the seeming invulnerability of the existing regime. He learns that most of them are motivated by idealistic aims. Yet when their deeds bring them into collision with the authorities, they cannot hope for justice. Inevitably they begin to use the same methods that have been used against them. Thus, there can be no end to the circle of violence leading to violence. This was the prophecy which Tolstoy had already begun to see fulfilled in the events that took place on a dreadful Sunday nearly six years before he died.[3]

IV.

In a number of his books Dostoevsky was concerned with the psychology of the criminal, whereas Tolstoy was concerned with the treatment of the criminal—with the court and penal systems and the whole economic and political framework which made such systems possible. When Nekhludov reviewed the terrible

[3] "Bloody Sunday" is discussed in Chapters XI and XII.

conditions he had observed—the cruelty and degradation, the indifference of the officials, and the resulting insanity and death—he sought to know what might be done to remedy the wrongs. He asked himself again the question: "Am I the madman, or have the authorities at whose bidding all these iniquitous dealings are visited upon the victims lost their reason?" He did not find an answer to this question, but in the New Testament he received the enlightenment he had been seeking:

> Now he knew the origin of all the horrors he had witnessed and he also knew where to find the remedy; In the answer given by Christ to Peter to forgive over and over again everybody and forever, never to grow weary in forgiving, for there are no men living who do not need forgiveness, and therefore there are no men who are fit to correct or punish others.

These words sound as though they might have been spoken by the Elder Zossima, but Tolstoy wore his saintliness as if it were a hair shirt, and even when he concludes with the injunction to forgive, there is thunder and threat in his tone instead of the benedictory sweetness of the Elder. Nevertheless, although Nekhludov was a less compelling spokesman than the Elder, there was no doubt about Tolstoy's sincerity or the earnestness of his interpretation of Christian doctrine. But in Russia in December, 1899, when *Resurrection* was completed, sincerity and earnestness were not enough. A few days after the novel was finished the wild bells rang out to the wild sky to signify the beginning, not only of a new year, but of a new century. The old century had grown increasingly troubled and determined and angry. The new century was to see the ripened grapes of wrath brought to the harvest. In that harvest Nekhludov would remain what he had always been—a straw man, another variety of "superfluous man," almost as inadequate as his brothers, Oblomov, Rudin, and Nezhdanov. Nekhludov was the epilogue to the dying year and the dying century. Yet it was not inadequacy which stood in the way of the fulfillment of Tolstoy's ideals. The insuperable obstacle was that his ideals had become anachronistic. In the vineyards of the twentieth century in Russia, the doers and the makers were the sons of Bazarov and perhaps of Peter Verkhovensky. They were the factory hand Kondratief (who was determined to set "others free from this state of bondage in which he had lived"), the peasant Nabatov ("for his comrades he demanded much"), and the university student Kryltzov ("who had left this world while his heart was filled with bitterness and wrath").

Tolstoy saw clearly the evils that must be remedied, and he formulated many plans for action. But his plans did not speak to the generation to which he addressed them. He set "the people" free, psychologically free, and he counted on their power to love. On this point he was mistaken. They were indeed possessed, but not by love. They had been forced to wait too long. They were possessed by hatred.

Tolstoy spoke majestically, but time was marching fast in Russia. His urgent words, his rebukes and warnings, soon faded away in the quiet glades of Yasnaya Polyana. The "place of the green stick" became a shrine, and a shrine is always a memorial to the past. Russia had done with her past. In the new century she turned resolutely to the future. Contrary to his hopes, it was not Tolstoy who opened the portals of the new day, but two other men. Their names were Marx and Lenin.

x/ Chekhov: The Axe to the Tree

In the company of Dostoevsky or Tolstoy one moves amid intense emotions and large ideas. The seasons vary. Sometimes the passionate heat of summer is sultry and lightning pierced. Sometimes the cold of winter shrouds the landscape in dead white, and the heart slowly turns to ice. At other times there is the rapture of spring—skies gloriously blue, the air caressed with fragrance, and the soul rising on wings. Then Chekhov comes, and all is changed. With him we are "in the ravine" (as one of his best stories is called), and the season is usually autumn. Occasionally we see a patch of color, but more often the skies are pale, the fields empty, and the hoarfrost cold at dawn. Men and women walk along the roads and on the streets of the villages and towns, but the sound of their steps is muted and their words often lost in silence. Life itself passes by, dismal and unvaried, leaving disappointment in its path. Chekhov never thought of himself as a pessimist, but with the trained perception of a physician he knew the pain of living, and he conveys the pain so clearly that the spirit longs for relief.

I.

When Chekhov began to be recognized as a writer, more than forty years had passed since the publication of Gogol's *Dead Souls*. During those four decades a change had come upon the Russian scene, transforming it, also, to autumnal tones. The 1840's had been a decade of idealism: a time for dreams, for glowing theories, and heady utterance. The "raging" Belinsky had led many intellectuals to white heat in the struggle for improvement, and others—Herzen and Bakunin among them—went abroad to woo the sweet form of freedom. The fifties brought a sense that something significant was ripening, and when the tyrant Nicholas II died, the night of his reign yielded a promise of dawn. The rule of Alexander II began auspiciously with the ending of the Crimean War and the gradual inauguration of reforms which, though only a suggestion of the reforms needed, were enough to keep hope alive. From London, Herzen in 1857 began to use *The Bell* as a clarion. When the Emancipation Act was signed in 1861, the long-awaited consummation seemed to have been achieved.

But the new day did not come. In the 1860's and 1870's the censorship, even if somewhat relaxed, still existed. The peasants, legally free, were still enslaved by poverty and ignorance, a slavery from which no one knew how to free them. The cultivated and idealistic radicals of the forties had given way to other types. Effete intellectuals like Turgenev's Nezhdanov (*Virgin Soil*), feeling guilty because of inherited privilege or the isolation imposed by learning, tried, often without success, to get down to the level of "the people." Stern young Nihilists wanted to destroy the decadent culture, including religion and the arts, and to substitute the realities of science and a tangible thing called "progress." The anarchists, pale imitations of Bakunin, loved violence for its own sake. The new radicals were no longer members of the nobility and the landed gentry. Coming from the middle class, they scorned the traditions of aristocracy and used utility as the basis for evaluation. For the most part they operated underground and made slow headway, actually perpetrating only a few terroristic activities. It was impossible, however, not to be aware of the ferment gathering just below the surface. As the culture of the West became increasingly suspect in Russia, with no adequate indigenous culture to substitute for it, and as leadership was transferred from aristocracy to *bourgeoisie*, the evils of inertia and complacency were superseded by brashness, disorganization, and iconoclasm. The new radicals were determined to reject the existing culture, but they had nothing to put in its place except materialism and negation. Although professing respect for work and the workers, they carried out few constructive measures.

The buoyancy of the early sixties, deflated by the discrepancy between anticipation and realization in the emancipation period, was for a time partially restored by the back-to-the-people movement of the late sixties. This effort, too, resulted in flagging hopes. "The people" revealed themselves as a sluggish mass, unresponsive and immobile. Meanwhile, the comparative freedom of the early part of the reign of Alexander II gave way to deepening tensions and suspicions. A feeling of painful disappointment paralyzed those who had expected much. Some, now permanently disillusioned, sank into cynicism and lethargy. They were similar to the "lost generation" after World War I who, their confidence in the possibility of bringing into existence a "world safe for democracy" destroyed, no longer hoped for or believed in anything. They had been willing to pay for freedom even if it were what Stephen Vincent Benét called "a hard-bought thing." But when it proved to be a mirage, that was too much to bear. Others became more radical than before, seeing no alternative to anarchy and terrorism. Through the seventies the pleadings of Dostoevsky for spiritual rebirth fell on ears growing deaf. The national harmony evoked by his Pushkin speech and a few months later by his death was but the pause before the storm. The assassination of Alexander II in 1881 marked the beginning of tumult. The whole country had to suffer for that sincere but ill-advised gesture in behalf of liberty.

Alexander III would take no chances. The eighties, therefore, began under a cloud of regression from the few hard-won gains toward freedom. The program of Nicholas I for the preservation of absolute autocracy was no more drastic than that of the new Czar. Alexander III resolved to make the penalty for any kind of radical activity so severe that not even fools or martyrs would take the risk. It was not necessary to be a political offender to receive a sentence of exile or imprisonment. Even acquaintance with an offender usually meant banishment. Inflexible censorship of the press and of university courses and activities resulted in the loss of many privileges granted by Alexander II. Religious minorities were persecuted with unprecedented ferocity. Especially for the Jews it was a period of despair and death. They were hounded and "purged" on a monstrous scale.

The tightening of monarchical authority with the inevitable increase of repression and surveillance meant the final collapse of hope. Even the fact that the reign of Alexander III was brief did not counteract the lethargy produced by expectations already too long unfulfilled. The succession to the throne in 1894 of his son, the weak-willed Nicholas II, made no difference. There was nothing in which to have faith. The spirit of the people was covered by a blanket of atrophied dreams and expectations like dead leaves. This was the autumnal scene from which Chekhov emerged as observer and recorder.

II.

Anton Pavlovitch Chekhov was born in 1860 in the town of Taganrog on the Sea of Azov in the southern part of Russia. His grandfather had been a serf who managed to accumulate more than enough wealth to purchase his freedom and that of his entire family. Chekhov's father, a grocer, was an unsuccessful businessman but had considerable musical talent and a strong religious bent. His primary interest was church music, and, whether they liked it or not, his sons were trained in the church ritual and spent long hours as choirboys. Although his father was not a bully, as some biographers of Chekhov have asserted, he was in many respects inflexible in his relations with his children. However, all of them—five boys and a girl—were given the benefit of musical training, an opportunity to indulge their varied hobbies, and the advantages of the best education available in the town. The fact that the boys often had to assist their father in his grocery store, in addition to spending arduous hours in the church choir, interfered with their leisure-time pursuits but did not stifle their spontaneous and ingenious pastimes. Their recreations included the dramatic improvisations later to bear fruit in Chekhov's literary productions. Despite the strain of inadequate finances, hard work, and a demanding father, the family was united by compatibility of interests and by the affection which prevailed when the children were small and throughout their maturity as well.

When Anton was only sixteen, his father's business failed, and the rest of the family went to Moscow to join the two oldest sons, who had previously gone there to pursue their education, one at the university and one at a school of art. Anton was left alone in Taganrog to complete his studies in the Latin School. This separation, entailing responsibility for his own livelihood, introduced Chekhov to the meaning of loneliness and insecurity, a lesson he never forgot. He proved capable of managing his affairs, however; already his balance and common sense were well developed. When he went to Moscow three years later, his adequacy resulted in his becoming the head of the family. The financial crisis had not been improved by the move to Moscow. There were debts to pay, and Anton quietly accepted the responsibility of paying them. From then on he was the main support of the entire family.

In Moscow in 1879, Anton entered the university to study medicine. There is every reason to believe he was deeply interested in his studies, but he was never able to give his whole attention to them. The fact that he had to support not only himself but the others as well made it necessary for him to find some source of income that could be carried on in conjunction with his activities as a student. Out of this necessity was born Chekhov's career as an author. Even before he left Taganrog, he had dabbled in playwriting, but now he must turn his dabbling to account. In 1880 he began to contribute to a comic paper. Tentatively at first, then with increasing momentum, he proceeded to pour out sketches, stories, short plays, and fillers of all kinds—anything and everything, from jokes to novelettes.

For several years Chekhov regarded his writing as nothing more than a means to provide shelter and food for the family. The writing was easy enough, and there was no problem about publication, but the pay was so poor that he was forced to an incredible output. Throughout his entire medical course he had to live two lives, that of student on the one hand and of hack writer on the other, and always he was surrounded by his large, noisy, sociable, disorganized family and their associates. It was no wonder that even his strong constitution began to show the strain of arduous living.

When Chekhov completed his medical studies at the age of twenty-four, he was already on the road to being established as a writer, and the practice of medicine became "the road not taken." He did not so much give up the practice of medicine as carry it on secondarily and intermittently. After the completion of his studies he worked for a short time in a hospital, and in later years he gave all his time and energy to medicine during several brief intervals of cholera epidemic, but there was never any real conflict between his two interests. If he was not a practicing doctor, he always continued to be a scientist, and his scientific bent had a strong effect on his writing. In 1890, when he was asked by a friend to supply certain autobiographical information, he was characteristically reticent, but he did avow his faith in science:

> My work in the medical sciences undoubtedly had a great influence on my writing; certainly it widened the area of my observations and enriched my knowledge. . . . My medical background has also been a guide to me. . . . Familiarity with natural sciences and the scientific method has always kept me on my guard, and wherever possible I have tried to write on the basis of scientific data.[1]

In 1886 the twenty-six-year-old Chekhov, having published a popular volume of stories and with another in preparation, became a regular contributor to the *Novoe Vremya* (*New Times*), probably the most influential daily paper in Russia. With its editor, Alexey Suvorin, he established the closest friendship of

[1] Most of the quotations from the Chekhov letters are from the translation by Sidonie Lederer, edited by Lillian Hellman. The others are from the Garnett translation.

his life, one which gave him the benefit of understanding and invigorating criticism. He also attracted the favorable notice of the well-known novelist Grigorovich, who had given initial encouragement to Dostoevsky forty years earlier. The attention of Grigorovich led Chekhov for the first time to recognize that he had a talent worthy of being put to serious use. In reply to the letter in which Grigorovich begged him not to squander his creative ability on "literary trifles," Chekhov wrote that he was "deeply moved," but he added with his usual modesty that he lacked the ability to judge whether he deserved such praise. His letter is full of significant clues to the circumstances of his life at that time:

> If I do have a gift to be respected, I can confess to you . . . that I have hitherto not given it any respect. I felt I had some talent, but had fallen into the habit of considering it trifling. . . . All my intimates have always referred condescendingly to my writing and have kept advising me in friendly fashion not to change a genuine profession for mere scribbling. . . .
>
> I am going to stop doing work that must be done in a hurry, but not just yet. . . . I am not averse to going hungry, an experience I have already had, but this is not a matter concerning me alone. . . .
>
> All hope is for the future. I am still only twenty-six. Perhaps I shall manage to accomplish something, although time does run out fast.

Chekhov did not realize how fast his own time would run out, but he had already begun to have unmistakable symptoms of the consumption which, although he did not acknowledge its existence for some years, pursued him relentlessly during the remainder of his short career, influencing both his external and, inevitably, his inner life.

From time to time Chekhov had been writing short plays, most of them little more than farcical vaudeville sketches. Several of his one-act plays were extremely successful, however, and from one of these, *The Bear*, he made so much money that he ceased to think of fiction as the only sure source of income. In 1887 his first full-length play, *Ivanov*, was written and produced. Despite its only moderate success (Chekhov's many revisions attested to his own uncertainty about the play), this new venture marked a turning point in his career. It is safe to assume that Chekhov was more interested in drama than in the short story. He was an excellent dramatic critic and was absorbed in every aspect of theatrical production. But he waited until he had achieved a degree of financial security before risking much time on dramatic composition. For the rest of his life after *Ivanov* he was always writing plays or evolving theories about what he believed drama should be. Although the Russian theater of the time was static, stodgy, and imitative, Chekhov was certain it could be revitalized if it had fresh, vigorous material, and he was determined to write plays that would show "life as it is" in place of the banalities of melodrama or the hackneyed conventionalities of plot and characterization.

During the late eighties and the early nineties almost all of Chekhov's time was given to writing, with two major interruptions. The illness and, after a comparatively short time, the death of one of his older brothers, Nikolai, plunged Chekhov into his first personal contact with sorrow. Chekhov's two older brothers, having been caught up in the Bohemianism of Moscow artists and would-be artists, had not done their share in support of the family. Chekhov's awareness of their faults, however, did not prevent him from feeling affection for them. Before his death Nikolai had done some effective illustrations for Anton's stories.

In his thirtieth year Chekhov had an experience quite different from anything else in his life. He spent nearly six months going to and observing conditions on the Russian penal island of Sakhalin. His unbelievably rigorous journey of three thousand miles across Siberia could easily have been too much for a man of robust health. Only his characteristic adaptability and liveliness of spirit enabled Chekhov to endure it. He traveled much of the way overland in what he called "a vehicle resembling a little wicker basket," across varied terrain, and through an extreme range of temperature, without any amenities. He stayed for three months on Sakhalin, where he was confronted with life in its rawest and most brutal form. He talked to literally every individual in the penal colony and made exhaustive notes of his observations.

The published findings of his investigation may have had some effect upon prison reforms. At any rate, they gave Chekhov the sense of having done something that desperately needed doing. Most of his relatives and friends had been unable to understand what seemed to them a pointless gesture. But the Sakhalin episode was not a gesture. It shows Chekhov as the man he was, a man who accepted his responsibility, not only as a son and brother and as an artist, but also as a member of the human family.

Back in Moscow after his unique experience he felt restless, uncertain whether he was justified in continuing to write when there was so much misery in the world to be relieved. After a short time he went with Suvorin on a trip to southern Europe, where he was especially pleased by Vienna and Venice. When he returned to Moscow the second time, he felt it was where he belonged; he had begun to love it as his spiritual home.

In the succeeding years Chekhov lived with his family on a country estate he bought near the village of Melikhovo, fifty miles from Moscow. Here he found much pleasure in country life. He enjoyed and assisted in all the activities of running a farm—planning, managing, building, and doing the farm work. The planting and nurture of trees was his special delight. Also, he took an active part in the organization of famine relief and later in the suppression of cholera, which threatened to move from southern Russia into the northern provinces. He was interested in community improvements—the building of roads and bridges and the establishment of schools and hospitals. The time he could give to writing was curtailed by all these activities and even more by the demands made upon him as a doctor by the peasants, whose woes he could not ignore, and by the unending procession in his home of guests, whose presence he always welcomed, for he was by nature gay and fond of people.

Chekhov had none of the artificiality or egocentricity of many creative temperaments. He never spared himself. Even when wracked by illness, he thought of the happiness of his family and guests, the welfare of his patients, and the continuation of his engrossing charitable activities. Yet, in spite of all the distractions, Chekhov produced many of his finest stories during the years at Melikhovo, years which were also punctuated by frequent trips to Moscow and Petersburg and, when health demanded it, by journeys abroad or to the Crimea. His letters during these years are full of his love of life, but a minor tone also appears. In the summer of 1894 he wrote to Suvorin: "I want so keenly to enjoy everything as if life were a perpetual Shrove Tuesday. . . . And some inner force, like a presentiment, nudges me to make haste. Perhaps it is . . . simply sorrow that life flows on in such a monotonous and pallid way. A protest of the soul, one might say."

In 1896, Chekhov's play *The Seagull* was performed in St. Petersburg. Because the director and actors failed to understand the quality of the drama, it was such a failure that Chekhov resolved never to write another play. The lack of appreciation and understanding was justifiably disheartening, but after the initial disappointment Chekhov took this failure as he had always taken success, with composure and good sense. A year later, however, when it was produced by the Moscow Art Theater under the direction of the great actor-director Stanislavsky and his associate Nemirovich-Danchenko, the play became an overwhelming success. From that time Chekhov's place at the center of the Russian theater was unchallenged. Stanislavsky and his fellow actors began to call their theater the Chekhov Theater, and a warm friendship existed between them and the dramatist until his death.

By 1897 the disease that was consuming him had begun to gain mastery of his body, and Chekhov could no longer hide the truth from his family. Coughing, hemorrhages, and almost incessant fever, as well as other minor ailments, sentenced him to semi-invalidism. Neither his iron will nor his optimistic clinging to the fullness of life could hold at bay the onrush of the fatal malady. During the seven years left to him he was compelled to live according to the terms levied upon him by the struggle to survive. Forced to seek a milder climate, either in the Crimea or southern Europe, he settled at Yalta. There he again acquired property and started to convert it into a place of beauty, giving personal attention to the planting of every tree and bush and the placing of every stone. In 1899, his father having died the previous autumn, Chekhov sold Melikhovo, and the family (now his mother and sister) joined him in Yalta. He undoubtedly had painful memories of his father's petty tyrannies, but they had long since been forgiven. He wrote after his father's death: "With his death the country place where I resided has lost all its delight for me. . . . Now I must begin a new life."

Although Chekhov had always been somewhat passive with regard to political issues, he became so much absorbed in the Dreyfus case that his long friendship with Suvorin was cooled by the latter's failure to champion the accused man. This was only one of several indications of Chekhov's increasing concern for public affairs as the diminution of his strength cut him off from the possibility of action. It has been customary to say that Chekhov was different from other great Russian writers because of his neutral attitudes and his unresponsiveness to public affairs. A careful reading of his stories and plays is all that is needed to disprove this assumption.

It gave Chekhov great pleasure to become acquainted with Tolstoy, whom he visited at Yasnaya Polyana. Tolstoy's views had a strong influence upon him. He was not a moralist, but the way he lived and many of the overtones of his writing show that his own ethic had much in common with Tolstoyism. A passage from one of his letters written shortly before he made the Sakhalin trip sounds like a foretaste of *Resurrection*:[2]

> From the books I have read and am now reading it is evident that we have let millions of people rot in prison . . . to no good purpose, barbarously, without giving the matter a thought; we have driven people in chains through the cold thousands of miles, infected them with syphilis, depraved them, multiplied criminals and shifted the blame onto the red-nosed prison overseers. . . . It is not the overseers who are the guilty parties, but all of us.

Still, he could not entirely sympathize with the views of the grand old man. "Something in me protests," he wrote in 1894. "Reason and justice tell me that in the electricity and heat of love for man there is something greater than chastity and abstinence from meat." Despite occasional outbursts of impatience with the Tolstoyan morality, however, Chekhov always asserted his reverence for the prophet of Yasnaya Polyana. In 1900, when Tolstoy was ill, Chekhov wrote in a letter to the journalist Menshikov a tribute which says much about both its author and its subject:

> I dread Tolstoy's death. His death would create a vacuum in my life. . . . I have never loved anyone as much as him. I am an unbeliever, but of all the faiths I consider his the nearest to my heart and most suited to me. Then again, as long as there is a Tolstoy in literature it is simple and gratifying to be a literary figure; even the awareness of not having accomplished anything and not expecting to accomplish anything in the future is not so terrible because Tolstoy makes up for all of us.

In exile in Yalta, Chekhov still wrote and tried gallantly to remain active. His enforced separation from the theater was very painful to him, for the theater had become the center of his world. He went to Moscow as often as possible, but one bout of

[2] Chekhov's letter was written several years before *Resurrection* was published.

illness after another assailed him. During the last five years of his life he was seriously ill a great deal of the time, yet he never lost his cheerfulness. Each time he rallied, he worked on a story or play, planted or pruned in his garden, caught up on the voluminous correspondence which was his means of contact with the world, made further plans for the library he was giving to his native town, and was indefatigable in his efforts to help the invalids who appealed to him, particularly the ones who came to Yalta in the hope of seeing him. During these years he became acquainted with Bunin and Gorky; the latter and Tolstoy he saw in Yalta a number of times. The measure of Chekhov's integrity is indicated by the fact that when shortly after his election to the Russian academy Gorky was expelled for thinly veiled political reasons, Chekhov requested the removal of his own name from the list of members.

In the spring of 1901, Chekhov married Olga Knipper, an actress in the Moscow Art Theater, whom he had known for three years and for whom he had written several parts in his plays. He loved her devotedly, both as a person and as a symbol of the theater he loved and from which he was cut off. Shortly after the marriage he went to take a cure, accompanied by his wife, but as always he was restless and could not wait to get back to work. He continued to go to Moscow whenever he could summon the strength, but he was separated from Olga for long intervals while she pursued her career, which he did not want to interrupt and she had no intention of giving up. Chekhov's personality is nowhere more clearly revealed than in his letters to his wife, filled with humor, whimsy, tenderness, and poignant loneliness. The marriage certainly brought him happiness—but with an undertone of pain. If ever a man needed the presence and care of a loving wife, it was he. The impression that Chekhov gave more devotion than he received is inescapable. It was his sister Marie, rather than his wife, who devoted herself to his welfare during the final phase of his illness and, after his death, to preserving his memory.

On January 17, 1904, Chekhov's last and greatest drama, *The Cherry Orchard*, was first performed. It marked the twenty-fifth anniversary of the beginning of his literary career. The play made an extraordinary impact by its almost breath-taking simplicity and beauty, and Chekhov received the plaudits of large numbers of theater-goers who paid him homage. His failing strength had been pushed too hard, however, and his life was almost over. A few months later he again went abroad with his wife to take a cure in the Black Forest. There, in June, 1904, he died. He had retained his resilience of spirit and his concern for others to the hour of his death.

Chekhov was not a morose man like Gogol. He was not motivated, like Dostoevsky and Tolstoy, by a passion for denunciation and reform. He did not consciously interpret his moment in history as did Goncharov or Turgenev. He was not a revolutionary like Gorky. He was not a prophet like Turgenev, Dostoevsky, or Andreyev. Although brought up in a religious atmosphere and intimately acquainted with the music and ritual of the Orthodox church, he was not a man of conventional faith. But lack of faith did not torment him or occasion ambivalence as it did Tolstoy and Dostoevsky. After the whirlpools of Dostoevsky's nature and the mountain peak of Tolstoy's talent, Chekhov seems like an ordinary man. But he was extraordinary, too.

Chekhov was the one among all great figures of Russian literature who would have always been a delight to know and a faithful friend. He had a droll wit, without acid, and a taste for fun—for mimicry and the ludicrous. He was kind, generous, and concerned for others. Yet there was nothing wishy-washy about him. He was contemptuous of posturing and irresponsibility. He never pelted other people with his own emotions. It would be an error to suggest that Chekhov was a simple man, yet he lived and acted simply, and he disliked all types of pretension, both in literature and in life. Gorky was impressed with this quality in him: "I think that in Anton Chekhov's presence everyone involuntarily felt in himself a desire to be simpler, more truthful, more oneself. . . . He loved everything simple, genuine, sincere, and he had a peculiar way of making other people simple."

Most important, Chekhov was a courageous and a modest man—too modest, perhaps—with a fine mental and spiritual equilibrium. He was, in the true sense of the word, mature—a whole nature. But he was not, after all, a demigod. If he had a defect in character, it was perhaps that he was too reasonable, too sane. He lacked the fire of high resolution. True, he yearned for a better life for all men, but his yearning was without passion. Like a good physician, he diagnosed his own disease and saw that it was the disease of a whole generation. In a remarkable letter written to Suvorin in 1892 he answered the question, "Now what about us?"

> We paint life such as it is . . . but that's as far as we'll go. We have neither immediate nor distant aims, and you can rattle around in our souls. We have no politics, we don't believe in revolution, we don't believe in God, we aren't afraid of ghosts, and personally I don't even fear death or blindness. He who doesn't desire anything, doesn't hope for anything and isn't afraid of anything cannot be an artist. . . . For the time being it would be rash to expect anything really good from us, regardless of whether or not we are gifted. . . . At least I don't conceal my illness from myself, don't lie to myself and don't cover my own emptiness with other people's intellectual rags.

It was characteristic of Chekhov that although he always intended to be honest, he was always more critical of himself than of others, more critical than he needed to be. The crowds who mourned him and followed him to his grave would not have known what he meant by what he called his "emptiness." They saw him as he really was—tender yet strong, a man of great heart and clear head, who had somehow stood for light in a time of darkness.

III.

Given the time and the circumstances of Chekhov's life, one can feel little surprise at the autumnal tone of his writing. As a scientist he formed the habit of minute and exact observation; as a writer he was untouched by the romantic sentimentality of the first decades of the nineteenth century. He loved Russia but viewed his country, like everything else, without illusion. His detachment from politics was a reflection of the general mood of resignation produced by the failure of the movement toward reform. On the personal plane he was perforce always conscious of the imminence of death. Therefore, though he was not a reformer and did not use his writing to bludgeon, prophesy, or exhort, his stories and plays offer what is not expressed so clearly anywhere else: an impression of the prevailing mood of the period immediately preceding the first outbreak of revolution in 1905. From 1880 for a quarter of a century Chekhov portrayed the temper of the times more sensitively than any other writer.

It is not wise to attempt generalizations regarding Chekhov's fiction, for it includes a wide variety of moods and a kaleidoscopic variety of character types; however, some observations can be made. Most of the farce and much of the humor is confined to the early stories, which lack the appeal of Chekhov's mature work. D. S. Mirsky in his *History of Russian Literature* states that from "A Dreary Story" (sometimes titled "A Tedious Tale") and succeeding stories, "We may date the meaning that has come to be associated in Russia with the words 'Chekhovian state of mind.' " He is referring to the quality which virtually all readers consider peculiarly Chekhovian. Intangible though this quality is, the reader can identify certain elements responsible for the highly individualized tone.

In the first place, the much heralded objectivity of Chekhov is a factor in the spirit and style of his writing. To Chekhov human beings were neither villains nor heroes, and he made no effort to interpret life on the grand scale. He saw it honestly and realistically, without sugar-coating; he saw both shadow and sunlight. The dark blots did not provoke his censure or disdain; he did not indulge in the luxury of passing judgment. Instead, he looked at human life against its background of nature and recorded what he saw. "To a chemist," he wrote a friend, "nothing on earth is unclean. A writer must be as objective as a chemist, he must lay aside his personal subjective standpoint and must understand that muck heaps play a very respectable part in a landscape, and that the evil passions are as inherent in life as the good ones." In 1890 he replied to a correspondent who had reproached him for being so objective that he did not make moral judgments:

> You abuse me for objectivity, calling it indifference to good and evil, lack of ideals and ideas, and so on. You would have me, when I describe horse-stealers, say: "Stealing horses is an evil." But that has been known for ages without my saying so. Let the jury judge them, it's my job simply to show what sort of people they are.

Even though the objectivity in Chekhov's writing is obvious, it is only part of the pattern. Whatever his intentions, he could not be only a "chemist." He did not judge people or events, but he did see them through his own prism. The subtle blend of the subjective elements with his objectivity is what gives his work its distinctive flavor.

One of the highly personal characteristics apparent in all Chekhov's writing is the lack of heroic proportions. Turgenev, Dostoevsky, and Tolstoy all sought leaders and looked for the splendor in mankind which might be the motive force to organize and move the mighty, yet slumbering, potentials of Russia. Turgenev did not succeed in finding a leader, and in Bazarov he revealed a premonition of the danger residing in science and the danger in the rejection of authority. Dostoevsky believed that Russia contained infinite resources of spiritual power, the raw materials for prophets and priests who could lead his country in the fulfillment of its divine destiny. He and Tolstoy saw the essence of greatness in the common people. Both glorified the elements of grandeur in Russia's past and saw her moving toward a heroic future. With Chekhov the dimensions are contracted. In his writing everything is small in scope—small stories, short plays—except for the few full-length plays made up, as it were, of a succession of small moments, flashes of life. His view of mankind is correspondingly small.

Chekhov's students are not Bazarovs or Raskolnikovs struggling to be "extraordinary," but insignificant young men who ride in the darkness on the mail wagon, unable to communicate with others ("The Poet"); or who end their cramped existences with bullets ("Volodya"); or who walk home from shooting ("The Student"), numbed by the wind and cold, reflecting—

> . . . that just such a wind had blown in the days of Rurik and in the time of Ivan the Terrible and Peter, and in their time there had been just the same desperate poverty and hunger, the same thatched roofs with holes in them, ignorance, misery, the same desolation around, the same darkness, the same feeling of oppression—all these had existed, did exist, and would exist, and the lapse of a thousand years would make life no better.

A Petersburg official ("An Anonymous Story") says: "We have grown feeble, slack—degraded, in fact. Our generation is entirely composed of neurasthenics and whimperers; we do nothing but talk of fatigue and exhaustion." In "Teacher of Literature" the main character realizes that "the illusion had evaporated." He is not a good teacher, he does not love his wife, and he is "surrounded by vulgarity." The man who has an impulse toward philanthropy ("The Wife") learns that his motives are selfish and his charity not wanted, for his egocentricity corrodes all he touches. The scientists discover that even science gives them no final satisfaction. In the most gaunt and unrelieved of Chekhov's stories, "Ward No. 6," the doctor soon gives up the attempt to improve conditions in the hospital because the weight of accumulated filth, inertia, and graft is too much for him. In the end he considers science as useless as all the rest, for the pygmies with whom he has to live and work are not able to make use of it. He is a superior man, but there is no place for superiority. Forced to join the patients in the mental ward, he becomes a symbol of the waste in human life. In "A Dreary Story" the famous old professor of medicine knows that, despite the respect of his colleagues and students, his whole life has been an empty shell. As he feels the approach of death, he is cut off from everyone and there is nothing for him to cling to. Alone and ill, he tries to think what he wants from life. But his desires are insignificant, as everything else about his life now seems to have been.

In many of the stories man is particularly paltry in comparison with the majesty and harmony of nature, which Chekhov felt deeply and used so perfectly as background for his characters that when he wrote of nature, it was as if he had at his command all the instruments of a symphony. "God's world is a good place," he wrote to Suvorin. "The only thing not good in it is we. How little justice and humility there is in us." One of the stories, "The Bet," is an almost allegorical treatment of the pettiness of human life. A young man voluntarily submits to fifteen years of solitary confinement to win a wager—to prove that he is willing to give up his freedom for two million rubles. During the years, however, the money ceases to have any meaning for him. A few hours before the expiration of the term of imprisonment he deliberately goes forth, disdaining the reward rightfully his, because he has come to realize, "It is all worthless, fleeting, illusory, and deceptive, like a mirage." He writes to his jailer, "You have lost your reason and taken the wrong path," and he says he despises all that most men live for.

Perhaps no other story gives more memorable expression to this unheroic, petty quality of human experience than "Gooseberries." It tells of a man who devotes his life to the realization of a dream: he wants a country estate, with a house, servants' quarters, kitchen-garden, and gooseberry bushes. He slaves, scrimps, and sacrifices everything that might have given meaning to life, until at last he gets all he wants. "Then he put one gooseberry into his mouth, looked at me with the triumph of a child who has at last received his favourite toy, and said: 'How delicious!' . . . They were sour and unripe." The sight of the man, now lazy and dull, his spirit extinguished by complacency, plunges his brother into despair. The latter is aware only of the bitterness of the fruit. Chekhov saw many men trading their souls for gooseberries!

Another of the most pervasive elements in the writing of Chekhov is irony, especially the irony of unfulfillment. Chekhov was not concerned with salvation, but he was acutely aware of frustration. Although personal to a certain extent, his irony is even more a symptom of the period when the writing was done. (Emancipation, for example, had come, but there was no freedom.) One form this irony takes is the realization that achievement, arriving at one's goal, seldom brings satisfaction. The bishop, in the narrative of that name, finds nothing but loneliness in his high position. He is not a success in his own estimation, and to others is only someone to fear. Irony is also expressed in the failure to realize hopes, in the pursuit of what proves to be a will-o'-the-wisp, and in lack of awareness of what the present offers. A man whose heart has been lifted up by a kiss received in a darkened room ("The Kiss") falls in love with the woman who kissed him, but he does not know who she is and cannot find her. A father ("The Requiem"), estranged from his daughter turned prostitute, has scarcely been aware that he has a daughter until her death leaves him with a sense of sudden desolation. A husband and wife, forgetting their existing blessings, are transported by the impression that they hold the winning number in a lottery. Then each becomes suspicious of what the other will do with the money. When they find it was all a mistake, that they did not win, their lives seem unspeakably small and wearisome ("The Lottery Ticket"). An old carpenter, taking his dying wife to the hospital, reflects that she has no right to die because he has not treated her well—though he never intended to abuse her—and he needs time to show her his true feelings ("Sorrow"). It is too late; the pelting snow is no colder than her waxen face on the wagon floor:

> He had not had time to live with his old woman, to show her he was sorry for her before she died. He had lived with her for forty years, but those forty years had passed by as it were in a fog. . . . And, as though to spite him, his old woman died at the very time when he felt he was sorry for her, that he could not live without her, and that he had behaved dreadfully badly to her.

To Chekhov marriage was not an idyllic relationship, but usually an unavailing struggle between two people to achieve compatibility. In "The Wife" the married couple, both well intentioned, can endure each other only by remaining apart; the wife lives upstairs, the husband down. Their only common language is quarreling, recrimination, and threats. In one of the most painful of the stories, "The Grasshopper," the unfaithful Olga ignores her husband and is oblivious to his sacrificial labors as a doctor. She wounds him beyond words, but he loves and forgives her, makes no demands upon her, and goes quietly about his work. Then all at once he is dead from diphtheria contracted from a patient: "Suddenly she understood that he really was an extraordinary, rare, and, compared with every one else she knew, a great man. . . . She wanted to explain to him that it had been a mistake, that all was not lost, that life might still be beautiful and happy." But his ears cannot hear the words he has longed for in vain. In "Enemies" the devastating grief of a doctor whose only child has just died must be put aside when he numbly heeds the plea of his wealthy neighbor whose stricken wife needs medical attention. When they go to the sick woman, however, they find she has used illness only as a ruse to enable her to run away with another man. The doctor is overwhelmed by the tawdriness of such emotions in the face of his own wretchedness. Sometimes people find too late the right person to love ("The Lady with the Dog"). Their love is genuine, but they are cheated of it by previously assumed responsibilities. They are sentenced to measure out their days in double desolation—that imposed by what they have but do not want and that of yearning for what they may not have though all their happiness depends upon it.

Chekhov sensed acutely and expressed the isolation of the human spirit. Like the husband and wife in "The Party," who love each other but cannot confess their love, people try in vain to communicate. "Misery" is the story of an old sledge driver whose son is dead. He needs desperately to tell someone, anyone, of his grief, but no one will listen. Finally he turns to his little mare; he is "carried away and tells her all about it." In "A Dreary Story" a young woman appeals to the old professor who is her only friend to help her overcome her loneliness and uselessness, but, although he needs her help as much as she needs his, he can only propose that they eat lunch together. Adults have no sense of the tremendous importance children often attach to what seems trivial to their elders. The little boy in "A Trifling Occurrence" is bewildered and deeply hurt by the treachery of the man who betrays his confidence. People are fearful and wrap themselves in conventionality, like "The Man in the Case," who always wore his galoshes and overcoat, slept in a heavily curtained bed, and seemed to welcome the protective shelter of his coffin, when nothing but his own nature had kept him from being able really to live.

Pettiness, disappointment, loneliness, and alienation—these are the elements of Chekhov's gray view of man's life. He saw what Thomas Hardy has called "life's little ironies" on all sides. This recognition did not cause him to rebel or even to despair; it caused instead a gentle melancholy which is marked by peace as well as pain—the peace that comes from not expecting much from life. This is the twilight tone in Chekhov's writings which blended so harmoniously into a twilight period in the history of Russia.

The stories to which reference has been made are only an intimation of the panorama of characters and moments produced by the inexhaustible resources of Chekhov's perceptive and creative powers. There is nothing to equal them in the whole range of the short story. No one has ever been able to surpass Chekhov in showing man as a laughable creature. Still, he was polite enough to make us laugh at ourselves more quickly than at others: he laughs with us instead of at us. Sudden moments of recognition are more likely to provoke a chuckle than a guffaw, but there is an occasional jab of robust humor. Chekhov was a master of the combination of understatement with anticlimax. He had a droll sense of the ridiculous, and his timing was perfect. He knew how to open the door just a crack; the hint stands for the whole.

An extremely significant element in the writings of Chekhov is his interpretation of the peasants. After the rising scale of adulation beginning in Turgenev's *Sportsman's Sketches*, progressing through Dostoevsky, and reaching a climax in Tolstoy's *Anna Karenina* and many of his late stories, it is something of a shock to find the Russian peasants presented impersonally and with no glorification. In Chekhov's tales there is little evidence of the peasants' humility and dignity, their reservoirs of inner strength, and their patient endurance or longing for a better life. Nor is there any of the Tolstoyan conception of the peasants as personifying the spirit of the Beatitudes. Chekhov's view of them was more realistic. He said, "Peasant blood flows in my veins, and you cannot astound me with the virtues of the peasantry." He showed even the idealist who went back to the people as being disconcerted by their lack of response. Chekhov recognized with regret that for the most part "the people" were not waiting with outstretched arms to come out of the mire.

In Chekhov's stories ("Peasant Wives," "Agafya," "Peasants," and many others) the peasants are dirty, dissolute, ignorant, shiftless, and completely aimless. The men do as little as possible, beat their wives, take for themselves the warm place on the stove, and drink to the point of stupefaction. The women become terrified and sullen drudges, old before youth is gone. There is neither health nor hope, tenderness nor fidelity. Brutality exists even within the family. Some are so stupid ("The Malefactor") that they cannot or will not understand that unscrewing nuts from the rails may cause train wrecks and endanger lives. Almost inarticulate, even when they make halfhearted efforts, they cannot communicate with or understand the educated because there is no common language ("The New Villa"). Some ("The Horse-Stealers") are absolutely unscrupulous; they resort to thievery and murder to get what they want with the least effort. A number of stories dealing with the children of peasants show them as pitiable creatures, doomed before they are born. Survival is limited to the fittest. In many of the peasant stories the weak suffer because of the strong, who wait callously for them to die. Poverty of body, however, is not the most distressing characteristic of the peasants as Chekhov presents them, but poverty of spirit. Almost completely lacking humane impulses, they combine the swinishness of the Yahoos with torpor of the mental and moral faculties.

If the peasants have initiative, if they manage to work their way up to become tradesmen, they are usually callous, scheming, hypocritical, and sometimes cruel. A masterful story dealing with such characters, "In the Ravine," starkly depicts the rapacity of those who have begun to be prosperous. The "viper," Aksinia, tyrannizes over an entire family and seizes control of financial affairs. The meekness of her sister-in-law, on the other hand, whose child she deliberately scalds to death (to prevent the division of the family properties) without eliciting even a reproach from the grief-stricken mother, is a reminder that emancipation could free the peasants legally but could not free them from their defects in character—rapacity at one extreme and servile endurance at the other.

In spite of the irrepressible cheerfulness of the face Chekhov turned toward his family and friends, life itself was often a "dreary story" to the gentle man. And Russia was dreary, too. "This Russia of ours," he said to Gorky, "is such an absurd, clumsy country." Against the breath-taking beauty of the steppes, the sound of wind rising in the trees, the song of the nightingales, the shape of luminous clouds, the sun shining on fields of rye, and the moonlight-drenched, fragrant air of evening—against that background the snow fell, freezing hearts and bodies to oblivion; the smoke gathered black in peasant huts; the pleas of children went unheard; people yearned for what they could not have; the word was spoken in vain; blows were given instead of blessings; and laughter was washed away by tears. Chekhov knew that freedom cannot be dispensed by law but must be achieved by the human spirit. And as he looked upon the pageant of humanity he saw little to give him assurance that mankind was ready to be free.

IV.

Chekhov's great plays repeat many of the same themes, although the irony is subtler, the interplay of relationships more complicated. The longing is painted on a broader canvas, but the tone is much the same as that of the best stories. Chekhov's plays reveal more clearly than the stories a deepening and maturing of his views. In order to understand the plays, one must be aware that as he began to make serious use of his talent, the objectivity for which Chekhov had always striven was no longer enough to satisfy him. He recognized that if he were to say anything significant as a writer he must be more than objective. In his letters to Suvorin and other friends he enunciated his artistic creed, and it is possible to see the changing attitude, a small change but nonetheless discernible, which proved to be the major development in his maturation. For example, in 1888 he wrote to Suvorin:

> It seems to me that it is not the business of novelists to solve such questions as those of God, pessimism, and the like. The novelist's business is only to describe who has been speaking or thinking about God or pessimism, how and in what circumstances.

The next year he was even more positive in insisting upon detachment for the writer:

> I am afraid of those who look for a tendency between the lines, and who are determined to regard me either as a liberal or as a conservative. I am not a liberal, not a conservative, not an indifferentist. I should like to be a free artist and nothing more.

These were the views of a young man still holding tenaciously to his right to be dispassionate. But Chekhov was too alive mentally and too responsible spiritually to be content with neutrality. It is not necessary to try to establish all the factors which contributed to his shift in attitude—of which the Sakhalin incident was clearly one. Whatever the causes, late in 1892 another letter to Suvorin reveals the new dimension in his viewpoint:

> Bear in mind that writers who are considered immortal or just plain good and who intoxicate us have one very important trait in common: they are going somewhere and call you with them; you sense . . . that they have an aim. . . . Looking at some of them . . . you will see that they have immediate aims—the abolition of serfdom, the liberation of their country, political matters; . . . others have remote aims. . . . The best of them are realistic and paint life as it is, but because every line is saturated with juice, with the sense of life, you feel, in addition to life as it is, life as it should be, and you are entranced.

It would be inaccurate to imply that Chekhov had been without aims in writing his stories. Many of them were obviously intended to show up the dreariness and ugliness, the waste and apathy, and the ignorance and brutality of Russian life. We have seen how resolutely Chekhov stuck to what he believed to be the truth about the peasants in his stories about them. At the other end of the social scale, the pomposity, irresponsibility, and corruption of political officials and the wealthy are often given graphic exposure. It would be impossible anywhere in Russian literature to find a more damning indictment of public ignorance and sloth than in the story "Ward No. 6," in which the truth-loving, selfless scientist is destroyed by human beings no better than animals. Many of the stories contain unmistakable echoes of the Tolstoyan morality, which Chekhov respected (except in moments of exasperation when he sometimes barked, "The hell with the philosophy of the great of this world!"). But because of their brevity and their dramatic intensity the stories have a static quality almost photographic in nature. The reader comes away from them with a mood rather than an idea.

Unfortunately, the same thing has been too often true of the effect of the plays, a fact which caused Chekhov discomfiture and annoyance. Yet he was caught in a situation as intractable as the impasses which sometimes beset his characters. Not until Stanislavsky and the Moscow Art Theater began to produce his plays could he be sure of effective productions, but even Stanislavsky and some of the other actors had their own ideas of how the plays should be interpreted, and these ideas only occasionally coincided with what Chekhov intended and wanted. When he was able to do so, Chekhov attended rehearsals and explained in detail how certain characters and scenes should be played, and when he could not attend, he wrote quantities of letters. He was, after all, ill and far from Moscow most of the time, and anyway the director always had the last word. Still, the plays were given artistic production, and the entire theater group felt such devotion to Chekhov that when he was too ill to come to Moscow, they once went to Yalta to perform for him there. The dramatist had to accept an interpretation of his plays which the reader of his letters will recognize as being sentimentalized and devitalized. Stanislavsky is largely responsible for the static, moody, even shadowy quality usually associated with Chekhov's plays. In his excellent book *Chekhov the Dramatist*, David Magarshack builds a strong case for what he considers a serious misinterpretation of the plays by the Moscow Art Theater. If he is right, and he probably is—considering Chekhov's wry sense of humor and his tendency to see comedy in what other people would regard as frustration, if not pathos—it must be admitted that the plays succeeded brilliantly partly because of the misinterpretation, for under Stanislavsky's direction they took on the tone of dreariness which accorded perfectly with the historical period in which they were written and produced. In fact, it is scarcely possible to dissociate the plays entirely from the stories, and whatever Chekhov's intentions, the gray which prevails in so many of the stories does cast its shadow on the plays.

In fairness to Stanislavsky it must also be said that his misconception was understandable because Chekhov's last plays differed not only from his own earlier plays, but also from all other conventional dramatic forms. It is often said of his plays that nothing happens, and there is little action in the ordinary sense. The action is all indirect. Stanislavsky interpreted this indirection as passivity. Yet if the plays are acted as Chekhov wanted them to be, they are nervously alive. As they unveil the "inner man," the acute but restrained emotions of the characters and the conflicts between them create effects of almost explosive intensity.

The first of Chekhov's plays written after the deepening of his aim was *The Seagull.* On the surface the play appears to be a chain of futility which tightens around a group of sensitive individuals. It seems to begin in hope and end in desolation. But this is only the surface impression of the play. Chekhov did not intend to depict characters who were victims of circumstances that bruised and battered them. He intended to show most of them as empty, useless, self-centered people, victims primarily of their own selfishness and aimlessness. The characters in this play accept no responsibility for their deeds. Chekhov does not accuse them, but neither does he excuse them. By exposing their weaknesses he ceased to be neutral.

The fact that Chekhov considered and called this play a comedy has always been mystifying, especially to English and American audiences and readers. Obviously it is not a comedy in the conventional sense, but it is not tragedy either, by anybody's definition. When Chekhov used the term "comedy," he was not considering the frustration which permeates the play or the death which concludes it; he was considering the small natures of the characters.

Perhaps the most interesting character in *The Seagull* is Trigorin, the author. He is a man of talent but without conviction. It is clear that Chekhov meant to condemn him for the same lack of purpose for which Chekhov had condemned himself and his fellow writers: "We have neither immediate nor distant aims." Trigorin lives by compromise and uses others. The beautiful but empty descriptive passages in his books are symptoms of an arrested soul. The young would-be playwright, Treplev, has some talent, too, but he has nothing to say. He wants to write only to make an impression. He kills himself because he must run away from his own inadequacy. He is, of course, the victim of his mother, but she could not have injured him so much if he had been capable of affirmation. The actress Arkadina, his mother, is the most selfish and egocentric of the characters. She can make hash of other people's lives without a twinge of self-censure, almost without awareness. Nina is the victim of Trigorin, but she at least has an aim. Yet her aim is useless because it has no basis in self-knowledge. All of them are people who do not know themselves.

In a fashion typically Chekhovian most of the characters are either made impotent by longing for what they can not have, or they are too anemic of spirit to long for anything meaningful. Masha wants Treplev; Treplev wants fame and Nina; and Nina wants Trigorin and a career. Trigorin, however, wants only an anesthetic for his soul, and Arkadina wants only to continue satisfying her own selfish desires.

The seagull is a symbol of the potential of man who is meant to soar. The death of the bird symbolizes the useless and wanton destruction of this potential. In this play and in the plays which follow Chekhov implies that being decorative is not enough and that melancholy is not a substitute for determination and honest effort.

In *Uncle Vanya* destructive forces are again at work in the personalities of the characters, but there is at least a beginning of vitality. The professor and his beautiful wife, Helen, are predatory and idle, too. The professor is only a pseudo-intellectual, and he knows how to exploit the illusions people have about him.

He has every intention of robbing his daughter Sonia and her Uncle Vanya, and he would have succeeded if Vanya had not seen through him in time to save them. Astrov, the doctor—the man of reason and constructive endeavor—is irresistibly drawn to Helen by her beauty, but he remains conscious of her idle parasitism and he knows that her idleness is like a taint upon her life. Sonia, Uncle Vanya, and Astrov are saved from the clutches of the professor and Helen, but saved for what? Their world has been turned upside down. They are tired, distrustful, and hopeless. All of them have been infected by the evil which might have destroyed them. Sonia looks ahead to the future with courage but without anticipation. These honest, warm-hearted people can not visualize any future for themselves except a long procession of empty days and weary evenings.

In this play a positive element appears in the personality of Astrov. This man is an indefatigable worker. He is both a conscientious doctor and a passionate advocate of the conservation of natural resources. It is as if Chekhov had shown in Astrov a part of his own nature which he respected, as Trigorin in the earlier play represented the part he condemned. Astrov is an admirable man, yet there is something missing. He is convinced that nothing is or can ever be satisfying or pleasant in his personal life, and he has no other hope than "that when we are asleep in our graves we may, perhaps, be visited by pleasant visions." He says he loves life, but there is an irreconcilable ambivalence within his nature: he loves life and hates it at the same time. He lacks faith, buoyancy, and eagerness. Astrov is probably more autobiographical than Chekhov knew or intended, but Chekhov had scant patience with Astrov's inclination to submit.

When Astrov asserted that he could not endure the routine provincial life in Russia, he had, of course, ample justification for his dislike. His description of the district in which he lived gave Chekhov a chance to explain what was wrong with Russia. It also, perhaps unintentionally, expresses the mood of the gray period out of which Chekhov was writing:

> Of the old settlements and farms and monasteries and mills there is not a trace. In fact, it's a picture of gradual and unmistakable degeneration. . . . You will say it is the influence of civilization—that the old life must naturally give way to the new. . . . If there were highroads and railways on the site of these ruined forests, if there were works and factories and schools, the peasants would be healthier, better off, more intelligent; but, you see, there is nothing of the sort! There are still the same swamps and mosquitoes, the same lack of roads, and poverty, and typhus and diphtheria and fires in the district. . . . We have a disintegration that is the result of too severe a struggle for existence. This degeneration is due to inertia, ignorance, to the complete lack of understanding. . . . Almost everything has been destroyed already, but nothing as yet has been created to take its place.

These were strong words to come from the pen of Chekhov.

The Three Sisters is the most subtle, complicated, and in some ways the most painful of Chekhov's plays. Tolstoy would not finish reading it; he and others called Chekhov cruel and unfeeling. How little they understood him. It was precisely his being the opposite of cruel and unfeeling that made Chekhov conscious of the sadness of existence. He well knew how precious life is (who had more reason to know than he, with death hovering close?), but he saw that few people manage to live it to the full or sense its preciousness until too late. Chekhov's last three plays are all remarkable for the degree to which they produce the impression of reality, but *The Three Sisters* accomplishes this end best of all. Its unanswered questions and unsatisfied longings bear the haunting image of truth.

In this play the forces of destruction and decay are again shown in conflict with dreams and idealism, and stultification in conflict with aspiration. There are two happy characters. The first, Chebutykin, is happy because he has lost touch with life. The second, Tusenbach, has to pay for his happiness and his goodness by dying when he is on the eve of realizing his hopes. Solyony and Natasha are ruthless egotists. Anyone who gets in their way is marked for disaster. So Tusenbach is destroyed by Solyony, and Andrey and his three sisters have no chance against Natasha. Is life like that? Does evil triumph over good? Chekhov implies that such is the case.

The drama is not, however, a simple morality play in black and white. There is another basic motif. Though Andrey and his sisters are not evil, they are unfulfilled. They are all looking for something—in vain. For all of them that elusive something is epitomized in the idea of Moscow. "To Moscow, to Moscow" is the refrain that rings through their lives. But if they did go to Moscow, it would make no difference. The dream would then change; they would want something else. Vershinin, wiser than they, tells them: "You won't notice Moscow when you live in it. We have no happiness and never do have, we only long for it." Irina cannot reconcile herself to this emptiness. In her wretchedness she cries:

> Where? Where has it all gone? . . . Life is slipping away and will never come back, we shall never, never go to Moscow. . . .
> . . . I am nearly twenty-four, I have been working for years, my brains are drying up, I am getting thin and old and ugly and there is nothing, nothing, not the slightest satisfaction, and time is passing and one feels that one is moving away from a real, fine life, moving farther and farther away and being drawn into the depths. I am in despair.

Tusenbach loves Irina selflessly, but she cannot return his love. Then, lacking what will satisfy her, she decides to accept his offer of marriage only to lose him when he is killed for her sake. Finally Masha's need is answered. She finds in Vershinin one to whom she can give her whole heart. But they have scarcely recognized and acknowledged their love when they are torn apart by circumstance. The three sisters want nothing else so much as to get rid of their property so that they can go to Moscow. When they finally realize they will never go to Moscow, they have lost their property to their brother's malicious wife.

Are people perforce the victims of their own weak and insatiable natures? Do they never get what they want or want what they can have? In place of answers Chekhov gives us melancholy intimations.

Yet Chekhov was apparently determined that his plays would not end in negation and that his characters would not be only empty or ineffectual. At the end the three sisters all make affirmative pronouncements. Masha suddenly asserts that, in spite of her stodgy husband and her lost love, "We must live." Irina has given up the hope of a great passion and decided to serve those who need her; she will find salvation in work. Olga will go on being a headmistress; she assures her sisters that their lives are not yet finished. Both Irina and Olga express the hope that some day they may know why they suffer. So Chekhov asked and left unanswered one of the basic questions of life.

The positive note which relieves the bleakness of *Uncle Vanya* and *The Three Sisters* is faith in work—Chekhov's personal faith which he communicates to some of his characters. In *Uncle Vanya*, Dr. Astrov is always preaching the gospel of work, and the disappointed Sonia concludes the play by avowing that they must work for the future. In *The Three Sisters* the lonely but gallant Vershinin is the apostle of work. If they work enough, he says, happiness will be the portion of their descendants. He is sure the time will come when everything will be changed for the better—will be as they want it to be.

The theme of work carries over to *The Cherry Orchard.* In this play the student Trofimov is Chekhov's spokesman. Trofimov is a rarity among Chekhov's characters: he is buoyant, enthusiastic, and filled with hope. "Humanity progresses," he says, "perfecting its powers. Everything that is beyond its ken now will one day become familiar and comprehensible; only we must work." Chekhov knew that improvement in Russia would come slowly and with difficulty. When he made Trofimov speak the following lines, Chekhov had at last accepted the role of social critic:

> Here among us in Russia the workers are few in number as yet. The . . . majority of the intellectual people . . . seek nothing, do nothing, are not fit . . . for work of any kind. They call themselves intellectual, but they treat their servants as inferiors, behave to the peasants as though they were animals, learn little, read nothing seriously, do practically nothing, only talk about science and know very little about art. . . . They all talk of weighty matters and air their theories, and yet the vast majority of us . . . live like savages, at the least thing fly to blows and abuse, eat piggishly, sleep in filth and stuffiness, bugs everywhere, stench and damp and moral impurity. . . . There is nothing but filth and vulgarity and Asiatic apathy.

The Cherry Orchard is the best loved of Chekhov's plays. Like the others it has little action, and yet it is pregnant with implication. The shades of gray are repeated, but there are also livelier tones. Perhaps this brightening was the product of the small degree of expectation which had developed during the reign of Nicholas II, who was less an absolutist than his predecessor. Perhaps it was owing to the mellowing of Chekhov's own spirit; he had not made friends with Death, but he had begun to feel accustomed to him. Perhaps it was inherent in the texture of the play, which Chekhov again spoke of as comedy. Sometimes he even called it a farce. Whatever the cause, the difference is unmistakable. In the other plays the characters are developed in relation to the immediate frame of their lives, whereas in *The Cherry Orchard* the characters step out of the immediate frame into a larger context.

Chekhov did not assume that he could say anything new about the passing of the old order and the emergence of the middle class, for that process had been going on for over half a century. Even if his material was not new, he at least treated it more memorably than had been done before. Yet there is something new here, the merchant Lopahin. He is not the crass, vulgar, unscrupulous bourgeois type which appeared in much of Russian literature during the period when the middle class was asserting itself.

He is an honest man, capable of appreciation and benevolence, loyal to what had been good in the past. He is genuine in his desire to save Madame Ranevskaya and her brother Gaev—the gentry—from their improvidence. Just as nearly fifty years earlier Stolz had been unable to save Oblomov, so Lopahin can do nothing to save these later Oblomovs. He tells them that only one word, yes or no, is necessary. "Forgive me," he insists, "but such reckless people as you are—such queer, unbusiness-like people—I never met in my life. One tells you . . . your estate is going to be sold, and you seem not to understand it." He cannot realize that any decisive action is beyond them. They implore him to tell them what to do, but when he repeats his proposal that they cut up their beautiful and famous cherry orchard into building lots, they reject it as impossibly "vulgar." Living dreamily in the past, they cannot cope with the present. They have suffered a paralysis of the will, and recovery is impossible. They are gracious, generous people, but the times demand more than they have to give.

While the gentry has become hopelessly enervated, those upon whose bent backs they formerly walked have become straight and strong. So Lopahin decides to buy the estate himself. Perhaps the most dramatic scene in all of Chekhov's plays is his announcement of what he has done. With typical inappropriateness Madame Ranevskaya gives a ball while she waits for news about what has happened to the estate. While the orchestra plays and dancing couples whirl by, Lopahin proclaims his ownership. He is sorry for his friends, but he is also wildly happy. This is the best moment of his life:

> I have bought it! . . . Now the cherry orchard's mine! Mine! . . . Tell me that I'm drunk, that I'm out of my mind, that it's all a dream. Don't laugh at me! If my father and grandfather could rise from their graves and see all that has happened! . . . I have bought the estate where my father and grandfather were slaves, where they weren't even admitted to the kitchen. I am asleep, I am dreaming! . . . Come, all of you, and look how Yermolay Lopahin will take the axe to the cherry orchard, how the trees will

> fall to the ground! We will build houses on it and our grandsons and great-grandsons will see a new life springing up there.

Madame Ranevskaya and Gaev adjust to the loss of their fortunes with the same compliant sweetness which has always made them lovable. Yet their displacement by Lopahin means for them the end of summer. Chekhov was, of course, aware that respectable houses for people to live in are more important than a cherry orchard so extensive that "it is mentioned in the 'Encyclopedia.' " Yet even in his comedy he could not avoid leaving the impression that something very special has passed. The spectacle of beauty being sacrificed to what Trofimov calls "progress" always brings a pang.

As the play ends, the ghost of Oblomov walks for the last time. Madame Ranevskaya, her daughter, and her brother bid farewell to the beloved home and step across the threshold of their uncertain future. With their customary inattention to practical matters they somehow leave behind their old servant Firs, who has devoted his whole life to their welfare. As they look back to say good-bye to the life they have cherished and wasted, Chekhov also was saying farewell, both to life and to the Russia he had known. After they have left the house:

> (*There is the sound of doors being locked up, then of carriages driving away. There is silence. In the stillness there is the dull stroke of an axe in a tree, clanging with a mournful, lonely sound. Footsteps are heard.* FIRS *appears in the doorway . . .*)
>
> FIRS (*goes up to the door, and tries the handles*): Locked! They have gone. . . . They have forgotten me. . . . Never mind. . . .
> Life has slipped by as though I hadn't lived. (*Lies down*) I'll lie down a bit. . . . There's no strength in you, nothing left you—all gone! Ech! I'm good for nothing. (*Lies motionless*).
>
> (*A sound is heard that seems to come from the sky, like a breaking harp-string, dying away mournfully. All is still again, and there is heard nothing but the strokes of the axe far away in the orchard.*)

With this play the curtain went down irrevocably on the nineteenth century, and the prologue of the twentieth century was spoken. Chekhov did not live to see the first outbreak of revolution, but he heard it when the axe was laid to the tree.

What did Chekhov really mean to say? Did he feel some kinship with Madame Ranevskaya and her brother, or did he have no regrets that their time was over? Did he loathe the smell of success which clung unmistakably to Lopahin, and would he have been glad to trade a dozen businessmen from the rising middle class for one cherry orchard—one haven of beauty kept free from the intrusion of "progress"? Chekhov made the student Trofimov a bungler (Madame Ranevskaya called him "funny"). Did he intend to make a fool of the only really optimistic character in the play? Chekhov gave no answer to these questions. One of the marks of his greatness is the fact that the transparent surface of his plays is misleading. Beneath the surface there is a blend of subtle implications—implications as subtle as life itself. There are no beginnings and no endings, and the answers are just beyond reach.

Whatever Chekhov thought of him, Trofimov is the only one who looks forward with assurance as he leaves the place where he had been happy and secure. Humanity is advancing, he has maintained. And now he is exultant: "Welcome to the new life!"

Welcome or not, the "new" had come to Russia.

XI/ INTERIM: ANDREYEV AND THE RED LAUGH

RUSSIAN LITERATURE of the nineteenth century reflects the progress of decadence. What Gogol and Goncharov anticipated and Dostoevsky feared, Chekhov realized. Relating at first to the gentry, this decadence gradually embraced the intelligentsia until many idealistic intellectuals became as lost and inert as Oblomov and far more despondent. Others resorted to dissipation and eroticism. The culmination of this process is recorded by Leonid Nikolayevitch Andreyev (1871–1919), who was at the height of his fame when the first attempt at revolution occurred in 1905. Even though not actively connected with this uprising or any of the subsequent political developments, as Gorky was, Andreyev was identified with the revolutionary period, which partially determined his mood and the substance of his thought. He continued to be a dominant figure in Russian literature during the sultry, disillusioned interim between the failure of the first attempt and the achievement of revolution in 1917. The collapse of the old regime and of Andreyev's fame and fortune occurred almost simultaneously.

I.

Leonid Andreyev was born at Orel, close to the birthplace of Turgenev. His family had some pretensions to culture, but little in the family background or way of life was conducive to either stability or positive attitudes in the excitable young man. He was obsessed with the idea of death, and had a more than Byronic passion for the morbid and extravagant. The family's comparative financial security was terminated by the father's death, which occurred while Leonid was still attending the gymnasium. Thereafter, in spite of being an indifferent student, engrossed by irrelevancies, and in spite of poverty almost reminiscent of Raskolnikov's, Andreyev completed his studies at the gymnasium and proceeded to the university, first at St. Petersburg and later at Moscow. Early in his university experience he attempted suicide. In fact, suicide attempts became commonplace for Andreyev. Poverty and disappointment in love may have had something to do with these melodramatic gestures, but he could not resist playing the part of a melancholy aesthete.

Because of the necessity to concentrate on something, Andreyev studied law, took his degree, and was admitted to the bar. He was, however, too restless, disorganized, and erratic to follow that or any other profession demanding routine. He tried to satisfy his craving for sensation by debauchery and such pranks as lying between the rails while a train passed over his body. When he had to start earning a livelihood, he was poorly prepared to do so. Having lost his first—and last—legal case, he began to work as a police court reporter on a leading Moscow paper. The subject matter appealed to him, and he wrote his reports with a flourish uncommon even in criminal journalism.

Like Chekhov, Andreyev had begun to write stories before the completion of his university studies, and also like Chekhov, he had the satisfaction of seeing his publications immediately successful. By 1898 he had begun to attract attention. His first collection of stories, published in 1901, became popular at once. When the early stories came to the attention of Gorky, the older author was much impressed and sought out Andreyev to give him encouragement. The two developed a friendship that lasted until it was disturbed by their conflicting political views. In his reminiscences Gorky offered the best clarification of Andreyev's personality and attitudes. He wrote of Andreyev's contempt for books and scholarship, of his distrust of people, his swift changes of mood, his insight, his egocentricity, his sensuality, his skill in conversation, and his deliberate cultivation of idiosyncrasy because he was convinced that geniuses are often insane.

Andreyev's popularity lasted for approximately ten years, during which time practically everything he wrote was the subject of controversy. His stories and plays usually took one extreme form or the other: the extreme of realism or of symbolism. Those in the former style aroused attention by their frank treatment, especially of sexual themes, which made them irresistible both to readers who considered themselves shockproof and to those looking for a shock. The symbolist pieces were equally tantalizing, because most readers could make nothing of them, whereas others read into them what they chose. Both types were the writings of a skeptic who believed in neither God nor man, who was morbidly attracted to the funereal and macabre, and for whom death was more real than life. Andreyev's characters are marked by the author's introspection and unbelief. They are what Dostoevsky's characters might have been if stripped of the cloak of faith and spiritual yearning.

As gray is the prevailing shade in the works of Chekhov, black is the dominant color in Andreyev's works. Surprisingly, the black prevailed increasingly as there was less occasion for it in his personal life. Poverty and the pedestrianism of police court reporting behind him, his books popular, his name on many tongues, his fortune made, his marital situation happy, and himself the center of an admiring circle of literary dilettantes—still he lived with and wrote of darkness. The influence of Poe and Nietzsche upon him is unmistakable, though whether he admired or feared the supermen who stalk through the pages of the latter is not always clear.

Before the beginning of World War I, Andreyev's creative energy and his popularity declined sharply. He was worn out—exhausted physically by dissipation and irregular habits and exhausted mentally and spiritually by too long immersion in a vacuum. The emergence of a school of writers who substituted vitality for his decadence was a decisive change. The literary vogue of death ended, paradoxically, before the real vogue of death began.

The war provided Andreyev with much needed distraction, but it came too late to resuscitate his failing talent. He became absorbed in patriotic activities, spending most of his efforts on pro-Russian, anti-German, and later, anti-Bolshevik propaganda. When the revolution broke out, he was plunged into a morass of genuine despair. He felt nothing but the bitterest loathing for the new regime. The last thing he wrote was a desperate appeal to the Allies to save Russia from the monster of Bolshevism. When he died in 1919, his fortune and fame had vanished, and the only thing he had ever really believed in aside from his own talent, the cause of czarist Russia, was lost. He did not live to see the final rout of the White Army and the triumph of the Bolshevik regime, but he did live long enough to prophesy accurately the disorder and bloodshed of the twentieth century.

II.

During his lifetime Andreyev's fame probably depended more on his plays than on his stories. More recently, however, the plays have been nearly forgotten—bloodless relics of a period almost lost in oblivion. They usually deal, even in the several attempts at realism, with destruction or negation. Their subject matter is repetitious, their effect impotent. They have none of the sense of life with which the dramas of Chekhov are charged to quivering intensity. Andreyev apparently had no talent for integrating scenes into a powerful dramatic structure or for creating memorable and individualized characters. The confused symbolism is an external manifestation of the inner darkness of the plays. Still, they have some authenticity as interpretations of the alienation of the intelligentsia, who had nothing to substitute for their lost faith. The catastrophe Dostoevsky feared had come to pass. Divorced from their belief in man and God, the intellectuals had become Nihilists, atheists, dilettantes, and lost souls. The only one of the plays widely known in America, *He Who Gets Slapped*, is actually one of the least interesting. But the title is a fitting clue to Andreyev's concept of man. "He" gets slapped by other people and by various dark forces "he" cannot name. "He" hides an anguished spirit behind the grease-painted mask-face of a clown. Andreyev's characters often belong to the fraternity of the dispossessed. They are the precursors of those who are waiting for Godot—or just waiting. Existential man peers forth from the eyes of most of them.

Andreyev's depiction of this paralysis of spirit and of some of the forces taking shape in his time may be suggested by reference to several of the better plays. For example, *King Hunger* (1907) has a legitimate place in the proletarian theater, having much in common with Hauptmann's *The Weavers* and other European reform dramas. It was one of the first plays which championed the workers and asserted that they would emancipate themselves from the tyranny of poverty, slavery, exploitation, and suffering. It indicated that even if hope for improvement had been dashed by the failure of early efforts at revolution, the waves of rebellion were gathering strength and becoming menacing. *The Black Maskers* (1908), the most complex of Andreyev's plays, is filled with symbolism which has been interpreted in a variety of ways. The play includes an argument in defense of the underprivileged, but primarily it allegorizes the plight of the Russian intelligentsia, who are presented as being able to resist the black evils which press in upon them only by giving up their lives.

Different in spirit from most of Andreyev's plays is *Anathema* (1909), which has some of the characteristics of a morality play. It is an indictment of the Nihilists and the intellectuals and radicals who have placed their faith in science and technology. Some commentators have been struck by the choice of a Jew for the Christlike central figure of the drama. This was Andreyev's attempt, they say, to defend not only the poor in general, but specifically the downtrodden Jewish minority. There is undeniable support for this assumption. Nicholas II was, if possible, more antagonistic to the Jews than Alexander III had been. During his reign the pogroms increased in frequency and brutality; the Jews suffered from innumerable forms of oppression. The treatment meted out to them was enough to arouse the conscience of Russia to indignation.

The detachment and spiritual decadence of the wealthy and

the intellectual and the reaching upward of the poor, who would not continue forever to endure their suffering—these are the recurring themes in the dramas of Andreyev which give their author claim to attention as a commentator during the first decade of the twentieth century in Russia.

III.

More memorable than any of the dramas and more clearly related to the outline of the future are two of Andreyev's narratives. Both added immensely to the author's prestige at the time of their publication. From the vantage point of more than half a century later they are interesting chiefly because of the accuracy of their prophecy. Although it would be an exaggeration to attribute to Andreyev the prophetic insight of Dostoevsky, the fact remains that these two narratives were heavy with portent. They offered a preview of two of the primary phenomena of the present century.

The Red Laugh (1904), inspired by Russia's conflict with Japan, is an allegorized treatment of war. Its first words, "horror and madness," supply the theme. A soldier, exhausted and driven past endurance by the hideous extravaganza through which he has been living, begins at last to understand what war is: "I recognized it—that red laugh. . . . Now I understood what there was in all those mutilated, torn, strange bodies. It was a red laugh. It was in the sky, it was in the sun, and soon it was going to overspread the whole earth—that red laugh!"[1] The soldier gradually recognizes that war is a form of insanity which spreads among all who participate in it: "And then I felt it for the first time. I clearly perceived that all these people, marching silently on in the glaring sun, torpid from fatigue and heat, swaying and falling—that they were all mad."

After a time the soldier is delivered from the horror; having lost both legs, he is sent home. At last he can see the light blue wallpaper of which he had often had a fleeting vision during the

[1] From the translation by Alexandra Linden.

frenzy of war. But even at home the horror does not leave him. He is mutilated, helpless. His family is overwhelmed by grief at his condition. When he tries to record his impressions, he finds that he can neither think nor remember. He is only the shell of a man. Then suddenly, as if there were some great illumination inside his head, he starts to write—to cover sheet after sheet with meaningless scrawls. He is happy, but he is completely mad. And he keeps on writing, almost without ceasing, never knowing that the marks on the paper are only marks, until he dies.

The soldier's death, however, does not cancel the dreadful account. His brother is also swept into the maelstrom of horror. The brother tries in vain to find some meaning or use in the wasteful carnage. Finally he understands that war is a form of madness which creatures who call themselves men create for their own destruction. But you are not men, he cries out; you do not deceive me: "I see claws under your gloves and the flat skull of an animal under your hat." And he adds that he can "hear insanity rattling its rusty chains" under the words of men which they consider clever conversation.

Finally the carnage becomes universal. The very earth itself spews up red corpses. They fill every available portion of space. Realizing that he will be smothered, the brother thinks he must try to escape. But the ghost of the dead soldier is realistic: " 'We cannot! We cannot! Look what is there!' . . . Behind the window, in a livid motionless light, stood the Red Laugh."

To the modern reader seasoned by the war novels of Hemingway and Koestler, by the stark etching of John Hershey's *Hiroshima*, and by the sobering realism of many war plays—to mention only a few of the reports of war in modern Western literature—*The Red Laugh* offers nothing new. It must be viewed against the background which produced it. At that time war was still regarded as romantic or heroic; the moonlight and magnolia tradition still hovered about the soldier. Readers were not then accustomed to coming into contact with war in such terms as the following:

"Are you afraid!" [the soldier asked a young volunteer who had come with a message from the general]. His lips twitched, trying to frame a word, and the same instant there happened something incomprehensible, monstrous and supernatural. I felt a draught of warm air upon my right cheek that made me sway—that is all—while before my eyes, in place of the white face, there was something short, blunt and red, and out of it the blood was gushing as out of an uncorked bottle. . . . And that short red and flowing "something" still seemed to be smiling a sort of smile, a toothless laugh—a red laugh.

Or in a passage like this, describing the madness of the doctor in the hospital in which the soldier's legs had to be amputated:

He was shouting now, that mad doctor, and seemed to have awakened by his cries the slumbering pain of all those around him with their ripped-open chests and sides, torn-out eyes and cut-off legs. The ward filled with a broad, rasping, crying groan, and from all sides pale, yellow, exhausted faces, some eyeless, some so monstrously mutilated that it seemed as if they had returned from hell, turned toward us. And they groaned and listened . . . while the mad doctor went on shouting. . . .

"Who said one must not kill, burn, or rob? We will kill and burn and rob. We . . . will destroy all; their buildings, universities and museums, and merry as children, full of fiery laughter, we will dance on the ruins. I will proclaim the madhouse our fatherland. . . .

"Friends!" continued the doctor, addressing himself to the groaning, mutilated shadows. "Friends! we shall have a red moon and a red sun, and the animals will have a merry red coat, and we will skin all those that are too white. . . . You have not tasted blood? It is slightly sticky and slightly warm, but it is red, and has such a merry red laugh!"

In such passages as these, Andreyev demonstrated that his lifelong preoccupation with death had given him good training. At the time it was written no one knew that *The Red Laugh*, a color symphony in red and black, had set the dominant motif of the century. It was ten years before the fatal shot was fired in

Sarajevo, but Andreyev could not have been more accurate in his prediction if that shot had already started to reverberate around the world.

Even more meaningful because it makes use of less familiar material, but material historically significant, is Andreyev's *The Seven That Were Hanged* (1908). This tale deals with the sentencing, imprisonment, and execution of seven people, two of them murderers and the others political terrorists. The story is written in a style and mood different from the majority of Andreyev's works. Without symbolism or confusing abstractions, it gives a straightforward account of events and characters. Although death is the principal theme, the narrative lacks the tortuous, cynical brooding characteristic of Andreyev's mind. When on rare occasions he wrote with simple realism, his style took on clarity and restraint in contrast to his more common introversive fulminations. In these instances there is some indication of the influence of Tolstoy, both in style and treatment. Another way in which this story is different from others by Andreyev is the sympathetic handling of subject matter. Death is not considered horrible, and the tone is not lugubrious. The important thing in Andreyev's thinking, for once, was not the fact of death, but the nobility with which most of the characters accepted it.

Apparently intended and received as a protest against capital punishment, *The Seven* implies that no individual or court has the right to decide that a prisoner deserves death. The story is presently interesting, however, for reasons entirely apart from any contribution it may have made to the controversy over capital punishment. Of significance now is the psychology of the five terrorists condemned to die because of an act performed in the line of duty. As anarchists committed to the effort to destroy the existing regime, they had to expose themselves to certain arrest and punishment. In them is little of the gloomy iconoclasm of Bazarov; they are not fallen angels driven by the spirit of negation. Nor have they any kinship with Nechaev. Violence for its own sake has no appeal for them; they are not by nature brutal and destructive. They are simple people, almost gentle, strong only because of their unwavering faith in the creed of revolution. They are idealists, made unselfish by their whole-hearted acceptance of their cause, of something bigger than themselves. When they took the "bombs, revolvers, and infernal machines" to the residence of the Minister, hoping to blow him up as he went to make a report, they knew they might fail. Even if they succeeded, they would almost certainly be caught, if not immediately, then after the next attempt. But they have no regrets. Only one of the five shows the slightest fear of death. It has been correctly said that they go to their death with the serenity and sense of mission of the Christian martyrs. During the trial, "In everything that happened they manifested that distrust and attenuated curiosity peculiar to people seriously ill or possessed by a single, all-powerful idea."

Two of the condemned terrorists are women. One of them, Tanya Kovalchuk, "sheltered her comrades with a maternal look":

> She seemed to be the mother of all the accused, so full of tender anxiety and infinite love were her looks, her smile, her fear. The progress of the trial did not interest her. She listened to her comrades simply to see if their voices trembled, if they were afraid, if they needed water. . . . She forgot that she was on trial too and would be hanged; her indifference to this was absolute.[2]

The other young woman, Musya, looks upon her coming death with joy. She believes there can be no higher blessing than to give her life for the cause. And despite her belief that a rare privilege has come to her, she remains humble.

> Now her sole desire was to explain, to prove, that she was not a heroine, that it was not a frightful thing to die, and that no one need pity her or worry on her account. . . .

[2] Modern Library of World's Best Books (Boni & Liveright, 1918). The translator is not named.

> And she is seized with unspeakable joy. There is no more doubt; she has been taken into the pale. She has a right to figure among the heroes who from all countries go to heaven through flames and executions. What serene peace, what infinite happiness!

During his imprisonment one of the men is transformed from being stern and cynical; his life begins to have new meaning. Formerly he had been contemptuous of people, but now the things which had once seemed disgusting and mean in human beings no longer bother him; he becomes aware of the admirable qualities in men. In death all of them, even the one who is afraid, achieve a nobility they probably would not have been capable of in life. Their devotion to their cause makes heroes of men and women who in other circumstances would have remained ordinary. Thus Andreyev paid tribute to the cause of freedom and to the people who made it their ideal, even if they had to destroy before they could create. It is ironical that just when such individuals as these had achieved their aims and the czarist regime toppled, Andreyev's sympathies were exactly reversed. He looked with loathing and fear upon Bolshevism and was certain that the oppression it would bring to Russia would far exceed anything that had existed under the Czars.

Andreyev's interpretation of character in *The Seven* was not unique. Terrorists occupied a place of high esteem in liberal and radical circles early in the century, and some were regarded as heroes. They were admired particularly by individuals who believed force was the only language which could combat the reaction that set in at the end of the nineteenth and the beginning of the twentieth centuries, but who were not willing or able to engage in dangerous enterprises themselves. *The Seven That Were Hanged* will prove illuminating to anyone who cannot understand the devotion of certain Communists to their cause and their willingness to disregard all personal considerations for the good of the party. It serves as a reminder that an individual's political beliefs may constitute his religion.

IV.

Like several of the earlier Romanovs, Nicholas II was a handsome man with considerable personal charm. But he had neither the education nor the character which makes a good ruler. As might have been expected, liberal influences had been absent from his training. When he took the throne in 1894, he announced that he would follow his father's policies, and he did exactly that. He was extremely weak-willed and also stubborn. When he made mistakes, he persevered in being wrong. Worst of all, he was almost completely dominated by his wife, a German princess disliked and distrusted in Russia. If at any point Nicholas had an impulse to follow a liberal course, he was dissuaded by her passionate determination to keep the design of autocracy intact.

Several years before his death Alexander III was instrumental in arranging an alliance between Russia and her old enemy, France. This compact was of some benefit in stabilizing Russia's financial balance, but it added to the tensions among the European powers. The building of the Trans-Siberian Railway, made possible by a loan from France, changed the whole picture of Russian relations in Asia and heightened the apprehensions of several European countries concerned with their own imperialistic policies. Nicholas was deficient in diplomatic acumen, but he recognized that Russia's position was far from secure. This misgiving caused him to call for a conference of the major European powers to consider techniques for the maintenance of peace. Since Alexander Herzen's concept of Russia—the "hostile, menacing empire"—has become fixed in modern Western ideology, it is difficult to recall that she ever took the initiative in urging peace. But such was the case. At her instigation the first peace conference met at The Hague in 1899. Perhaps the fact that it was prompted by selfish motives was responsible for its failure to accomplish anything constructive. The second conference eight years later produced no more lasting results.

Between these two peace conferences Russia was again involved in a war. The conflict with Japan (1904–1905) weakened Russia's international prestige, brought further havoc to her financial condition, and increased the unrest within the country. The war was in no sense inevitable. Overambitious imperial goals, combined with shortsightedness and irresponsibility, caused Russia to be drawn into the venture. Some of Nicholas' advisers convinced him that war would unite the people and reduce their dissatisfaction with the regime. From the beginning, however, the war offered no hope for the realization of the Czar's ambitions. Japanese forces proved superior on both land and sea. Instead of arousing patriotism among the Russian people, news of the reverses increased the already widespread antagonism toward the sovereign, his policies, his ministers, and everything the regime stood for. The people were beginning to feel their power. Before the inglorious adventure was completed, the government was more concerned with its attempt to control the internal situation than with the losses abroad. When the Russian soldiers returned from war, they had to quell an uprising at home which had begun to take on startling proportions.

During the latter part of the nineteenth century two of the most important developments in Russia were the emergence of political parties and the emergence of the workers as a force to be reckoned with. The first major party to achieve identity was the Social Democratic Workers' party, known by that name from 1898 onward. It had actually existed for some time as scattered groups, prevented from coming into the open by the surveillance and oppression of the regimes of Alexander III and Nicholas II. The leaders of this party were staunch Marxists. The fact that in order to stay alive they had to direct party policies from abroad and that party work had to be kept underground did not diminish the zeal or the energy of these leaders—or of their followers. The party organ was a newspaper called *Iskra* (*The Spark*) edited by a man named Vladimir Ilyitch Ulyanov, soon to be known as Lenin. A later member of the editorial staff was Leon Trotsky.

The aim of the Social Democrats was the emancipation of the working man. Most of the leaders as well as the members of the party were from the proletariat.

The second congress of this organization in 1903 culminated in a party split, the results of which had dire consequences for the future of Russia and all the world. The group separated into two factions, the Mensheviks and Bolsheviks. The Mensheviks believed in education rather than violence. They contended that the people must be slowly and methodically prepared for citizenship in order to fulfill the challenge of democracy. The Bolsheviks, on the other hand, advocated the forcible overthrow of the existing order. Both desired the elimination of the monarchy and the political and social system associated with it. The Mensheviks had a long-range view in mind, whereas the Bolsheviks might have said with Bazarov that they liked "to deny" and to destroy. The Bolshevist aim had been anticipated several decades earlier by Pyotr Verkhovensky: "We are going to make a revolution. . . . We are going to make such an upheaval that everything will be uprooted from its foundation." When the split occurred, the Bolsheviks had only a slight majority. Under the leadership of Lenin, however, their power increased rapidly. They soon learned that the way to handle opposition was to liquidate it. At the 1912 Congress the Mensheviks (and their inclinations toward moderation) were summarily ejected from the party. Thereafter the Bolshevik program became the platform of the Social Democratic party. From this embryo developed the pattern of politics in the Soviet state.

The Social Revolutionary party was similar in purpose and procedures. This organization, however, worked for the welfare of the peasants in contrast to the Social Democrats' absorption in the interests of urban workers. Another difference was that the philosophy of the Social Revolutionary party was not derived exclusively from Marxist doctrines. Terrorist acts were perpetrated by members of both parties, but more frequently by members of the latter group. In all probability the five anarchists among "the seven that were hanged" were Social Revolutionaries. Lenin's Marxist organization was, of course, quite as much committed to the principle of social revolution as the party called by that name. The Social Democrats resorted to violence less often, only because they believed in giving evidence of the importance and power of the workers through strikes. The strike was the technique upon which their program was based.

A third party, the Constitutional Democratic party (or Kadets), came into being only slightly later than the other two. It was much more conservative than the others but shared with them the aim of substituting a government by and for the people in place of the existing autocracy. Its members included outstanding representatives of the intelligentsia. In spite of the ideational restraints which limited its appeal among large sections of the population, this party exerted considerable influence. If the Constitutional Democrats could have gained control, the history of Russia, and perhaps of the world, would have been different. This was the party most attractive to the moderate liberals.

The government expended prodigious effort upon tracking down and eliminating party leaders and revolutionaries. In large numbers they were put to death or sent to Siberia. No matter how extensive and severe the government controls, however, they were unable to check more than superficially a movement now gathering irresistible momentum. Even while still largely underground, this movement had begun to determine the future of Russia.

The year 1905 was a memorable one in Russian history. In the first month an event occurred which cast its shadow over the entire year. A clergyman named Father Gapon had developed great influence among the workingmen. He was apparently sincere in trying to persuade them that they would obtain a better hearing from the authorities and be more likely to find their lot improved if they used peaceful measures than if they resorted to violence. He was convinced that the Czar was genuinely concerned for the people but knew little of their predicament. On a

Sunday in January, Father Gapon led thousands of workingmen and their families to the Winter Palace for the purpose of making an appeal directly to the Czar. Most of the marchers had been attending services in various churches. The large crowd moved through the snowy streets in good order, many individuals talking with confidence of the monarch's interest in "the people." But the confidence was misplaced. Instead of recognizing the moment for what it was—an opportunity to endear the monarchy to the people, strengthen monarchical authority, and cement public feeling into unity—the Czar and his advisers made a fatal mistake. They answered the reasonable, peaceful multitude with bullets. Soldiers were directed to fire upon the crowd without even giving their spokesmen a chance to be heard. Those bullets sounded the death knell for the house of Romanov. After this inexcusable mistake, as stupid as it was cruel, the government had no chance to survive. No exact figures are available to indicate the number killed and wounded on that "Bloody Sunday." The fear and sense of outrage of the thousands of survivors and their determination to have revenge were like flood waters that could not be contained.

Throughout the remainder of the year the internal situation in Russia was marked by one crisis after another. Disorders of all kinds took place. Workers began openly to defy authority. At one time nearly two million workmen were out on strike. Finally even the railroads were forced to cease operating because of widespread strikes. In rural areas highly destructive peasant uprisings added to the general disorganization. When the government made the spiritless gesture of calling a congress, or Duma, which had only deliberative, not legislative, power, the disorders increased. In this period of confusion the Soviet (Council) of Workers' Deputies emerged. This organization was composed of members from various socialist parties. One of the most influential leaders was Leon Trotsky, a Menshevik. The Bolsheviks, at this time still a minority, disagreed with the Soviet program of reasonableness, but the conflict was not sharp enough to nullify the aims of the council. Swift emergency measures by the government were all that prevented this organization from launching into positive action.

Recognizing that a decisive step must be taken to keep the various uprisings from becoming full-scale revolution, the government issued a manifesto in October, 1905, which was unexpectedly generous in its promise of reforms. It did not go far enough to satisfy the socialists but met practically all the demands of the liberals. The latter, however, hesitated too long in taking advantage of the opportunities offered them to have a share in the formulation of new government policies. Perhaps the shadow of Rudinism still clung about them. Like the earlier Hamlets of Russia, they were still unable to harness ideas to deeds. The capacity for action resided in men of different temperament and, for the most part, different background. The liberals never again had a good chance to play a prominent part in shaping public affairs. Meanwhile, the Bolsheviks under the leadership of Lenin were growing in strength, assurance, and aggressiveness.

Although the October Manifesto postponed the collapse of the monarchy, the year closed with overt rebellion. During a revolt which broke out in December, many more were killed and wounded than in the Bloody Sunday outbreak eleven months before. Even though the soldiers returning from the war with Japan were able to put down the insurrection, this time it was clear that "the people" were not to be held in check much longer. The Revolution of 1905, though short lived, indicated the course of future events in Russia.

In the following twelve years the government endeavored to preserve itself by granting a measure of constitutionalism as promised by the October Manifesto. This measure permitted the intermittent assembling of a legislative body (or such it was supposed to be) to admit the people to participation in government affairs. Presumably the Duma was to be the instrument of democratic representation and expression. Four Dumas were called during these years. Their history, however, is a record of the gradual loss of the small power they endeavored to assume as the monarchy cut backward from the program provided by the manifesto. Although certain positive reforms were achieved by the Duma and by the few enlightened leaders in the political machine of Nicholas II, the over-all condition of Russia became worse instead of better. Internal agitation continued. The economy of the country was completely unstable. The socialist parties, especially the Bolsheviks, could no longer be kept underground. Externally the situation was equally serious. Germany and Austria were harshly antagonistic. The Czar had gambled heavily on adding to Russia's prestige through diplomatic maneuvers in the Balkans, but without success. When Europe stood "on the eve" of World War I, the Red Laugh was ready to break into a raucous crescendo across all of Russia.

XII/ Gorky: The End of the Beginning

When Chekhov died in 1904, the first overt attempt at revolution was still several months away. When Andreyev died in 1919, the Revolution had succeeded, and the people long chained by the absolutism of a tyrannical, corrupt monarchy were rising to a new day. What that day would bring only Maxim Gorky (1868–1936), of all the authors of the "golden age," lived to see. Gorky's influence was largely confined to the writers of his own generation, but some of his subject matter anticipates the Soviet writing of the following generation. In no sense a genius, Gorky lacked the artistry which distinguished the finest authors in Russian literature, from Pushkin to Chekhov. Still, he had narrative power, and in the best of his work, such as his early story "Chelkash" and the later autobiographical volume *My Childhood,* he created unforgettable characters, drawing them with economy and insight. A good many of his publications, however, were deliberately intended for propaganda. Almost all of his work rises above the sterility of Soviet writing, but that does not prevent it from being at times closer to sociological or political pamphleteering than to art.

From Gogol to Tolstoy, Russian literature chronicles the decline of the gentry, the mute misery of the serfs, and their inchoate struggles to effect more than legal emancipation. In the background, of less interest to most of the authors of the period, loomed the shadow of the emerging *bourgeoisie,* becoming ever larger. Not until the twentieth century did Russian writers devote much attention to the proletariat. To do this was the function of Gorky. At one bound the industrial workers came into their own, with Gorky as interpreter and defender. What Turgenev and Tolstoy did for the peasants, Gorky did for the proletariat. Nearly half a century earlier, Mrs. Gaskell, Charles Kingsley, Charles Dickens, and other reform writers had performed the same task in English literature. It must be remembered, however, that large-scale industrialization developed more slowly in Russia than in England and other sections of western Europe. Therefore, the individuals and problems connected with industrialization did not find their way into Russian literature until the expansion of the factory system had produced what might be called a serf class in the cities, a class victimized by capitalistic exploitation as the serfs had been victimized by the landowning gentry. In *Virgin Soil,* Turgenev showed the intelligentsia attempting in the late sixties and seventies to enlighten the peasants and to spread among them a form of socialism to help them toward the solution of their economic and social problems. In spite of the well-intentioned but sentimental efforts of the intelligentsia, this movement met with small response from the peasantry, which was not yet ready for it. Meanwhile the urban workers, who possessed a vigor and a capacity for organization unknown to the peasants, began to show evidence of a determination to improve their lot. For several reasons the seeds of revolution produced quick growth in the milieu of the urban proletariat. For one thing, their predicament was, in a sense, more acute than that of the peasants because of the hardships of city life. Moreover, many of the most alert among the peasants had chosen to give up the wretchedness of country life in an attempt to find something better in the city. When they failed to do so, often their disillusionment ripened into rebellion. Also, leadership of the urban workers' movements came from within their own ranks, and these leaders found sure response in their comrades and co-workers. Thus the need and the means for reform and revolution were at last synthesized. By the time Gorky began to serve as mouthpiece for the proletariat, the revolutionary movements had begun to have tangible form.

I.

Maxim Gorky (Alexey Maximovitch Pieshkov) was not only the first major Russian writer who interpreted the proletariat, he was also the first who belonged to that class. A slowly developing transition was consummated with Gorky: literature had ceased to be the prerogative of the cultivated intellectuals. When he became one of the most popular of Russian authors, he represented a new phenomenon, the emergence of a people's literature. Born in 1868 at Nizhny Novgorod (now called Gorky), the author was the son of an artisan who died of cholera when Gorky was four years old. Thereafter the boy lived in the home of his grandparents. In that setting life in its rawest form was unrolled before him. His grandfather Kashirin was the owner of a dye works. After having managed to establish a degree of financial security, he met with reverses which led to bankruptcy. More distressing than poverty, however, were the conditions prevailing within the Kashirin family life. Except for one mitigating influence, the features of that life were violent passions, wife beating, drunkenness, greed, tyranny, and servility. The brief period the lad spent with his mother and stepfather offered nothing better. He had to watch while her second husband reduced his once imperious mother to a state of abjectness and exhaustion. After her death, when Gorky was ten years old, he was ordered by his grandfather to get out and make his own way. His one or two short intervals of schooling had been terminated by an attack of smallpox, from which he barely recovered. When his childhood came to a premature end, he had scant preparation for facing the world.

The one compensation in Gorky's childhood was his grandmother, a woman of simple dignity, great faith, imagination, and warm humanity; a lover of nature and of people. In spite of the passions and meanness of her husband and sons, she somehow managed to retain her sprightliness, her sense of humor, and her optimism. Gorky owed to her whatever he knew in childhood of security and understanding. She had a gift for storytelling. From her the boy learned to appreciate the flavor of an episode well told and characters sharply depicted. She also taught him to perceive the beauty of the Russian landscape and to know intimately the creatures of forest and meadow. In *My Childhood*, Gorky evokes with stunning clarity the personalities of his grandmother and other members of his family, some tempestuous, some browbeaten. A book rare among records of childhood, it represents the writer at his best.

The experiences of Gorky after he was forced to make his way in the world cause the life of David Copperfield to appear tranquil by comparison. First he served as flunky in a shoe store, an intolerable situation from which he was released when he had to be hospitalized for the treatment of serious burns. His next job, as apprentice to a draftsman, was no better. Instead of being given some opportunity to learn the trade, he was kept at the most menial drudgery. He escaped from this impasse to become a dishwasher on a Volga steamer. Here, although his eighteen-hour day in the scullery was no relief from his former slavery, one opportunity provided a turning point in his life. The ship's cook supplied him with books that literally opened a new world before him. From this time on he read everything he could find. Perhaps the most exhilarating of his discoveries was the fact that many notable people had begun life as workers. After an interval of apprenticeship to an icon painter and then a brief experience in the theater—not as the actor he had hoped to be, but as an extra and handy man—he resolved to get an education. A chance acquaintance told him about the university at Kazan. He made his way there, assuming that education would be free. The reality he discovered offered a startling contrast to his dream. It also pointed the way to his future.

When Gorky wrote *My Universities*, he did not refer to the educational institution at Kazan, from which he was excluded by poverty, but to the education he received from the beggars, petty thieves, outcasts, and workers with whom he associated on the wharves. His real training began when they introduced him to several revolutionaries and when he started to read the works of Adam Smith and Karl Marx. After spending some time as a laborer on the wharf, Gorky became a baker's helper in a pretzel establishment. There the conditions were so inhumane that his life was little better than it would have been in jail. This situation furnished the basis for one of Gorky's most memorable stories, "Twenty-Six Men and a Girl," in which the girl always greeted the men appropriately as "poor prisoners." Later Gorky worked in a bakery, the profits of which were contributed to revolutionary activities.

In this period Gorky was reading during every available minute. Such minutes usually occurred only at night when he went without sleep for the sake of his self-education. He also began to write furtive pieces, poems, and jottings in a notebook. His life was hard. He dreamed of a better life without seeing any way to achieve it. When he was nineteen, he tried to commit suicide. Fortunately, his body was found in the snow in time for him to be saved by a hospital surgeon. Thereafter he went to a village in the country to assist in disseminating propaganda among the peasants, a short-lived effort terminated by the violence of the villagers, who killed the leader of the movement.

After all these experiences Gorky began to wander, to see his country on foot. He was a fisherman on the Caspian Sea and a night watchman at two or three lonely railway stations almost lost in the steppes; he tramped through the Don country; made his way to Moscow, where he attempted in vain to see Tolstoy; worked in a brewery; and offered himself for military service, but was rejected as unfit because of the condition of his lungs. He continued to write, but after showing a poem to the author Korolenko, whose criticism discouraged him, he resolved to write no more. Meanwhile he maintained his contacts with revolutionaries and intellectuals and began to attract the attention of the police. For nearly two years he tramped across the southern part of Russia, observing life, studying people, storing up impressions, and becoming firm in his belief that the world of wanderers, outcasts, criminals, and workers—the "have-nots"—could and must be better. His natural optimism and verve were supplemented by an increasing faith in "the people"—poor people like himself who did the work of the world and got few of the rewards. In Tiflis he became acquainted with a man who had given himself to revolutionary activities. This man saw potentials of great usefulness in Gorky and encouraged him to write. Inspired by the friendship of someone who believed in him, Gorky began again to express himself, this time drawing on the experiences of his own life. In 1892 a Tiflis newspaper editor published his first story, "Makar Chudra," and gave him the pen name under which he soon became famous—Maxim Gorky—Maxim "the Bitter." Gorky was then twenty-four years old, the same age as Dostoevsky when *Poor Folk* was published.

Back in Nizhny Novgorod, Gorky worked by day as a lawyer's clerk; at night he continued his omnivorous reading. Now he began to write in earnest. To his astonishment he found no difculty in having his stories published. A future which had appeared forbidding and unalterable began to reach out its arms toward him. He revived his acquaintance with Korolenko, who now gave him invaluable encouragement and criticism. Gradually he freed himself from the conventions of romantic writing. Limiting himself to the realities he knew, he became the voice of the tramps, the outcasts, and the workers—the "creatures that once were men." In 1895 his story "Chelkash" brought him fame. He continued for a while to contribute to the many newspapers and periodicals which avidly accepted anything from his pen, but soon he left journalism to spend all his time on the narratives that had begun to make him famous. In 1898 his stories were published in two volumes, and immediately Gorky became a major constellation among Russian writers.

Gorky's rise to fame was unprecedented in Russian literature. His experience was a fairy tale come true. From slavey in a shoeshop, dishwasher on a Volga boat, odd-job man on the Kazan docks, sweatshop worker in a pretzel factory, watchman at lonely stations, wanderer, and friend of outcasts, criminals, and revolutionaries, to the most talked of and most widely read writer in Russia—that was the span of his early experience. Soon none but the old and ailing Tolstoy could compete with him in reputation.

In 1901 his works, published in five volumes, were read all over Russia, and international fame followed swiftly. Perhaps the peak of his career occurred with the production a year later of his most famous play, *The Lower Depths*, which whipped public interest to high excitement, in Russia and throughout Europe. In Berlin the play had a record-making run of five hundred nights. The same year Gorky was elected to honorary membership in the Imperial Academy of Science—an extraordinary distinction for so young a man. As might have been expected, the government promptly vetoed the election on the ground of Gorky's sympathy with revolutionary activities. Even this official slap did not detract from his popularity, however. Chekhov and Korolenko withdrew from the Academy in protest, and there was general indignation at the stupid shortsightedness of the authorities. Gorky stood for a new force in Russian culture. "The people" had made a contribution to what had formerly been the exclusive property of the privileged. It was time to begin to recognize that contribution.

It is significant that fame did not alter Gorky's profound concern for the oppressed. He became a Marxist, a Social Democrat, and a regular contributor to a Marxist paper, but he never permitted party theories to divert him from humanitarian impulses. In 1901 his poem "The Song of the Stormy Petrel," which promised, "Soon the storm will break!" became a rallying cry for the revolutionary movement. When Gorky was arrested and imprisoned on a charge of sedition, public protest forced the government to release him. His influence upon the workers proved so strong that the government was disconcerted by his power. Since they could not imprison him, the authorities banished him to a remote spot, but even there he continued active participation in the writing, printing, and spread of inflammatory material.

At the outbreak of the revolution of 1905 the author played an important role. On the evening of Bloody Sunday he joined Father Gapon, who had led the workers to the palace of the Czar only to have them stopped by bullets, in a protest against the horrifying slaughter.[1] As a result, he was again imprisoned, this time in the infamous fortress of Peter and Paul. Again the government was compelled to release him, for his imprisonment became a *cause célèbre* throughout all of Europe and in America. Not even the unyielding machinery of czardom could hold out against the indignation aroused by his detention. Near the end of the year 1905, Gorky was back in Moscow, doing everything he could to encourage the uprising which marked the end of the initial revolutionary effort. The uprising was suppressed, but the forces which provoked it were only temporarily checked. The determination of the revolutionaries, Gorky among them, was not diminished. At this time Gorky first met Lenin. In spite of ideological differences which sometimes separated them, the two men remained friends until Lenin's death.

In 1906, having been warned that remaining in Russia would certainly lead again to arrest, Gorky decided to go abroad in an attempt to raise money for the cause of freedom in his unhappy country. He traveled by way of Finland and the Scandinavian countries to New York, where he received a tremendous welcome that soon changed to an undisguised snub. For some years the author had been separated from his wife, with whom he continued on amicable terms. Now he was living with a young actress who had accompanied him to New York as his interpreter. Gorky considered her his wife, but when the facts became known, the American public, inflamed by hysterical journalism, saw her in a different light. An outburst of the most violent prudery resulted in the ejection of Gorky and his mistress from their hotel (indeed, from more than one) and in Mark Twain's refusal to be toastmaster at a banquet in the writer's honor. The whole American tour turned into a fiasco. Baffled by public reaction to what seemed to him a personal matter in no sense reprehensible, Gorky

[1] Gorky told the details of the march and slaughter on Bloody Sunday in his story "The Ninth of January." The narrative account adds nothing, however, to the drama and terror of the actual events.

recorded his resentment in a series of sketches called *The City of the Yellow Devil.* It is not difficult to imagine the state of mind in which he wrote to Andreyev, "I could write ten volumes about America of five hundred pages each, and not one good word!"

Fortunately, private individuals offered Gorky and his mistress asylum from the public wrath. During several quiet months in the Adirondacks, Gorky wrote most of his novel *Mother.* Although undistinguished by literary standards, this book is of all his works the most helpful as an interpretation of the significant currents of the times. It acted also as a stimulus to the oppressed. American readers can scarcely fail to be interested in visualizing the composition of this book, which became the testament of the anarchic proletariat, in the tranquil setting of rural New York State. *Mother* is a handbook for revolutionaries. It gives a clear, if simplified, explanation of the procedure as well as the ideology of the peoples' resistance movement in Russia during the first decade of the present century. A comparison of the rarefied histrionics of Rudin and his impotent defiance as he died on the barricades, with the systematic, purposeful dedication of Pavel Vlasov, the hero of *Mother*, provides a commentary on the change in characteristics of the leaders who shaped the revolutionary policies.

The remainder of Gorky's life was devoted to writing and to a variety of activities, always motivated, though sometimes indirectly, by his sympathy with the forces working for political and social change. Much of the time he lived abroad, partially for political reasons, probably more often because of his health. The rigors of his early life had left him tubercular, and since Gorky never spared himself or took account of the limitations imposed by his illness, he came time after time to physical crises during which physicians gave him slight hope for survival. He became accustomed to brushing close to death, but the resilience of his constitution and spirit enabled him to keep on living and working with rich abandon.

Upon his return to Europe from the American trip, Gorky attended the fifth congress of the Russian Social Democratic party in London. At that time his friendship with Lenin was strengthened. Thereafter he settled at Capri, where he remained for six years. In 1913 he returned to Russia, taking advantage of the amnesty granted political exiles in one of the government's rare efforts to woo public favor. During the Capri interval he maintained, largely at his own expense, a school for the training of revolutionary leaders. There is evidence that Stalin was among the pupils who took the course of training. Although Lenin disagreed with Gorky in regard to some of the techniques and the ideology of the school, he visited the writer at Capri and was eager to have Gorky return to Russia. Lenin was always solicitous about the health of the author and the continuance of his activities.

Back in Russia, Gorky established a periodical (*Letopis*) which did little to augment his now diminishing prestige. In 1913 and two years later he published the first two parts of a rambling autobiography (*My Childhood* and *In the World*), completing it some years later with *My Universities*. Each of these volumes, especially the first, contains some of Gorky's best writing. During World War I, Gorky was international in his viewpoint but continued his attacks upon the czarist regime. When the revolution of 1917 matured, he gave his support to the Bolsheviks, though he did not become an active member of the party. Indeed, he had many reservations about the policies pursued, especially in the period of upheaval and chaos following the breakdown of the monarchical institutions, when the Bolsheviks practiced more violence than Gorky considered necessary or justifiable. Many of the leaders resented his detachment from the party and his objective attitude, but they recognized in him a force for the control of public opinion which they could not afford to suppress.

During the three or four years following the collapse of the old regime, Gorky rendered what was probably the most valuable of all his services to his country. Acting independently, without the aegis of party or office, he became a bulwark of reasonableness and humanity in troubled times. He waged a one-man war to preserve the best of Russian culture and civilization from the onslaughts of the iconoclastic new regime. Through his efforts authors and artists who would otherwise have been lost were enabled to survive. He understood what the Bolsheviks could not or would not understand—that the past offered priceless treasures by which the future could be enriched. D. S. Mirsky in *Contemporary Russian Literature* goes so far as to say: "The debt of Russian culture to him is very great. Everything that was done between 1918 and 1921 to save the writers and other higher intellectuals from starvation was due to Gorky. This was chiefly arrived at by a whole system of centralized literary establishments where poets and novelists were set at work at translations."[2] In the light of later developments Gorky's attempts now appear to have been rather futile, but the fact that almost insurmountable barriers were put in his way does not detract from the worth of his aims or the honor to which his efforts entitle him.

The last fifteen years of Gorky's life were not filled with the drama of the earlier years. In 1921 he again went to western Europe to benefit his health and because of disagreement with Bolshevist policies and leaders. He lived in Germany and Italy until 1928, when he returned to Russia for the celebration of his sixtieth birthday. This event occasioned widespread attention and showed that he still occupied a place of high regard, both in literature and in the affection of the common people, to whom he had given dignity and to whose need of humane treatment and improved living standards he had given expression. A year later he returned to his native land for good. During all these years he continued to write, but none of his later works had the spontaneity or the impact of the early narratives. He did not again duplicate the sweeping success of *The Lower Depths* or write anything else so influential as the novel *Mother*. Still, he

[2] Page 111.

occupied a position of eminence in literature which none of the new Soviet writers could challenge.

During the 1930's until his death in June, 1936, he continued to uphold literary standards, to encourage young writers, and to do whatever he could to preserve and vitalize the culture of the old and new regimes. The details of his activities during these years are almost entirely obscure. He seems to have given at least tentative approval to the Stalinist government, but he may have done so hoping that he could in slight measure mitigate some of its errors and excesses. Varied and contradictory reports about his death lead to the conclusion that it was somehow caused by political intrigue. It cannot be fully determined whether he was liquidated by a Trotskyite plot (as the Soviets once claimed), or in a Stalinist purge,[3] or died from a breakdown in spirit and health brought about by the circumstances under which he had to live in Soviet Russia. In any event, Gorky's idealism was not a quality the Soviets would have cared to preserve. No man worked harder than Gorky for a "people's" government. He did not foresee what that government would do to him or to the country he loved.

In addition to the early works already mentioned, Gorky's reminiscences of other writers, particularly his *Recollections of Tolstoy*, and the lengthy novel written in his later years, a trilogy having the general title *Klim Samghin*, are representative of his best achievement. He occupies a unique place in Russian literature. Although not a writer of first rank, he exerted as much influence as if he had been. Belonging to two different periods in the history of his country, he was able to blend and harmonize the two as no other major literary figure could. As the first outstanding Russian author produced by "the people," he proved that they could make a contribution to the culture of their country, and at the same time he was capable of appreciating the culture of the effete minority against whom the proletariat re-

[3] It is reasonably well established that a doctor confessed to having poisoned Gorky by order of certain political officials.

belled. He is the most forceful and clearest spokesman for that proletariat. Literally, he gave words to the inarticulate masses. His books furnish an introduction to the group who accomplished what the intelligentsia and the liberals from the gentry and the middle class had failed to do, that is, a revolution.

II.

In his *Days with Lenin*, Gorky gave an appealing account of the man who played one of the leading parts in the emergence of the new Russia. With customary generosity he passed over the defects and emphasized the attractive features of Lenin's personality. The following is one of his many interesting comments:

> Lenin was exceptionally great, in my opinion, precisely because of this feeling in him of irreconcilable, unquenchable hostility towards the sufferings of humanity, his burning faith that suffering is not an essential and unavoidable part of life, but an abomination which people ought and are able to sweep away.

Whether or not this "feeling" was characteristic of Lenin may be debatable, but it was true of Gorky. His compassion, his faith in the inherent goodness of mankind, and his belief in the possibility of a better future are expressed in all his writings, most notably in the narratives and dramas dealing with the underprivileged. The "creatures that once were men" may be battered by repeated blows, and they may be weak of will and mind and faulty of character, but all deserve better than they have, and all are infused with an essential goodness that makes them beings different from the gloomy, frustrated figures in the world of Chekhov. Paradoxically, he felt most concern for the outcasts, sometimes even for petty criminals. In them he found integrity, basic kindness, and freedom from pretense or hypocrisy. He felt only contempt, on the other hand (in such novels as *Foma Gordyeff*), for the smug *bourgeoisie* who were grasping and mercenary and in whom the impulse for sympathy or charity was blotted out by the drive for possession and social superiority.

It has often been pointed out that Gorky was most at home and most effective when dealing with underworld characters. These scarred remnants of humanity at times suggest some of Dickens' characters, but there is a difference. Dickens treated his characters with indulgence, but he stood aloof and often made them grotesques or caricatures. Gorky, in contrast, saw his "people from the depths" with compassionate eyes. He made them bigger than they could possibly have been. What matter that the teacher in *Creatures That Once Were Men*[4] was a drunken weakling. When he died, a valuable human spirit was lost, and he became for a moment as important as any Hamlet of princely blood. Gorky stood with head uncovered before the miracle of humanity.

"It's the same human beings everywhere. At first you don't see it. Then, you get a good look at them, and it turns out they're all human beings—they're all right." This statement by one of the characters is the theme of the play *The Lower Depths*, the most famous of Gorky's writings. Its characters are a group of people from the dregs of society. Some have fallen from higher positions as a result of a combination of ill luck and weakness of character. Others have always been and always will be as they appear in the drama. Some try to work and feel contempt for those who refuse to do the same. Others live by their wits, convinced that work is unnecessary. Some are honest, others opportunistic. Gathered together by circumstance in a basement lodging where each has only a corner or a few feet of space, they live out their days in squalor. They are quarrelsome, hungry, insecure, and sure of nothing except death. For them the amenities of life do not exist. Nothing happens except the reiteration of misery, or if something does happen, it makes no difference. Life is cheap. Human beings are small creatures. This play is the *Dead End* of the Russian slums.

One thing does make a difference, however, and that is the point of the play. One character stands out from the gray mass of

[4] One of Gorky's most famous stories.

victims and weaklings. The pilgrim Luka, a warm-hearted old man, pauses briefly in his wanderings to live amid the tattered fragments of humanity who dwell in the particular "lower depths" of this play. Luka's past is uncertain, but his spirit is whole, and his wholeness brings healing to the others. He is a doer, not a preacher. The kindly act and cheerful word are as natural to him as brawling, suspicion, and meanness are to the others. Moreover, he believes in them and in their goodness. Knowing such a man is a new experience for them. They do not understand him, but they feel the difference as soon as he comes among them. When they ask whether God exists, he gives them exactly the answer they need: "If you believe in him, he exists. If you don't, he doesn't. Whatever you believe in exists." After he has gone on his way, the others try to explain the source of his faith and of the inspiration he has left behind. The cardsharp Satin summarizes it in the words Luka spoke to him:

> "Everybody, my friend, everybody lives for something better to come. That's why we have to be considerate of every man—Who knows what's in him, why he was born and what he can do? Maybe he was born for our good fortune—for our greater benefit."[5]

Satin is deeply impressed by Luka's belief in humanity. Inspired by the contagion of the old man's spirit, he says:

> "It's tremendous! . . . Everything in man, everything for man. Only man exists, the rest is the work of his hands and his brain. Man! It's magnificent! It has a proud ring! Man! We have to respect him, not pity him, not demean him—Respect him, that's what we have to do. . . . It's good to feel oneself a man!"

Satin's words afford a good statement of the religion of Gorky. Further, it is no exaggeration to suggest that they represent the view of a number of the radical idealists and some of the early revolutionaries of nineteenth-century Russia. This transcendent belief—which enables the terrorists in *The Seven That Were*

[5] *The Lower Depths* and *Enemies* were translated by Alexander Bakshy.

Hanged to go serenely to their deaths, confident that they are dying for something meaningful and important—is what Gorky saw even in the "depths" among men and women made strong by belief in a better future. No matter how melancholy the present, it can be endured while they create tomorrow for their children. Working and hoping for "something" gives them courage. In the light of that hope they become the protagonists of the revolution.

It is small wonder that the Russian proletariat looked upon Gorky as their deliverer from anonymity and hopelessness or that he became their hero. *The Lower Depths* is the climax of what Gogol started in "The Cloak." The poor clerk in Gogol's story has a job and a small pittance he can count on, and he is a man of complete rectitude. The lodgers in Gorky's play are outcasts, existing from day to day, victims of their own weakness as well as of crushing social and economic forces. But the clerk and the lodgers alike were all forgotten until Gorky finished what Gogol began, the process of giving them a right to be heard and a sense of their importance.

It is necessary to add, however, that several years before his death Gorky wrote with regret about the stand he had taken in *The Lower Depths.* He repudiated Luka, who is obviously a spiritual brother of the meek but inspiring peasants from whom Tolstoy's heroes received the formula for salvation. The idealism of Luka was perhaps too much a by-product of the gospel propagated by Orthodoxy for Gorky's taste. He had apparently come to believe that men should not find appeasement of their hunger only in dreams of a better future. This stand was not, however, really a shift in viewpoint, for consistent with his pity for the oppressed was his lifelong condemnation of man's inhumanity to man. Even as early as 1905, in the month after the Bloody Sunday calamity, he wrote to Andreyev:

> Life is built on cruelty, horror, force; for reconstruction a cold, rational cruelty is necessary, that's all. They are being killed? They must be killed. Otherwise what will you do? Go to Count

Leo Tolstoy and wait with him for the wild beasts to become senile and the slaves, their legal food, to be eaten up?

Marc Slonim has asserted that after 1927, Gorky "gave unconditional support to the Soviet leaders."[6] Whether he supported them unconditionally or not, he had ceased to oppose them and was so sympathetic with their ideology as to see the idealism expressed in *Lower Depths* as nothing other than the "opiate" that was all Marx could find in religion. In his last years Gorky's influence was almost as great as it had been during the period when he was most popular in the early part of the century. His position was, in effect, that of a "prose" laureate; he served sometimes as arbiter, sometimes as apologist, for the regime. Whatever the circumstances of his death may have been, he was given funeral pomp and eulogy on a scale seldom equaled, and Stalin played the role of conspicuous mourner. Gorky was loved and respected by multitudes of his fellow countrymen, however, not for his political allegiance, but for his humanitarianism, which transcended all the machinery of politics. They also loved him because his yearning to see a better future for all Russians was linked to a consistent pattern of action calculated to help bring that future into being. This quality of participation is graphically set forth in the following statement from one of the most interesting of his letters to Andreyev:

> Many, allured by the corrupt chatter of the Asiatic and nihilist Ivan Karamazov, preach, most vulgarly, about "nonacceptance" of the world, in view of its "cruelty" and "senselessness." Were I Governor General, I wouldn't hang revolutionists, but these same "nonaccepters," for these tongue-lechers are more harmful for our country than plague rats.

III.

By no means as popular or well known as the earlier play, but more enlightening in relation to later developments in Russia,

[6] *Modern Russian Literature*, p. 150.

Gorky's play *Enemies* (1906) records a step forward in the emergence of the proletariat. It is one of a number of European dramas depicting the clash between the owners (capitalists) and the workers, after the workers became determined to free themselves from the enslavement of industry. At the time the play was written, strikes were forbidden by law, and participation in a strike—whether agitating for it or taking a more active part—was regarded as a political offense.

When the action of the play begins, the workers in a factory have threatened to strike. The two owners and managers have opposing views of their relationship to the workers and of the rights the workers should be permitted. One of them prefers to close the factory rather than give in to the laborers' ultimatum. He is angry because he knows "illicit handbills" are circulating through the factory, and he blames all the problems on "socialism." When he becomes involved in an argument with one of the workmen, he is shot. The evidence is clear. Those who labor are no longer willing to be regarded as slaves. If the owners will not give them freedom, they will take it for themselves.

When the question arises about who is to take the penalty for the murder, the author's attitude is that none of the workers is at fault; the guilt lies elsewhere. The niece of the dead man, a young woman who has been "corrupted" by talking to the workers and reading what members of her class seldom read, speaks for Gorky. She says to the man who fired the shot: "Listen to me, you didn't kill that man. It's they who kill everybody—they kill all life by their greed—by their cowardice." One of the workmen echoes her words: "You're right. . . . It's not the one that strikes who kills, but the one that plants bitter hatred." The strength of the masses, says another of the characters, comes from the fact that they have faith in their rightness. At the conclusion of the play a spokesman for the laborers makes their position plain: "We've lived long enough in dark lawlessness. We've caught fire now, and you'll never put that light out."

It was inevitable that Gorky, a worker himself, should be the spokesman for all the oppressed masses of Russia. It was also inevitable that what he said should make a powerful impact, because his themes were taken directly from the basic issues of a society in ferment against many forms of tyranny.

IV.

Mother is scarcely a novel. It is a case history of the workers' revolutionary activities in a factory town. Gorky had no other intent than to inform the proletariat and stir them to action. The message of the book is, "Go and do likewise!"

Though probably suggested by real people, the characters are highly idealized. It is unlikely that agitators were so enlightened, considerate, and philosophical in outlook as Pavel Vlasov or the Little Russian, and even more unlikely that a living model could have been found for the mother. The setting, however, was certainly taken from life. Gorky had both observed and labored in conditions such as he presents. The book deals with the period just following the failure of the 1905 revolution. At that time the workers were still compelled to stay underground in their efforts to become educated and to organize against the existing tyranny.

Unlike a number of other European writers, Gorky never inveighed against industrialization. Some of the others, nostalgic for the past, yearned to return to an age when society was based upon an agricultural economy and the independent craftsman was his own master. They blamed all the abuses of modern life upon the "age of steam." Gorky held no such view. He recognized industrialization as an inevitable and constructive step in the process of civilization. But he could not regard the hardships and misery introduced by the Industrial Revolution as inevitable. He saw that those who had capital were determined to increase it, an end to be accomplished only by the sacrifice of those who supplied the labor. The remedy as he saw it was not less industry, but more profits for those who did the work. Gorky sympathized with most Slavophile attitudes, but he disagreed with the traditional Slavophile championship of agrarianism. He believed that the future of Russia depended not upon the peasants, but upon the urban workers.

The plot of *Mother*, if it can be said to have a plot, is only a convenient line from which to hang the ideas. The central characters are a mother and son who are workers and representatives of the downtrodden masses. The son, Pavel Vlasov, is studying socialist literature and has joined the movement to educate and emancipate the workers. "I want to know the truth," he tells his mother. He explains that he will not be able to escape prison, yet he must persist in his self-appointed task. Finally, "she understood with her heart that her son had consecrated himself forever to something mysterious and awful."[7] As she listens to the endless discussions of her son and his comrades, she begins to have a sense of their mission. One of them explains it:

> . . . The world is ours! The world is for the workers! For us there is no nation, no race. For us there are only comrades and foes. All the workingmen are our comrades; all the rich, all the authorities, are our foes. When you see how numerous we workingmen are, how tremendous the power of the spirit in us, then your heart is seized with such joy, such happiness, such a great holiday sings in your bosom! . . . We are all children of one mother —the great invincible idea of the brotherhood of the workers of all countries over all the earth.

Gradually the mother is filled with admiration for these earnest young people dedicated to their dream of a better world for all. As she absorbs strength from the others and from her own growing convictions, she begins to learn what they are learning, and in time she becomes one in spirit and belief with them. Finally she can say with certitude:

> . . . a new heart is coming into existence. . . . This bell rings forth the message: "Men of all countries, unite into one family! . . ."
>
> . . . there is still much suffering in store for the people, much of their blood will yet flow, squeezed out by the hands of greed;

[7] The quotations from *Mother* are taken from the first American edition, published by D. Appleton Co., New York, 1927. The translator is not identified.

> but all that . . . is a small price for that which is already stirring in my breast, my mind, in the marrow of my bones! . . . I will bear all, I will suffer all, because there is within me a joy which no one, which nothing can ever stifle! In this joy there is a world of strength!

It is to be expected that Pavel, one of the leaders of the group, will be apprehended for inciting the workers to strike. While her son is in prison, the mother is anxious until the moment comes when she knows what she must do. She becomes active in the movement, going into the factory to distribute books and leaflets to the workers under the pretense of carrying food. When Pavel is released, he is proud of her, and she feels a satisfaction she has never known before, both in the approval and affection of her son and in her new sense of usefulness. Soon Pavel is arrested again, this time for leading a May Day parade in which the workers are dispelled only when a detachment of soldiers uses violence against them. Pavel had rallied his comrades with these words:

> "Brothers! The hour has come to give up this life of ours, this life of greed, hatred, and darkness, this life of violence and falsehood, this life where there is no place for us, where we are no human beings. . . .
>
> "Comrades! We have decided to declare openly who we are; we raise our banner today, the banner of reason, of truth, of liberty! . . .
>
> "Long live the working people!" he shouted. . . .
>
> "Long live the Social Democratic Workingmen's Party, our party, comrades, our spiritual mother."

In her son's absence the mother, going into many places with the leaflets, becomes acquainted with working people of all types. She realizes that although many are weak and do not yet understand what she and her comrades are trying to do, their response is growing. She rejoices at the recognition that: "A day is coming when the workingmen of all countries will raise their hands and firmly declare, 'Enough! We want no more of this life.' . . . And then the fantastic power of those who are mighty by their greed will crumble; the earth will vanish from under their feet, and their support will be gone."

Pavel's speech in the courtroom before he receives the sentence of exile is the summation of his and his comrades' faith and their goal for the future. It is the familiar oratory of revolt. In fairness to Gorky it must be observed that he (and Pavel speaking for him) was absolutely sincere. These revolutionaries were genuine idealists, much closer to the Herzens of the forties and fifties and to the Solomins (*Virgin Soil*) of the seventies than to the ruthless anarchists spawned by the Revolution. Pavel and his comrades used resistance and violence only as a means to fulfill their vision of a brighter future.

The mother's affirmation of faith, spoken as she started to carry out her last mission, explains the lightning effect this book had upon Gorky's public. These words went straight to their hearts:

> . . . how good it is when you know that light for all the people already exists in life, and that there will be a time when they will begin to see it, when they will bathe their souls in it, and all, all, will take fire in its unquenchable flames. . . .
>
> Why, this is like a new god that's born to us, the people. Everything for all; all for everything; the whole of life in one, and the whole of life for everyone, and everyone for the whole of life!

In *Mother*, Gorky answered the question raised by Turgenev when he asked where a leader for Russia might be found. After Turgenev considered the possibilities within the gentry and intelligentsia, only to find them negative, he half-heartedly suggested that the search would have to be carried into the broader base of Russian life, among "the people." The foreman, Solomin, in *Virgin Soil*, is the only resolute and firmly motivated man among all Turgenev's characters, except for the Nihilist Bazarov. Gorky went much farther. The leader for Russia, he asserted, is not some massive figure who will emerge like the heroes in the epics and sagas of old to lead the masses forward and become a great national symbol. No, the leader is "the people" themselves —ordinary men and women like Pavel Vlasov and his mother who transcend their ordinariness through the power of their worthy idea. According to Gorky's view the ideal society is that in which great men are common and common men are great.

Mother is in many respects similar to the proletarian fiction written by American novelists between 1910 and the late 1930's, for example, the novels of John Steinbeck, both *The Grapes of Wrath* and the earlier and less well-known *In Dubious Battle*. In the latter book several of the characters have the same motivation and use some of the same expressions as Gorky's characters. A still closer parallel is *The Jungle*, by Upton Sinclair, which exposed with shocking lucidity the predicament of the workers in the Chicago stockyard area before World War I. Ernest Poole in *The Harbor* showed the laborers on the wharves of New York working in conditions little better than those Gorky encountered on the docks at Kazan. These and many others are stories of the "forgotten man" who during the present century has managed to emerge from obscurity.

There is, of course, one marked difference between these American novels (and their counterparts in England) and the Russian proletarian writings. The American studies show the desperate plight of the workers and call for reform, but there is no intimation that the existing political regime will be a barrier in the way of reform. In the Russian proletarian novels, on the other hand, the protest is not only against an unfair and crippling economic system, but also against a system of government. Although Pavel in *Mother* says he "must declare—that to us the Czar is not the only chain that fetters the body of the country," there is no suggestion that the economic system can be improved without a change in the political machinery as well. Thus a double task confronted the workers in Russia. They believed that change within the existing framework was impossible. They believed, moreover, that evolution was not enough; it had to be supplemented by revolution. Western readers can scarcely fail to understand that in the difference between these two basic concepts is to be found the explanation for many of the disturbing phenomena which have followed the Russian Revolution.

One notable similarity in the proletarian novels—in Russia, western Europe, and America—is the unwavering faith of "the people" in their cause. The words of Pavel might have come from the lips of Tom, Ma Joad, or Casy in *The Grapes of Wrath*. "The consciousness of their great role unites all the workingmen of the world into one soul," Pavel declared. "Our energy is a living power, founded on the ever-growing consciousness of the solidarity of all workingmen." Steinbeck's Ma Joad was inspired by the power of this feeling of togetherness. "The people are strong," she affirmed; and so in the novel *Mother* they are shown to be, in contrast to the enslaved masses which for centuries had remained inert and helpless.

Gorky's novel shows that in the first decade of the twentieth century the laborers of Russia had found their work—not the daily drudgery in mills, factories, and sweatshops by which they earned the pittance that enabled them to exist—but the work of bringing about what the pilgrim Luka in *The Lower Depths* calls "something better to come." Moreover, they had found their religion. This religion had nothing to do with incense, icons, and sumptuously robed priests; it was not the Orthodox faith which Dostoevsky loved. It was a religion as much concerned with the bodies of men as with their souls. It favored re-creation and rehabilitation over redemption. It assumed that whether or not heaven is his destination, the human being is entitled to a reasonable number of comforts and privileges in the present life. He should not have to wait and endure in the vague hope of being compensated in the life to come.

It was a long-awaited infant which Pavel Vlasov and his mother received from the hands of the liberal and socialist midwives in 1917. What he thought of the creature that infant grew up to be, under the tutelage of Lenin and his successors, Gorky was never free to tell.

V.

The assassination of the Austrian archduke, Franz Ferdinand, in June, 1914, afforded the pretext needed by the European powers to start the chain of violence that has disfigured the twentieth century. The Russian government was eager for war, as had been the case a decade earlier when the leaders made the blunder of entering the conflict with Japan. They again clung to the hope that external pressures would arouse patriotic fervor and thus restore internal unity. After Germany declared war on Russia on August 1, 1914, the immediate response gave gratifying evidence that these hopes might be realized. But the temporary respite was only an anticlimax. The Czar's government had been operating on borrowed time since 1905.

From the beginning of the war the Russian forces were hopelessly inadequate to combat the superior numbers, organization, and strategy of the Germans. Actually, the Russian Army played a much larger part in the war than is usually supposed in America. The closer and, in Western eyes, more dramatic events of the Western front make difficult the realization that the existence of the Russian "second front" was of incalculable help to the Allies. Only a few months after the beginning of the war, however, the Russian soldiers became dispirited, not alone because of what appeared to them the impregnability of their opponents, but also because of the distressing conditions within Russia. The military losses, in turn, added to the breakdown of public morale. While the war dragged on through one inconclusive year after another, the Russian spirit was more and more paralyzed by the inevitability of the disintegration and collapse of the Russian Army.

After a brief interval of quiet following the outbreak of international hostilities, the agitation by all the radical groups within Russia was resumed and increased. The reverses of the Russian forces were accompanied by depletion of the national treasury, by acute food shortages, and by complete and almost universal distrust of everything connected with the government. Most serious of all was the widening chasm between the Czar (and his immediate family and favorites) and practically the whole of the Russian people. He had not kept his promises; he had blocked move after move that might have averted a final break between the government and the masses. The Duma had been permitted to exist, but it had been stripped of power and representativeness. Dissatisfaction had now spread from "the people" to the gentry—even to the aristocracy and some members of the nobility. The whole country was a vast, churning storm of confusion and antagonism. There was no longer any possibility of calm except through a change of government.

The Czar was encouraged in obstinacy and error by his wife, against whom the public hatred mounted month by month. Even more pernicious than her influence was that of the self-styled "monk," Rasputin, an evil adventurer who became the virtual ruler of the country. The rise to power of Rasputin and the way he used his power form one of the most fantastic chapters in the history of a country whose story can only be told in extremes. He apparently had some type of personal magnetism that enabled him to win the confidence of those he wanted to use. The road to royal favor was built by the reassurance he gave the Czarina in connection with the illness of her son. Alexis, the only male heir to the throne, was cursed with the disease of hemophilia. On several occasions the Czarina, whose tendencies toward mysticism were highly developed, gave credit to Rasputin for saving the child's life, or at least predicting his recovery when no doctor would give the parents reason to hope. As a result, Rasputin's least wish became her will and in large measure that of the Czar. No one could shake the belief of the Czarina that the "monk" was divinely inspired. Consequently, as a final indignity, Russia had to endure the calamity of being subjected to policies dictated by the whim, self-interest, or bestial characteristics of a man who was probably mad and certainly a scoundrel. When Rasputin was put to death in December, 1916, it was not by a group of terrorists or political idealists, but by members of the nobility closely associated with the Czar. They made a desperate play to save Nicholas and Russia, but, like so many of the gestures of the Russian officials, their action came too late. Even after the death of Rasputin, the royal couple were so dominated by his influence that those who wanted to do so could not approach them or get a hearing.

The final collapse of the government of Russia did not occur through a Bolshevist coup, as is generally supposed. It was the result of an accumulation of forces, probably the most important of which was the deadlock between the Duma and the Czar. The latter, under pressure from within the palace, favored making a separate peace with Germany. The pro-Ally Duma was opposed to a move which would make Russia appear weak and irresponsible. On this, as on all other points of friction, it was impossible for the monarch and the Duma to agree. In March, 1917, the acute food shortage and the widespread spirit of rebellion smouldering just below the surface stimulated the Duma once more to appeal to the Czar to make extensive changes in the personnel of his cabinet. His reply was a formal dissolution of the Duma. This was the signal for revolt.

The Duma proceeded to make plans for a provisional government. When the plans were complete, the new government asked the Czar to abdicate. On March 15, 1917, he gave up his throne in favor of his brother, the Grand Duke Michael, because the invalidism of the young Alexis made him unfit to rule. The Grand Duke, however, read the handwriting on the wall and relinquished his claim. The reign of the Romanovs was finished.

The Czar and his family were sent into exile in Siberia. A little more than a year later, in July, 1918, they were slaughtered by terrorists. Their murder had not been intended or decreed by the government then in power; at least, the government officials disclaimed responsibility for the unfortunate event. Because the circumstances of their death were surrounded by secrecy, the royal family became the subject of numerous legends in which they played parts far more attractive than their roles in life. The

Czar, indeed, had failed to meet the challenge to direct constructively the destiny of his great but chaotic country, which had looked long and in vain for a worthy leader.

Only a small number of Bolsheviks took an active part in the events which led to the actual fall of the Czar's government. In a short time, however, the fanatic energy of the Bolsheviks enabled them to challenge the authority of the provisional government under the leadership of Kerensky.[8] When the Bolsheviks stormed the Winter Palace in October, 1917, there was no turning them back—as the masses had been driven back on the Bloody Sunday in 1905. The provisional government was too moderate; the revolutionaries would not be satisfied with less than the seizure of power in their own hands. The October Revolution was the beginning of the new Russia, and the Bolsheviks under Lenin assumed the leadership of the new society. What that society may become is a chapter in the history of Russia which has not been fully recorded. For a considerable time after the establishment of the new regime it seemed that the doleful premonitions of Andreyev had been justified. But throughout the course of their history the Russian people have proved their strength—strength not only to endure but also to create. When the second Nicholas lost his duel of monarch *versus* people, the way was open at last for the people to make their own future.

Because of the disorder of the period in which he lived and because he was intimately connected with a regime which used evil means for the accomplishment of good ends, it is difficult to see Gorky the man objectively. Perhaps his humaneness in a harsh time makes him loom larger than he was. His books are not great literature, but in his expression of aspiration he established a link with Dostoevsky and Tolstoy at the same time that he was interpreting what was new in Russia. His detractors in the West condemned him for his allegiance to a cause which

[8] Alexander Kerensky, a Menshevik, had been head of the provisional government since the time of the abdication of the czar in March, 1917. He and other moderates could not match the decisiveness and ruthlessness of the Bolsheviks under Lenin.

added new horrors to old. Gorky was a Russian as well as a humanitarian. He knew all too well that the old patterns had failed; it is no wonder that, no matter what his misgivings, he was willing to give new patterns the benefit of the doubt. The Bolsheviks definitely used him to cover certain of their nefarious deeds. At times he resisted, but at other times he probably was willing to be used, in the hope that some time the day would come when there would not be so much to hide. Whatever the real stature of the man, he was genuine in the midst of falseness, and he was compassionate in a time of cruelty. He worked for mankind, and he is a hero of the Russian people. The first writer who convinced them that their dreams could be realities, he was indeed their "stormy petrel." They revere him as one of the creators of modern Russia.

In August, 1934, Gorky was one of the speakers at the first All-Union Congress of Soviet Writers. His words pointed the direction in which he hoped and believed his beloved country would go. He urged his listeners to understand the importance of labor, for, he said, there must no longer be superfluous people in Russia. He reassured his hearers that the process by which all workers were being reborn to a new life was developing throughout the entire Soviet nation. To follow the record of this development, the reader will need to turn to modern Russian literature, the literature of the Soviet people.

EPILOGUE: PUSHKIN TO PASTERNAK

THE VISITOR TO Moscow is certain to make the acquaintance of Gorky Street, which leads to the Kremlin. One of the squares fronting on that street is distinguished by the statue of a man whose face—if the statue is a faithful likeness—must have been a fitting mirror of the soul. It requires little imagination to see in that sculptured likeness both melancholy and a haunting premonition. One wonders what Pushkin would say if he could speak now or what he would think if he could step down from the marble pedestal and mingle with the throngs who pass the square which bears his name.

The poet's face is turned a little to one side, his gaze withdrawn, directed inward. If the visitor, however, looks straight ahead, he will see at some distance, at the end of a tree-lined plaza, another statue which bears a familiar aspect. The heavy-lidded eyes and enigmatic smile of Gogol do not convey any of the vision or the pain of Pushkin's sculptured countenance, but they give the beholder both a sense of sharing in the smile and an uneasy feeling that the expression has in it more of disdain than pleasantness.

The traveler who leaves Pushkin Square and proceeds along Gorky Street away from the Kremlin will soon pass a statue of the beloved Soviet poet Mayakovsky. Farther still, the likeness of Gorky dominates the small square adjacent to one of the Moscow railroad stations. It is fitting that this statue has been placed in a location where it seems to preside over travelers, for Gorky spent much of his life wandering across the massive reaches of his country, and across other countries too. The face of Gorky in marble does not suggest the "stormy petrel." The mouth and chin are firm, but the direct, warm gaze and the benign expression reveal the spirit of the man who became the spokesman of the people struggling to rise from the depths.

These images in stone are a partial answer to the question, What has happened to the great Russian authors in the Soviet period? The recognition of major literary figures is to be explained in part, no doubt, by the Soviet compulsion for external manifestations of culture. But there is a truer explanation. The respect of the Russian people for great writers (and artists in general) is widespread and genuine. During the first thirty-five years of the Soviet regime, literature was distorted and emasculated by pressures frightful even in retrospect. Even yet the artist is not free. But the signs of recovery are reassuring. The denigration of the outstanding nineteenth-century authors has now been replaced by a heartening acknowledgment of their real significance. There is a plan for the erection at strategic locations in Moscow of statues of all the major classical authors. Nor are these tributes limited to Moscow. They are to be found from Leningrad in the north to Yalta in the south. Everywhere in Russia—in schoolroom, hotel lobby, station waiting room, office, and factory—the pictured countenance of Gorky may be seen. Indeed, the frequent appearances of Gorky and Pushkin in sculpture and on canvas are exceeded only by the ubiquitous likenesses of Lenin and (less frequently) of Marx.

The most popular writer in Russia today is not the creator of the Marxist dialectic, but the poet who died eighty years before the Revolution. Pushkin is loved and quoted by school children and their elders alike. "He is our contemporary!" the Russians say. Their feeling for him is far warmer and more personal than the veneration of Shakespeare in English-speaking lands. The village in which he went to school has been renamed for him and is now better known for its Pushkin museum than for the palace which dominates it. One of the stations of the Leningrad subway bears his name; the only ornamentation in its magnificently simple decor is a statue of the poet placed in an unforgettable setting. Many of the theaters of Russia—and theater in Russia is a lively art—are named for him. He has fully achieved the immortality of which he dreamed.

Next to Pushkin, probably the best loved of nineteenth-century writers in Russia is Chekhov. There are many reasons for his being thus cherished and widely read, not the least of which is the fact that his plays are still the backbone of Russian theater. The Moscow Art Theater is still called by many the Chekhov Theater. It is easy to feel the presence of Chekhov there, when one sees the seagull insignia above the entrance and watches the actors playing characters who are like emanations of the playwright himself. In the garden of his home in Yalta, Chekhov seems even closer. Knowing he would not live to enjoy them, he still planted trees and started a rose garden. Now his cypress trees reach toward the sky, a reminder of the warm-hearted man who believed that "everyone should add one touch of beauty to this earth."

Dostoevsky is not regarded in his own country as its foremost writer, as he is increasingly considered in western Europe and America. His grave, though located in the crowded burial ground of the Alexander Nevsky cemetery in the heart of Leningrad, is somehow lonely. Perhaps the dark granite tomb appears more somber because of the contrast with several brighter memorials in the musicians' corner nearby. There Moussorgsky, Arensky, Rimsky-Korsakov, Rubinstein, and Borodin are always well remembered with wreaths of brilliant carnations and bouquets of roses. Probably the image of Dostoevsky's tortured spirit fixed in marble will be one of the last to look upon the Moscow throngs from a lofty eminence, for the Communists have been troubled by his horror of "the possessed." But they have never been able to forget him. His books are now widely read in Russia, the favorite being *The Idiot*. Perhaps the continuing appeal of this book is the best reply to Dostoevsky's sense of failure in the creation of Prince Myshkin.

There can be no doubt that the Russians are working systematically and conscientiously to give permanence to the finest achievements of their literature. Since World War II, complete and handsome editions of the works of all their great writers have been published, and new editions appear frequently. Scholarly studies in considerable number are being carried on; there is constant enrichment of biographical and critical material as well as publication of hitherto unpublished manuscripts. The homes of Pushkin, Dostoevsky, Tolstoy, Chekhov, and Gorky—and numerous other sites connected with them and other authors—have become state-supported museums, with collections irresistible to all lovers of Russian literature.

The most famous and, in some ways, most significant of these shrines is the country house of Tolstoy, Yasnaya Polyana, the "beautiful glade." There one may see the room where *War and Peace* was created and where the charming face of Anna Karenina became real to the mind and eyes of the author. As one stands at Tolstoy's grave, surrounded by a grove of towering beech trees, one can understand why he asked to be buried at "the place of the green stick." The quiet which reigns there is like the quietude of the faith Tolstoy spent his life seeking.

In his book *American in Russia*, Harrison Salisbury made the statement that "no one who has read Dostoevsky or Tolstoy or Chekhov is ever lost for long in Russia because very quickly you will see something or something will happen which comes right out of the pages of *The Brothers Karamazov*, *Anna Karenina*, or *The Cherry Orchard*." He is right. Familiarity with the great books of Russia is still the best introduction to Russia itself. The carriage of Anna Karenina was probably burned for whatever heat it might supply during the dreadful winters of the revolutionary period. But Anna may still be seen—at the opera or perhaps in the schoolroom or in the park. And if you look a second time at the man stepping off the street car, you will recognize Dr. Chekhov—or is it Dr. Zhivago?

In spite of all the violence and nightmare chaos which attended the birth of the "new" Russia and in spite of the travesty of freedom which still exists, the arts have survived. When you talk with students and the people on the street, the conversation is certain to come to literature, and you discover that, although political regimes come and go, the great writers are immortal. When you see the crowds of people buying books, the bulging reading rooms in the libraries, the intent faces of theater-goers—and, even more, when you go to Peredelkino and stop for a while beside the peaceful hillside grave of Pasternak—you are sure that there will not soon be an end to the making of great books in Russia.

BIBLIOGRAPHY

THE HISTORY OF RUSSIA—GENERAL

Adams, Arthur E., ed. *Imperial Russia After 1861.* Boston, Heath, 1965 (paper).

Baring, Maurice. *The Mainsprings of Russia.* London, Nelson, 1914.

Chadwick, N. K. *The Beginnings of Russian History: An Enquiry into Sources.* Cambridge, Eng., Cambridge Univ. Press, 1946.

Charques, Richard D. *A Short History of Russia.* New York, Dutton, 1956 (paper).

———. *Twilight of Imperial Russia.* New York, Oxford Univ. Press, 1959.

Clarkson, Jesse D. *A History of Russia.* New York, Random House, 1961.

Crowson, Paul. *A History of the Russian People.* London, Arnold, 1948.

Deutscher, Isaac. *Russia in Transition.* New York, Coward, 1957.

Ellison, H. J. *History of Russia.* New York, Holt, Rinehart & Winston, 1964.

Florinsky, Michael T. *Russia: A History and Interpretation.* 2 vols. New York, Macmillan, 1953.

———. *A Short History.* New York, Macmillan, 1964.

Graham, Stephen. *Tsar of Freedom: The Life and Reign of Alexander II.* New Haven, Yale, 1935.

Grey, Ian. *Peter the Great: Emperor of All Russia.* Philadelphia, Lippincott, 1960.

———. *Catherine the Great: Autocrat and Empress of All Russia.* Philadelphia, Lippincott, 1962.

Gribble, Francis H. *Emperor and Mystic: The Life of Alexander I of Russia.* New York, Dutton, 1931.

Harcave, Sidney. *Russia: A History.* New York, Lippincott, 1959.

Jones, Dorsey D. *Russia: A Concise History.* New York, Stackpole, 1955.

Karpovich, Michael. *Imperial Russia, 1801–1917.* New York, Holt, 1932.

Kerner, R. J. *Urge to the Sea: The Course of Russian History*. Berkeley, Univ. of California Press, 1946.

Kluchevsky, Vasily O. *A History of Russia*. 5 vols. New York, Russell & Russell, 1960.

Kohn, Hans. *Basic History of Modern Russia*. Princeton, Van Nostrand, 1957.

Kornilov, Alexander. *Modern Russian History*. New York, Knopf, 1924.

Latimer, Robert S. *Under Three Tsars: Liberty of Conscience in Russia, 1856–1909*. London, Morgan & Scott, 1909.

Lensen, George A. *Russia's Eastward Expansion*. Englewood Cliffs, Prentice Hall, 1964.

Makieev, Nikolai, and Valentine O' Hara. *Russia*. New York, Scribners, 1925.

Maynard, Sir John. *Russia in Flux*. New York, Macmillan, 1948.

———. *The Russian Peasant and Other Studies*. London, Gollancz, 1942.

Mazour, Anatole G. *The Rise and Fall of the Romanovs*. Princeton, Van Nostrand, 1960.

———. *Russia: Past and Present*. Princeton, Van Nostrand, 1958.

———. *Russia: Tsarist and Communist*. Princeton, Van Nostrand, 1962.

Mirsky, D. S. *Russia, A Social History*. London, Cresset, 1931.

Mosse, W. E. *Alexander II and the Modernization of Russia*. Collier (paper).

Pares, Sir Bernard. *A History of Russia*. New York, Knopf, 1944.

Platonov, S. F. *A History of Russia*. Tr. by E. Aronsberg. New York, Longmans Green, 1932.

Riasanovsky, Nicholas V. *A History of Russia*. New York, Oxford Univ. Press, 1963.

———. *Nicholas I and Official Nationality in Russia, 1825–1855*. Berkeley, Univ. of California Press, 1959.

Seton, Watson Hugh. *The Decline of Imperial Russia, 1855–1914*. New York, Praeger, 1960.

Skrine, Francis. *The Expansion of Russia, 1815–1900*. Cambridge, Eng., Cambridge Univ. Press, 1903.

Spector, Ivar. *First Russian Revolution*. Englewood Cliffs, Prentice Hall, 1962.

———. *An Introduction to Russian History and Culture*. New York, Van Nostrand, 1949.

Strakhovsky, Leonid I. *Alexander I of Russia.* New York, Norton, 1947.

Sumner, B. H. *Peter the Great and the Emergence of Russia.* New York, Macmillan, 1951.

———. *A Short History of Russia.* New York, Harcourt Brace, 1947.

Thaden, Edward C. *Conservative Nationalism in Nineteenth Century Russia.* Seattle, Univ. of Washington Press, 1964.

Treadgold, Donald W. *Twentieth Century Russia.* New York, Rand McNally, 1959.

Vernadsky, George V. *Origins of Russia.* New York, Oxford Univ. Press, 1959.

———. *Russia at the Dawn of the Modern Age.* New Haven, Yale Univ. Press, 1959.

———, and Michael Karpovich. *A History of Russia.* 4 vols. New Haven, Yale Univ. Press, 1959.

Von Eckhardt, Hans. *Russia.* Tr. by C. A. Phillips. New York, Knopf, 1932.

Walsh, Warren B. *Readings in Russian History.* 3 vols. Syracuse, Syracuse Univ. Press, 1959.

———. *Russia and the Soviet Union.* Ann Arbor, Univ. of Michigan Press, 1958.

THE RUSSIAN MIND AND SPIRIT

Baring, Maurice. *The Russian People.* London, Methuen, 1911.

Berdyaev, Nicholas A. *The End of Our Time.* New York, Sheed & Ward, 1933.

———. *The Origin of Russian Communism.* New York, Scribners, 1939; Ann Arbor, Univ. of Michigan Press, 1960.

———. *The Russian Idea.* Tr. by R. M. French. New York, Macmillan, 1948.

Bunt, Cyril G. E. *Russian Art from Scyths to Soviets.* London, The Studio, 1946.

Carr, Edward H. *Michael Bakunin.* London, Macmillan, 1937.

———. *The Romantic Exiles.* London, Gollancz, 1933; Boston, Beacon Press, 1961.

Casey, Robert P. *Religion in Russia.* New York, Harper, 1946.

Chamot, Mary. *Russian Painting and Sculpture.* New York, Macmillan, 1963.

Cherniavsky, Michael. *Tsar and People.* New Haven, Yale Univ. Press, 1961.

Conybeare, Frederick C. *Russian Dissenters.* New York, Russell & Russell, 1962.

Curtiss, John S. *Church and State in Russia: The Last Years of the Empire, 1900–1917.* New York, Columbia Univ. Press, 1940.

De Grunwald, Constantin. *Saints of Russia.* New York, Macmillan, 1960.

Eastman, Max. *Since Lenin Died.* New York, Boni & Liveright, 1925.

Edie, James M., James P. Scanlon, and Mary-Barbara Zeldin. *Russian Philosophy.* 3 vols. Chicago, Quadrangle Books, 1956.

Fedotov, G. P. *The Russian Religious Mind.* New York, Harper, 1960.

Fischer, George. *Russian Liberalism: From Gentry to Intelligentsia.* Cambridge, Harvard Univ. Press, 1958.

Fülöp-Miller, René. *Rasputin, the Holy Devil.* Tr. by F. S. Fint and D. F. Tait. New York, Viking, 1928.

Haimson, L. H. *Russian Marxists and the Origins of Bolshevism.* Cambridge, Harvard Univ. Press, 1955.

Hare, Richard. *Pioneers of Russian Social Thought.* New York, Oxford Univ. Press, 1951.

———. *Portraits of Russian Personalities between Reform and Revolution.* New York, Oxford Univ. Press, 1959.

Hecht, David. *Russian Radicals Look to America, 1825–1890.* Cambridge, Harvard Univ. Press, 1947.

Herzen, Alexander. *My Past and Thoughts (1852–55).* 6 vols. Tr. by Constance Garnett. London, Chatto & Windus, 1924–27; New York, Knopf, 1924–26.

Kohn, Hans. *Pan-Slavism, Its History and Ideology.* South Bend, Univ. of Notre Dame Press, 1955.

———, ed. *The Mind of Modern Russia: Historical and Political Thought of Russia's Great Age.* New Brunswick, Rutgers Univ. Press, 1955.

Kucharov, Samuel. *Courts, Lawyers and Trials under the Last Three Tsars.* New York, Praeger, 1953.

Kucharzewski, Jan. *The Origins of Modern Russia.* New York, Polish Institute of Arts and Sciences in America, 1948.

Lampert, Evgenii. *Sons against Fathers: Studies in Russian Radicalism and Revolution.* Oxford, Clarendon, 1965.

———. *Studies in Rebellion.* New York, Praeger, 1957.

Leary, D. B. *Education and Autocracy in Russia.* Buffalo, University Studies, 1919.

Liddell, R. S. *Actions and Reactions in Russia.* New York, Dutton, 1918.

Lossky, N. O. *History of Russian Philosophy.* New York, International Universities, 1951.

Matlaw, Ralph E. *Belinsky, Chernyshevsky, and Dobrolyubov: Selected Criticism.* New York, Dutton (paper).

Mazaryk, Thomas G. *The Spirit of Russia: Studies in History, Literature, and Philosophy.* New York, Macmillan, 1919.

Mazour, Anatole G. *The First Russian Revolution, 1825: The Decembrist Movement.* Stanford, Stanford Univ. Press, 1961.

Miliukov, Paul N. *Outlines of Russian Culture.* Ed. by Michael Karpovich. Vol. I: *Religion and the Church*; Vol II: *Literature*; Vol. III: *Architecture, Painting and Music.* Philadelphia, Univ. of Pennsylvania Press, 1942.

Naryshkina, Elizaveta. *Under Three Tsars.* Ed. by René Fülöp-Miller. New York, Dutton, 1931.

Nomad, Max. *Apostles of Revolution.* Boston, Little, Brown, 1939.

Riasanovsky, Nicholas V. *Russia and the West in the Teaching of the Slavophiles.* Cambridge, Harvard Univ. Press, 1952.

Rice, Tamara Talbot. *A Concise History of Russian Art.* New York, Praeger, 1963.

Salisbury, Harrison. *American in Russia.* New York, Harper, 1955.

Simmons, Ernest J., ed. *Continuity and Change in Russian and Soviet Thought.* Cambridge, Harvard Univ. Press, 1955.

Soloviev, A. V. *Holy Russia.* Gravenhage, Mouton, 1959.

Souvarine, Boris. *Stalin, A Critical Survey of Bolshevism.* New York, Longmans Green, 1939.

Spinka, Matthew. *The Church and the Russian Revolution.* New York, Macmillan, 1927.

Tompkins, Stuart R. *The Russian Intelligentsia: Makers of the Revolutionary State.* Norman, Univ. of Oklahoma Press, 1957.

———. *The Russian Mind from Peter the Great Through the Enlightenment.* Norman, Univ. of Oklahoma Press, 1953.

Utechin, Serge. *Russian Political Thought.* New York, Praeger, 1963.

Venturi, Franco. *Roots of Revolution: A History of the Populist and Socialist Movements in Nineteenth Century Russia.* New York, Knopf, 1960.

Wallace, Donald M. *Russia.* London, Cassell, 1912.

———. *Russia on the Eve of War and Revolution.* Vintage (paper).

Zenkovsky, V. V. *A History of Russian Philosophy.* 2 vols. Tr. by G. L. Kline. New York, Columbia Univ. Press, 1953.

———. *Russian Thinkers and Europe.* Tr. by Galia S. Bodde. American Council of Learned Societies, 1953.

Zilliacus, Koni. *The Russian Revolutionary Movement.* New York, Dutton, 1905.

THE RUSSIAN REVOLUTION

Adams, Arthur E. *The Russian Revolution and Bolshevik Victory: Why and How?* Boston, Heath, 1960.

Berdyaev, Nicholas. *The Russian Revolution.* Ann Arbor, Univ. of Michigan Press, 1961.

Breshkovskaia, Katerina. *Hidden Springs of the Russian Revolution.* Stanford, Stanford Univ. Press, 1931.

———. *The Little Grandmother of the Russian Revolution (Letters and Reminiscences).* Boston, Little, Brown, 1917.

Bunyan, James, and Harold H. Fisher. *The Bolshevik Revolution, 1917–18.* Palo Alto, Stanford Univ. Press, 1934.

Carr, Edward H. *The Bolshevik Revolution, 1917–1923.* 6 vols. New York, Macmillan, 1951.

Chamberlain, William H. *The Russian Revolution, 1917–1921.* New York, Macmillan, 1952.

Chernov, Victor M. *The Great Russian Revolution.* New Haven, Yale Univ. Press, 1936.

Curtiss, John S. *The Russian Revolution of 1917.* Princeton, Van Nostrand, 1957.

Deutscher, Isaac. *The Prophet Armed: Trotsky, 1879–1921.* New York, Oxford Univ. Press, 1954.

Hill, Christopher. *Lenin and the Russian Revolution.* New York, Macmillan, 1950.

Kerensky, Alexander. *The Catastrophe: Kerensky's Own Story of the Russian Revolution.* New York, Appleton Century Crofts, 1927.

———. *The Crucifixion of Liberty.* New York, Day, 1934.

Luxemburg, Rosa. *The Russian Revolution and Leninism or Marxism.* Ann Arbor, Univ. of Michigan Press, 1961.

McNeal, Robert. *The Russian Revolution: Why Did the Bolsheviks Win?* New York, Holt, Rinehart & Winston (paper).

Mavor, James. *The Russian Revolution.* London, Allen & Unwin, 1928.

Meyendorff, Baron A. *The Background of the Russian Revolution.* New York, Henry Holt, 1929.

Moorehead, Alan. *The Russian Revolution.* New York, Harper, 1958.

Nomad, Max. *Aspects of Revolt.* New York, Twayne, 1959.

Olgin, M. J. *The Soul of the Russian Revolution.* New York, Holt, 1917.

Pares, Sir Bernard. *Fall of the Russian Monarchy.* Vintage (paper).

———. *Russia: Reform and Revolution.* New York, Schocken (paper).

Prawdin, Michael. *The Unmentionable Nechaev.* New York, Roy, 1963.

Reed, John. *Ten Days That Shook the World.* New York, Modern Library, 1935.

Rodzianko, M. W. *The Reign of Rasputin.* London, Philpot, 1927.

Ross, Edward A. *The Russian Bolshevik Revolution.* New York, Century, 1921.

Sazanov, Serge. *Fateful Years, 1909–1916.* New York, Stokes, 1928.

Sukhanov, N. N. *The Russian Revolution, 1917: A Personal Record.* 2 vols. Ed. by Joel Carmichael. New York, Oxford Univ. Press, 1955.

Treadgold, Donald W. *Lenin and His Rivals.* New York, Praeger, 1955.

Trotsky, Leon. *The History of the Russian Revolution.* Tr. by Max Eastman. New York, Simon & Schuster, 1932.

Vernadsky, George V. *Lenin, Red Dictator.* Tr. by M. W. Davis. New Haven, Yale Univ. Press, 1931.

———. *The Russian Revolution, 1917–1931.* New York, Holt, 1932.

Wilton, R. *The Last Days of the Romanovs.* London, Thornton Butterworth, 1920.

Wolfe, Bertram. *Three Who Made a Revolution.* New York, Dial, 1948.

Yarmolinsky, Avrahm. *Road to Revolution: A Century of Russian Radicalism.* New York, Macmillan, 1959.

Russian Literature—General

Baring, Maurice. *Landmarks in Russian Literature.* London, Methuen, 1910.

———. *An Outline of Russian Literature.* New York, Holt, 1914.

Bruckner, A. A. *Literary History of Russia.* Tr. by H. Havelock. London, Unwin, 1908.

Hare, Richard. *Russian Literature from Pushkin to the Present Day.* New York, Barnes & Noble, 1947.

Jackson, Robert L. *Dostoevsky's Underground Man in Russian Literature.* New York, Humanities, 1959.

Kropotkin, Peter A. *Ideals and Realities in Russian Literature.* New York, Knopf, 1919.

Lavrin, Janko. *An Introduction to the Russian Novel.* London, Methuen, 1942.

———. *From Pushkin to Mayakovsky.* London, Sylvan, 1948.

———. *Russian Writers, Their Lives and Literature.* New York, Van Nostrand, 1954.

Lindblom, Thaïs. *Concise History of Russian Literature.* Vol. I: *From the Beginnings to Chekhov.* New York, New York Univ. Press, 1966.

Mathewson, R. W., Jr. *The Positive Hero in Russian Literature.* New York, Columbia, 1958.

Mirsky, D. S. *A History of Russian Literature.* New York, Knopf, 1949.

Muchnic, Helen. *An Introduction to Russian Literature.* New York, Doubleday, 1947.

———. *From Gorky to Pasternak.* New York, Random House, 1961.

Olgin, M. H. *A Guide to Russian Literature (1820–1917).* New York, Harcourt Brace, 1920.

Phelps, Gilbert. *The Russian Novel in English Fiction.* New York, Rinehart, 1957.

Phelps, W. L. *Essays on Russian Novelists.* New York, Macmillan, 1911.

Poggioli, Renato. *The Phoenix and the Spider, Essays on Some Russian Writers.* Cambridge, Harvard Univ. Press, 1957.

Simmons, Ernest J. *An Introduction to Russian Realism.* Bloomington, Univ. of Indiana Press, 1965.

———. *An Outline of Modern Russian Literature.* Ithaca, Cornell Univ. Press, 1943.

Slonim, Marc. *The Epic of Russian Literature: From Its Origins through Tolstoy.* New York, Oxford Univ. Press, 1950.

———. *From Chekhov to the Revolution: Russian Literature 1900–1917.* New York, Oxford Univ. Press, 1962.

———. *Modern Russian Literature: From Chekhov to the Present.* New York, Oxford Univ. Press, 1953.

———. *An Outline of Russian Literature.* New York, Oxford Univ. Press, 1958.

———. *Russian Theater: From the Empire to the Soviets.* Cleveland, World, 1961.

Spector, Ivar. *The Golden Age of Russian Literature.* Caldwell, Idaho, Caxton, 1943.

Verneke, B. *History of the Russian Theater (17th–19th Century).* New York, Macmillan, 1951.

Wiener, Leo. *The Contemporary Drama of Russia.* Boston, Little, Brown, 1924.

Yarmolinsky, Avrahm. *Russian Literature.* Chicago, American Library Assn., 1931.

RUSSIAN WRITERS

Pushkin

Brasol, Boris. "Pushkin" in *The Mighty Three.* New York, Payson, 1934.

Cross, Samuel H., and E. J. Simmons. *Alexander Pushkin, 1799–1837: His Life and Heritage.* New York, American-Russian Institute for Cultural Relations with the Soviet Union, 1937.

Mirsky, D. S. *Pushkin.* New York, Dutton, 1963.

Simmons, Ernest J. *Pushkin.* Cambridge, Harvard Univ. Press, 1937.

Gogol

Brasol, Boris. "Gogol" in *The Mighty Three.* New York, Payson, 1934.

Driessen, F. C. *Gogol as a Short Story Writer.* Tr. by I. F. Finley. New York, Humanities, 1965.

Fanger, Donald L. "Gogol: The Apotheosis of the Absurd" in *Dostoevsky and Romantic Realism.* Cambridge, Harvard Univ. Press, 1965.

Lavrin, Janko, *Nikolai Gogol, 1809–1852.* New York, Macmillan, 1952.

Magarshack, David. *Gogol, A Life.* New York, Grove, 1957.

Nabokov, Vladimir V. *Nikolai Gogol.* New York, New Directions, 1961.

Setchkarev, Vsevolod. *Gogol: Life and Works.* Tr. by R. Kramer. New York, New York Univ. Press, 1965.

Tsanoff, Radoslav, *The Russian Soil and Nicholas Gogol.* Houston, Rice Institute, 1917 (pamphlet).

Goncharov

Lavrin, Janko. *Goncharov.* New Haven, Yale Univ. Press, 1954.
Phelps, W. L. "Goncharov" in *Essays on Russian Novelists.* New York, Macmillan, 1911.
Poggioli, Renato. "On Goncharov and His Oblomov" in *The Phoenix and the Spider.* Cambridge, Harvard Univ. Press, 1957.

Turgenev

Freeborn, Richard. *Turgenev, The Novelist's Novelist.* London, Oxford Univ. Press, 1960.
Garnett, Edward. *Turgenev.* London, Collins, 1917.
Gettman, Royal A. *Turgenev in England and America.* Urbana, Univ. of Illinois Press, 1941.
James, Henry. "Ivan Turgenieff" in *Partial Portraits.* London, Macmillan, 1919.
Lloyd, J. A. T. *Ivan Turgenev.* London, Hale, 1942.
Magarshack, David. *Turgenev, A Life.* New York, Hillary, 1954.
Moxom, Philip S. *Two Masters: Browning and Turgenieff.* Boston, Sherman, 1912.
Tsanoff, R. A. *The Art of Ivan Turgenev.* Houston, Rice Institute, 1917 (pamphlet).
Yarmolinsky, Avrahm. *Turgenev, The Man, His Art and His Age.* New York, Orion, 1959.
Zhitova, Varvara N. *The Turgenev Family.* New York, Roy, 1954.

Dostoevsky

Berdyaev, Nicholas A. *Dostoevsky, An Interpretation.* Tr. by Donald Attwater. London, Sheed, 1936.
Brasol, Boris. "Dostoevsky" in *The Mighty Three.* New York, Payson, 1934.
Carr, Edward H. *Dostoevsky.* New York, Macmillan, 1949; London, Allen & Unwin, 1931.
Coulson, Jessie. *Dostoevsky: A Self-Portrait.* New York, Oxford Univ. Press, 1962.
Curle, Richard. *Characters of Dostoevsky.* London, Heineman, 1950.
Dostoevskaia, Anna Grigorevna. *Diary of Dostoevsky's Wife.* Ed. by René Fülöp-Miller and Frank Eckstein. London, Gollancz, 1928.

———. *Diary and Reminiscences of Mme. Dostoevsky.* Ed. by S. S. Koteliansky. New York, Dutton, 1926.

Fanger, Donald L. *Dostoevsky and Romantic Realism.* Cambridge, Harvard Univ. Press, 1965.

Fülöp-Miller, René. *Fyodor Dostoevsky: Insight, Faith, and Prophecy.* New York, Scribners, 1950.

Gide, André. *Dostoevsky.* New York, New Directions, 1961 (paper).

Harper, Ralph. *Seventh Solitude: Man's Isolation in Kierkegaard, Dostoevsky, Nietzsche.* Baltimore, Johns Hopkins Univ. Press, 1965.

Hubben, William. "Dostoevsky" in *Four Prophets of Our Destiny.* New York, Macmillan, 1958.

Ivanov, Vyacheslav. *Freedom and the Tragic Life: A Study in Dostoevsky.* Tr. by Norman Cameron. New York, Noonday, 1957.

Jackson, Robert L. *Dostoevsky's Quest for Form.* New Haven, Yale Univ. Press, 1966.

———. Dostoevsky's *Underground Man in Russian Literature.* New York, Humanities, 1959.

Kaufmann, Walter, ed. *Existentialism from Dostoevsky to Sartre.* New York, Meridian Books, 1956.

Lavrin, Janko. *Dostoevsky.* New York, Macmillan, 1947.

Lloyd, J .A. T. *Fyodor Dostoevsky.* New York, Scribners, 1947.

Magarshack, David. *Dostoevsky.* New York, Harcourt Brace & World, 1963.

Maurina, Zenta. *Fyodor Dostoievsky, A Prophet of the Soul.* London, J. Clarke, 1940.

Meier-Graefe, A. J. *Dostoevsky, The Man and His Work.* New York, Harcourt Brace, 1928.

Murry, John M. *Fyodor Dostoevsky.* Boston, Small, Maynard, 1924.

Pachmuss, Tamira. *F. M. Dostoevsky: Dualism and Synthesis of the Human Soul.* Carbondale. Southern Illinois Univ. Press, 1963.

Passage, Charles E. *Dostoevsky the Adapter.* Chapel Hill, Univ. of North Carolina Press, 1954.

Payne, Robert. *Dostoevsky: A Human Portrait.* New York, Knopf, 1961.

Powys, John Cowper. *Dostoievsky.* London, Lane, 1946.

Sajkovic, Miriam. *F. M. Dostoevsky: His Image of Man.* Philadelphia, Univ. of Pennsylvania Press, 1962.

Seduro, Vladimir. *Dostoevsky in Russian Literary Criticism, 1846–1956*. New York, Columbia Univ. Press, 1957.

Simmons, Ernest J. *Dostoevsky, the Making of a Novelist*. New York, Oxford Univ. Press, 1940; London, Lehmann, 1950.

Slonim, Marc. *Three Loves of Dostoevsky*. New York, Rinehart, 1955.

Soloviev, Evgenii. *Dostoevsky, His Life and Literary Activity*. New York, Macmillan, 1916.

Steiner, George. *Tolstoy or Dostoevsky*. New York, Knopf, 1959.

Thurneysen, E. *Dostoevsky*. Tr. by K. R. Crim. Richmond, John Knox, 1964.

Troyat, Henry. *Firebrand: The Life of Dostoevsky*. New York, Roy, 1946.

Tsanoff, R. A. *From Darkness into Light: Fyodor Dostoevsky*. Houston, Rice Institute, 1917 (pamphlet).

Wasiolek, Edward. *Crime and Punishment and the Critics*. San Francisco, Wadsworth, 1961.

———. *Dostoevsky: The Major Fiction*. Cambridge, M.I.T. Press, 1964.

Wellek, René. *Dostoevsky: A Collection of Critical Essays*. Englewood Cliffs, Prentice Hall, 1962.

Yarmolinsky, Avrahm. *Dostoevsky: His Life and Art*. New York, Criterion, 1957.

Yermilov, Vladirir V. *Fyodor Dostoevsky, 1821–1881*. Tr. by J. Katzer. Moscow, Foreign Languages Publishing House, n.d.

Zernov, Nicholas. "Dostoevsky" in *Three Russian Prophets*. New York, Macmillan, 1944.

Zweig, Stefan. "Dostoevsky" in *Three Masters*. New York, Viking, 1930.

Tolstoy

Asquith, Cynthia. *Married to Tolstoy*. New York, Houghton Mifflin, 1961.

Berlin, Isaiah, *The Hedgehog and the Fox: Tolstoy's View of History*. New York, Simon & Schuster, 1953.

Christian, R. F. *Tolstoy's War and Peace*. New York, Oxford Univ. Press, 1962.

Crosby, Ernest H. *Tolstoy and His Message*. New York, Funk, 1904.

———. *Tolstoy as a Schoolmaster*. Chicago, Hammarsmark, 1904.

Davis, H. C. *Tolstoy and Nietzsche: A Problem in Biographical Ethics*. New York, New Republic, 1929.

Dillon, E. J. *Count Leo Tolstoy: A New Portrait.* London, Hutchinson, 1934.
Dole, Nathan H. *The Life of Count L. N. Tolstoi.* New York, Crowell, 1911.
Duffield, Holley G., and M. Bilsky. *Literature and Aesthetics: Tolstoy and the Critics.* Scott Foresman, 1965 (paper).
Farrell, James T. "Tolstoi" in *Literature and Morality.* New York, Vanguard, 1947.
Garnett, Edward. *Tolstoy: His Life and Writings.* London, Houghton, 1914.
Garrod, H. W. *Tolstoy's Theory of Art.* Oxford, Clarendon, 1935.
Gibian, G. *Tolstoy and Shakespeare.* New York, Humanities (paper).
Gorky, Maxim. *Reminiscences of Leo N. Tolstoi.* London, Hogarth, 1920.
———. *Reminiscences of Tolstoy, Chekhov, and Andreev.* London, Hogarth, 1948.
Howells, W. D. "Lev Nikolayevitch Tolstoy" in *Scandinanian and Slavonic Literature.* New York, Columbia Univ. Press, 1928.
Kuzminskaia, Tatiana A. *Tolstoy As I Knew Him.* New York, Macmillian, 1948.
Lavrin, Janko. *Tolstoy, An Approach.* New York, Macmillan, 1946.
Leon, Derrick. *Tolstoy: His Life and Work.* London, Routledge, 1944.
Maude, Aylmer. *Life of Tolstoy.* New York, Dodd Mead, 1911.
———, ed. *Family Views of Tolstoy.* London, Allen & Unwin, 1926.
Merejkovsky, D. S. *Tolstoy As a Man and Artist.* New York, Putnam, 1902.
Míček, Eduard. *Tolstoy, the Artist and Humanist.* Austin, Czech Literary Society, 1961.
Nazaroff, Alexander. *Tolstoy, the Inconstant Genius.* London, Harrup, 1930.
Noyes, George R. *Tolstoy.* London, Murray, 1919.
Polner, Tikhon I. *Tolstoy and His Wife.* Tr. by N. Wreden. New York, Norton, 1945.
Redpath, Theodore. *Tolstoy.* New York, Hillary, 1959.
Rolland, Romain. *Tolstoy.* Tr. by B. Niale. London, Unwin. 1911.
Simmons, Ernest J. *Leo Tolstoy.* Boston, Little, Brown, 1946.

Steiner, E. A. *Tolstoy, the Man and His Message.* New York, Outlook, 1904.

Steiner, George. *Tolstoy or Dostoevsky.* New York, Knopf, 1959.

Sukhotina-Tolstoy, Tatiana. *Diaries of the Tolstoy Home.* New York, Columbia Univ. Press, 1951.

Tolstoy, Alexandra. *A Life of My Father.* Tr. by E. R. Hapgood. New York, Harper, 1953.

———. *The Tragedy of Tolstoy.* Tr. by E. Varneck. New Haven, Yale Univ. Press, 1933.

Tolstoy, Count Ilya L. *Reminiscences of Tolstoy.* Tr. by G. Calderon. New York, Century, 1914.

Tolstoi, Sergei L. *Tolstoi Remembered.* Tr. by Moura Budberg. New York, Atheneum, 1962.

Tolstoia, Sofia A. *Diary of Tolstoy's Wife, 1860–1891.* Tr. by A. Werth. London, Gollancz, 1928.

———. *The Final Struggle: Countess Tolstoy's Diary for 1910.* New York, Oxford Univ. Press, 1936.

Tsanoff, R. A. "Tolstoy the Novelist" in *The Problem of Life in the Russian Novel.* Houston, Rice Institute, 1917 (pamphlet).

Zweig, Stefan. *Presenting Tolstoy.* New York, McKay, n.d.

Chekhov

Avilova, Lidia Alekseevna. *Chekhov in My Life.* New York, Harcourt Brace, 1950.

Bruford, W. H. *Anton Chekhov.* New Haven, Yale Univ. Press, 1957.

———. *Chekhov and His Russia.* New York, Oxford Univ. Press, 1948.

Chandler, Frank W. "Chekhov and the Moscow Art Theater" in *Modern Continental Playwrights.* New York, Harper, 1931.

Ehrenburg, Ilya. *Chekhov, Stendhal, and Other Essays.* Ed. by Harrison Salisbury. New York, Knopf, 1963.

Elton, Oliver. *Chekhov.* Oxford, Clarendon, 1929.

Gerhardi, William A. *Anton Chekhov, A Critical Study.* London, Cobden-Sanderson, 1923.

Gorky, Maxim. *Reminiscences of Tolstoy, Chekhov, and Andreev.* London, Hogarth, 1948.

Hingley, Ronald. *Chekhov: A Biographical and Critical Study.* New York, Macmillan, 1950.

Magarshack, David. *Chekhov, A Life.* New York, Grove, 1952.

———. *Chekhov, The Dramatist.* New York, Hill & Wang, 1960.

Nemirovsky, Irina. *A Life of Chekhov.* Tr. by Erik de Mauny. London, Gray Walls, 1950.

Saunders, Beatrice. *Tchekov, The Man.* Chester Springs, Penn., Dufour, 1961.

Simmons, Ernest J. *Chekhov: A Biography.* Boston, Atlantic, Little, 1962.

Stanislavsky, Constantin. *My Life in Art.* Tr. by J. J. Robbins. Boston, Little, 1924.

Toumanova, Princess Nina. *Anton Chekhov, The Voice of Twilight Russia.* New York, Columbia Univ. Press, 1937.

Wiener, Leo. *The Contemporary Drama of Russia.* Boston, Little, Brown, 1924.

Winner, T. G. *Chekhov and His Prose.* New York, Holt. Rinehart & Winston, 1966.

Yermilov, Vladimir V. *Anton Pavlovich Chekhov.* Tr. by Ivy Litvinov. Moscow, Foreign Languages Publishing House, 195?.

Andreyev

Chandler, Frank W. "A Major Eccentric—Andreyev" in *Modern Continental Playwrights.* New York, Harper, 1931.

Gorky, Maxim. *Reminiscences of Tolstoy, Chekhov, and Andreyev.* London, Hogarth, 1948.

Kaun, Alexander. *Leonid Andreyev, A Critical Study.* New York, Huebsch, 1924.

Kuntz, Joshua. *Russian Literature and the Jew.* New York, Columbia Univ. Press, 1929.

Manning, Clarence A. "Leonid Nikolayevich Andreyev" in *Scandinavian and Slavonic Literature.* New York, Columbia Univ. Press, 1917.

Gorky

Dillon, E. J. *Maxim Gorky, His Life and Writing.* New York, McClure, 1903.

Gourfinkel, Nina. *Gorky.* New York, Grove, 1960 (paper).

Hare, Richard. *Maxim Gorky, Romantic Realist and Conservative Revolutionary.* New York, Oxford Univ. Press, 1962.

Huneker, J. G. *Iconoclasts.* New York, Scribners, 1905.

Kaun, Alexander. *Maxim Gorky and His Russia.* New York, Cape & Smith, 1931.

Levin, Dan. *Stormy Petrel: The Life of Maxim Gorky.* New York, Meredith (Appleton), 1965.

Muchnic, Helen. *Gorky to Pasternak.* New York, Random House, 1961.

Olgin, Moissaye J. *Maxim Gorky, Writer and Revolutionist.* New York, International Publishers, 1933.

Roskin, Alexander. *From the Banks of the Volga: The Life of Maxim Gorky.* New York, Philosophical Library, 1946.

Weil, Irwin, *Gorky.* New York, Random House, 1966 (paper).

Wiener, Leo. *The Contemporary Drama of Russia.* Boston, Little, Brown, 1924.

Introduction to Soviet Literature

Alexandrovna, Vera. *A History of Soviet Literature.* Garden City, Doubleday, 1963.

Brown, Edward J. *Russian Literature Since the Revolution.* Collier (paper).

Dana, H. W. L. *Handbook on Soviet Drama.* New York, American Russian Institute, 1938.

Eastman, Max. *Artist in Uniform, A Study of Literature and Bureaucratism.* New York, Knopf, 1934.

Ehrhard, Marcelle. *Russian Literature.* New York, Walker, 1963.

Gibian, George. *Interval of Freedom: Soviet Literature During the Thaw, 1954–57.* Minneapolis, Univ. of Minnesota Press, 1960.

Hayward, Max and Leopold Labedz, eds. *Literature and Revolution in Soviet Russia, 1917–1962, A Symposium.* New York, Oxford Univ. Press, 1963.

Kaun, Alexander. *Soviet Poets and Poetry.* Berkeley, Univ. of California, Press, 1943.

Lavrin, Janko. *Russian Writers, Their Lives and Literature.* New York, Van Nostrand, 1954.

MacLeod, J. T. G. *The New Soviet Theater.* London, Allen & Unwin, 1943.

Mirsky, D. S. *Contemporary Russian Literature, 1881–1925.* New York, Knopf, 1926; London, Routledge, 1926.

Muchnic, Helen. *Gorky to Pasternak: Six Writers in Soviet Russia.* New York, Random House, 1961.

Reavey, George. *Soviet Literature Today.* New Haven, Yale Univ. Press, 1947.

Simmons, Ernest J. *An Outline of Modern Russian Literature (1880–1940).* Ithaca, Cornell Univ. Press, 1943.

———. *Russian Fiction and Soviet Ideology.* New York, Columbia Univ. Press, 1958.

———. *Through the Glass of Soviet Literature.* New York, Columbia Univ. Press, 1953.

Slonim, Marc. *Modern Russian Literature: From Chekhov to the Present.* New York, Oxford Univ. Press, 1953.

———. *Soviet Russian Literature: Writers and Problems.* New York, Oxford Univ. Press, 1964.

Struve, Gleb. *25 Years of Soviet Russian Literature.* London, Routledge, 1944.

———. *Soviet-Russian Literature.* Norman, Univ. of Oklahoma Press, 1951.

Vickery, Walter N. *The Cult of Optimism: Political and Ideological Problems of Recent Soviet Literature.* Bloomington, Indiana Univ. Press, 1963.

Zavalishin, Vyacheslav. *Early Soviet Writers.* New York, Praeger, 1958.

Index

The Great Books of Russia has been set on the Linotype in eleven-point Caledonia with two-point spacing between the lines. Handset Perpetua was selected for display to complement the calculated character of Caledonia.

The paper on which this book is printed bears the watermark of the University of Oklahoma Press and is designed for an effective life of at least three hundred years.